The Wiley Finance series contains books written specifically for finance and investment professionals as well as sophisticated individual investors and their financial advisors. Book topics range from portfolio management to e-commerce, risk management, financial engineering, valuation, and financial instrument analysis, as well as much more. For a list of available titles, visit our Web site at www.WileyFinance.com.

Founded in 1807, John Wiley & Sons is the oldest independent publishing company in the United States. With offices in North America, Europe, Australia, and Asia, Wiley is globally committed to developing and marketing print and electronic products and services for our customers' professional and personal knowledge and understanding.

Successful Defined Contribution Investment Design

How to Align Target-Date, Core, and Income Strategies to the PRICE of Retirement

STACY L. SCHAUS, CFP® with
YING GAO, Ph.D., CFA, CAIA

WILEY

Published by John Wiley & Sons, Inc., Hoboken, New Jersey.
Published simultaneously in Canada.

For general information on our other products and services or for technical support, please contact our Customer Care Department within the United States at (800) 762-2974, outside the United States at (317) 572-3993 or fax (317) 572-4002.

Wiley publishes in a variety of print and electronic formats and by print-on-demand. Some material included with standard print versions of this book may not be included in e-books or in print-on-demand. If this book refers to media such as a CD or DVD that is not included in the version you purchased, you may download this material at http://booksupport.wiley.com. For more information about Wiley products, visit www.wiley.com.

Library of Congress Cataloging-in-Publication Data:

ISBN 978-1-119-29856-4 (Hardcover/)
ISBN 978-1-119-30254-4 (ePDF)
ISBN 978-1-119-30256-8 (ePub)

Printed in the United States of America

10 9 8 7 6 5 4 3 2 1

*This book is dedicated to all of the plan sponsors
and defined contribution professionals who inspire us
with your commitment to improve retirement security;
to my husband, John, and children, Robert and Julia,
and to all of our families and yours.*

Disclosure

The author of this book is employed by Pacific Investment Management Company, LLC (PIMCO) at time of publication. The views contained herein are the author's but not necessarily those of PIMCO. Such opinions are subject to change without notice. This publication has been distributed for educational purposes only and should not be considered as investment advice or a recommendation of any particular security, strategy, or investment product. Information contained herein has been obtained from sources believed to be reliable, but not guaranteed.

This publication contains a general discussion of defined contribution plans and is intended for plan sponsors of such plans. The analysis contained herein does not take into consideration any particular investor's or plan's financial circumstance, objectives, or risk tolerance. Investments discussed may not be suitable for all investors or plans.

This book may contain hypothetical simulated data and is provided for illustrative purposes only. Hypothetical and simulated examples have many inherent limitations and are generally prepared with the benefit of hindsight. There are frequently sharp differences between simulated results and actual results. There are numerous factors related to the markets in general or the implementation of any specific investment strategy that cannot be fully accounted for in the preparation of simulated results and all of which can adversely affect actual results. No guarantee is being made that the stated results will be achieved.

Nothing contained herein is intended to constitute accounting, legal, tax, securities, or investment advice, nor an opinion regarding the appropriateness of any investment, nor a solicitation of any type. This book includes discussions of financial concepts that are theoretical in nature such as the "risk-free rate" or "risk-free asset"; readers should be aware that all investments carry risk and may lose value. The information contained herein should not be acted upon without obtaining specific accounting, legal, tax, and investment advice from a licensed professional.

Contents

Acknowledgments

This volume was brought into being as a result of countless conversations about the increasing importance of defined contribution pension plan design for workers around the globe. My first volume, *Designing Successful Target-Date Strategies for Defined Contribution Plans: Putting Participants on the Optimal Glide Path*, was published in 2010 and focused on designing and implementing custom target-date strategies within DC plans. This volume, in turn, broadens and deepens the dialogue about plan design—looking not only at custom target-date strategies, but also the whole of DC investment design from governance to investment defaults, through the core lineup and ending with retirement income. My goal in preparing this book is to further contribute to plan sponsors', consultants', and other professionals' understanding of how to design a DC plan to help participants succeed in building adequate and sustainable retirement income.

Like its predecessor, this book is the result of extensive collaboration and participation among a very long list of colleagues, plan sponsors, consultants, lawyers, and investment and other DC professionals. Among my colleagues, Ying Gao, PhD, CFA, CAIA is noted on the cover as she has worked tirelessly over the past six years in developing and enhancing the PIMCO DC analytic toolset, including the methodology for PRICE. We worked together in coauthoring a long list of DC design papers; analytic work from these papers is updated and woven into the analytic sections of the book. Outside of PIMCO, I worked closely with talented financial editor Alexandra Macqueen CFP®, who skillfully guided the project and helped shape, refine, and polish every chapter. Her financial depth of understanding, coupled with superb writing skills, eased the process and improved the book's readability.

Once again I extend my deepest gratitude to the plan sponsors whose passionate work to "get DC right" has paved the way for increasing the retirement success of workers today and tomorrow, and who have shared the details of their plan design through our PIMCO DC Dialogues and in the various summits, forums, conferences, and other ways in which they keep the DC conversation alive. My gratitude extends to Karin Brodbeck at Nestlé, USA; Judy Mares, formerly of Alliant Techsystems Inc. (now part of Orbital); Stuart Odell at Intel Corporation; Brad Leak, CFA of The Boeing Company;

Sharon Cowher and Christine Morris at Halliburton; Cindy Cattin at Exelon Corporation; Karen Barnes of McDonald's Corporation; Gary Park at Schlumberger; Dan Holupchinski formerly of Deluxe Corporation; Dave Zellner at Wespath Benefits and Investments (formerly United Methodist Church); Georgette Gestely at New York City Deferred Compensation Program; David Fisser formerly of Southwest Airline Pilots' Association; and Pete Apor at Fujitsu.

Each chapter of this book delves into a specific topic and I have called upon the insights and expertise of many experts to review and comment on the content. For this volume, my appreciation for their assistance and global plan pension design insights, both in the opening and close of the book, extends to Brigitte Miksa, Head of International Pensions, and Greg Langley, Editor-in-Chief, Allianz PROJECT M, both of Allianz Asset Management AG; Sabrina Bailey, Global Head of Defined Contribution at Northern Trust Asset Management; and former PIMCO colleague Will Allport. For plan and investment design, I'm thankful for the expertise and careful review by Lori Lucas, DC Practice Leader at Callan Associates; Matthew Rice, Chief Investment Officer at DiMeo Schneider and Associates, LLC; Kevin Vandolder, DC Client Practice Leader, Partner, Investment Consulting, and Bill Ryan, Associate Partner at Aon Hewitt Investment Consulting; Ross Bremen, Rob Fishman, and Tim McCusker, partners at NEPC; Thomas Idzorek, Chief Investment Officer at Ibbotson Associates; Mark A. Davis, Senior Vice President, Financial Advisor at CAPTRUST Financial Advisors; Philip Chao, Pension Consultant and Chief Investment Officer at Chao & Company; Donald Stone, Director of DC Strategy and Product Development and Senior Consultant at Pavilion Advisory Group Inc.; Josh Cohen, Head of Defined Contribution at Russell Investments; Chris Lyon and Lisa Florentine, partners at Rocaton Investment Advisors, LLC; Tim Burggraaf, DC Leader at Mercer in the Netherlands; Jody Strakosch, Founder of Strakosch Retirement Strategies, LLC; Kelli Hueler, Founder of Hueler Companies; Susan Bradley, Founder of Sudden Money Institute; and Lee Baker, Financial Planner at Apex Financial Services.

In addition, I'm deeply appreciative of the extensive research, writing, and insights from many of the world's most noted academic thought leaders, including Harry Markowitz, Nobel Prize winner, recognized Father of Modern Portfolio Theory, and professor of finance at the Rady School of Management at the University of California, San Diego (UCSD); Zvi Bodie, retired Norman and Adele Barron Professor of Management at Boston University; Richard Thaler, Charles R. Walgreen Distinguished Service Professor of Economics and Behavioral Science at the University of Chicago Booth School of Business; Shlomo Benartzi, professor at University of California at Los Angeles; Brigitte Madrian, Aetna Professor of Public Policy and Corporate

Management at the Harvard Kennedy School; Olivia S. Mitchell, Professor of Insurance and Risk Management, International Foundation of Employee Benefit Plans, also Executive Director, Pension Research Council, and Director, Boettner Center on Pensions and Retirement Research, The Wharton School; Jeffrey R. Brown, the Josef and Margot Lakonishok Professor of Business and Dean of the College of Business at the University of Illinois in Urbana-Champaign, Illinois; Joshua Grill at University of California at Irvine; Michael Drew, Professor of Finance at Griffith Business School, Griffith University, and Partner at Drew, Walk & Co.; and Julie Agnew, Associate Professor of Finance and Economics at The College of William and Mary.

I also am thankful for the research, insights, and contributions to DC by many extraordinary professionals and organizations, including Jack VanDerhei, Research Director at the Employee Benefit Research Institute (EBRI); Lew Minsky, Executive Director at Defined Contribution Institutional Investment Association (DCIIA); Chris J. Battaglia, Vice President and Group Publisher at Crain Communications, Inc.; Joshua Franzel, PhD, Vice President, Research Center for State and Local Government Excellence; Juan Yermo, Deputy Chief of Staff to the OECD Secretary-General; Helen Monks Takhar at the NEST Corporation; Gina Mitchell, President of the Stable Value Investment Association (SVIA); and Hattie Greenan, Director of Research and Communications at the Plan Sponsor Council of America (PSCA).

I am grateful for the additions to content, thoughtful editing, and suggestions by ERISA legal professionals, including Marla Kreindler, Partner at Morgan, Lewis and Bockius; James Fleckner, Securities and Investment Management Litigator at Goodwin Procter LLP; David Levine, Principal at Groom Law Group, Chartered; R. Bradford Huss, Partner at Trucker Huss APC; and Sally Nielsen of Kilpatrick, Townsend and Stockton LLP.

PIMCO colleagues also contributed significantly to the content development, review, and editing of all of the chapters. I would like to extend heartfelt gratitude to Joe Healy, DC institutional leader for his review and contribution to the entire book; and Steve Sapra, PhD, and Justin Blesy for meticulous review of the glide path and benchmarking content found in multiple chapters. By topic, we thank: Steve Ferber and former colleague Michael Esselman for review of investment structure; Brett Gorman, Brian Leach, Paul Reisz, Ronnie Bernard, and David Berg for capital preservation and fixed income; Nick Rovelli for shaping and editing the fixed income chapter, plus David Fisher and Loren Sageser for their careful edits; Andy Pyne, Raji Manasseh, and Markus Aakko for contribution to content and editing the equity section; Bransby Whitton, Klaus Thuerbach, and Kate Botting for contributing to and editing the inflation chapter; John Cavalieri, Ashish Tiwari, and Ryan Korinke, as well as Rob Arnott and Lillian Yu of

Research Affiliates for review of additional strategies and alternatives; Mike Cogswell and Theo Ellis for review of the retirement income section; and Ken Chambers and Chantal Manseau for their review of the closing. I also appreciate the review by colleagues in Australia, including Adrian Stewart, Sara Higgins, and Manusha Samaraweera; in Canada by Stuart Graham; and in The Netherlands by Patrick Dunnewolt.

PIMCO leadership, as well, stood behind the creation and fulfillment of this project, including Tom Otterbein, managing director and head of institutional Americas, and Rick Fulford, executive vice president and head of U.S. retirement. I also extend gratitude to PIMCO managing directors Susie Wilson; James Moore, PhD; Kim Stafford; and Candice Stack for their review of materials and support of discussions with consultants and plan sponsors.

In addition, our highly professional team at PIMCO tirelessly and individually had a hand in producing this final work, including reviewing, adding to content, editing, designing, and confirming numbers, names, graphics, and figures. These include Daniel Bradshaw and Carla Harris, who reviewed the entire book from a compliance perspective; Blayze Hanson, who worked on all of the charts and graphs throughout the book; Barry Lawrence, who contributed to analyses and helped shepherd the project; and Candi Barbour, who served as marketing assistant to the project. In addition, I would like to thank our editors who contributed to materials, including Steve Brull and Matt Padilla.

My partners at John Wiley & Sons, Sheck Cho, Judy Howarth, and Vincent Nordhaus assisted greatly in editing and publishing this book, and I owe them, too, my appreciation.

And last but never least, I owe a continuing debt of thankfulness to my family, whose generous patience, support, and encouragement helped me produce this work—through many time zones, late nights, weekends, and other moments and hours dedicated to this project. Thank you, once again, for allowing me the time to continue to contribute to global defined contribution plan advancement.

Introduction

Today, workers around the globe are increasingly dependent on defined contribution plans to reach their retirement income goals. In the United States, fewer than one in five workers have access to a traditional defined benefit pension program. To retire financially secure, workers need well-designed defined contribution (DC) plans—as most will rely on such plans for at least a third of retirement income. Those who have access to a well-designed plan and are contributing at a sufficient level are likely to succeed. Unfortunately, not all workers are offered a DC plan . . . and plans that are offered may have a less-than-optimal design.

As of 2015, we estimate that only about half of U.S. workers have access to a DC plan; in particular, people working part-time or for small employers often lack plan access. Some countries such as the United Kingdom and Australia have addressed DC plan availability by mandating that employers must offer and enroll employees into such programs. At this writing, we anticipate retirement plan availability will increase in the United States as multiple states and possibly the federal government will roll out compulsory programs or regulatory change to ease the burden of offering plans.

As plans become increasingly available, our hope is they offer an investment structure that places participants on a path to success.

This book is designed to assist plan sponsors and providers to structure investment menus that help participants meet their retirement goals. Our earlier book, *Designing Successful Target-Date Strategies for Defined Contribution Plans: Putting Participants on the Optimal Glide Path* (2010), provided a framework for understanding the growing role DC plans have come to play for Americans planning for and transitioning into and through retirement. In that volume, we reviewed the origins of DC plans with a focus on building custom target-date strategies, an innovation that is now widely adopted, particularly within the largest U.S. plans. Our earlier book was a resource that helped plan sponsors and their consultants as they considered how to create their own custom target retirement-date strategies. It was written at a time when DC plans were experiencing significant growth in both prevalence and assets.

In the intervening years, the trends we identified have accelerated. Global DC assets in seven major markets (representing more than 90 percent of total assets) swelled to $15.6 trillion in 2015, a 7.1 percent 10-year annual growth rate that was more than double the 3.4 percent pace for defined benefit plan (DB) assets, according to Willis Towers Watson. At the end of 2015, DC assets in these markets represented 48.4 percent of combined DC/DB assets, up from 39.9 percent in 2005. With continued adoption of DC plans and higher contribution rates—fueled increasingly by automatic enrollment—DC assets will eclipse those of DB plans in the near future.

As contribution rates climb, DC assets will increasingly flow into investment defaults. In the United States, more than 80 percent of plans use a qualified default investment alternative (QDIA, an investment vehicle used for retirement plan contributions in the absence of direction from the plan participant); target-date funds dominate, being offered by about 75 percent of plans. According to PIMCO's ninth annual Defined Contribution Consulting Support and Trends Survey (published in 2016 with data collected in 2015), 96 percent of consultants supported target-date funds as the QDIA.

As a result of the increasing popularity and importance of DC plans, plan sponsors, consultants, advisors, investment managers, attorneys, academics, and other professionals are keenly interested in DC plan design. But as they seek information and guidance, they often find only piecemeal information on how to thoughtfully structure a DC plan. They are left not knowing where and how to begin. To help answer the questions of those interested in and responsible for DC plans, this book offers a framework, information, analytics, and ultimately a guide to building successful DC plans.

Throughout these pages, we focus the discussion first and foremost on meeting the DC plan's objective—which for nearly all plans today is *to provide participants with sustainable retirement income*. This retirement income objective may differ from the past when many plans may have been considered supplemental savings programs. Those days are over and new approaches are required. By identifying and focusing first on the plan objective, plans can be managed to meet that objective, both during asset accumulation and retirement-income drawdown.

We believe this outcome-oriented approach presents the best path to success. Our interest in focusing on outcomes extends from our collective experience over the past decade. We have learned that the old approaches to DC plan design are often misaligned to a plan's objective and can present participants with untenable risk. By aligning investment design to the plan objective and managing both to maximize return and minimize risk, workers are likely to succeed; and what's more, plan sponsors are able to meet their fiduciary duty to participants.

At PIMCO, we understand that meeting the objective of outcome-oriented investing may be easier said than done. To help plan fiduciaries grapple with this challenge, we have developed proprietary analytics and other resources to help inform and guide DC investment development. Our commitment to contribute to the effective design and success of DC plans for sponsors and participants alike is what motivates us to return to the printing press with a new book for 2017.

HOW THIS BOOK IS ORGANIZED—AND HOW TO USE IT

The book is divided into three parts. Part One (Chapters 1–4) provides the background that readers will need to build their understanding of DC plan design rudiments. Part Two (Chapters 5–9) sets out a guide to understand the overall DC investment structure and menu of choices plan sponsors and participants face. In Part Three (Chapters 10 and 11), we return to a focus on the individual, both in the U.S. and other markets around the world. In it we explore the specific plan features and investment choices retirees seek as they consider whether to stay in their plans, and how a DC plan balance could be turned into a lifetime of retirement income.

Here's what's happening, chapter by chapter:

Chapter 1: We start with an overview of the new reality. For most workers success is up to the individual, as DC plans have replaced traditional pension plans as the primary source of employer-provided retirement income. While the objective is often the same, design around the globe varies significantly so we look at the types of plans by major market. Then we discuss what this shift means as fiduciaries design DC plans: What are a fiduciary's responsibilities? How can consultants and advisors help? How can plans be designed to succeed? Where does a plan sponsor begin? This chapter includes an assessment of the extent to which workers globally may rely on DC plans for retirement income, showing how the audience for DC plans continues to expand. We discuss the challenges that plan sponsors face in governing plans and share views on the importance of both contribution and investment design. We also consider automatic enrollment and contribution escalation, and then turn our attention to investment design.

Chapter 2: In this chapter, we introduce a framework for evaluating and structuring DC plans. We discuss how to align investment design to the plan objective and introduce the innovative PIMCO Retirement Income Cost Estimate (the "PRICE" approach) as a methodology to quantify both the historical and prospective cost of buying a lifetime income stream. The PRICE approach helps fiduciaries to identify the number, or amount of savings, a worker needs to retire. In this chapter, readers will be able to ask—and answer—the questions: What is the PRICE of retirement? Is your company's DC plan on track? We also reach into the world of behavioral finance to help understand why numeric or quantitative frameworks can provide an important counterpoint to the biases that may otherwise shape our behavior.

Chapter 3: Here we turn to plan investment structure, including an investigation of the number of tiers and investment structures available in plan design. We consider qualified default investment alternatives (QDIAs), including the types of investments and prevalence of each. Then we look at the core investment lineup, helping readers understand how to think about the number and type of investment offerings. We also consider active versus passive investment choices, and brokerage windows (whether full or mutual-fund-only). Finally, we consider the investment structure, whether mutual fund, collective investment trust (CIT), or separately managed account. We also explore white label or multimanager approaches, including considering when a delegated or outsourced chief investment officer approach might make sense.

Chapter 4: In Chapter 4, we delve into target-date funds. We consider the types available, including packaged, custom, and semicustom. What type of fund may be desirable by plan size? Why may a custom or semicustom approach make sense? We review evaluation criteria and how to apply these during both selection and monitoring of the funds. Among the criteria, we include the objective of the fund, diversification, investor loss tolerance versus capacity, and more.

Chapters 5–9: Part Two includes Chapters 5 to 9 in which we review core investment offerings in DC plans, including options for capital preservation, fixed income, equity, and real assets. In Chapter 9, we consider whether and how alternative assets fit within plan offerings. Together these chapters allow readers to gain insight into the full range of investment options for DC plans, and the trade-offs, benefits, and costs of different approaches—including how to evaluate plan options in the face of a changing regulatory and economic backdrop. How might an environment of equity levels at record highs and interest rates at record lows, for example, require plan sponsors to review their core lineups? What is the role of active strategies with global exposure, or the importance of inflation hedging? In these chapters, we evaluate how considering options from both return and risk perspectives can help provide the assortment of solutions retirees will likely need.

Chapter 10: In Part Three, we shift from accumulation to distribution with a more in-depth look at the options available for retired plan participants. We grapple with how retirees make the decision to stay in or exit their plans; and we investigate what plan features and investment choices retirees need, both from the point of view of expert observers and the retiree. Questions include: What role should plans play in encouraging retirees to leave assets in the plan at retirement, and what features cause retirees to stay? How do individuals think about and accommodate the impact that increasing longevity may have on their retirement income plans?

Chapter 11: We wrap up with the best ideas for improving defined contribution plan success, including a summary of suggestions made throughout the book. We will consider how retirement plan coverage might be improved, including ideas from outside the United States. Among potential improvements, we'll look at increasing contribution rates, reducing plan leakage, and aligning investment design to a retirement objective.

Finally, in our closing comments, we'll identify some top priorities for future action. These include 1: increasing plan coverage and savings rates, 2: moving to objective-aligned investment approaches, and 3: broadening options for retirement income.

As readers proceed through the book, they will find dozens of design examples and insights from plan sponsors such as Intel Corporation, The Boeing Company, and Nestlé USA, among others. We also draw on the rich insights and perspectives that DC plan design consultants can offer, including Aon Hewitt, Callan, Mercer, NEPC, Rocaton Investment Advisors, LLC, Russell Investments, and more.

In this volume, we have likewise turned to prominent and insightful academics in the world of retirement income planning—including the father of modern finance, Harry Markowitz. Through our interviews with these masterful observers, we broaden the scope of our discussion to include everything from the impact of the field of behavioral finance on individual behavior and DC plan design, to demographic issues such as the effect of increasing longevity for Americans on DC plan design and outcomes, among other topics.

And while this book focuses primarily on U.S. DC plan design, we intend that non-U.S. readers find the framework, case studies, and consultant insights relevant and helpful. We also hope that U.S. readers will be enriched by the information and insights we pull in from other economies around the world.

How should readers use this book? You might think of it as akin to a cookbook, or car-repair manual, to give two examples. While it has been designed to flow logically from start to finish, readers might find it most useful to dip into or refer to specific ideas or chapters—without necessarily reading in a linear fashion. To that end, we've written it so the sections and chapters can function independently, versus requiring you to build knowledge that carries from one section to another. And both the Contents and Index can help readers locate specific conversations that are of particular interest. All that said, readers should engage with this volume in whatever way best suits their needs.

A CONTINUING COMMITMENT TO MEET THE NEED FOR INFORMATION

By publishing this handbook, PIMCO is continuing our tradition of dedication to helping clients and the consulting community build more successful DC plans. We bring this commitment to life by identifying and exploring questions and issues active participants and retirees alike face in preparing to enter retirement, and by proposing ways in which we can work together to optimize outcomes for all participants.

Over the past years, we have produced a range of publications to help plan sponsors evolve their retirement programs. Our DC Design series focuses on ways plan sponsors can modify plan lineups to promote the potential of improved participant outcomes, and examines issues plan sponsors face in globalizing their plan offerings.

In 2006, we launched the PIMCO DC Dialogue to showcase the thinking of a wide range of retirement leaders and innovators including consultants, academics, lawyers, financial advisors, not-for-profit executives, and, most important, plan sponsors from both the private and public sectors. In this volume, as in our previous volume, we draw upon the generous contributions we have gleaned from our Dialogue series to contribute to readers.

In addition to our Dialogue series, PIMCO also publishes targeted research and analytic papers that carefully examine elements of DC plan structure. These include our PIMCO DC Research, DC Analytics, and Viewpoint series. In this volume, we use the findings pinpointed in these series to more fully develop our analysis—however, as in our earlier volume, our motivation is not to promote only the suggestions or philosophies of PIMCO, but to add PIMCO's voice to the various perspectives cultivated from across the industry. In addition, we note that in order to preserve an objective and balanced viewpoint, each chapter of this handbook has been reviewed and edited by professionals from across the country.

Over the past decade, PIMCO has also undertaken an annual Defined Contribution Consulting Support and Trends Survey to help plan sponsors understand the breadth of views and specific consulting services available within the DC marketplace. Through this survey, we capture data, trends, and opinions from 66 consulting firms across the United States, which in 2016 served over 11,000 clients with aggregate DC assets in excess of $4.2 trillion.

The data and observations from these surveys—10 in total—are cited throughout this book, providing practical "on the ground" intelligence about DC plans in America.

We have cultivated the input of these many voices because we recognize that there are a range of approaches, viewpoints, and solutions—both here at home and from around the world—that can contribute to plan sponsors' and plan members' understanding of defined contribution plans. And that enhanced understanding, in turn, can help produce plans that are more likely to succeed. So whether you are reading this as a plan sponsor who is new to DC plan oversight, a consultant with decades of experience, or an individual (perhaps planning for your own or another's retirement) who is keen to learn about plan design, we hope engaging with the ideas in this book will be a valuable experience.

WHY SHOULD YOU READ THIS BOOK?

Finally, if you're on the fence about whether to carry on reading beyond this introduction, we've compiled a partly tongue-in-cheek list of our top 10 reasons to continue. Without further ado, we think you should read this book to:

1. Understand and embrace a framework for considering the world's most important retirement plan structure: the DC plan.
2. Develop the knowledge that will help improve retirement income security for employees.
3. Learn about how to reduce risk for all employees, as well as the cost of older workers who lack sufficient means to retire.
4. Get up to speed on a concrete approach to structure and benchmark target-date and other investment strategies for DC plans.
5. Receive plan design tips from many of the world's largest employers.
6. Gain design insights and benefit from the diverse points of view and experiences of consultants and DC experts from around the world.
7. Quickly get up to date on recent DC design trends.
8. Stimulate your own thinking for how to evolve your plan.
9. Gather design concepts from peers and other experts.
10. And last but not least, in order to be able to discuss DC plan ideas and suggestions at cocktail parties!

DC Plans: A Cornerstone of Retirement

CHAPTER 1

DC Plans Today

An Overview of the Issues

PREFACE: A CAREER AND A NEW FORM OF PENSION PLAN ARE BORN

I started my career in 1981, at the age of 21 . . . which also happened to be the year 401(k) plans were launched. As a new employee at Merrill Lynch Capital Markets, I had the great fortune of working with financial professionals who immediately recognized the power of tax-deferred retirement investing. One experienced colleague told me, "If you participate in this plan, you'll be a millionaire someday." That's all I needed to hear to sign up for automatic payroll deductions into my plan—a practice I have never stopped. Today, I am among the many millions of workers around the world who will fund retirement primarily with my defined contribution assets. I am very fortunate to have been advised to start saving early, and to have ignored others' suggestions to postpone retirement savings and "enjoy being young." I'm also lucky that I've had access to an employer-sponsored plan funded via automatic payroll deduction, and to have a healthy investment menu from which to choose.

In short, I've spent my working years with a defined contribution (DC) pension, versus the "traditional" defined benefit (DB) pension. I believe that my personal experience, as someone who started working just as 401(k) plans came into being, has helped me understand the power and importance of "getting DC right." In 1989, I joined Hewitt Associates in Lincolnshire, Illinois, and shortly thereafter turned 100 percent of my professional focus toward consulting to DC plan sponsors and research, including creating the Hewitt 401(k) Index to track participant reaction to stock market movements. Since that time, and in the 10-plus years I've spent working at PIMCO, getting DC right has not only been a personal but also a professional passion. As my career is exactly as old as 401(k) plans, this means that DC plans and I have "grown up" together.

Part of growing up for DC plans has been the evolution toward more institutional structures, which some refer to as "DB-izing" DC. This movement includes shifting away from retail-priced packaged products, such as mutual funds and closed-architecture target-date funds, and toward collective investment trusts, separately managed accounts, and custom multi-manager structures. These shifts can be beneficial for plan participants: Using institutional investment vehicles and improving asset diversification may lower plan costs and improve risk-adjusted investment returns for participants. For example, if an investor could earn an additional 100 basis points (1 percent), over a 40-year career, this expense and return difference adds up. Indeed, for someone starting with a salary of $50,000—and assuming annual real wage gains of 1 percent; contribution rates, including the employer match, of 9.5 percent (in the first 10 years) and 15.5 percent (for the next 30 years); and conservative portfolio returns of 4 percent per year—an additional portfolio return of 1 percent plus the reduction in expenses resulting from the shift from retail-priced products compounds after 40 years into about $210,000 when retirement starts. This extra sum may be sufficient to boost the retirement income replacement rate by 16 percent throughout retirement (that is, the extra sum can be used to provide yearly income in retirement that is equal to 16 percent of yearly preretirement pay).

To support the ongoing transition of DC plans toward more institutional structures, in 2010 I worked with Lew Minsky, Executive Director of the Defined Contribution Institutional Investment Association (DCIIA), to launch and serve as the founding Chair of this organization. DCIIA is a community of retirement leaders that is passionate about improving the retirement security of workers by improving the design and outcomes of DC plans. DCIIA brings together professionals from across the DC market, including consultants, asset managers, plan sponsors, recordkeepers, insurers, lawyers, communication firms, and others, all working together on this common goal.

Today, as DC plans are poised to become the dominant form of retirement savings around the world, I am inspired to provide a book to help guide the development of successful DC plans primarily for the benefit of employers and workers now and in the future. My hope is that plan sponsors, consultants, and other plan fiduciaries, by engaging with the materials in this book, will take away an empowering framework and insights to help structure and further evolve DC plan design.

DC PLANS: BECOMING THE NEW REALITY . . . NO TURNING BACK

DC plans are a large and growing market globally, representing nearly half the world's $36 trillion in estimated total pension assets. Over the past decade, the global share of pension assets held in DC plans in the world's major pension markets has increased dramatically, from 39.9 percent in 2005 to 48.4 percent in 2015—and DC assets have also grown at a faster pace than DB assets, at a rate of 7.1 percent per year compared to the slower pace of 3.4 percent per year for assets in DB plans (Willis Towers Watson, Global Pension Assets Study 2016, covering 19 major pension markets). While DC pension assets are increasing around the world, the United States, Australia, and the UK represent roughly 90 percent with 76 percent, 7.5 percent, and 6 percent of the global DC pension assets.

In 2014, we spoke to Brigitte Miksa, Head of International Pensions (and Executive Editor of PROJECT M at Allianz Asset Management AG), about the development of retirement systems around the globe. We discussed the shift in weight among the pillars or sources of retirement income, including the first source of public pensions, such as Social Security, and the second source of occupational programs, both DB and DC. We also contrasted reliance on the different sources of retirement income and DC developments within three market segments: Anglo-Saxon countries, developed European countries, and emerging pension markets.

Looking forward, as each market develops and DC assets grow, Miksa expects the plans in these markets will become increasingly "professionalized," such that decision-making about asset allocation and more will shift over time to professionals, away from individual participants. (These shifts mirror the evolution toward institutionalized structures for DC plans discussed above.) She told us:

> *Starting in the early 1990s, many countries initiated pension reforms and we began to see shifts in the dependency on different retirement income pillars. The initial wave of reforms focused on sustainability of the first pillar—government-funded public pensions such as Social Security. With the recent financial crisis, more pressure has been placed on reforming public pensions, and fortunately, these efforts have been quite successful in many cases. For instance, increasing the age for public pension qualification will help with the sustainability of public pensions in many countries.*

Another significant global shift is occurring in the second pillar—employer-sponsored or occupational pension schemes. We continue to see rapid movement away from defined benefit pension plans and toward defined contribution systems. This shift started in the Anglo-Saxon countries, including the U.S., Australia, Canada and the U.K., and continues to spread to other developed markets like the Netherlands and Norway, as well as to the emerging markets.

Over the past decade, Miksa told us, more than half of the 34 countries in the Organisation for Economic Co-operation and Development (OECD) have rolled out DC programs. While the Anglo-Saxon countries continue to dominate in their percentage of global DC assets accumulated, other markets are showing rapid development; these include Denmark, Israel, Italy, and Turkey.

As the move away from traditional DB pension plans continues, workers are increasingly reliant on DC pension schemes to build their own retirement income. Employers, too, are reliant on DC plans to both attract and retain talent, and to manage their workforce—reducing the cost and the potentially detrimental effect of retaining workers beyond their desired retirement age. Multinational corporations commonly manage their DC plans worldwide with the aim of providing a valuable retirement savings vehicle as well as local-market competitive benefits (PIMCO's 2015 Global DC Survey for Multinational Corporations). Over a third of these organizations have a written global retirement plan philosophy, while another third say they are likely to write one over the next year or two. These employers view "the ability to attract and retain talent" as the top return on investment for offering retirement benefits—this motivation is followed by a "sense of doing what's right."

SETTING GOALS FOR SUCCESS: INCOME REPLACEMENT TARGETS

Whether you're a multinational plan sponsor, a single market, or a public employer, we know that for a DC plan to succeed, that plan may need to deliver an old-age income stream to last 20 to 30 years in retirement—or perhaps even longer. Consultants surveyed in PIMCO's 2016 Defined Contribution Consulting Support and Trends Survey suggest that plan sponsors set an income replacement target at 80 percent of final pay, including Social Security and other income sources. They suggest that a DC plan will need to replace 60 percent of a worker's final pay for those who lack both a DB plan and paid retiree medical coverage—which is the case for the vast majority of U.S. workers. We know that the percentage of income replacement will vary broadly based on the income level and personal circumstances of workers. Whatever the percentage, most DC plans share a common goal: to help workers retire at their desired age and with sufficient income to maintain their lifestyle throughout retirement. For organizations that also provide a DB plan, the DC income replacement target may be only 30 percent. What's important is to consider the objective for your plan and set a reasonable target.

In December 2014, we interviewed Philip S. L. Chao, Principal and Chief Investment Officer of Chao & Company Ltd., a retirement plan and fiduciary consulting firm, about their approaches to DC investment design. He shared the followed comments:

> We begin with a basic question: "What is the objective for this plan?" It is rare for us to set up a new plan; rather, we're typically asked to advise on an existing plan. With that said, it may be surprising how much time we spend on the plan's objective. We ask the plan sponsor to forget about how the plan is designed today; they are encouraged to step back and identify what they are trying to accomplish. This often leads to a refreshing discussion of the DC plan as a benefit program and the outcome they seek for their participants. Yet, plan sponsors are rarely specific about the desired outcome. Instead, we often initially hear they simply want a competitive plan, or they may tell us how a DC plan is the only retirement savings vehicle employees have. We then work with the plan sponsors to articulate and document the objective for the plan. Once the objective is set, then we work on crafting the investment structure to help meet this objective.

Chao goes on to tell us more about setting an income replacement target, saying:

> We consider the organization's workforce (i.e., thinking in sole interest of the participants) and the retirement income sources for the typical employee. A law firm's demographics, income distribution and other factors may differ greatly from a retail chain store. The law firm may have higher-paid workers and lower turnover. These are important considerations as we think about the median worker profile. Median is not perfect either, but it's a start. We consider Social Security, likelihood of the existence of other retirement plans, housing wealth, and other retirement income sources.

In general, plans consider a 75% to 80% income replacement as the default target, including Social Security. About half of that need can be covered by Social Security and other income sources. This leaves DC plans to fill in the remaining 35% to 40% of income for the median worker over the course of a working career. This isn't exact and won't fit all workers, but a general target helps us as we consider the plan design. We ask ourselves whether the median participant is likely to meet their income needs. We want the plan sponsor to understand the probability of failure and whether the plan is likely to meet the set objective. This goes beyond investment return and pulls in the average deferral rate, employer contribution amount and other assumptions. Assessing the likelihood of meeting the plan's objective can help plan sponsors evaluate target-date funds and other QDIAs [Qualified Default Investment Alternatives] as well as test the balance in and portfolio construction adequacy of their core lineup.

While DC plans need to focus on meeting participant needs and consultants tell us that the number one driver of plan sponsor decisions is to "meet participant retirement goals," they also note that the second driver is to "manage litigation risk" (PIMCO's 2016 Defined Contribution Consulting Support and Trends Survey). Sound plan governance and plan oversight are central to both of these. Before delving deeply into meeting a retirement objective, let's take a look at litigation and fiduciary duties.

REDUCING DC LITIGATION RISK: PROCESS AND OVERSIGHT

In 2014, we sat with James O. Fleckner, Partner and Employee Retirement Income Security Act of 1974 (ERISA) Litigation Practice Leader at Goodwin Procter LLP, to talk about how plan sponsors can reduce the risk of litigation. Fleckner first provided some background on the Employee Retirement Income Security Act, a 1974 federal law that is intended to "help protect the interests of employee benefit plan participants and their beneficiaries by establishing fiduciary duties of care, plan disclosure requirements and more. This federal statute governs most private employee benefit plans, including defined contribution plans."

To protect themselves against lawsuits, "Plan sponsors should understand and fulfill their fiduciary duties," Fleckner comments. These include the duties of loyalty, prudence, diversification, and fidelity to plan documents. Loyalty focuses plan sponsors on doing what is in the best interest of participants, rather than on what may be of value to themselves or their company. "We've seen this duty raised in cases that have alleged that the plan fiduciaries cared more about saving money for the company than they did about doing what was right for the participants," he notes.

Prudence, in contrast, focuses on the process for making fiduciary decisions; for those lacking expertise to make decisions such as about investments, the government suggests they hire experts. Fleckner also discussed the duty of diversification, which is intended to help reduce the risk of losses. Plan sponsors are guided by the provisions of ERISA section 404(c) in offering at least three diversified investment choices within the plan. And, finally, there is the duty to follow plan documents.

ERISA litigation may arise when it is alleged that a plan sponsor has failed to meet any of these fiduciary duties, or to challenge technical violations of ERISA's prohibited transaction rules. Unlike in DB plans, where the company bears the cost in the event of an error or misjudgment, in DC plans the participants bear both the upside and downside risk—hence Fleckner commented that "we see few DB lawsuits and many DC cases. Also, since many of these fiduciary duties are left open to interpretation or to the particular facts and circumstances of a given case, this area exposes plan sponsors to litigation risk."

In the end, says Fleckner, fiduciaries need to demonstrate that they care about their participants: "In defending against any litigation involving those choices, it is most helpful to have a written record of the consideration that the fiduciaries gave in arriving at their decision. That way, we can show the judge that, in fact, the fiduciaries were evaluating options and landed on the ones that they felt were most appropriate for their participants."

WHO'S A FIDUCIARY?

ERISA requires that a DC plan have at least one fiduciary—that is, a person or entity either named in the written plan, or through a process described in the plan, as having control over the plan's operation. The Employee Benefits Security Administration (EBSA) explains: "The named fiduciary can be identified by office or by name. For some plans, it may be an administrative committee or a company's board of directors. A plan's fiduciaries will ordinarily include the trustee, investment advisers, all individuals exercising discretion in the administration of the plan, all members of a plan's administrative committee (if it has such a committee), and those who select committee officials. Attorneys, accountants, and actuaries generally are not fiduciaries when acting solely in their professional capacities. The key to determining whether an individual or an entity is a fiduciary is whether they are exercising discretion or control over the plan."

For plan sponsors who lack expertise in a specific area such as investment oversight, they may want to engage an investment consultant or other experts to help them fulfill their fiduciary responsibility. In 2011, we spoke at length to David Levine of Groom Law Group regarding fiduciary rules played by plan sponsors and outside advisors, including how to understand primary ERISA fiduciary categories, and what responsibilities fit with each.

In the U.S. system, the core concept of *fiduciary*, Levine told us, is contained within a single category—an ERISA "3(21) fiduciary." Beyond this basic definition are various additional roles, such as the concept of the *named fiduciary*, which generally is a fiduciary named either in a plan document or by a plan sponsor. A named fiduciary is the default plan fiduciary. Others, including advisors, can also be 3(21) fiduciaries. Further, a person can be a 3(16) plan administrator responsible for certain core administrative duties under ERISA. The determination of when a person is a fiduciary or not depends on their exact duties, on whether the duties are discretionary in nature, and on the financial relationship of the person to the plan. The bottom line, Levine says, is that "It's important to carefully evaluate each situation to determine whether an individual is a fiduciary or not."

We asked Levine about the plan design and oversight issues that require fiduciary oversight, including selecting the investment lineup and manager. In the case that the plan sponsor would prefer to outsource these duties, what should they consider? Here's what he told us:

> *The role and responsibilities for each advisor should be clear and documented within a contract and, depending on the exact circumstances, potentially in the plan document as well. In some cases, the administrative and investment issues are split and managed by different advisors. It's important that both the investment and administrative issues be addressed, and to clarify who is actually administering the plan. Without clarity, all fiduciary responsibility will, under many standardized plan documents, rest with the plan sponsor—that is, the company.*
>
> *Within advisor contracts, it's helpful to identify the exact fiduciary status of the advisor to minimize confusion as to what role the advisor is playing. Of course, each contracting situation is unique, so there is no one-size-fits-all solution.*
>
> *As plan sponsors and fiduciaries finalize their agreements with providers, you need to understand if this person is really saying, "I will be named as the main fiduciary in the plan document." Or are they saying, "I will be your co-fiduciary with you," which really means, "I'm just a fiduciary with your existing plan fiduciary, so we're all on the hook together"?*

The bottom line, Levine told us, is that outsourcing many fiduciary duties to a third party is doable, but "it's important to really dot the *i*s and cross the *t*s because this is where people may get caught, especially if they only focus on the investments and not on the administration."

HOW TO APPROACH OUTSOURCING DC PLAN RESOURCES

Levine told us that smaller plans will often end up with a prototype plan offered by a third-party administrator or a bundled-service provider; while larger plans may have a custom plan document but still use a third-party administrator, bundled-service provider, or independent recordkeeper. These administration providers will oftentimes manage the administration of the plan, handle all the day-to-day responsibilities, and make nondiscretionary recordkeeping decisions. Whether these providers are fiduciaries will depend on the exact circumstances of each situation, but "An advisor or consultant can play a key role in helping you figure out exactly what fees are being charged and what services are being provided by the recordkeepers and other providers." Levine adds, "They can help you confirm and document that the fees your plan is paying are reasonable."

The most common and typically the biggest role played by most advisors is in relation to the plan investments. In this case, the advisor can act as the fiduciary in the selection, monitoring, and retention of investment offerings for the plan. This includes vetting the managers, evaluating risk and return, and determining how the investments have done relative to peers and benchmarks. The advisor can either lead or help go through this process if the default plan fiduciary doesn't have the time, resources, or skills to do this work internally. A plan might even hire the advisor to assume full control or discretionary oversight of the investments for the plan. In all cases, the plan fiduciary needs to define the breadth of responsibility as well as agree to the advisor's fees. Says Levine, "Fiduciaries have a duty to properly appoint an investment manager. But once the decision is made, the risk is mostly shifted to the investment manager at that point (subject to a duty to monitor the investment manager)."

When we asked Levine what final words he had with respect to the changing role of plan sponsors and external advisors, he commented that "Too often, plan sponsors are bombarded from so many sides with information about these issues. Good advice and good support from outside parties doesn't have to be overwhelming to plan sponsors and plan fiduciaries. In fact, it appears to be moving us in a good direction where, hopefully, it will advance the entire system's objective as we move forward."

HIRING AN INVESTMENT CONSULTANT

DC investment consulting is a growing profession. In PIMCO's 2016 Defined Contribution Consulting Support and Trends Survey, the 66 participating DC consultant and advisory firms reported serving over 11,000 plan sponsor clients who together represent combined plan assets of over $4.2 trillion. These firms say they provide a broad range of services, including investment policy development and documentation, investment design, recordkeeping searches, and total plan cost or fee studies. Nearly all said they are willing to serve as a 3(21) nondiscretionary advisor—that is, they will make recommendations with respect to which investments a plan sponsor may want to select. The majority of consultants also are willing to serve in a 3(38) discretionary fiduciary capacity over such functions as manager selection, glide path oversight, and investment management. This allows the consultant to make decisions for the plan sponsor, such as which investment managers to hire. Consultants expect continued growth in discretionary services for clients, as clients may initially hire the consultant as a nondiscretionary advisor and then migrate the consultant to a discretionary role.

While hiring a consultant can help fulfill a plan's fiduciary duty, it is important to note that plan sponsors are not necessarily protected by going with the consultant's recommendation (no matter how well-documented that decision may be). In commenting on a recent lawsuit that followed a line of decisions that held that "independent expert advice is not a 'whitewash,'" Fleckner said: "The court explained that a fiduciary who relies on an expert, like a consultant, should make certain that reliance on the expert's advice is reasonably justified under the circumstances. The court cautioned that the sponsor cannot reflexively and uncritically adopt investment recommendations."

Ultimately, plan sponsors may take a different direction than recommended by their consultant and still meet their fiduciary duty. In fact, "if the sponsor believes that the consultant's recommendation is contrary to the interests of the plan and participants," comments Fleckner, "or it believes that the consultant did not engage in a rigorous enough process, then the fiduciary may be obligated to reject the recommendation. As discussed with any fiduciary decision, the plan sponsor should document its rationale for taking action that differs from the consultant's recommendation."

GETTING STARTED: SETTING AN INVESTMENT PHILOSOPHY AND GOVERNANCE STRUCTURE

In 2015, in collaboration with our UK-based colleague at the time, Will Allport, and a host of multinational plan sponsors, we created a guide to achieving a consistent philosophy and governance structure for global DC plans, Global DC Plans: Achieving Consistent Philosophy and Governance (DC Designs, November 2014). Whether you are a plan sponsor offering a plan only in the United States or via multiple plans around the world, it may be helpful to consider the following five-step process for DC retirement plan design.

1. Establish a plan philosophy and guiding principles
2. Set retirement plan objectives and design
3. Create a governance oversight structure
4. Formulate objective measures of success
5. Outline implementation considerations

We'll look at each of these steps in turn.

Establish Global Philosophy and Guiding Principles

It is sometimes a great challenge for organizations that already have a complex employee benefits and pensions landscape to step back and consider the basic question: "Why do we offer a DC plan?"

Although it seems simplistic, we believe asking this question is a critical first step in establishing a philosophy for DC design. Does an organization want to be paternalistic to its employees, to educate, guide, and empower them toward successful retirement outcomes, to be an attractive employer, and to retain and nurture talent? Or alternatively, does an organization offer pensions simply to satisfy legal or fiduciary requirements, or perhaps simply to meet the market norm? The reality is often a combination of all of the above, but establishing which motivations are most important will aid organizations in creating the guiding principles for all of their pension plans.

While an overarching philosophy to apply to pension benefits is somewhat intangible, the principles through which an organization ensures this philosophy is delivered should be anything but! The guiding principles that each organization should develop need to be clear, rigorous, and tangible. Each local plan will be able to prove whether it meets the requirements of these clear principles. The UK's Pensions Regulator put a great deal of effort into proposing effective principles for high-quality DC design, and we have drawn upon their work and others' in the suggestions that we include in the following.

Suggestions for Core DC Plan Guiding Principles
- **Principle 1:** Plans should be designed to target appropriate outcomes, for example, replace 50 percent of final pay throughout retirement.

- **Principle 2:** Plans should identify, evaluate, monitor, and manage key DC risks, for example, volatility, potential loss (value at risk), inflation, and longevity.
- **Principle 3:** Plans should have a clear governance framework to implement a global retirement benefits philosophy, with clear and transparent accountabilities and responsibilities.
- **Principle 4:** Plans should provide ongoing governance, regulatory oversight, and investment training to plan fiduciaries necessary to competently fulfill their duties.
- **Principle 5:** Plan design, investments, service providers, and fees should be reviewed annually by the organization's global DC plan oversight body or other designated bodies.
- **Principle 6:** Plans should seek recordkeepers that provide timely, accurate, and comprehensive records as well as appropriate disclosure on error resolution, fees, and services.
- **Principle 7:** Plan member communications should educate and guide participants toward informed retirement planning and investment decisions.

Set Retirement Plan Objectives and Design

Having established the overarching philosophy for retirement program design, and the core guiding principles that guide every plan, organizations next need to consider local factors and finalize the retirement benefit objectives for each plan.

This is the point at which most companies recognize that a one-size-fits-all approach to DC design probably will not work. For plans operating in more than one market, understanding the local labor market demands for each country in which the organization is operating is critical. No matter how many markets a plan serves, organizations need a clear view of the design of *first pillar* or *first source* Social Security benefits and the resulting income replacement targets, the competitive landscape benchmarked against other employers competing for the same talent pool, and statutory requirements. These and other considerations will help each plan to define its specific retirement benefits objectives.

Please note we are not suggesting that for multinational organizations, every plan within the organization should have similar objectives, or have the same design or providers. Rather, we would expect to see retirement benefit objectives that are philosophically consistent across all plans, and with the same core principles underpinning their design.

We believe that organizations that have not established the core objectives for each local plan risk a great deal. Without objectives, measuring the local plan's success—and therefore measuring return on investment for pension costs that affect the financial performance of the entire company—is virtually impossible.

Once objectives are set at the local level, most organizations find the design and investment structures underpinning each local plan are broadly similar, again excepting for local market nuances (for example, providers or legal restrictions).

Create Governance Oversight Structure

The first two steps of the five-step process require high-quality and clear communication across all the retirement benefits teams within an organization. Adhering to the core philosophies and guiding principles would be challenging without effective monitoring, along with engagement of senior leadership and broader stakeholders. Organizations should periodically revisit their guiding principles and objectives to ensure they evolve to meet the changing objectives of the corporation itself, alongside the needs of its employees. To achieve this, organizations should create a governance oversight structure that taps into the expertise of both in-house and retained investment, benefits, and other experts. The oversight structure establishes and evolves the guiding principles and philosophy for DC design, engaging key stakeholders throughout the organization. Critically, the structure allows for monitoring the plans for adherence to those core principles and for measuring the success of each plan relative to its objectives.

Formulate Objective Measures of Success

To effectively monitor DC efforts, organizations should establish clear success metrics. Since most DC plans aim to provide retirement income replacement, a percentage of final pay may be an appropriate success metric. Such a metric may be used internally to evaluate the plans; it need not be communicated to participants for fear they may construe the objective as a promise. Without clear objectives and the means to demonstrably measure progress against them, any retirement benefits program will be effectively "flying blind."

Outline Implementation Considerations

The final step in the process will be to assess and manage key implementation considerations that will underpin the final plan designs. These will include recordkeeper and custodian capabilities among many other considerations.

A PLAN SPONSOR'S PLAN DESIGN GUIDING PRINCIPLES

In July/August 2011, Judy Mares, at the time Chief Investment Officer of Alliant Techsystems Inc. (ATK), shared in a PIMCO DC Dialogue the five guiding principles that they established to guide the plan changes. She explained the following:

> To start, we established a set of five guiding principles to help our policy committee as they thought about the plan design.
>
> - First, we decided that we wanted to continue to deliver retirement benefits consistent with the company's business objective of providing employees with a solid foundation for retirement income.
> - Second, we wanted to encourage and facilitate our participants' establishment of a final income replacement rate based on personal facts and circumstances and desired retirement income.
> - Third, we needed to continue to educate participants about the factors that influence retirement income adequacy, such as cost-of-living increases, medical costs, longevity—the various factors that are key to the development of a financially successful retirement.
> - Fourth, we sought to offer a plan design and fund lineup that seek to minimize the negative effects of participant behavior. We looked at as many behavioral finance studies as we could get our hands on, and certainly that body of literature suggests that we should imbed structures in the plan that are more opt-out than opt-in.
> - Fifth, we strove to implement a plan fee and expense methodology that's understandable, transparent and reasonably applied across all participants. We could see that the Department of Labor was moving in that direction. But equally important was the sense that individuals could be better consumers when they know what things cost. Fee transparency helps people understand that component of decision making.

Finally, we presented these principles to our policy committee and gained approval. Then we started to look at the plan design, asking how the plan design addresses these principles, and whether we should think about doing things differently.

PIMCO PRINCIPLES FOR DC PLAN SUCCESS: BUILDING AND PRESERVING PURCHASING POWER

A key tenet of PIMCO's own DC principles is that success is defined as "building and preserving purchasing power to meet retirement income needs for the majority of participants, regardless of the prevailing economic environment." This definition has a subtle but incredibly important undertone, namely that the average outcome for participants is not enough on its own as an objective. Instead, as shown in Figure 1.1, the distribution of those outcomes across participants is critical. Think of it as a principle: *Avoiding failure for some is as important as marginal gains for the majority.* Said another way, we seek good outcomes for all plan participants. This principle requires a success metric (and accordingly an objective threshold to be defined) for avoiding failure, not just for achieving success. In Figure 1.1, we show people on the left standing in a shadow; this represents a probability distribution of those who may fail to reach 30 percent income replacement. You'll see on this distribution that there are many on the right who may achieve more than 75 percent income replacement. We believe plans should set a target income replacement level and design their plans to minimize the risk of failure (i.e., people in the shadow) even if that means they will reduce extreme winners (i.e., people on the right).

We define *success* as building and preserving purchasing power to meet retirement income needs for the *majority* of the people regardless of the economic environment.

Income Replacement Target

Sample for illustrative purposes only
The income replacement target illustrates an example of the percentage of their income that most plan participants will need to replace at retirement.

FIGURE 1.1 Consider Distribution of Potential Income-Replacement Outcomes: Identify Both Target and Failure
Source: PIMCO.

PIMCO believes that using an objective-aligned framework will lead to improved outcomes for DC participants, giving employees greater comfort over their retirement, human resource professionals greater confidence in their ability to perform effective workforce management, and corporate treasurers an improved sense of return on investment for retirement benefits spending.

Moving to an objective-based framework begins with acknowledging the retirement income objective—that is, the ability of the plan to help participants fund future consumption of goods and services. By aligning the investment management to this objective, the asset allocation structure shifts. Similar to DB, DC plans are not focused on maximizing returns. Rather, they aim to meet a future liability, and unlike DB assets that may not be required to keep pace with inflation, DC participants' objectives must meet the pace of inflation. Thus, shifting the asset allocation to inflation-hedging or "real" assets may better align DC assets to the objective and thereby reduce risk of failing to meet the plan's objective.

DCIIA Executive Director Lew Minsky shared, in PIMCO's January 2012 DC Dialogue, his views on defining DC plan success:

> At the end of the day, designing DC plans and their investment structures to "succeed" means designing them so that participants are more likely to have the money they need to retire and maintain their lifestyle in retirement. For most plan sponsors, defining success in terms of a retirement income target or outcome is a big shift. In the past, plan sponsors focused on other success measures, such as "What is my participation rate?" and "What's the savings rate of the non-highly compensated group that's going to allow me to meet my testing goals and not have to worry about the contributions of the highly compensated groups?"
>
> Redefining success as meeting a retirement income goal involves shifting from a strictly tactical view of DC plan management to a much more strategic view that asks, "Why are these plans in place?" and "What is the policy goal behind having these retirement savings plans?"

Minsky discusses how to achieve an outcome-focused design by referencing a DCIIA paper, "Institutionalizing DC Plans: Reasons Why and Methods How". This paper lays out the consultants' "building-block" approach for improving DC plan outcomes. In accordance with this approach, the consultants suggest focusing first on governance, then funding (i.e., increasing contribution rates), restructuring investments to an institutional model, and finally improving participant engagement and distribution options.

Aligning the investment design to the DC plan's retirement income objective will be the primary focus for the majority of this book. Before we turn to that topic in earnest, we must comment on the most critical first step in DC plan success: getting people into the plans and contributing at a sufficient rate.

MAXIMIZING DC SAVINGS: JUST DO IT!

One of the greatest advances in DC plan design is the leveraging of human behavior to improve contribution and investment behavior. Professors Richard Thaler at University of Chicago and Shlomo Benartzi at UCLA helped plan sponsors increase contribution rates with a concept they called "Save More Tomorrow" or SMART. In the June 2007 DC Dialogue, Professor Thaler explained:

> *The idea is to use simple principles of behavioral finance to design a program that helps people save more.*
>
> *We have three components in our version of auto escalation [with auto-escalation, your participation level is automatically increased at regular intervals, typically 1 percent a year, until it reaches a pre-set maximum]. First, we invite people to sign up for auto escalation a few months before it takes effect. Second, we link contribution increases to pay raises and, third, we leave things alone until the person opts out or reaches an IRS or plan savings cap. All three components are based on research principles.*
>
> *We ask people to sign up in advance because we know from other research that they're more willing to entertain self-control ideas if the control occurs in the future. As St. Augustine prayed, "Oh, Lord, make me chaste. But not yet!"*
>
> *People don't think they can afford to save more right now. Rather, they think they can later, perhaps. Linking savings increase to raises mitigates what we call "loss aversion"; people hate to see their pay go down, but they can imagine taking some of their raise and contributing it to the defined contribution plan.*
>
> *Then we let the power of inertia work for us. Once people sign up for a plan, they remain in unless they opt out. Fortunately, for both auto enrollment and escalation, the dropout rates are tiny. It's comforting because we worry that somehow we're tricking people into saving more. If people wake up and think that it's a mistake to save 10 percent, and they should return to 3 percent, then some people would return to 3 and ultimately hurt their retirement security.*

In fact, people almost never reduce their escalation contribution rates. A small percentage drops out of auto escalation, but typically that's to stop future escalation. It's rare for anyone to set his or her saving rate back to a lower percentage.

All these factors together lead us to think that auto programs help the vast majority of people save more. We don't hear complaints.

In July 2006, shortly prior to the enactment of the Pension Protection Act's (PPA) release in August, we conducted our first PIMCO DC Dialogue interview with Lori Lucas, CFA and now DC Practice Leader at Callan Associates. We titled the piece "Look, Ma! No Hands!" as she focused on how "autopilot" programs such as automatic enrollment and contribution escalation fuel DC asset accumulation without requiring action by the participant. Lori commented: "After years of trying to get people to participate actively in 401(k) plans, sponsors have learned that autopilot programs are most effective because they leverage inertia. The auto programs play into participants' inertia and make the plans work for employees—instead of against them—even if the employees do nothing."

Prior to autopilot programs, American employers spent millions of dollars trying to persuade workers to contribute to their DC plans. Among other reforms, the PPA gave plan sponsors statutory authority to auto-enroll eligible employees into the plan (yet allow participants to opt out if they preferred), thus finally providing sponsors with an alternative to begging workers to opt in. This "just do it" auto-enrollment approach, now adopted by 52.4 percent of U.S. employers (in 2014, according to Plan Sponsor Council of America's 58th Annual Survey), has successfully offset natural human inertia and improved DC participation and contribution rates, with about 80 percent of all eligible participants now making contributions. What's more, auto-escalation of the contribution rate, a feature utilized by almost 40 percent of plans that auto-enroll, may help pump up the percentage of salary that Americans contribute each year to 401(k) and other employer-provided DC plans.

In November 2011, DC Dialogue spoke with financial planner Lee Baker, CFP®, President of Apex Financial Services about automatic enrollment and contribution escalation, as well as retaining assets in the DC plan. He shared the following suggestions:

. . . automatic enrollment and contribution escalation can help a lot. Rather than putting [participants] into a plan at 3 percent of pay and escalating them up by 1 percent a year, I think they would be

better off to go in at the matched savings rate, often 6 percent, and then escalate up at 2 percent a year. This is a tolerable contribution rate and may help get folks to save over 10 percent of their pay, which they will need to meet their goals. What's important is to make sure they receive the full match.

Baker also encourages plan sponsors to offer participant education. He talks about how participants learn at seminars:

We help people get over these concerns [with investing in a DC plan] by explaining the value of their plan's matching contribution. There is a cost in that you have to give money to get money . . . you have to give up whatever else you could have done with that money. You put a hundred bucks in there and with many plans you're going to get an extra 50 bucks contributed by the employer.

There are always some light bulbs that go off when we say that, because often no one has ever explained it that way before. And here's the kicker. We may say, "You get this match money even if you put your money into the money market, cash, or stable value option."

Sometimes it can take a while, but if you're willing to provide some education, you'll see some attitudes change. Even if they start out investing in the conservative investment option, I would not be at all surprised if, over time, they begin to invest some of their dollars into a more broadly diversified portfolio. While diversification is important, just getting them started and saving in these plans has to be the first step.

Baker also notes the importance and power of retaining assets in a DC plan rather than cashing out or rolling the money over to an IRA. He comments:

Cash-outs are a problem. We believe people need to be educated—they need to understand the dangers of cashing out. You've got to help them understand what's going to happen if they cash out, particularly if they're under age 59 and $\frac{1}{2}$. They're going to give the government a 10 percent early withdrawal penalty, and they're not ever going to see that money again. It's just gone, because they're going to have to pay a huge hunk in taxes right up front.

At one session, one of the participants shared a story about cashing out a past 401(k). She decided to take the cash and buy *a car, but got a really nasty surprise when it came time to do her taxes. Participants need to hear, "Hey, listen, this lady thought she was going to go buy a car, so she took $30,000 out of her retirement account because she wanted to pay cash for the car. But she was shocked when she ended up with a $3,000 tax bill the next year." If nobody's ever told you, it's easy to make that kind of mistake.*

Baker encourages retirees to retain assets in an employer plan rather than rolling to an IRA, especially for those who have access to a large and well-managed plan. He also notes that "we can do more to help folks that remain in the plan during retirement by improving the distribution flexibility and offering retirement income options."

In a February 2016 Defined Contribution Institutional Investment Association (DCIIA) paper titled "Plan Leakage: A Study on the Psychology Behind Leakage of Retirement Plan Assets," they address the problem of leakage out of the DC system as follows:

According to a study by the Federal Reserve Board, $0.40 of every dollar contributed to the DC accounts of savers under age 55 eventually "leaks" out of the retirement system before retirement.* This phenomenon, often referred to as plan leakage, has a disproportionate incidence in those workers least prepared for retirement: of those who cashed out their DC retirement accounts upon a change in employment, 41 percent had less than $25,000 in household retirement savings.

A recent survey of 5,000 retirement plan participants sheds light on leakage patterns, as well as on the thought process of job changers who are confronted with the challenge of "rolling in" retirement savings from a former employer.**

Cash-outs occur at all income levels. Even among the highest income level (those earning over $150,000 annually), 33 percent reported they have cashed out at least one account during their career. However, cash-outs occur more frequently among those with lower wealth levels. More than 40 percent of workers with a modest level of wealth (defined as those with less than $25,000

---

* Robert Argento, Victoria L. Bryant, and John Sabelhaus, "Early Withdrawals from Retirement Accounts During the Great Recession," *Contemporary Economic Policy* 33, no. 1 (2015): 1–16.

** Warren Cormier, *Boston Research Technologies on behalf of Retirement Clearinghouse, Actionable Insights for Your Mobile Workforce,* 2015.

in household retirement savings) cashed out at least once in their working lifetime compared to only 23 percent of workers with more than $150,000 in retirement savings.

Approximately half of survey respondents reported leaving their retirement assets in their former employer's plan, a finding consistent across generational groups. Only about 20 percent of all generations expressed a well-thought-out reason for leaving their money in the previous employer plan, such as preferring the prior plan's investment menu or customer service. On the other hand, barriers such as not knowing how to roll over assets, not having time to do so, or not prioritizing the issue were each mentioned by about 20 percent of all generations as reasons for not moving retirement assets to their new employer's plan.

DCIIA's paper concludes that leakage remains an issue and undermines the goal of building retirement security. Removing obstacles or barriers to the rollover process is suggested. Unfortunately, it is much easier for a person to cash out than it is to roll the money into another employer's plan. The U.S. government is working to help minimize these barriers and complexities. While a far smaller issue compared to cash-outs, the failure to pay back loans is another way in which money may leak out of the DC system; this is particularly problematic when a participant loses his or her job and the loan is immediately due—if it goes unpaid, the loan becomes a distribution that is typically taxable to the participant. Offering a program to pay back a loan even after termination or perhaps even with a grace period (e.g., suspend payments for six months) is one way to help address leakage from loans. Among the many advantages of automatic enrollment and contribution escalation programs are that they may help participants start savings at an earlier age, and participants also may remain in the plans longer. In a July 2010 DC Dialogue with Jack VanDerhei, PhD, CEBS Research Director at the Employee Benefit Research Institute, he observed that:

Auto-enrollment can be a huge benefit particularly for the lowest income quartile. Two things we've seen over and over again in our research is that among the younger, lower-income employees, participation rates in traditional 401(k) plans without automatic enrollment are very low, in many cases under 50 percent. But if you switch to automatic enrollment, the percentage of individuals opting out, even in that young and low-income cohort, is quite small. You get the advantages of the increased participation rate, which should help increase overall balances in that group significantly.

VanDerhei also commented on how auto-enrollment may lead to higher retention of retiree assets:

There's no quantitative data thus far from which to draw conclusions because it's much too early. But I'm willing to predict that, as you find more of these 401(k) participants who are auto-enrolled, you also will find that more of them have never made any active investment decisions during the time they participated in a 401(k).

As a result, by the time these individuals reach retirement age, they may have very little desire to roll that money over to an IRA and then have to start actively managing it. Even if this IRA has the same funds available as in their former employer's DC plan, these individuals may be much more likely to keep their money with the 401(k) sponsor and continue to participate in a plan where they don't have to manage the asset allocation actively.

Beyond the U.S. borders, Australia and the UK have taken a more aggressive approach toward DC savings and asset retention. In Australia, employers are required to contribute 9.50 percent of pay, rising to 12 percent by 2025, to a tax-advantaged retirement plan (overwhelmingly a superannuation DC program). Between 2012 and 2017, the UK is phasing in a requirement for employers to auto-enroll participants at a rate that will increase to 8 percent of pay with at least 3 percent contributed by the employer (employees may still opt out). In contrast to the United States, once the money is in the Australian or UK programs, participants generally cannot withdraw funds until retirement age. Clearly, DC account values will build far more swiftly in the Australian and UK systems, given their higher contribution rates and their firmer control of leakage. In addition, the opting-out approach seems to function more effectively in the UK where many companies report that more than 85 percent of members defaulted into plans do not opt out.

IN CLOSING

In this chapter, we've set the stage for those that follow. We started with a review of the growing size and scope of DC plans in the United States and worldwide, and thus the growing importance of "getting DC right" as the future of an ever-increasing number of workers will depend on the income they receive in retirement from their DC plans. We introduced a number of core concepts that we'll further develop in the remainder of this volume, including the income replacement target for DC plans, and the question of "what is a fiduciary?" We also outlined the importance of establishing an overall investment philosophy and governing structure for DC plans. Developing these guiding elements for a DC plan will help plan sponsors walk through the "how" and "why" they are implementing DC plans, and can help workers understand how and why they should participate to help meet their personal retirement goals.

This chapter also draws on some of the work that PIMCO has undertaken to develop principles for DC plan success, including how both the success and, crucially, the failure of a DC plan is to be evaluated and measured. We noted that for PIMCO, success is defined as "building and preserving purchasing power to meet retirement income needs for the majority of participants, regardless of the prevailing economic environment." Folded into this definition of the objective for DC plans is the underlying idea that success must be measured by considering the outcomes for all participants, not just the average outcome for all. That is, the distribution of results is important—as the goal is to avoid failure for every participant, versus maximizing "winning" for some. With that objective in mind, we can ask: How might plans be designed to produce this outcome, and how does current plan design differ from the objective-aligned framework we've laid out in this chapter? With the continued global evolution toward a DC-based pension system and increasing reliance on these plans to meet retirement income needs, we're now ready—in subsequent chapters—to consider the investment design for these critical plans. Before we start, however, we end this chapter with a set of questions for plan fiduciaries to consider as they reflect on the discussion we've undertaken so far.

QUESTIONS FOR PLAN FIDUCIARIES

1. What is the objective for the DC plan(s)? If there are multiple plans, does the objective vary by plan?
2. What is the income replacement objective for the plan?
3. Who is the plan fiduciary? Who are the stakeholders?
4. Do you need external experts—such as an investment consultant, glide path manager, ERISA counsel, or others—to help oversee the plan?
5. Are your plan documents current and accurate?
6. Do you have governing principles?
7. Have you considered how you will benchmark your plan investments?

CHAPTER 2

Aligning DC Investment Design to Meet the PRICE of Retirement

Solving every asset allocation problem is the same mutatis mutandis—that is, changing only those things that need to be changed. There is always an objective for the investment, which is either real or nominal. For DC participants, the investment objective is usually to replace income in retirement—in real terms. Risk is the failure to meet the objective. Then DC investment choices, as well as the asset allocation and constraints, can be defined to align to the objective and within the risk capacity of the investors.

—Harry Markowitz, Nobel Prize–winning economist and father of modern portfolio theory

In 2013, I had the great honor, along with colleagues Ying Gao and Michael Esselman, of meeting Nobel Laureate and acknowledged father of modern portfolio theory Professor Harry Markowitz in his San Diego office. As plan fiduciaries consider the objective for their DC plan and structure the plan's investments to help meet it, Markowitz's words are influential. He tells us that for DC participants, the objective is to replace income in retirement—in real terms. In other words, a DC plan investment lineup should be designed and managed to meet a retirement income objective—one that builds sufficient assets to maintain a participant's lifestyle during retirement. To accomplish this goal, DC assets and the retirement income distributions must keep pace with inflation.

FIGURE 2.1   My 2013 Meeting with Dr. Harry Markowitz
Left to right: Michael Esselman, Dr. Harry Markowitz, Stacy Schaus, and Ying Gao (PIMCO).

Professor Zvi Bodie, The Norman and Adele Barron Professor of Management at Boston University (now retired), also underscores the importance of inflation protection in DC plans. In fact, he notes that DC plans offer an advantage relative to most defined benefit plans that lack inflation protection. Bodie shared with us (in PIMCO's March 2007 DC Dialogue): "Inflation protection makes the DC option stronger than traditional DB plans in this country, because DB plans don't offer inflation protection typically. Rather, a retiree's retirement income erodes over time as his or her dollars buy less in retirement."

Professor Bodie goes on to recommend that DC plans offer, as a retirement risk-free asset, treasury inflation-protected securities (TIPS) as these individual bonds contractually keep pace with inflation. He identifies TIPS as the most prudent asset for retirement investing. In Bodie's book, *Worry-Free Investing*, he tells readers that "If you want to sleep nights secure in the knowledge that you will achieve your savings goal, you must invest in a way that eliminates the possibility that inflation will undercut your efforts. If you try to do it by saving less and expecting the stock market to do the heavy lifting, you may not get there at all." He adds, "There are circumstances when you will want to take calculated risks by investing in the stock market in the hope of increasing your future income or wealth. . . . . But if you want to hit specific targets for certain, then worry-free investing with inflation-protected securities is the way to go."

Both Professors Markowitz and Bodie influence and guide our thinking about investing for retirement, starting with the objective to create a real income stream in retirement and seeking appropriate assets to help meet this objective.

In this chapter, we'll take a close look at the DC plan objective and setting a specific target replacement income rate. Then we'll suggest a methodology to quantify the income-replacement target using the PIMCO Retirement Income Cost Estimate (PRICE). We will show you how the PRICE methodology can help determine how much it may cost to retire, whether the investment default and other plan investments are aligned to meet a retirement income objective, and finally how to consider whether the retirement income offerings are likely to keep pace with the cost of retirement.

BEGIN WITH THE END IN MIND

As Steven Covey tells us in *The 7 Habits of Highly Effective People*, we should "begin with the end in mind." We agree with this thinking and encourage plan fiduciaries to think first about the investment objective for their DC plan. As discussed earlier, for most that objective is to help provide sustainable retirement income for participants. Over the past 10 years, we have interviewed dozens of DC plan sponsors and consultants about plan design. In the DC Dialogue series, we often begin with the question "What is the philosophy for design or objective for your DC plan?" In PIMCO's November/December 2012 DC Dialogue, Karin Brodbeck, Director of Retirement Investments at Nestlé USA, Inc., shared Nestlé's philosophy for retirement plan design:

> *Our management style is to look at our retirement plans holistically. For most workers, we have a three-legged retirement stool, including Social Security, DB, and DC. Speaking specifically to DC, our general philosophy is that our plans need to be designed to deliver a reasonable likelihood of meeting the participants' income needs. As we designed our plans, we aimed for the combined sources of*

income to replace 70 percent of an employee's final pay. For those who only have a DC plan, they may need 40 percent of their pay replaced by the DC plan.

While many plan sponsors consider the DC plan the primary retirement plan for employees, they often do not state a specific income replacement target. However, they may be aware of the retirement income replacement need and take this into account as they design their plan and investment defaults. For instance, Brad Leak, CFA, managing director of public markets at The Boeing Company, tells PIMCO in a 2012 DC Dialogue that "We don't have a specific income replacement goal. However, we did consider whether various glide paths were likely to maintain a retiree's consumption pattern throughout retirement. We focused on glide path designs that had at least a 90 percent chance of maintaining the modeled consumption pattern." (The term "glide path" refers to a formula that defines the asset allocation mix of a fund, based on the number of years to a target date. The glide path typically creates an asset allocation that becomes more conservative—that is, includes more fixed-income assets and fewer equities—the closer a fund gets to the target date.)

Generally, corporate plan sponsors tell us that the defined benefit plan is no longer open to new hires and instead participants must look to the DC plan as the primary occupational pension scheme. But what about employers that do offer a DB plan? Is their DC plan objective different? Not necessarily.

Over the years, we've spoken with many DC plan sponsors that also offer a DB pension plan to participants. For instance, nearly all of the public employers continue to offer a DB benefit. Nonetheless, these plan sponsors acknowledge that retirees increasingly will look to DC plans to replace at least a certain percentage of a participant's final pay. In the May/June 2015 DC Dialogue, Joshua Franzel, PhD, Vice President of Research at the Center for State and Local Government Excellence (slge.org) in Washington, DC, shared an overview on retirement income sources for public workers:

Public workers may have one or more sources of retirement income, including Social Security, a DB plan, a DC plan, or a hybrid program, which may be a DB/DC combination or cash balance plan. According to [the Bureau of Labor Statistics], as of 2014, 86 percent of state workers and 82 percent of local workers had access to a DB plan, while only 43 percent and 30 percent had access to a DC plan, respectively.

According to NASRA [the National Association of State Retirement Administrators], about 75 percent of state and local workers participate in Social Security through their current jobs. About 40 percent of all public school teachers don't participate in Social Security in their current roles, and about two-thirds of public safety workers don't participate in Social Security. There are some states, such as Alaska, Colorado, Louisiana, Maine, Massachusetts, Nevada, and Ohio, where essentially all public employees don't participate in Social Security.

A couple of states—Alaska and Michigan—offer only a DC plan for state workers. Eight states offer a hybrid plan that is either a combination of DB and DC or a cash balance plan. Nine states offer workers a choice between plan types. There has been growing interest in the hybrid plan design.

He goes on to explain the increasing importance of DC plans:

Changes to DB as well as to health care plans increase the importance of supplemental DC savings in the state and local sector. While we refer to DC as "supplemental savings," these plans are a growing part of building retirement security. For workers to retire on time and support a reasonable standard of living, they will likely need a DC plan, other personal savings, and Social Security, if they participate. While there is no set retirement income objective, many folks are thinking 85 percent of final pay is an appropriate goal.

WHAT IS A REASONABLE PAY REPLACEMENT TARGET?

Several factors influence the pay replacement target, including the public pension (e.g., Social Security) amount, availability of a DB plan, worker income level, tenure, and assumed retirement age. We are often asked, "How do you have a target income replacement percentage for a population that is highly diverse?" While imperfect, focusing the plan to the median worker may be most appropriate. Workers with lower incomes may have more of their pay replaced by Social Security, while higher-income individuals may have other compensation programs or personal savings to help meet retirement income needs. It is also important to note that the overall income replacement level will vary by individual and income band. Those with the highest income may need a far lower income replacement level, while those with the lowest income may need more.

While beyond the scope of this book, retiree medical cost coverage is also a significant factor to consider. Only a small percentage of U.S. private employers cover retiree medical costs, and this number continues to decline according to unpublished Employee Benefit Research Institute estimates from the Medical Expenditure Panel Survey: "Very few private-sector employers currently offer retiree health benefits, and the number offering them has been declining. In 2014, 16.6 percent of workers were employed at establishments that offered health coverage to early retirees, down from 28.9 percent in 1997."

By contrast, many public employers do cover retiree medical, although according to Franzel this is beginning to change:

> *A few public employers have dropped retiree medical altogether or changed to a DC model for retiree health coverage. Unlike DB plans that may be protected by state constitutions or statute, health care benefits typically do not have the same protections. As a result, health care benefits are more likely to be cut. That's another reason why DC plan availability and contributions will likely grow— retirees may look to their DC plan to help fund more of their retiree medical expenses.*

Workers outside the United States are far more likely to have retiree medical coverage via the government. Given that the majority of U.S. workers lack both a retiree medical and a DB plan, we asked consultants in our 2016 Defined Contribution Consulting Support and Trends Survey: What total income replacement percentage should the median worker seek? At the median, consultants suggested 80 percent as the total replacement target, yet some suggested as little as 50 percent and others as much as 120 percent. That's quite a range. Let's look at income sources that can help fill this need.

Public pension income such as Social Security is the first building block in real retirement income replacement. Today, U.S. Social Security provides 35 percent of retirees' income. In the OECD's Pensions at a Glance, 2015, they provide expected public pension income replacement by country for various worker income levels. As shown in Figure 2.2, the public pension expected income replacement level for the median worker ranges from 4 percent in Mexico to 70 percent in Italy. This means DB, DC, or personal savings must fill the gap.

The OECD also projects what percentage of pay replacement may come from occupational pension programs, such as DC plans. Figure 2.2 shows that countries may have mandatory or voluntary DB or DC systems. For instance, Australia requires participation in a DC plan (i.e., superannuation), whereas the UK requires auto-enrollment in a DC plan. The difference in the latter case is that participants may decide to opt out of the DC plan. Based on this OECD data, U.S. plan sponsors may consider an income

FIGURE 2.2   Expected Retirement Income from Public Pension

| Market | Funded Pension System | Gross Pension Replacement Rates | | |
| | | Mandatory | | |
Country	Structure	Public	Private	Voluntary DC Total
Australia	Mandatory DC	14%	31%	0%	45%
Canada	Voluntary DC/DB	37%	0%	29%	66%
Denmark	Mandatory DC	22%	46%	0%	68%
France	Voluntary DC/DB	55%	0%	0%	55%
Germany	Voluntary DC/DB	38%	0%	13%	51%
Italy	Auto-enrollment DC	70%	0%	0%	70%
Japan	Voluntary DC/DB	35%	0%	0%	35%
Mexico	Mandatory DC	4%	22%	0%	26%
United Kingdom	Auto-enrollment DC	22%	0%	30%	52%
United States	Voluntary DC/DB	35%	0%	33%	68%

Source: OECD, *Pensions at a Glance 2015.*

replacement target from DC of 40 percent or more. Consultants place this target for U.S. workers higher at 60 percent, yet some suggested as low as 20 percent.

Plan sponsors also may vary the replacement income target based on the demographic characteristics of their organization's population. For instance, airline pilots may have shorter careers but higher pay than employees in many organizations. David Fisser, consultant and former chairman of the Southwest Airline Pilots' Association 401(k) Committee in a July 2009 DC Dialogue said this about pilots: "They have higher incomes. They also have a mandatory retirement age of no later than 65 years, which works well because our average new-hire age is about 35 now. If participants can work until they're 65, they have around 30 years to accumulate enough funds to provide a decent retirement."

By comparison, university professors may have longer careers but possibly lower pay levels. Yet, the pilot may not have a DB plan while the professor may. As a final example, retail organizations may have both short tenure and lower pay levels—and no DB plan.

As we consider an appropriate income replacement target, plan sponsors should also consider what would be considered failure. For instance, if the target is to replace 60 percent of final pay, would replacing only

30 percent be considered failure? As we consider DC design throughout this book, we use as an example income replacement target of 50 percent and consider achieving less than 30 percent as failure. Plan sponsors may set higher or lower targets and apply the same evaluation methods to determine likely success.

CALCULATING THE INCOME REPLACEMENT RATES

How do plan fiduciaries calculate the replacement rate historically as well as prospectively? While few participants actually buy an annuity, a common approach to calculating income replacement ratios is to consider the cost of buying a lifetime income stream via an immediate annuity.

For example, consider a 65-year-old male who has accumulated $400,000 in DC assets. This is a substantial sum, but is it enough to deliver an adequate income in retirement? One way to answer the question is to look at the income that could be delivered by purchasing an annuity. Based on average annuity quotes between March 2013 and December 2015 provided by Hueler Companies (Figure 2.3), he may have received an annuity payout equal to a 6.47 to 7.17 percent return, providing an annual income of $25,899 to $28,665 a year. If we assume his final pay was $75,000, his income replacement rate would be 35 to 38 percent, depending on the year in which he retired.

But what if he wanted to purchase a *real* annuity in which the payout is adjusted annually consistent with the Consumer Price Index (CPI)? Over

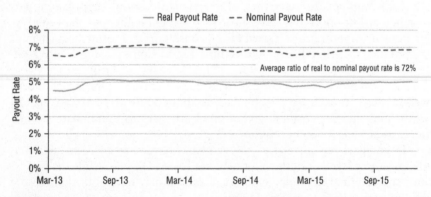

FIGURE 2.3 Immediate Annuity Income: Real Payout Rate versus Nominal Payout Rate
Sources: Hueler Companies, Inc., and PIMCO, as of December 31, 2015. Hueler data is © 2015 Hueler Companies, Inc. All Rights Reserved.

the period from March 1, 2013 to December 31, 2015, real annuity quotes averaged 72 percent of the nominal payout (see Figure 2.3). This means the dollars paid would have delivered $17,885 to $20,501 a year, or 4.47 to 5.13 percent annually, in real terms. His real income replacement rate would then equal 24 to 27 percent of his final salary.

To consider a longer time frame historically or to model prospectively, we need a proxy for annuity pricing. At PIMCO, we developed a methodology for this proxy that we refer to as the PIMCO Retirement Income Cost Estimate (or PRICE). PRICE is calculated as the discounted present value of a 20-year annual income stream using the historical zero-coupon U.S. TIPS yield curve. After considering many alternatives, we have found that a 20-year ladder of zero-coupon TIPS provides the best available proxy for annuity rates. If we compare real annuity rates to the TIPS ladder (which is a portfolio of TIPS with different maturities), we see a 91 percent correlation and a small difference in the payout rate (Figure 2.4).

In our view, a 20-year inflation-adjusted income stream from TIPS makes sense as a proxy for inflation-adjusted income, particularly as we

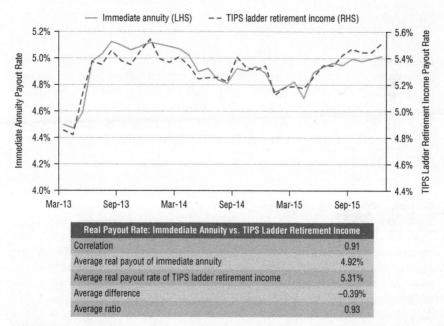

Real Payout Rate: Immdediate Annuity vs. TIPS Ladder Retirement Income	
Correlation	0.91
Average real payout of immediate annuity	4.92%
Average real payout rate of TIPS ladder retirement income	5.31%
Average difference	−0.39%
Average ratio	0.93

FIGURE 2.4 Correlation of Real Annuity Rates with TIPS Ladder Retirement Income
Sources: Hueler Companies, Inc., and PIMCO, as of December 31, 2015. Hueler data is © 2015 Hueler Companies, Inc. All Rights Reserved.

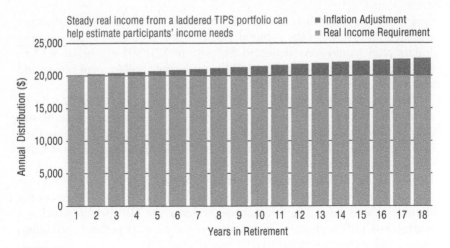

FIGURE 2.5   Real Income in Retirement from a TIPS Ladder

The chart above depicts the components for the total distribution that an investor receives over time. The cumulative inflation accruals may be adjusted higher or lower as a result of increases (inflation) or decreases (deflation) in the Consumer Price Index (CPI). Due to the laddered structure, the amount of principal in the distributions is higher in later years.

Source: PIMCO. For illustrative purposes only.

consider life expectancy for a 65-year-old male today is 17.4 years, and for a female 20.4 (according to the 2010 life expectancy tables from the Society of Actuaries). Thus if a retiree bought a 20-year ladder of TIPS bonds, as shown in Figure 2.5, he or she would have real purchasing power over those 20 years. We considered adjusting the TIPS ladder for a mortality credit or otherwise, but found a simple ladder to have the best fit to the actual real annuity pricing.

HISTORIC COST OF RETIREMENT: PRICE IS A MOVING TARGET

Participants often ask, "How much do I need to retire?" Or "What's my number?" Unfortunately, this is not an easy question to answer as the cost to retire will depend largely on prevailing interest rates at the time of retirement. Using PRICE helps us look both at the historic cost of retirement as well as the potential future cost.

How much people need for retirement is a moving target. Over the last decade, using PRICE as the definition of the cost of retirement, near-retirees have faced an escalating retirement price tag. This change is shown

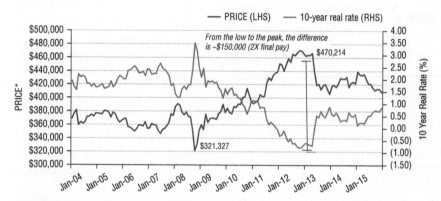

FIGURE 2.6 PRICE Is a Moving Target: How Much Does a Participant Need to Replace 30 Percent of Final Pay?

Hypothetical example for illustrative purposes only.

Assumptions: (1) a participant has $75,000 in final salary regardless of the time period; (2) his or her goal is to achieve a 30 percent income replacement rate after retirement.

*The retirement income cost is calculated as the discounted present value of the 20-year annual income stream of $22,500 by using the historical zero-coupon U.S. TIPS yield curve.

Sources: PIMCO, Bloomberg Finance L.P., and Haver Analytics, as of December 31, 2015.

in Figure 2.6, which graphs the change for a typical participant with final pay of $75,000 and a 30 percent real retirement income replacement goal (i.e., $22,500 CPI-adjusted annual income). As you can see in Figure 2.6, from a 2008 low to a peak in 2013, the near-retiree saw her retirement cost jump by about $150,000—or twice her final pay.

Because the retirement cost is calculated as the discounted present value of future cash flows, it is not surprising to see that it is inversely correlated with interest rates: As interest rates move up, the cost of retirement moves down, and vice versa. This relationship underscores why retirees desperately need rates to rise!

Figure 2.6 only takes us so far, however; as while understanding historical retirement costs is useful, and can provide insight into cost over time, workers and plan fiduciaries likely care more about *future* costs.

This is where PRICE can help. Figure 2.7 shows the cost of retirement based on a participant's age, an assumed retirement at age 65, and desired annual income stream, as of December 2015. Looking at Figure 2.7, you can see that at the end of 2015, for a 25-year-old to buy an annual CPI-adjusted income stream of $50,000, the cost would have been just under $530,000. In contrast, for participants age 45 or 65, buying the same real annual income would have cost about $685,000 and just over $900,000,

FIGURE 2.7   Cost for Future Retirement Income Stream

As of December 31, 2015		Cost for Future Annual Retirement Income Stream		
Age	PRICE Multiplier	$25,000 Annual Income	$50,000 Annual Income	$100,000 Annual Income
25	10.59	$264,794	$529,589	$1,059,178
35	12.02	$300,471	$600,942	$1,201,884
45	13.70	$342,559	$685,118	$1,370,237
55	15.79	$394,726	$789,453	$1,578,906
65	18.15	$453,836	$907,671	$1,815,343

Hypothetical example for illustrative purposes only. Multiplier is rounded so annual income amounts differ.

Sources: PIMCO, Bloomberg Finance L.P., and Haver Analytics, as of December 31, 2015.

respectively. The discount rate (used to determine the present value) differs depending on the years to retirement. The closer a participant is to retirement, the higher the retirement cost.

To consider the cost of different annual income streams, readers may use the "PRICE multiplier" shown in Figure 2.7. The PRICE multiplier is the cost of one dollar of annual retirement income, and is calculated as the discounted present value of the 20-year zero-coupon TIPS ladder. It shows, for example, that for a 25-year-old seeking $100,000 of real annual income in retirement (with an assumed retirement at age 65—meaning they are 40 years from retirement, 20 years from retirement, or have reached retirement), the purchase price was simply the annual retirement income times the PRICE multiplier, or approximately $1.06 million. Figure 2.8 shows the PRICE multiplier change over time (January 2004 to December 2015) for participants at 25, 45, and 65 years old.

As you can see in Figure 2.8, since inception in February 2004, the annualized change in the PRICE multiplier is *highest* for the 40 years to retirement vintage at 3.7 percent and *lowest* for the at-retirement vintage at 0.9 percent. This change is largely a function of the longer duration of retirement liability and the declining interest-rate environment.[1] Looking at the volatility of the PRICE metric, from inception to December 2015, the PRICE multiplier had annualized volatility of 7.3 percent at retirement (i.e., age 65). PRICE multiplier volatility is much higher 20 and 40 years prior to retirement at 20.4 percent and 34.7 percent, respectively. What this means for prospective retirees is that a considerable amount of uncertainty remains in retirement planning as the years from retirement increase and

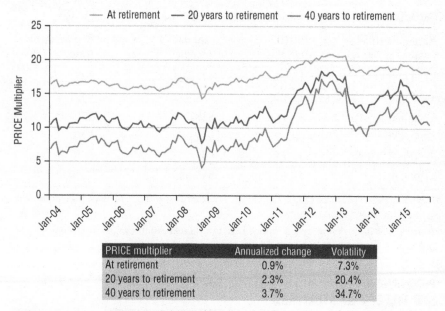

PRICE multiplier	Annualized change	Volatility
At retirement	0.9%	7.3%
20 years to retirement	2.3%	20.4%
40 years to retirement	3.7%	34.7%

FIGURE 2.8   Price Multiplier for Different Age Groups

Hypothetical example for illustrative purposes only.

Sources: PIMCO, Bloomberg Finance L.P., and Haver Analytics, as of December 31, 2015.

uncertainty about the prospective cost of retirement declines as the retirement date approaches.

A FOCUS ON INCOME, NOT COST

Some participants may flip the "What's my number?" question and ask, "How much income can I buy given my current savings?" Similarly, plan fiduciaries may consider what percentage of income can be replaced based on the median balance in their DC plan.

The PRICE multiplier can help give insight to these questions as well. Figure 2.9 shows how much income (and what replacement rate) various levels of savings could confer as of December 2015. For a 65-year-old with $500,000, the multiplier is 18.15, leading to a projected annual income of about $27,500—or a 37 percent income replacement rate, assuming her final pay is $75,000. If her accumulated balance increases to $700,000, the income replacement rate increases to 51 percent.

FIGURE 2.9 Estimated Income Replacement from Various Levels of Savings

Accumulated Balance at Age 65	PRICE Multiplier	Annual Income	Income Replacement Rate
$500,000	18.15	$27,543	37%
$600,000	18.15	$33,052	44%
$700,000	18.15	$38,560	51%
$800,000	18.15	$44,069	59%
$900,000	18.15	$49,577	66%
$1,000,000	18.15	$55,086	73%

Assumes a participant has $75,000 in final salary regardless of the time period. Hypothetical example for illustrative purposes only.

Sources: PIMCO, Bloomberg Finance L.P., and Haver Analytics, as of December 31, 2015.

PRICE-AWARE: APPLYING PRICE TO CONSIDER DC ASSETS AND TARGET-DATE STRATEGIES

Now that we have identified PRICE as a proxy for the historic and future cost of retirement (i.e., the real liability), we can evaluate assets and asset allocation structures relative to PRICE. To reduce risk relative to the retirement-income replacement objective, DC plans—like their DB cousins—should seek assets that are liability-aware. PRICE tells us the cost of the DC liability. If we look at asset classes, we can determine which ones correlate best to the liability. Figure 2.10 shows a low correlation of 0.11 between the monthly returns of the S&P 500 Index and the retirement liability from

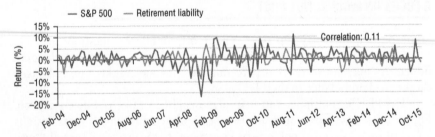

FIGURE 2.10 S&P Index versus Retirement Liability

Retirement liability represented by a 20-year zero-coupon TIPS ladder.

Sources: Bloomberg Finance L.P., Haver Analytics, and PIMCO, as of December 31, 2015.

FIGURE 2.11 Long-Duration TIPS versus Retirement Liability

Retirement liability represented by a 20-year zero-coupon TIPS ladder. Long TIPS represented by Barclays U.S. TIPS Index > 10 Years.

Sources: Bloomberg Finance L.P., Haver Analytics, and PIMCO, as of December 31, 2015.

January 2004 through December 2015. In contrast, Figure 2.11 shows the correlation between the retirement liability and long-duration TIPS is very "tight" (0.95).

In Figure 2.12, we show the absolute risk (volatility) side-by-side with the risk relative to retirement income generated by the TIPS ladder. This illustrates the reduced retirement income risk of long-duration TIPS compared to stocks, nominal bonds, and even cash.

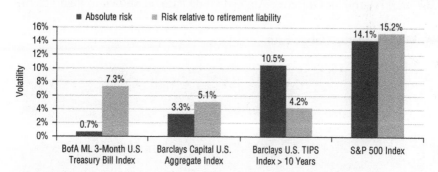

FIGURE 2.12 Considering Absolute Risk of Selected Assets versus Risk Relative to Retirement

Absolute risk is measured by the standard deviation of monthly returns of the asset class from February 2004 to December 2015; relative risk to retirement liability is measured by the standard deviation of surplus returns over retirement liabilities (represented by a 20-year zero-coupon TIPS ladder) from February 2004 to December 2015.

Sources: Bloomberg Finance L.P., Haver Analytics, and PIMCO, as of December 31, 2015.

Selecting assets that correlate with PRICE better aligns the investments to the DC plan objective. Unlike a DB plan, DC plans are unlikely to fully match the assets to the liabilities. In the February 2011 DC Dialogue, Professor Zvi Bodie shared with us a basic formula which shows that if participants want to replace 50 percent of their income in retirement and desire to retire at age 65, they need to begin saving 25 percent of their pay at age 25, assume a zero real interest rate on their savings, and expect to live to age 85. In reality, on average the DC participants' saving rates are far below 25 percent, according to 2016 EBRI Retirement Confidence Survey. DC plan fiduciaries would not buy only TIPS—rather, they will likely include other assets that may offer additional return and accept the risk (i.e., tracking error) relative to PRICE. Target-date funds offer the most prevalent example of a DC asset allocation structure. In Chapters 3 and 4 we will take a close look at investment structures and target-date strategies. For now, let's take a quick look at how an asset allocation glide path may be evaluated relative to PRICE.

EVALUATING GLIDE PATHS

By aligning the target-date design to the retirement liability PRICE, DC participants have a higher likelihood of meeting their income goals. Let's consider two glide paths: the Market Average Glide Path (which is constructed by NextCapital and is an average of the 40 largest target-date strategies in the market) and an Objective-Aligned Glide Path, as shown in Figure 2.13.

A. Market Average Glide Path

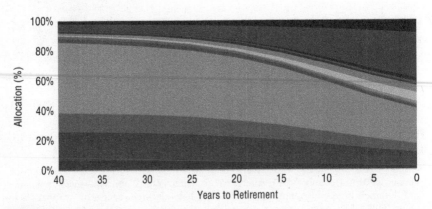

FIGURE 2.13   Glide Path Asset Allocation
Market Average data is as of September 30, 2015. Objective-aligned data is as of December 31, 2015.

Sources: PIMCO and NextCapital.

B. Objective-Aligned Glide Path

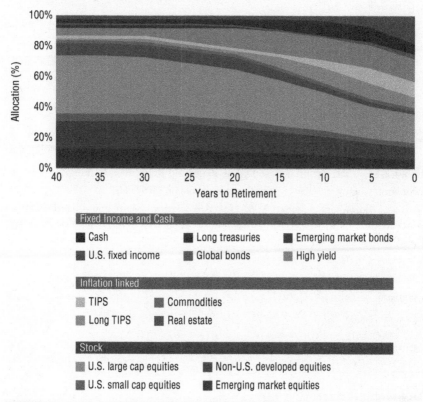

FIGURE 2.13 (*continued*)

The Objective-Aligned Glide Path has a greater proportion of assets allocated to TIPS, including an allocation of between 1 percent and 10.0 percent to long-duration TIPS. Back-tested results from January 2004 to December 2015 (see Figure 2.14) show that the Objective-Aligned Glide Path at-retirement vintage has a tighter correlation to the retirement liability at .51 than the Market Average Glide Path at-retirement vintage at .38.

Plan fiduciaries may worry that a tighter correlation relative to PRICE may result in lower investment returns. This is not necessarily the case. According to back-tested results from February 2004 to December 2015, the Objective-Aligned Glide Path yields greater inflation-adjusted capital appreciation. For instance, assume participants started with $350,000 and invested in the Market Average Glide Path and the Objective-Aligned Glide Path at age 55 (from January 2004 through December 2015). Figure 2.15 shows that the accumulated real balance is $42,751, or 6.1 percent higher, for the Objective-Aligned Glide Path compared to the Market Average Glide Path.

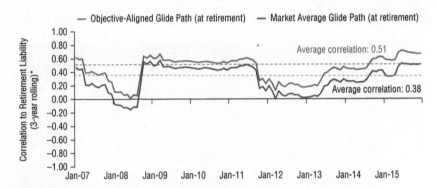

FIGURE 2.14   Correlation between Glide Paths and Retirement Liability

Retirement liability represented by a 20-year zero-coupon TIPS ladder.

Sources: Bloomberg Finance L.P., Haver Analytics, NextCapital, and PIMCO. Market Glide data is as of September 30, 2015; Objective-Aligned Glide Path data is as of December 31, 2015.

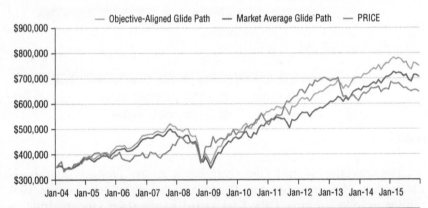

	Objective-Aligned Glide Path	Market Average Glide Path
A: Average deviation in accumulated balance (vs. PRICE)	$26,851	–$5,913
B: Tracking error in accumulated balance (vs. PRICE)	$48,050	$52,130
Ratio of average deviation to tracking error in accumulated balance (A/B)	0.56	–0.11

FIGURE 2.15   Accumulated Real Balance

Hypothetical example for illustrative purposes only. Salary at age 55: $67,000; real annual wage growth: 1 percent; savings rate: 12 percent; employer match: 3.5 percent.

Sources: PIMCO, NextCapital, Bloomberg Finance L.P., and Haver Analytics, as of December 31, 2015.

As fiduciaries evaluate DC plan investments, they will need to bring together both risk and return considerations. As the most prevalent DC investment default, target-date funds rise to the top in requiring scrutiny and benchmarking. We suggest plan sponsors evaluate target-date strategies relative to their investment objective, which consultants define as "to maximize asset returns while minimizing volatility relative to the retirement liability."

Evaluating asset structures relative to this objective can be done using an *information ratio*, that is, a risk-adjusted return measure calculated using active return divided by tracking error, where active return is the difference between the return of the security and the return of a selected benchmark index, and tracking error is the standard deviation of the active return. Figure 2.16 shows how target-date glide paths can be evaluated relative to PRICE within an information ratio context. Again, comparing the two glide paths—the Market Average Glide Path and the Objective-Aligned Glide Path—we see in Figure 2.16 that across all "vintages" (years in which income will start to be required from the portfolio—such as the at-retirement vintage, or the 20-years-to-retirement vintage), the Objective-Aligned Glide Path has a higher excess return, lower tracking error, and higher information ratio. The at-retirement vintage shows a 0.72 information ratio for the Objective-Aligned path compared with 0.60 for the Market Average path.

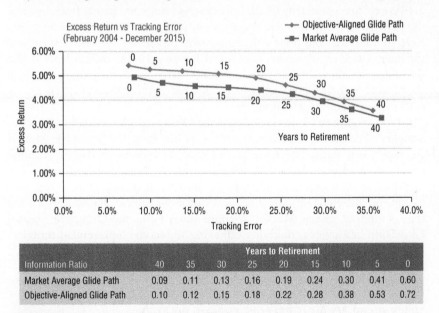

Information Ratio	Years to Retirement								
	40	35	30	25	20	15	10	5	0
Market Average Glide Path	0.09	0.11	0.13	0.16	0.19	0.24	0.30	0.41	0.60
Objective-Aligned Glide Path	0.10	0.12	0.15	0.18	0.22	0.28	0.38	0.53	0.72

FIGURE 2.16 Excess Return versus Tracking Error to Price (February 2004–December 2015)

Hypothetical example for illustrative purposes only.

Sources: PIMCO, Bloomberg Finance L.P., and Haver Analytics, as of December 31, 2015.

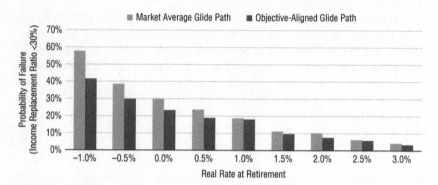

FIGURE 2.17   Probability of Failure (Income Replacement Ratio <30 Percent)
Hypothetical example for illustrative purposes only.
Sources: PIMCO, NextCapital, as of December 31, 2015.

This assessment tells fiduciaries whether participants have been compensated for taking on the added risk, or tracking error, as measured by the information ratio (which for our purposes is the ratio of excess return to tracking error, both relative to PRICE). The downward slope that you can see in Figure 2.16 is explained primarily by the lower excess return and higher tracking error over PRICE of the farther-dated vintages (i.e., 20 or more years to retirement). Keep in mind that the slope will change over time based on asset returns and the interest-rate environment. Looking at Figure 2.16, the overall story is that the Objective-Aligned Glide Path has been a better choice for participants than the Market Average Glide Path, when compared on the metrics of excess return, tracking error, and information ratio.

From Figure 2.13, we know that the Objective-Aligned Glide Path has a higher allocation to liability aware assets like long TIPS than the Market Average Glide Path. The level of real rates at retirement has a profound effect on income replacement. An allocation to long duration assets late in the glide path can help mitigate the likelihood of achieving a very low income replacement ratio during a low rate environment. Figure 2.17 shows that compared to the Market Average Glide Path, the Objective-Aligned Glide Path has lower probability of having an income replacement ratio less than 30 percent under different real rate environments and the difference is larger when real interest rate is lower.

TRACKING DC ACCOUNT BALANCE GROWTH RELATIVE TO PRICE

Taking our analysis further, plan sponsors may also want to evaluate how the default investment strategy performs relative to PRICE by taking into account the impact of savings.

Here's how it works. Assume a participant at age 55 has accumulated $350,000 in retirement savings. Her personal savings rate and the employer match from age 55 through 65 are 12 percent and 3.5 percent per year, respectively. Her salary at age 55 is $67,000 and the real annual wage growth rate is 1 percent per year. Given this information, we can calculate and compare the DC account balance that would have accumulated by investing in the Objective-Aligned Glide Path and the Market Average Glide Path, both relative to PRICE.

Figure 2.15 tells us that the average deviation from PRICE in the accumulated balance has been *positive* for the Objective-Aligned Glide Path and *negative* for the Market Average Glide Path between January 2004 and December 2015. Although both glide paths outpaced PRICE—they ended ahead of the retirement cost—from the perspective of relative risk, the Objective-Aligned Glide Path had significantly lower tracking error in its accumulated balance than the Market Average Glide Path. Thus, the Objective-Aligned Glide Path had a positive ratio of average deviation to tracking error in accumulated balance at 0.56, whereas the corresponding ratio for the Market Average Glide Path was –0.11. Again, the overall story is that the Objective-Aligned path presented a more successful outcome for participants over this timeframe.

SUMMARY: THE IMPORTANCE OF KNOWING YOUR PRICE

As with reaching any goal, a concrete objective—knowing one's number—can be helpful. Although it is a theoretical construct, not a prediction or projection of investment return, PRICE can help in this regard. It can translate accumulated account balances into future retirement income potential. And it can help plan sponsors benchmark target-date strategies.

Plan fiduciaries, especially those in the United States, will want to keep a close eye on how their target-date funds have performed, and how likely they are to deliver the retirement income plan participants need. PRICE is a simple yet compelling methodology to address this most fundamental of retirement planning questions. We believe that by helping to keep track of and projecting one's progress in real terms, the PRICE metric can be an invaluable aid for individuals and plan sponsors alike.

IN CLOSING

In the first and second parts of this chapter, we've taken on several of the biggest questions about DC plans; questions that ask and seek to answer how plans might be best positioned to deliver the retirement income workers need. They are:

- What might retirement cost, and what kinds of plans provide the best shot at meeting the PRICE of retirement?
- How can plan fiduciaries evaluate default investment options in DC plans—particularly target-date strategies—and determine which default options are most likely to allow retirees to retire, both on time and with sufficient lifetime income?

In the last section, we also looked beyond the quantitative aspects of plan development and performance to consider the qualitative aspects, or human factors that influence and shape plan design—and we've drawn on the expertise of knowledgeable observers to suggest ways in which plans can take those factors into account to deliver a higher chance of meeting plan, sponsor, and retiree objectives.

QUESTIONS FOR PLAN FIDUCIARIES

1. What is the investment objective for your DC plan?
2. How is the plan design aligned to this objective?
3. What does it cost to retire?
4. Are your DC investments aligned to the retirement cost?
5. What assets may better align to the cost?
6. How much tracking error are you willing to take versus the cost?
7. Are you benchmarking to the cost?

NOTE

1. Duration is a measure of the sensitivity of the price, or the value of principal, of a fixed-income investment—in this case, TIPS—to a change in interest rates. Duration is expressed as a number of years. Rising interest rates mean falling bond prices and a shorter duration, while declining interest rates mean rising bond prices and a longer duration.

CHAPTER 3

Plan Investment Structure

Make everything as simple as possible, but not simpler.

—Albert Einstein

Behavioral economists have taught us the importance of investment menu design. In the early days of DC plans, an investment menu may have been as simple as offering just a few investment choices; often these were limited to a single choice each for capital preservation, bonds, and stocks. This narrow set of at least three core investment offerings was not surprising given limited government direction as to the investment structure offered in plans. Under the Employee Retirement Income Security Act (ERISA) section 404(c), participants must be able to select from at least three investment alternatives, each of which is diversified and has materially different risk and return characteristics. According to the Callan Investments Institute's 2016 Defined Contribution Trends report, most DC plans (81.3 percent) are designed to comply with ERISA section 404(c).[1] Today, participant-directed retirement plans maintain far more than three investment choices, and, though there may be overlap among asset classes within an investment array, in the vast majority of retirement plans at least three investments with materially different risk and return characteristics can be identified.

UNDERSTANDING THE ERISA REGULATIONS FOR INVESTMENT CHOICES IN DC PLANS

Under the DOL regulations pursuant to ERISA section 404(c), fiduciaries are offered a safe harbor: 404(c) compliant plans will not be liable for losses resulting directly from participants' or beneficiaries' exercise of control over their accounts if the plan satisfies all of the regulations' requirements. Generally, plan participants and beneficiaries must be able to:

- Exercise control over assets in their individual accounts
- Choose, from among a broad range of investments, how their accounts will be invested

A broad range of investments exists when there is a reasonable opportunity for a participant or beneficiary to:

- Materially affect the potential return in his individual account
- Materially affect the degree of risk the account is subject to
- Choose from at least three diversified core investment categories
- Diversify so that the portion of the account that the participant controls has minimum risk of large or inordinate losses

The core investment categories must contain investment choices that have materially different risk and return characteristics, and must enable participants to achieve portfolios with risk and return characteristics that are normal and appropriate. The regulations do not require specific types of investment options, but employer stock does not qualify as a core investment. The core investment categories must permit investment instruction at least once within every three-month period, or more frequently as appropriate in light of the market volatility of the investment. In addition, one of the three core investment categories must accept transfers as often as they may be made out of any available investment in the plan. Alternatively, the plan sponsor can provide a low risk fund or subfund as a transfer vehicle.

Participants' current choice of investment alternatives within DC plans stands in contrast to the 1980s, when offering a balanced strategy or mix of bonds and stocks seemed unnecessary as it was thought that participants could (and would) create their own balance by allocating assets across the investment choices offered. Since that time, however, DC plan investment menu design has continued to evolve. First, we saw the introduction of balanced funds, and then a focus on offering more investment choice; often by filling the equity style box—that is, plans would make sure to offer large cap and small cap as well as value and growth choices. At the same time, education efforts directed at plan participants aimed to increase their understanding of stocks, bonds, and asset allocation, hoping participants would then make informed investment decisions.

Unfortunately, education was not enough. As DC call centers answered seemingly endless calls from participants asking, "How should I allocate my money?" more plan sponsors offered solutions to help people make asset allocation decisions. These included asset allocation guides and modeling tools, followed by the development of a series of balanced or target-risk funds (e.g., conservative, moderate, and aggressive). Despite the guides, tools, and target-risk offerings, inertia still often thwarted success as participants generally failed to reallocate their assets over time; with the result that what may have been an appropriate asset allocation when participation began (say, at age 30) was potentially far too risk-laden as the participant aged (say, at age 40). The solution: target-date strategies (or, in the UK, the "lifecycling" approach) which automatically shifts the asset allocation for the DC participant over time, typically reducing investment risk as the target retirement date approaches. While target-date strategies help simplify the selection and asset allocation decisions, they need not be simple in their underlying structure.

Today, target-date funds are the most prevalent DC investment default, followed by target-risk or balanced funds. Yet, these strategies are rarely offered alone. Rather, participants typically are given a core investment lineup as well, allowing them to create their own asset allocation. Plus, about a third of DC plans also offer participants a brokerage window, whether for access to mutual funds only or to full brokerage. As a rule, behavioral economists generally support this multitier structure as an improvement over simply presenting participants with a long list of funds from which to make choices.

In 2012, PIMCO's DC Dialogue spoke with Brigitte Madrian, Aetna professor of public policy and corporate management at the Harvard Kennedy School, about DC investment menus. She shared the following:

> From a behavioral perspective, investment menus should be simple on the surface, yet well diversified underneath. Offering a three-tier structure is one such approach that may help from a behavioral

perspective. The first tier, for the novice investor or the investor who wants to cede control to someone else, would include a set of low-fee target date funds. The second tier, for the investor who wants some control over their asset allocation, would be comprised of a small set of broadly diversified core investment options. For instance, instead of offering growth and value equity choices, perhaps offer a blend by market size, or offer a single global equity strategy that includes developed and emerging markets. A third tier, for the do-it-yourself investor, could include a wider range of investment funds, or a brokerage window. For the novice investor, this type of tiered investment menu is less overwhelming.

TIERS AND BLENDS: INVESTMENT CHOICES FOR DC PARTICIPANTS

In our opinion, it may be beneficial to offer participants a simple menu, but not one that precludes the option of a broadly diversified portfolio. The asset classes that build diversification within target-date strategies are also needed as core options. Yet, we believe the best way to diversify assets in the core menu may not be with stand-alone investment choices, but rather perhaps as components within a blended strategy. As we will discuss, blended strategies may help both simplify a menu and reduce risk; both may help curb behaviors that may harm investment returns over time, such as performance chasing or fleeing an investment or, worse, the entire plan.

In a three-tier structure, target-date strategies offer an approach that we believe works well for the default (or first tier). A second tier of a limited set of broadly diversified core investments can allow for diversification without unacceptable risk. Finally, a third tier for a mutual fund or full brokerage window accommodates plans that want to respond to the small but vocal minority of participants who want to run their own show by investing in brand-name mutual funds, ETFs, or individual securities.

While consultants suggest that DC plans offer a multitier investment structure, to date there is no consensus on which investment choices belong within each tier. In PIMCO's 2014 Defined Contribution Consulting Support and Trends Survey, we asked whether plans should offer multiple investment tiers; nearly all respondents (98 percent) suggested a target-date or target-risk investment tier and all firms (100 percent) recommended that clients offer a core fund tier (with both active and passive investment choices). (Note that the vast majority did not recommend a separate investment tier for passive only or active only.) Over three quarters of consultants (76 percent) also suggested, as an additional investment tier, that either a mutual fund-only brokerage window (41 percent) or a full brokerage window (35 percent) be offered. In the 2016 survey, those suggesting a brokerage window declined to just under half of consultants (47 percent), with 25 percent recommending mutual fund only and 22 percent suggesting full brokerage, while another 18 percent said "it depends on the client situation."

From a communication perspective, some plans label the investment default or asset allocation tier as the "do-it-for-me" choice, the core fund tier as "help-me-do-it," and a brokerage window as the "let-me-do-it" option. If managed accounts are offered, they may be a choice within the "do-it-for-me" choice. Let's take a look at the possible choices, considerations, and consultant suggestions for each tier.

TIER I: "DO-IT-FOR-ME" ASSET ALLOCATION INVESTMENT STRATEGIES

The "do-it-for-me" tier is the most important of all options, given that this is the tier to which plan sponsors often default DC participants. For this tier, plan fiduciaries typically select a qualified default investment alternative (QDIA) as identified by the Department of Labor (DOL). With the intent of ensuring the QDIA is appropriate as a single investment capable of meeting a worker's long-term retirement savings needs, the QDIA regulations offer four types and examples of each, as follows:

1. A product with a mix of investments that takes into account the individual's age or retirement date (an example of such a product could be a life-cycle or targeted-retirement-date fund)
2. An investment service that allocates contributions among existing plan options to provide an asset mix that takes into account the individual's age or retirement date (an example of such a service could be a professionally managed account)
3. A product with a mix of investments that takes into account the characteristics of the group of employees as a whole, rather than each individual (an example of such a product could be a balanced fund)
4. A capital preservation product that is available for only the first 120 days of participation

A QDIA must be managed by one of three options: by an investment manager, a plan trustee, or a plan sponsor; by a committee composed primarily of employees of the plan sponsor that is a named fiduciary; or by an investment company registered under the Investment Company Act of 1940.

A QDIA generally may not invest participant contributions in employer securities. (A copy of the regulations is available on the DOL's website at www.dol.gov/ebsa under "Laws and Regulations.")

Prior to the establishment of the QDIA regulations, many plans defaulted participant assets to either a capital preservation fund (such as stable value or a money market fund), while some defaulted to company stock. Through the QDIA regulations, the DOL made it clear that they viewed neither capital preservation funds nor company stock as appropriate long-term savings vehicles. The regulations thus allow for capital preservation "only for the first 120 days" as a way to simplify administration for those who may opt out of auto-enrollment.

While the DOL did not specifically state which investment products or strategies plan fiduciaries should select among, the categories and examples communicate support for three product types: target-date strategies, managed accounts, and balanced or target-risk funds. Today, plans most commonly default to target-date strategies. The Plan Sponsor Council of America (PSCA) reports in their 58th Annual Survey of Profit Sharing and 401(k) Plans (reflecting 2014 plan experience) that 81 percent of plans use a QDIA and among those, 74 percent offer target-date funds, 14 percent offer balanced or target-risk funds, 8.5 percent use managed accounts, and only 3 percent default to a stable value fund.

Consultants suggest that over time, plans will continue moving toward target-date funds as the most common default. In PIMCO's 2016 Defined Contribution Consulting Support and Trends Survey, 89 percent of respondents generally recommend target-date strategies as the QDIA, while 8 percent recommend balanced or target risk and 3 percent suggested multiple defaults—and no consulting firm suggested managed accounts as a default. Now, let's take a quick look at each default type.

Target-Date Strategies

Target-date strategies are also known as life-cycle, age-based, or dynamic-risk strategies. They generally follow a *glide path* that reduces risk as a participant gets closer to retirement age; Figure 3.1 shows how a glide path may be structured over time to move from growth assets to capital preservation assets, with allocations changing as participants age and move closer to retirement.

Typically, these funds are offered in 5- or 10-year retirement year vintages (e.g., 2050, 2045, and Income funds for those near or at retirement). As the QDIA, participant assets generally are defaulted to the target date based on the participant's expected retirement date. For example, a 30-year-old participant may be defaulted into the 2050 fund assuming a retirement

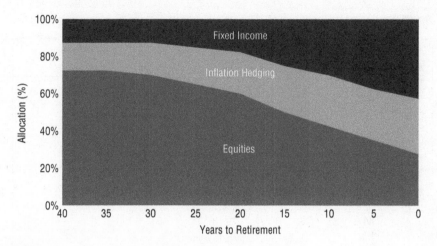

FIGURE 3.1 A Sample Diversified Glide Path Allocation
Source: PIMCO. For illustrative purposes only.

age of 65. These strategies are used in many markets although their asset allocation structure may differ significantly. For instance, in the UK the National Employment Savings Trust (NEST) offers single-year target-date funds that manage investment risk over three phases throughout members' savings careers. When members join NEST, their contributions are invested by default into a NEST Retirement Date Fund unless they make an active investment choice of a different fund. The default single-year Retirement Date Fund will match either their State Pension age or age 65, depending on their date of birth. Each of the three phases sets allocations to both growth and income-seeking assets in varying proportions to meet the different objectives throughout members' time savings (Figure 3.2).

In Morningstar's 2016 "Target-Date Fund Landscape" research paper, lead authors Jeff Holt and Janet Yang comment:

> *Target-date funds continue to play an increasingly crucial role in delivering successful retirement outcomes for investors. Target-date fund assets have grown from $116 billion to $763 billion in the past 10 years, as the retirement landscape has shifted to defined-contribution over defined-benefit plans. However, target-date series often vary significantly from one another, as managers impart their different philosophical approaches to balancing risks and implementing their asset-allocation decisions, among other factors. These differences may cause investors' results to diverge, and target-date funds' relatively short history combined with their decades-long in-*

FIGURE 3.2 Indicative Glide Path of NEST Retirement Date Funds

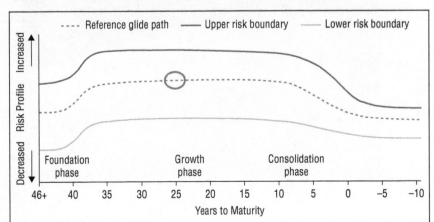

Foundation Phase Objectives

- Preserve capital while seeking sufficient return to match inflation after all charges
- Target a long-term investment volatility average of 7 percent
- Significantly reduce the likelihood of extreme investment shocks

Growth Phase Objectives

- Target investment returns equivalent to inflation plus 3 percent and cover all scheme charges
- Target a long-term volatility average of 11 percent
- Aim for steady growth in real terms over the life of the fund
- Maximize retirement incomes by taking sufficient investment risk at appropriate times while reducing the likelihood of extreme investment shocks

    This is the main phase where members could spend 30 years. The position of an indicative fund in the Growth phase is depicted by the grey circle on the diagram above.

Consolidation Phase Objectives

- The primary objective of the Consolidation phase for funds maturing from 2021 is to outperform CPI after all charges while aiming to progressively dampen volatility as a scheme member's fund approaches maturity.
- For NEST Retirement Date Funds maturing up to 2020, the Consolidation phase objective is to manage the risks associated with converting a member's accumulated savings into a cash lump sum.

Source: NEST Corporation, 2016 (nestpensions.org.uk).

vesting horizons can muddle the assessment of those results. Still, the U.S. Department of Labor stressed the importance of evaluating target-date series in its "Target Date Retirement Funds—Tips for ERISA Plan Fiduciaries."[2]

Target-date strategies are offered as mutual funds or collective investment trusts (CITs), or they may be customized using separate accounts. In Chapter 4 we will consider the DOL's "Target-Date Retirement Funds—Tips for ERISA Plan Fiduciaries" and will delve into the types, structures, and considerations for target-date strategies.

Balanced or Target-Risk Strategies

Many plan sponsors and consultants prefer offering a single balanced fund or a series of funds that target a specific risk level. For instance, they may offer a set of three: a conservative, moderate, and aggressive fund. This target-risk series also may be referred to as lifestyle funds. (Note: this label may be confusing as in the UK they call target-date-like strategies that modify risk over time "lifestyling.") Plans that offer these types of strategies may believe it more appropriate to default participants into a risk level that will not change over time—they may believe that the participant is the one who should decide whether they should change their risk by moving their assets to a different fund or creating their own asset allocation. While this group often views target-date strategies as too paternalistic, they are in the minority. The majority of plan fiduciaries have moved away from defaulting to balanced or target-risk strategies as they worry participants may take on an inappropriate level of risk given their time horizon for investment.

Over the past decade, plans that offer target-risk or balanced funds increasingly have migrated to target-date funds. PIMCO's DC Dialogue in October/November 2013 spoke with Sharon Cowher, Director of Trust Investments, and Christine Morris, Assistant Treasurer at Halliburton, about how to evolve from custom target-risk to custom target-date strategies. They explained:

> *We had four risk-based funds, with the moderate risk-based fund serving as the default fund. Because it had a substantial amount of assets, we did consider whether or not to offer both target-date and risk-based options, but decided that it would be too confusing.*
>
> *To gain confidence with the decision to eliminate the target-risk strategies, we evaluated whether participants in these strategies changed their asset allocation over time. Not surprisingly, we found a high level of inertia. The default allocation was approximately*

60 percent equities and 40 percent bonds. When we looked at our population by age bands in 10-year intervals, we found the vast majority stayed in the default strategy. This was true until we looked at participants over 50 years of age.

Target-risk funds require action by the participant, because the risk of a moderate fund always stays moderate and the aggressive fund always stays aggressive, etc. What we saw, based on the asset allocation of our participants, is they aren't taking action until they were in their 50s.

And then, when they did change, they swung it too far on the conservative side—often fully to stable value.

While rare, some plans offer participants both target-date funds as a default and target-risk funds as a core investment option. The 2015 survey from the Plan Sponsor Council of America (their 58th Annual Survey of Profit Sharing and 401(k) Plans, reporting on the 2014 plan year experience of 592 companies) shows that while only 16 percent of plans offer target-risk/lifestyle funds, 56 percent offer a balanced or asset allocation fund. Consultants in PIMCO's 2016 Defined Contribution Consulting Support and Trends Survey said they expect growth in the custom target-risk/balanced category; this growth expectation may be surprising given the shift from target-risk to target-date offerings. We believe that for many plans, the increase in balanced offerings may reflect the addition of a single balanced strategy such as a global tactical asset allocation (GTAA) strategy. Nearly two fifths of consultants (39 percent) recommended the addition of such strategies as a core investment option, while even more (61 percent) suggested adding GTAA to a blended strategy (i.e., multimanager/white label or in a sleeve of a custom target-date/risk portfolio). We will return to the topic of how GTAA strategies may fit into plans in Chapter 9 when we consider additional strategies, including alternatives.

Managed Accounts

In PIMCO's 2015 Defined Contribution Consulting Support and Trends Survey (referencing 2014 data), 60 percent of consultants showed support for managed accounts as an opt-in choice, but few (7 percent) supported them for the QDIA or opt-out option (note: this dropped to zero in the 2016 survey). Consultants shared various concerns about managed accounts, including the additional cost versus the potential alpha (the excess return over a benchmark) available, the appropriateness and relative impact of personalization factors, the inability to use multiasset portfolios, and biases toward or away from active management and diversifying asset classes.

While assets overseen within U.S. managed-account programs now exceed $150 billion, plan fiduciaries also raise concern about how best to benchmark these strategies. The importance of evaluating these strategies was noted in a June 2014 report by the U.S. Government Accountability Office (GAO) entitled "401(k) Plans: Improvements Can Be Made to Better Protect Participants in Managed Accounts."[3] In PIMCO's February 2015 DC Design article, DC experts Steve Ferber and Michael Esselman shared both the need for and approach to benchmarking managed accounts:

The GAO report stated that plan sponsors often have had limited or insufficient information to evaluate potential providers and monitor ongoing services. Importantly, the GAO also noted that participants face similar challenges. The good news is that these challenges can be overcome. Providers typically disclose basic aspects of their offerings, such as fees and service levels. And when advice providers disclose details of their methodology, the evaluation can be fairly straightforward.

Interest in managed accounts is expected by many to increase over time as improvements are realized in technology, cost efficiencies, participant engagement, and benchmarking. Yet, the majority of interest may come from those who opt-in rather than default into this option. Also worth noting as the managed-account market develops is the rise of robo-advisors, online wealth management services that provide automated, algorithm-based portfolio management advice, including for DC plans. While the robo-advisor offering is still new and developing, some observers expect that robo-advisor offerings and approaches will increasingly be integrated into managed account offerings, meaning plan participants may come to rely on a mix of managed and robo account services.

TIER II: "HELP-ME-DO-IT" STAND-ALONE OR "CORE" INVESTMENT OPTIONS

DC plans, with rare exception, offer a set of stand-alone or core investment funds for participants to select among. By selecting a short list of investment options, plan fiduciaries help the participant in making an investment selection. Looking back, we believe the economic environment that 401(k) plans grew up in may have significantly influenced this DC investment lineup. At the 1981 inception of 401(k) plans, the United States entered one of the strongest bull markets in global economic history. As shown in Figure 3.3, from 1981 to 2000 DC participants benefited from the rise in stocks and

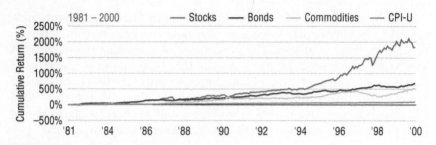

FIGURE 3.3   U.S. Market Returns, 1981–2000

Stocks are represented by the S&P 500; bonds are represented by the 10-year U.S. Treasuries; commodities are represented by an equally weighted index constructed by Gorton and Rouwenhorst from 1962 to 1990. Beginning January 1991, commodities are represented by the DJ-UBS Commodity TR Index.

Sources: PIMCO, Bloomberg Finance L.P., "Facts and Fantasies about Commodities Futures": Gorton and Rouwenhorst.

bonds without much worry about inflation eroding their returns, as the Consumer Price Index averaged 3.5 percent during this time period.

This market experience, along with research on the value of diversifying equity across styles and market cap sizes, likely encouraged many plan sponsors to "fill the equity style box" shown in Figure 3.4 and lengthen the list of core equity choices. The work of academics Eugene Fama and Kenneth French on the importance and benefit of diversifying asset allocation

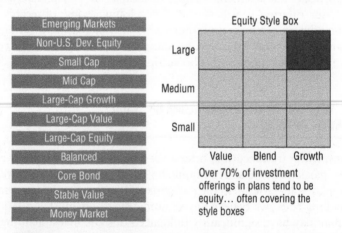

FIGURE 3.4   Typical DC Core Menu Choices—Driven by Bull Markets and a Need to "Fill the Style Box"
Source: PIMCO. For illustrative purposes only.

by three factors (company size, company price-to-book ratio, and market risk)—hence, the Fama-French three-factor model—also encouraged increasing asset diversification beyond equities and fixed income.

PSCA's 58th Annual Survey shows that from 2003 to 2014, the average number of funds made available for participant contributions increased from 16 to 19 (note that this approach counts target-date/target-risk funds as one fund rather than counting each of the funds in the series). PSCA finds that the funds most commonly offered to participants are actively managed domestic equity (80 percent of plans), actively managed international equity (75 percent of plans), indexed domestic equity (78 percent of plans), and actively managed domestic bond (73 percent of plans). On average, plans offer two balanced funds, two bond funds, six domestic equity funds, and two international equity funds. Notably (and as shown in Figure 3.4), 8 out of 12 funds mentioned here are equity strategies; it thus appears that close to 70 percent of investment choices are equity funds.

Academics who have studied these issues often raise concern with menu design, explaining that the number and types of investment choices may be perceived by participants as offering an appropriate balance when evenly allocating contributions across the set. Looking back, early DC education efforts made clear the need to diversify, often by using tactics such as showing pictures with the message "don't put all of your eggs in one basket." This may have led many plan participants to spread their money evenly across all available investment choices without regard to the risk or other considerations. Academics label this phenomenon as the "one over n ($1/n$) heuristic" or "naive diversification," explaining that the plan design itself may be interpreted as providing unintended advice regarding an appropriate asset allocation (that is, if there are 10 choices available, an appropriate strategy is to allocate 10 percent of assets to each choice). Shlomo Benartzi and Richard Thaler have studied whether the $1/n$ effect manifests itself among investors making decisions in the context of defined contribution saving plans. They found that "some investors follow the '$1/n$ strategy': they divide their contributions evenly across the funds offered in the plan. Consistent with this Naïve notion of diversification, we find that the proportion invested in stocks depends strongly on the proportion of stock funds in the plan."[4] Therefore, as plan fiduciaries consider the core fund menu, both the number of investment options and the types of asset class—and, more importantly, risk categories that encompass various asset choices—should be carefully considered.

In PIMCO's 2016 Defined Contribution Consulting Support and Trends Survey, respondents suggested a far shorter list of investment choices than the 19 reported by PSCA. For the past several years, consultants have suggested, at the median, a core lineup of 10 investment offerings. As shown in Figure 3.5, you can see that 98 percent of consultants suggest that plans offer

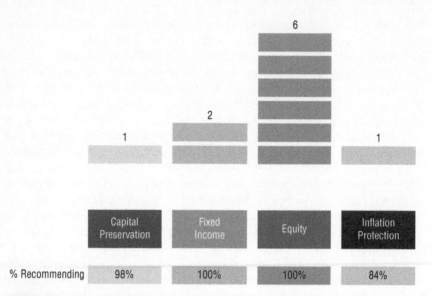

FIGURE 3.5 PIMCO Defined Contribution Consulting Support and Trends Survey 2016: What Is the Optimal Number of Core Menu Options?
Source: PIMCO, 2016 Defined Contribution Consulting Support and Trends Survey.

a capital preservation option and at the median, suggest only one option in this category. All of the consultants suggest fixed income and equity choices with a median number of two and six, respectively, and the vast majority recommend that an inflation-protection choice be made available. In addition, over a third of consultants suggest additional strategies for the menu such as a balanced fund or alternatives. In Chapters 5 through 9 we will review each of these investment categories.

Compared to the PSCA survey data average core lineup, the consultant-suggested menu offers slightly more balance, with 60 percent of the investment choices sitting in the equity asset class. But considering the asset-class label alone may be insufficient. We suggest taking a closer look at this lineup from the perspective of what is driving the risk of each fund. For instance, if we consider high-yield bonds, they may be considered in the bond asset class, yet their risk may be driven largely by the equity markets.

Breaking down each of the investment options by risk factors allows us to consider how the investment options may respond to different economic environments. As you can see in Figure 3.6, stocks, bonds, and real assets may respond differently to the economic factors of inflation and growth.

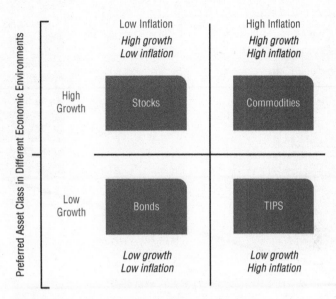

FIGURE 3.6 Asset Class Performance Is Dependent on the Economic Environment
Source: PIMCO. For illustrative purposes only.

For example, a high-growth economic environment favors stocks, but only when inflation is low—when both inflation and growth are high, the environment favors commodities. When inflation is high but growth is low, TIPS are the preferred asset class. Finally, when both growth and inflation are low, investors should consider bonds.

Ultimately, we believe plan fiduciaries should seek to balance the risk across the investment choices offered. One way to think about the menu is like a scale—as shown in Figure 3.7—which can balance equity risk with other risk types, such as risks within capital preservation, fixed income, inflation-hedging assets, and possibly additional diversifying strategies.

DC Plan Investment Choices: Farewell to Company Stock?

Plan fiduciaries often ask how to manage company stock in the core investment lineup. Plans that do not offer company stock are unlikely to add this option, given the risk that participants may overallocate to an undiversified security, plus the added risk of being overexposed to that company—for

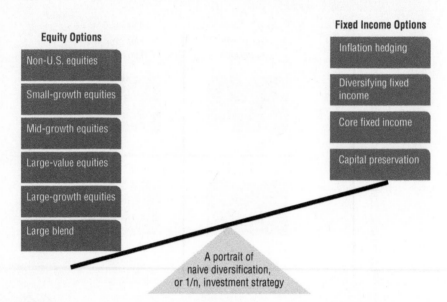

FIGURE 3.7 Balancing Investment Menu Risk by Adding Diversifying Assets
Source: PIMCO. For illustrative purposes only.

instance, if the employee is laid off and the value of the stock falls at the same time. That's a double whammy fiduciaries try to avoid. Given this risk and company stock litigation, fiduciaries are wise to not add company stock to a DC plan. For plans that offer stock, fiduciaries consider how best to manage this risk.

The Plan Sponsor Council of America's 58th Annual Survey of Profit Sharing and 401(k) Plans reflecting 2014 plan experience found that 19.0 percent of all plans make company stock available as an investment option and 16.0 percent of all plan assets are invested in this option. Company stock is most prevalent among the largest plans (5,000+ participants) where 43.8 percent of plans make the option available and 17.2 percent of plan assets are invested. About a third of plans (30.4 percent) limit the amount of plan assets that can be invested in company stock, while over a third (36.7 percent) make contributions in company stock. Among plans that offer company stock, 42.1 percent of them have less than 10 percent of plan assets invested in the stock, while 6.6 percent of plans report that more than 50 percent of plan assets are invested in company stock.

In 2014, we sat down with James O. Fleckner, Partner and ERISA Litigation Practice Leader at Goodwin Procter LLP, to talk about defined contribution litigation, how plan sponsors reduce the risk of litigation, and how company stock fits into DC plans.

According to Fleckner, there are two primary DC litigation areas: first, lawsuits involving fees, and second, cases involving company stock, which often relate to a drop in the stock price and are thus referred to as "stock-drop" cases. In order to protect themselves against lawsuits, Fleckner comments:

> *Plan sponsors should understand and fulfill their fiduciary duties. These include the duties of loyalty, prudence, diversification, and fidelity to plan documents. Loyalty focuses plan sponsors on doing what is in the best interest of participants, rather than on what may be of value to themselves or their company. We've seen this duty raised in cases that have alleged that the plan fiduciaries cared more about saving money for the company than they did about doing what was right for the participants.*

Stock-drop lawsuits arise when a company DC plan includes company stock, which then drops in value. Most often, claims in these cases allege imprudent selection and maintenance of a sponsor stock on a 401(k) lineup, improper monitoring of other fiduciaries and investment options, and concealment or misrepresentation of material facts. In 2014, a Supreme Court decision on a stock-drop case was issued in *Fifth Third Bancorp v. Dudenhoeffer*, which was about offering company stock to DC plan participants.

Fleckner told us that the best litigation defense against a stock-drop case is "having a documented, conscientious process for evaluating company stock. Process is an important defense for fiduciaries. Documentation should reflect the deliberation and process followed by the fiduciaries in making a decision about company stock. With the Supreme Court saying, in the Fifth Third case, that prudence trumps the plan document, a plan sponsor would not have a complete defense to a stock-drop suit in saying that 'I just followed what the plan said.' "

Companies may also want to consider hiring an independent fiduciary to oversee the ongoing evaluation of the stock and its appropriateness for the plan. Unlike other investment options in the plan, company stock has no obvious benchmark. Hiring an independent fiduciary allows a disinterested professional to evaluate the stock, and it eliminates the concern with inside information. It is important to note, however, that courts have also said that a plan sponsor who has some fiduciary responsibility under a plan document cannot fully offload its responsibility by hiring an independent fiduciary. Instead, the sponsor would likely still need to evaluate, hire, and monitor the independent fiduciary's work.

The issue or risk of company stock in DC plans can also be seen when the stock is removed from the plan. Comments Fleckner, "We have seen stock-drop cases alleging that the plan sponsor forced the participants to sell and forced them to lock in losses, claiming that the participants were robbed of a future increase in the stock's price."

Reduce Company Stock Exposure with "Sell More Tomorrow"

Plan fiduciaries often ask how they can help reduce participants' allocation to company stock. As noted above, about a third of plans may limit the percentage of assets that may be allocated to company stock. Others may consider ways to help reduce the stock allocation over time. One idea from behavioral economists is to implement a dollar-cost averaging way to slowly sell out of company stock over time.

In PIMCO's June 2007 DC Dialogue, and updated at the time of writing, University of Chicago Professor Richard Thaler told us about the work he had been undertaking in this area with his fellow behavioral economist colleague Shlomo Benartzi, at the UCLA School of Management. In particular, Dr. Thaler told us that "plan sponsors who find that participants have high concentrations of their retirement wealth invested ought to work on reducing that." He added, however, that many plan sponsors are reluctant to announce a major sell-off of their stock by employees, either because it appears to show a lack of confidence in the stock or employees might complain if the timing were unfortunate. "That is why I think the best approach is to help participants reduce their positions in company stock gradually," he noted. He explained:

> To address this, Professor Shlomo Benartzi and I have come up with the program "Sell More Tomorrow." We're looking for a plan sponsor willing to try the approach. The idea is gradually to sell off stock automatically over several years until the participant divests down to a reasonable holding—say, a 10 percent cap. The money earned by selling company stock would be invested in the firm's default investment fund (unless the employee chooses something else).
>
> This plan addresses plan sponsors' concerns of a sudden sell-off, as well as the fear that removing it from the plan sends a negative signal about the stock. We suggest sponsors implement Sell More Tomorrow as an opt-out. Given a gradual stock sell down, people won't worry about divesting at exactly the right or wrong moment. Rather, they benefit from dollar-cost averaging. Effectively, this can reduce the risk of holding a single security and prevent the unfortunate situation we saw at Enron.

As plan fiduciaries decide how best to address company stock issues, they may be best advised to seek assistance from ERISA counsel.

Evolution of Investment Menu Design

With balance in mind, many plans have migrated from a style box approach to an asset class or even an ultra-simplified *risk pillar* approach, in which the primary driver of returns is identified. As shown in Figure 3.8, the number of diversifying asset classes increases, yet the number of choices decreases as the menu shifts from the style-box focus to an asset-class focus and finally to a risk-pillar approach. In considering the approach to offer, plan fiduciaries may ask, "If a participant allocates evenly across the core investment lineup, what portfolio would result?" Then, the fiduciary can consider the risk and return characteristics for this naive diversification portfolio.

Comparing the three approaches on a naive diversification basis gives us the following characteristics as shown in Figure 3.9. As you can see, in the hypothetical example risk-adjusted returns improved as core lineup design moves from the style-box focus to an asset-class focus and then to the risk-pillar focus. While the risk-pillar shows lower return at 3.63 percent, volatility is also significantly lower at 7.71 percent. Notably, the risk of loss dropped in half from 21 percent in a single year to 10.51 percent. Also,

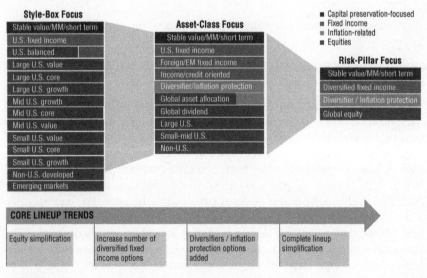

FIGURE 3.8 Core Lineup Trends in DC Plans: From Style-Box Focus to Risk-Pillar Focus
Source: PIMCO. For illustrative purposes only.

FIGURE 3.9   Comparing the Characteristics of Three Approaches to Investment Plan Design

	Style-Box Focus	Asset-Class Focus	Risk-Pillar Focus
Estimated return	4.04%	3.70%	3.63%
Esimated volatility	14.21%	8.90%	7.71%
Sharpe ratio[1]	0.17	0.23	0.26
Loss potential[2]	−21.00%	−12.25%	−10.51%
Correlation to S&P 500	0.96	0.93	0.86

For illustrative purposes only.
For indices, return estimates are based on the product of risk factor exposures and projected risk factor premia. The projections of risk factor premia rely on historical date valuation metrics and qualitative inputs from senior PIMCO investment professionals. Other factors include slope, convexity, country, swap, municipal spread factors, and Idiosyncratic (specific) risk.
[1]Sharpe ratio is calculated as estimated return minus the return estimate for cash, 1.72 percent, divided by estimated total volatility.
[2]Loss potential is proxied by Value-at-Risk (VaR) at 95 percent confidence level.
VaR is an estimate of the minimum expected loss at a desired level of significance over 12m horizon.
Source: PIMCO, as of December 31, 2015.

you can see the lower correlation to the equity markets in the risk-pillar approach.

Active versus Passive Approaches: DC Consultants' Views

Once the number and types of investments are identified, plan fiduciaries may then consider whether each investment choice should be actively or passively managed, or rely on a blend such as multimanager or *white-label* approaches. Data from the PSCA (2014), shown in Figure 3.10, shows that plan sponsors commonly offer both active and passive investment choices. While 77.7 percent of plans offer passively managed equity such as the S&P 500, only 53.9 percent of plans offer passively managed fixed income. This difference is partly explained by relative performance: The median active intermediate U.S. fixed income manager has historically outperformed the benchmark (i.e., the Barclays U.S. Aggregate Bond Index), whereas the median active U.S. large blend manager has failed to beat the S&P 500 Index benchmark.

Looking specifically at investment choices for fixed income, there are many reasons that passively investing in fixed income is suboptimal and must be differentiated from equity index investing. In a 2014 PIMCO

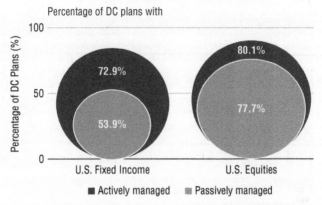

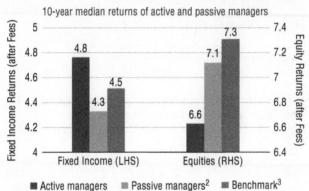

FIGURE 3.10 Active versus Passive Approaches in DC Plans

[1]58th Annual PSCA Survey.
[2]Morningstar: Based on median peer group returns for Intermediate-Term Bond (Passive) for fixed income and U.S. Large Blend (Passive) for equities.
[3]Equities benchmark represented by the S&P 500 index; fixed income benchmark represented by Barclays U.S. Aggregate Bond Index.

Sources: eVestment, Morningstar, PIMCO, Bloomberg Barclays, as of December 31, 2015.

Viewpoint by James Moore, PhD, titled "Sorry, Mr. Bogle, But I Respectfully Disagree. Strongly," Moore summarizes five reasons why, in his view, active bond investing should be viewed distinctly from passive equity investing. These are: the variety of investor objectives other than maximizing total return, the mechanics of bond index construction, the importance of the

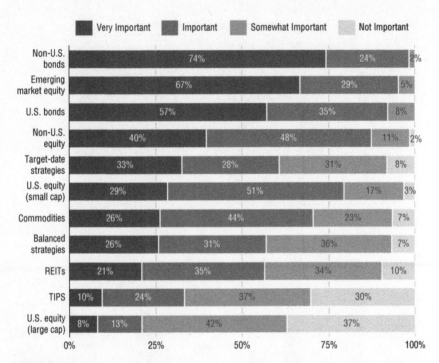

FIGURE 3.11 PIMCO Defined Contribution Consulting Support and Trends Survey 2016: The Importance of Active Management in DC Plans
Source: PIMCO, 2016 Defined Contribution Consulting Support and Trends Survey.

new-issue market for bonds, the predominance of over-the-counter transactions, and the highly skewed returns on individual bonds versus stocks.

Consultants agree with Dr. Moore on the importance of actively managed fixed income globally. As shown in Figure 3.11, nearly all of the consultants (98 percent) surveyed in 2015 believe it is very important or important to actively manage non-U.S. bonds, while 92 percent believe the same for U.S. bonds. Notably, the majority of consultants also say active management is very important or important for emerging-market and small-cap equity as well as target-date, balanced strategies, commodities, and real estate investment trusts (REITs); however, the group views active management of TIPS and U.S. large-cap equity as less important. This data underscores the importance of including active management among the core and particularly within the default investment strategies, for example, target-date funds.

Consultants also shared their views on which asset classes should be active only, passive only, an active/passive blend, or provide multiple active and passive strategies or mirrored active and passive (e.g., a large-cap

	Capital Preservation	Fixed Income	Equity	Inflation Protection
# of stand-alone options	1	2	6	1
Active only	80%	37%	2%	37%
Passive only	2%	0%	2%	10%
Active/passive blend	19%	25%	41%	42%
Multiple active and passive	0%	19%	34%	3%
Mirrored active and passive	0%	17%	20%	0%

FIGURE 3.12   Consultant Views on Management Approaches for Various Investment Strategies
Source: PIMCO, 2016 Defined Contribution Consulting Support and Trends Survey.

passive and a large-cap active fund). As show in Figure 3.12, the majority of consultants (80 percent) recommend active only for capital preservation. In fact, not one suggested passive only for fixed income, and instead over a third (37 percent) recommend active only while another 25 percent suggested a blend. These responses were similar for equity and inflation-protection assets; the majority suggests either a blend or multiple active and passive equity options, while over a third suggest active only for inflation protection (37 percent) or an active/passive blend (42 percent). Notably, a fifth or fewer of the consultants suggested offering a mirror of active and passive fixed income or equity choices.

Active versus Passive: Reduced or Heightened Litigation Risk?

Plan fiduciaries often ask whether they may be more insulated from litigation if they offer passively managed index funds, versus actively managed investments. ERISA attorneys tell us that plan sponsors should focus on prudent choices with "reasonable"—not necessarily the lowest—fees. Plans are not required to offer passively managed or the cheapest investment choices.

In the October 2014 PIMCO DC Dialogue, ERISA attorney James O. Fleckner told us that "the focus in the cases challenging investment management fees is usually on the fund itself, not necessarily on whether it is actively or passively managed. At the same time, fiduciary committees may have specific views about whether active management is worth the additional cost; and may decide that active management is the best way to allow participants to maximize outcomes and minimize downside risk, or that participants should be given a choice between active and passive invest-ing. Those all seem to me to be perfectly defensible decisions," comments Fleckner, "and judges [in lawsuits arising on investment management fees] typically do not like to second-guess informed fiduciaries."

The DOL requires plan fiduciaries to understand plan fees and expenses. In support of this outcome, the DOL has published a guide, *Understanding Retirement Plan Fees and Expenses* (available online at the DOL website at www.dol.gov) to help plan sponsors understand their responsibilities. The guide explains why to consider fees:

> *Plan fees and expenses are important considerations for all types of retirement plans. As a plan fiduciary, you have an obligation under ERISA to prudently select and monitor plan investments, investment options made available to the plan's participants and beneficiaries, and the persons providing services to your plan. Un-derstanding and evaluating plan fees and expenses associated with plan investments, investment options, and services are an important part of a fiduciary's responsibility. This responsibility is ongoing. After careful evaluation during the initial selection, you will want to monitor plan fees and expenses to determine whether they continue to be reasonable in light of the services provided.*

There are many types of fees that may be imposed within plans. The DOL outlines three categories for plan sponsors to consider: plan administration such as recordkeeping, investment fees generally charged as a percentage of assets, and individual service fees such as loan initiation. Investment fees tend to be the largest percentage of total plan fees; it is important to evaluate and confirm that the fees are reasonable for the value of the management. Evaluating value, in turn, should take into consideration both the oppor-tunity to deliver returns as well as to manage risk. Plan sponsors should use their buying power to get the best price for the investment strategy and structure desired. The larger the plan assets, the greater the buying power. Plans with sizable assets may seek institutionally priced vehicles, including institutionally priced mutual funds, collective investment trusts, and sepa-rately managed trusts.

Plan sponsors can also work to leverage the organization's buying power to add investments with the highest perceived value at the lowest price. In PIMCO's March/February 2015 DC Dialogue, we spoke with Cindy Cattin,

Managing Director of Investment Operations and Risk Management at Exelon Corporation, about how Exelon used the scale of their $35 billion retirement and other assets to drive down DC investment costs:

> *We have the processes and procedures in place to identify best-in-class managers, and we have the scale to drive down cost. . . . We believe that over a market cycle, best-in-class active management will outperform passive management. We believe the investment management fees are worth it given the opportunity for improved risk-adjusted returns of active managers. Despite our belief in active management, we acknowledged that some participants prefer passive management and value the lower cost of this approach. That recognition drove us to offer both active and passive choices in the core.*
>
> *We spent a lot of time educating our participants on the changes and the cost differences. We explained the difference in active and passive management as well as the fees. We also showed them a comparison of costs they might incur in the retail market relative to our plan. They could see the significant cost savings our plan offers. Again, leveraging our scale drove down our costs, and we made sure participants understood that advantage.*

For plan fiduciaries who select passively managed investments, there's more work to do than simply comparing fees. Josh Cohen, CFA, Managing Director, Head of Defined Contribution at Russell Investments, comments in a January 2016 "A Conversation" article, "Going Passive Is Still an Active Decision":

> *I've observed some sponsors pick passive investments based on the belief it can reduce fiduciary risk and due diligence requirements and obligations. But, there are still a lot of active decisions being made when passive investments are implemented, and thus meaningful due diligence requirements remain. We have identified eight of them here.*
>
> 1. *Review the index provider's organization*
> 2. *Review the index provider's methodology*
> 3. *Review the passive fund manager's implementation quality*
> 4. *Review the fund manager's ability to replicate the index and the costs to do so*

5. *Review the fees charged by the passive fund provider*
6. *Determine whether active management opportunities might be more prudent*
7. *Review Target Date Fund glide path methodology* *
8. *Review Target Date Fund asset allocation* *

*Additional considerations for Target Date Funds.

For a detailed look at each of the above decisions, see the November 2015 guide provided by Russell Investments on their website (at www. russell.com/institutional) called "Passive Management and the False Premise of Fiduciary Relief: Going Passive Is an Active Decision," by Josh Cohen and Kevin Knowles. The Russell Investments January 2016 piece also points out:

> *One of the most important things to remember is that low fees don't necessarily translate to better outcomes for participants. Passive funds with low cost have opportunity costs—that's the cost of giving up potentially higher returns that active management aims to provide for some asset classes. For example, there could be a fairly significant wealth differential if participants' actively managed funds generated 50 basis points more per year than their passive counterparts, compounded over a 40-year working career. Our analysis finds it could generate up to seven years of additional spending in retirement.*

One consideration that may significantly influence fees is the investment structure selected. Plan fiduciaries should understand the alternative structures.

Investment Structure: Mutual Fund, Collective Investment Trust, or Separately Managed Account

In general, DC plans tend to invest in investment structures that pool the assets of many investors. Mutual funds are the most prevalent investment-pooling vehicle used within both DC and retail individual retirement accounts (IRAs). Each investor in a mutual fund owns shares of the fund that represents the mutual fund's holdings. Mutual funds typically offer many share classes for different types of investors and fee arrangements. They may carry sales charges, including front-end or back-end loads and ongoing sales fees labeled "12(b)1" fees. Large DC plans tend to seek funds that carry no sales charges; rather, they seek the lowest-cost, institutionally priced share class that covers the fund's management and administrative fees.

Unlike retail retirement accounts such as IRAs, ERISA plans including 401(k)s have the ability to invest in bank- or trust company–managed trust funds; these include collective investment trusts (CITs) and separately managed trusts. Similar to a mutual fund, a CIT pools investments of tax-qualified assets such as DB plans, profit-sharing plans, government employee benefit plans, and again 401(k)s. (Note that non-ERISA plans such as 403(b)s and endowments/foundations are generally excluded from participating in CITs.)

Each CIT investor has a proportionate interest in the trust fund assets. For example, if a collective investment fund holds $10 million in assets and your investment in the fund is $10,000, you have a 0.1 percent interest in the fund. As with mutual funds, collective investment funds may have a variety of investment objectives. There are no front- or back-end fees associated with a collective investment fund, but there are investment management and administrative fees. As shown in Figure 3.13, CIT fees may be considerably lower than mutual fund fees, yet this is not always the case—so each available investment structure should be considered. Notably, CITs allow investment managers to vary their fee based on account size; this is not the case for mutual funds which hold the management fee constant, but may vary the distribution, operation and, other costs. The Callan Investments Institute estimates that 70 percent of DC plans offer at least one CIT-structured investment choice. Assets in CITs in 2015 were estimated to exceed $2.3 trillion according to the Coalition of Collective Investment Trusts.

While operationally CITs and mutual funds function similarly, there are other considerations for CITs relative to mutual funds. Most importantly, there is a difference in the regulatory oversight of mutual funds, which are registered with the Securities and Exchange Commission (SEC) and follow SEC rules and guidelines; whereas CITs are regulated by banking

FIGURE 3.13 Mutual Fund and Collective Investment Trust Fund Fee Differentials on an Assumed $50 Million Mandate

Asset Classes	Mutual Fund (%)	Collective Fund (%)
Intermediate-Term Bond	0.58%	0.28%
Large Value	0.80%	0.55%
Large Growth	0.80%	0.59%
Small Value	1.19%	0.90%
Small Growth	1.00%	0.90%
International	0.97%	0.70%

Source: Callan Investments Institute, March 31, 2016.

authorities; for federally chartered banks, by the Office of the Comptroller of the Currency (OCC), an independent bureau within the United States Department of the Treasury; and for state banks, by the state banking authorities (which largely defer to the OCC rules). Notably, CITs are subject to ERISA law while mutual funds are not. DOL, IRS, and potentially Commodities Futures Trading Commission (CFTC) rules/law also apply. To participate in a CIT, the plan fiduciary must adopt the terms of the CIT through the execution of a participation or joinder agreement. This requirement does not exist for mutual funds. Given these different governance structures, trading restrictions, redemption fees, and SEC 22c-2 regulations (which govern specific mutual fund redemption fees) do not apply in CITs as they may for mutual funds.

For more information on CITs, readers may want to visit the website of the Coalition of Collective Investment Trusts website (www.ctfcoalition.com).

Another type of trust structure that large plans may consider is a separately managed trust or separate accounts. This type of offering allows the plan to tailor the investment guidelines of the fund, and not pool assets with other investors. Separate accounts may pool both ERISA DB and DC

FIGURE 3.14 Comparison of Mutual Funds and Collective Trusts (CITs): Similar but Not Identical

	Mutual Funds	Collective Trusts
Pooled Vehicle	Yes	Yes
Regulation	Registered with SEC	Overseen by OCC, DOL
Governing Document	Prospectus	Plan Document (Declaration of Trust)
Enrollment Requirements	According to prospectus	Investment management or trust agreement
Availability	Available to general public	Limited availability
Portfolio Composition	Pooled	Pooled
Valuation	Daily	Not always daily
Clearing	NSCC	NSCC
Advertisement	Yes	No
Ticker Symbol	Yes	No
Third-Party Coverage	Yes	Some
Operational Oversight	Board of Directors	Bank as Trustee

For more information on CITs, readers may want to visit the website of the Coalition of Collective Investment Trusts web site (at www.ctfcoalition.com).

Source: Callan Investments Institute, 2016.

assets via a master trust arrangement, thereby gaining pricing and oversight advantages for both plans. Typically, fees for separate accounts are on a sliding scale, declining as assets grow. These fee schedules often level off at around $300 million in assets under management, according to the Callan Investments Institute. Keep in mind that investment management fees are just one component of separate account costs; additional fees for trust services or other costs may range from four to over ten basis points.

Understand Revenue Sharing: Consider Paying Administration and Other Plan Fees

For plans that select mutual funds, they need to carefully consider the share classes available and whether revenue sharing, which is commonly used to help offset recordkeeping or other plan costs, is offered. Revenue sharing may be available from mutual fund share classes that include fees such as distribution 12(b)1, subtransfer agency, shareholder servicing, profit-sharing payments, or other fees. The DOL refers to these fees as indirect payments. Note that plaintiff attorneys may often view revenue sharing as padding a mutual fund's expense ratio with general plan administration, marketing, and other noninvestment-related fees, then passing these expenses to participants—often without ensuring they understand the costs.

Mutual funds typically offer a range of share classes that may or may not offer revenue sharing. For instance, a Class A share class may include a 12(b)1 fee based on a percentage of assets (typically 0.25 percent, paid annually by investors). Alternately Class R, also known as retirement-class shares, may include, for example, an administrative services fee of 25 basis points; this fee income, based on DC assets allocated to the funds, is often shared directly with the recordkeeper to offset the cost of services. For instance, if recordkeeping costs total $500,000, this cost may be reduced by the revenue sharing from funds (e.g., $100 million invested with 0.25 percent revenue sharing provides $250,000 in revenue, thus reducing plan fee costs by 50 percent).

Mutual funds often offer Class I shares, also known as institutional-class shares, typically available only to institutional investors making large fund-share purchases. With minimum investments often of $1 million or more, this class of shares is out of reach for most retail investors—but not DC plans. By pooling the assets across participants, the DC plan may thus offer these institutional share classes to all participants regardless of their individual DC account balances. What plan sponsors need to be wary of, however, is whether revenue sharing is attached to these share classes; while they are institutionally priced, they may nonetheless include a small amount of revenue sharing (e.g., 15 basis points or less) to recordkeepers or others.

In 2012, Congress enacted fee disclosure requirements with ERISA 408(b)(2). These rules support a plan sponsor's ability to gather and evaluate all fees and revenue-sharing arrangements. In fact, 408(b)(2) made it clear that plan fiduciaries have a duty to monitor and control service provider fees.

While revenue sharing may appear attractive, plans increasingly are moving away from any revenue-sharing funds, seeking rather the lowest cost for investment management and managing other plan costs such as recordkeeping separately. In fact, consultants suggest both *evaluating fees* and *moving away from revenue sharing* as two of the most important actions plan fiduciaries can take, both to fulfill fiduciary duty and to reduce litigation risk. In PIMCO's Defined Contribution Consulting Support and Trends Survey, 2016, in order to manage fiduciary risk, the vast majority of consultants (86 percent) suggest benchmarking plan costs; and over half (54 percent) recommend that plan sponsors move away from revenue sharing funds. Some plan sponsors not only have moved away from revenue sharing, but also have decided to cover plan fees as a benefit cost—they may cover administration or include all costs, even investment management. Karen Barnes, former ERISA Counsel at McDonald's Corporation, shared with us in PIMCO's December 2007 DC Dialogue:

> *Our company covers all plan administrative fees, except for loan origination, which the participant pays. Participants pay the investment management fees of the funds in which they invest. We try to use separate accounts or institutional funds to minimize investment management expenses. So plan participants cover investment fees, which are disclosed to all participants in our annual explanation-of-fees report, but don't cover administrative fees.*

While rare, some companies cover not only DC administration fees, but also investment management costs. For instance, Gary Park, Director of Trust Investments at Schlumberger, shared with us in PIMCO's September/October 2015 DC Dialogue:

> *The U.S. [DB] plan closed in 2004, and our international DB plan closed in 2014. In exchange for DB, we have enhanced our DC plans, including increasing the employer contribution and covering all DC fees—investment management and administration. While our total cost of running the DC plans may be higher than the DB plans, we prefer the known cost of DC relative to the unknowns of DB, such as the volatility in pension expense, liquidity requirements and balance sheet impact. The trend is in just one direction—toward DC plans.*

To offset DC plan cost coverage, plan sponsors may consider offering a lower employer match. However, reducing a match may be viewed as a "take away" (of a benefit previously offered to employees) so the communication to participants requires conveying the value of the employer-covered fees. By covering fees outside the plan, participants' accounts may grow more rapidly over time. Employers who are closing a DB plan and considering compensating with an unmatched or higher-matched DC contribution may thus consider cost coverage and a lower contribution increase.

Blended Multimanager or White-Label Investment Options

Many plans offer one or multiple blended core options. In PIMCO's 2015 Defined Contribution Consulting Support and Trends Survey, over two-thirds of consultants said they actively promote or support client interest in fixed income (70 percent), equity (72 percent), and real asset (69 percent) multimanager/white-label core structures. Support for multimanager/white-label alternative strategies is weaker, but still promoted or supported by over half (53 percent) of consultants.

In PIMCO's 2016 Defined Contribution Consulting Support and Trends Survey, respondents reported a total of $330 billion in white-label/multimanager assets across their clients. They anticipate, at the median, that another 10 percent of their clients will implement these strategies in the next three years. The majority of consultants suggest plans with over $500 million in assets consider a white-label/multimanager approach.

In summary, there are many potential benefits to these types of strategies, including the following.

- **Simplicity:** Mutual fund names can be confusing, and sponsors want to consolidate the number of options. White-labeling can help simplify the core offering and enhance clarity for participants, leading to increased likelihood of better decisions.
- **Improved diversification:** Single-manager risk can be reduced while improving diversification and increasing the potential for higher alpha by combining "best-of-breed" managers. White-labeling also allows the addition of more volatile asset classes (e.g., emerging markets) without exposing participants to the risk of investing directly in these higher-risk options. Increased diversification may lead to reduced volatility, which can also help guard against behavioral mistakes of chasing high performance or fleeing from a fund or the plan altogether given poor performance.
- **Reduced costs:** Plans can potentially reduce costs by:
  - Using a combination of active and passive investment strategies, and
  - Benefiting from relationship pricing by leveraging the same managers (e.g., those used in a DB plan if available)

■ **Increased flexibility:** Plan sponsors have increased flexibility to add or replace fund managers within a white-label/multimanager structure without altering the lineup from the participant perspective or requiring broad communication that can be onerous, time-consuming, and costly. Due diligence and investment monitoring may also be eased by using white-label structures.

Figure 3.15 outlines the traditional and white-label/multimanager approaches, including the potential drawbacks of the traditional approach and the benefits of the white-label/multimanager approach.

Plan fiduciaries must also consider some potential concerns with white-label/multimanager approaches. These are summarized along with potential solutions in Figure 3.16.

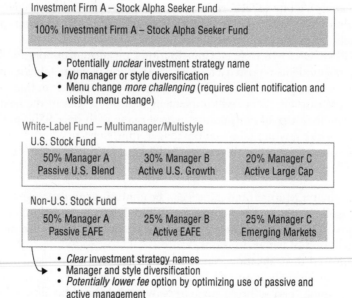

FIGURE 3.15 Traditional and White-Label/Multimanager Investment Options Compared
Source: PIMCO. For illustrative purposes only.

FIGURE 3.16 Challenges in White-Label/Multimanager Investment Options

Consideration	Concern	Solution
Simplified Investment lineup	Some participants want more granular options	Generally applies to small subset of participants; needs can be addressed with brokerage window
No Ticker Symbol	Fund data is not publically available	Make data readily available on web portals, which participants are increasingly accustomed to using
Short Historical Performance	Participants lack information to make informed decisions	■ Historical composite performance can be made available through appropriate disclosure ■ Stress the fund's desired outcome versus past performance
Challenging Communication	Participants may not understand underlying investment strategies	■ Underlying investments can be reported similarly to target-date fund communications ■ Redirect participant focus to benefits of the strategy rather than underlying investment
Implementation	Costs associated with developing fund structure, record keeper fees, and trustee's fees for fund administration	■ Additional costs may be offset by lower manager change costs, improved investment performance, and/or lower underlying investment management fees ■ Leverage partners with strong expertise in implementing white-label strategies

Source: PIMCO, 2016.

TIER III: "DO-IT-MYSELF" MUTUAL-FUND-ONLY OR FULL BROKERAGE WINDOW

Brokerage windows can be defined as a type of defined contribution plan investment choice that allows plan participants to select a much larger number of investments from a brokerage provider. These plans enjoy the same tax advantages as regular defined contribution investment choices. As discussed earlier, brokerage windows can allow a participant to invest in only mutual funds, or to invest in both mutual funds and individual securities. The 58th Annual PSCA Survey reports that 29 percent of all plans have brokerage windows; notably, 39 percent of the largest DC plans (i.e., those with more than 5,000 participants) offer brokerage windows as an option. The PSCA also reports that assets allocated to the brokerage option are meager at 4 percent across all plan sizes.

Consultants are split on whether offering a brokerage window makes sense. In PIMCO's 2016 Defined Contribution Consulting Support and Trends Survey, 25 percent recommend a mutual-fund-only window, and 22 percent suggest full brokerage, while over a third (35 percent) advised against offering either type of window. While only a small fraction of DC plan participants will likely invest via a brokerage window, providing this option may help plan sponsors streamline the core menu without the perceived "take away" of investment choices.

In March 2011, DC Dialogue talked with Mark A. Davis, Senior Vice President, Financial Advisor, CAPTRUST Financial Advisors, about the inclusion of a brokerage tier. He shared the following:

> We may suggest a brokerage account capability of some sort for what I call "hyper-engaged" people—the kinds of folks who want, for example, the gold fund and various sector funds. This group may have more customized needs or advisors who can help them.
>
> I'm a big supporter of giving my clients a brokerage capability, as long as it's appropriately documented that participants have the chance to use the target strategies or traditional core funds that are monitored and overseen by the sponsor and our firm. But if participants willingly accept the risks of going outside that circle, then there's a real place to use the brokerage account.

He goes on to talk about the types of companies that may find brokerage most appealing:

> It depends on the construct of the company. For some organizations, like professional service firms, again, as long as it's docu-

mented properly, I think full brokerage is more than reasonable. Companies with a more diversified workforce may want to stick just their toes in the water and go mutual funds only. Honestly, I think that once you go into the brokerage world, you might as well open it up to everything, including stocks, bonds, ETFs, and mutual funds. The important thing is making sure the fiduciary is protected, that the participant signs the piece of paper that says, "I know I can have the core, but I willingly choose to accept the cost and the risk of this other option."

From a behavioral perspective, just knowing more choice is available may increase participants' overall plan satisfaction even for those who do not use this offering. On the other hand, many plan fiduciaries prefer not offering such broad choice given concerns that participants may invest unwisely—such as chasing a hot stock tip or selecting a high-priced share class of a mutual fund. What's more, plan fiduciaries may be concerned with potential future DOL regulations that may affect brokerage windows, such as a duty to monitor brokerage-window investments by participants under a prudence standard. At this time, the 404(c) regulation limits the duties to prudently select and monitor investments to *designated investments* as defined in the regulations. That definition does not included unspecified brokerage-window investments. While DC experts do not expect this to change, we nevertheless need to keep watch on DOL action related to brokerage windows.

CONSIDERING AN OUTSOURCED CHIEF INVESTMENT OFFICER

Plan fiduciaries may prefer delegating responsibility for the selection, oversight, or management of the core investment lineup. As more plan sponsors acknowledge a lack of resources or expertise to manage their investment lineup, they may turn for help to an existing consultant relationship or another provider. In PIMCO's 2016 Defined Contribution Consulting Support and Trends Survey, consultants at the median reported that 5 percent of their clients use their discretionary services and that over the next three years, they expect 14 percent to do so. Consultants tell us they believe many factors, outlined in Figure 3.17, may drive growth in delegated services; at the top of this list is the perceived mitigation of fiduciary risk and the ability to hand over the reins on investments.

Consultants in PIMCO's 2016 Defined Contribution Consulting Support and Trends Survey noted the following delegated services (i.e., 3(38)

FIGURE 3.17   Factors Driving Growth in Delegated Services

Factors Driving DC OCIO Growth	
Perceived mitigation of fiduciary risk (e.g., litigation)	80%
Ability to hand over reins on investments	78%
Clients outsource DB already and wish to do the same with DC	49%
Desire multimanager custom strategies and prefer to fully delegate this outside	43%
Costs may be lower	35%
Ability to hand over reins on administration	28%
Access to investment managers may increase	23%
	11%

Other: time saver for committees; lack of internal resources; corporate reorgs/spinoffs; perceived improved participation; committee fatigue.

Source: PIMCO, 2016 DC Consulting and Trends Survey.

services) that have grown the most over the past year and the percentage of consultants that provide each of these services. As outlined in Figure 3.18, about a third of the respondents have experienced the most growth in a broad range of investment manager selection and due diligence categories; in the right column, you can see that over two-thirds of the consulting firms provide such services.

FIGURE 3.18   Top Discretionary Services Growth and Availability by DC Plan Consultants

Discretionary Services	Top Five Growth Areas	Consultants Who Provide
Measure, monitor, and negotiate fees	34%	67%
Conduct/document due diligence on managers	33%	78%
Conduct manager searches	33%	81%
Decide when to replace managers	33%	78%
Decide menu of investment choices	31%	77%
Develop multimanager/white-label portfolios	30%	53%
Develop custom glide path	25%	63%
Decide mapping policy	22%	69%
Decide investment default	19%	66%

Source: PIMCO, 2016 DC Consulting and Trends Survey.

IN CLOSING

In this chapter, we've started to dig into the nitty-gritty of investment plan structure, including how plan structure has evolved over the past three decades. We explored the ways in which options for plan participants have moved from simplistic asset allocation questionnaires and tools in the 1980s to today's sophisticated and professional solutions designed to help ensure participants are best set up for retirement success. We also reviewed the regulatory requirements under the ERISA that set out minimum standards for the kinds of investment choices plans must offer participants.

Today, target-date funds are the most prevalent DC investment default, followed by target-risk or balanced funds. Yet, these strategies are rarely offered alone. Rather, participants typically are given a core investment lineup as well, allowing them to create their own asset allocation. Plus, about a third of DC plans also offer participants a brokerage window, whether for access to mutual funds only or to full brokerage. As a rule, behavioral economists generally support this multitier structure as an improvement over simply presenting participants with a long list of funds from which to make choices.

As a result of their evolution over time, today's plans may offer a full range of options for participants so they may select the amount of direct involvement they want in allocating their plan assets. Options can range from "do it for me" (lots of plan sponsor involvement) to "help me do it" (a balance of participant and sponsor involvement), to "let me do it" (an option in which the plan sponsor facilitates the participant's asset allocation decisions). Today's plan design is also informed by insights from the field of behavioral finance, which explores how plan participants make decisions—including the pitfalls, such as naive diversification, that can thwart the intentions underlying plan design.

In this chapter, we've also touched on a variety of topics that are important considerations in plan design, including the role of company stock in DC plans, the active versus passive decision with respect to the options for managing plan assets, and the choice of mutual funds, collective investment trusts, or separately managed accounts for plan investment options.

In creating the appropriate investment structure, plan fiduciaries should consider many factors including behavioral, investment, cost management, and oversight for plan fiduciaries. Most important in the investment menu is the plan's investment default option, most commonly target-date strategies. In the next chapter, we will look in depth at this important investment choice.

QUESTIONS FOR PLAN FIDUCIARIES

1. Should we offer multiple investment tiers?
2. What type of investment default is appropriate?
3. How many investment options should be offered on the core lineup?
4. What asset classes or risk categories should be offered?
5. Should the options be actively managed, passively managed, or both?
6. What investment structures should be used: mutual fund, CIT, or separately managed account?
7. Does multimanager/white-labeling make sense for any of the core choices?
8. Should some or all of the investment oversight be delegated?

NOTES

1. Callan Investments Institute, 2016 Defined Contribution (DC) Trends Survey. Available at www.callan.com/research/DC/.
2. Jeff Holt and Janet Yang, "2016 Target-Date Fund Landscape: Morningstar's Best Practices in Target-Date Evolution," Morningstar Manager Research Series, April 12, 2016. Available at www.morningstar.com.
3. U.S. Government Accountability Office, *401(K) Plans: Improvements Can Be Made to Better Protect Participants in Managed Accounts*, GAO-14-310: Published June 25, 2014. Publicly released July 29, 2014. Available at www.gao .gov/products/GAO-14-310.
4. Shlomo Benartzi and Richard H. Thaler, "Naive Diversification Strategies in Defined Contribution Saving Plans," *American Economic Review* 91 (2001): 79–98.

CHAPTER 4

Target-Date Design and Approaches

You must unlearn what you have learned.

—Yoda

Selecting a plan's investment default is by far the most important investment decision plan fiduciaries will make. Indeed, when a default is in place, plan participants may essentially hand over the investment decision-making reins to the plan, trusting that the selected default will help them achieve a secure retirement. If a plan participant makes no investment election, his or her contributions are typically automatically allocated typically to a *qualified default investment alternative* or QDIA—which might be a balanced, target-risk, or target-date asset allocation fund. Thus active decisions made by plan sponsors, including the selection of the investment default, will largely dictate, if not hardwire into place, whether workers will succeed in meeting the PRICE (refer to Chapter 2 for an in-depth discussion on PRICE) of their retirement. Since participants have only *one chance to get it right*—just one lifetime to build retirement savings—plan fiduciaries need to select the most appropriate default to help them succeed.

As discussed in Chapter 3, target-date funds are most prevalent and recommended among investment default alternatives. Yet there is not just one type of target-date fund or approach. Rather, there is a broad range of target-date types and structures. In this chapter, we'll consider the selection and evaluation criteria for target-date strategies. We'll discuss the types of solutions—custom, semicustom, and packaged—and why they may be attractive. We'll take a close look at active versus passive decision-making for target-date strategies. Then we'll consider target-date evaluation criteria, including modeling approaches to compare glide paths. While we focus on target-date strategies in this chapter, most of the selection and evaluation factors we discuss can be applied to any type of asset allocation strategy, such as target-risk or balanced strategies. These solutions can be compared within and across countries, using the asset allocation, asset classes, and relevant assumption sets. For example, we can use the factors in this chapter to compare non-U.S. DC asset allocation structures, such as the UK's lifestyling strategies and Australian balanced strategies, to a U.S. target-date fund.

During the U.S. financial crisis, dramatic losses occurred in some at-retirement target-date fund vintages (e.g., 2010 target-date funds at that time) even though participants expected their investments to be more conservatively invested that close to retirement. The U.S. Government Accountability Office (GAO) found that the returns of the largest 2010 target-date funds (those with at least five years of returns) ranged from a 31 percent loss to a 28 percent gain. Not surprisingly, given the QDIA status of target-date funds, the U.S. government spoke up to emphasize the important role of target-date structures and to suggest that plan sponsors take increased care in selecting such vehicles for plan participants. In February 2011, the Government Accountability Office released a report arguing that the financial crisis of 2008 showed that target-date funds varied widely in asset allocations and risk levels, leaving plan participants vulnerable to having inadequate retirement assets.[1]

The report recommended to the Department of Labor (DOL) that:

- Fiduciaries take into account additional factors when considering target-date funds as qualified default investment alternatives.
- The DOL provide guidance to plan sponsors on target-date benchmarks and the importance of considering the long-term investment allocations and assumptions used to develop target-date funds.
- The DOL should require plan sponsors to provide information to participants about the impact of taking withdrawals from or changing contributions to target-date funds.

As stated in a news release (on February 23, 2011) from U.S. Rep. George Miller (D-Calif.) of the House Committee on Education and the Workforce in reaction to the Government Accountability Office's report on target-date funds:

While these new options promised to help workers invest more wisely over a career, GAO's investigation shows that target-date funds are not all created equally. Employers who choose options for their employees and workers building their retirement security need clear and complete information in order to make the best choice. GAO raises serious concerns and highlights the need for employers to undertake a higher level of due diligence [as they select target-date strategies] in order to fulfill their duties under the law to act in the best interest of workers.

In essence, a target-date strategy or other asset allocation default investment can be thought of as taking discretionary control over a participant's account balance not only by offering advice, but also by implementing that advice for the participant. Plan sponsors should thus carefully evaluate whether the advice embedded in the asset allocation structure or glide path is appropriate relative to the plan's goals. With the control a sponsor holds in determining the default, the advice provided should be carefully considered and intentionally selected.

DOL TIPS ON TARGET-DATE FUND SELECTION

To help plan sponsors as they evaluate and select target-date funds, in February 2013 the DOL responded to the GAO with a fact sheet titled "Target Date Retirement Funds: Tips for ERISA Plan Fiduciaries."[2] In the guide, the DOL advises plan sponsors on issues to consider when choosing target-date funds:

- **Establish a process for comparing and selecting target-date funds.** In general, plan fiduciaries should engage in an objective process to obtain information that will enable them to evaluate the prudence of any investment option made available under the plan. For example, in selecting a target-date fund you should consider prospectus information, such as information about performance (investment returns) and investment fees and expenses. You should consider how well the fund's characteristics align with eligible employees' ages and likely retirement dates. It also may be helpful for plan fiduciaries to discuss with their prospective target-date fund providers the possible significance of other characteristics of the participant population, such as participation in a traditional defined benefit pension plan offered by the employer, salary levels, turnover rates, contribution rates, and withdrawal patterns.

(continued)

(continued)

■ **Establish a process for the periodic review of selected target-date funds.** Plan fiduciaries are required to periodically review the plan's investment options to ensure that they should continue to be offered. At a minimum, the review process should include examining whether there have been any significant changes in the information fiduciaries considered when the option was selected or last reviewed. For instance, if a target-date fund's investment strategy or management team changes significantly, or if the fund's manager is not effectively carrying out the fund's stated investment strategy, then it may be necessary to consider replacing the fund. Similarly, if your plan's objectives in offering a target-date fund change, you should consider replacing the fund.

■ **Understand the fund's investments—the allocation in different asset classes (stocks, bonds, cash), individual investments, and how these will change over time.** Have you looked at the fund's prospectus or offering materials? Do you understand the principal strategies and risks of the fund, or of any underlying asset classes or investments that may be held by the fund? Make sure you understand the fund's glide path, including when the fund will reach its most conservative asset allocation and whether that will occur at or after the target date. Some funds keep a sizeable investment in more volatile assets, like stocks, even as they pass their target retirement dates. Since these funds continue to invest in stock, your employees' retirement savings may continue to have some investment risk after they retire. These funds are generally for employees who don't expect to withdraw all of their 401(k) account savings immediately upon retirement, but would rather make periodic withdrawals over the span of their retirement years. Other target-date funds are concentrated in more conservative and less volatile investments at the target date, assuming that employees will want to cash out of the plan on the day they retire. If the employees don't understand the fund's glide-path assumptions when they invest, they may be surprised later if it turns out not to be a good fit for them.

■ **Review the fund's fees and investment expenses.** Target-date fund costs can vary significantly, both in the amount and types of fees. Small differences in investment fees and costs can have a serious impact on reducing long-term retirement savings.* Do you understand the fees and expenses, including any sales loads, for the target-date fund? If the target-date fund invests in other funds, did you consider the fees and expenses for both the target-date fund and the underlying funds? If the expense ratios of the individual component funds are substantially less than the overall target-date fund, you should ask what services and expenses make up the difference. Added expenses may be for asset allocation, rebalancing, and access to special investments that can smooth returns in uncertain markets, and may be worth it, but it is important to ask.

■ **Inquire about whether a custom or nonproprietary target-date fund would be a better fit for your plan.** Some target-date fund vendors may offer a prepackaged product that uses only the vendor's proprietary funds as the target-date fund component investments. Alternatively, a custom target-date fund may offer advantages to your plan participants by giving you the ability to incorporate the plan's existing core funds in the target-date fund. Nonproprietary target-date funds could also offer advantages by including component funds that are managed by fund managers other than the target-date fund provider itself, thus diversifying participants' exposure to one investment provider. There are some costs and administrative tasks involved in creating a custom or nonproprietary target-date fund, and they may not be right for every plan, but you should ask your investment provider whether it offers them.

■ **Develop effective employee communications.** Have you planned for the employees to receive appropriate information about target-date funds in general, as a retirement investment option, and about individual target-date funds available in the plan? Just as it is important for the plan fiduciary to understand target-date fund

---

* A difference of just one percentage point in fees (1.5 percent as compared with 0.5 percent) over 35 years dramatically affects overall returns. If a worker with a 401(k) account balance of $25,000 averages a 7 percent return, the worker will have $227,000 at retirement with the lower fee and $163,000 with the higher fee, assuming no further contributions. U.S. Department of Labor, Employee Benefits Security Administration, A Look at 401(k) Plan Fees, at www.dol.gov/ebsa/publications/401k_employee.html.

(*continued*)

(continued)

basics when choosing a target-date fund investment option for the plan, employees who are responsible for investing their individual accounts need information, too. Disclosures required by law also must be considered. The Department published a final rule that, starting for most plans in August 2012, requires that participants in 401(k)-type individual account retirement plans receive greater information about the fees and expenses associated with their plans, including specific fee and expense information about target-date funds and other investment options available under their plans. The Department of Labor is also working on regulations to improve the disclosures that must be made to participants specifically about target-date funds. For example, in addition to general information about target-date funds, the proposed regulations call for disclosures to include an explanation that an investment in a target-date fund is not guaranteed and that participants can lose money in the fund, including at and after the target date. Check EBSA's website for updates on regulatory disclosure requirements.

- Take advantage of available sources of information to evaluate the target-date fund and recommendations you received regarding the target-date fund selection. While target-date funds are relatively new investment options, there are an increasing number of commercially available sources for information and services to assist plan fiduciaries in their decision-making and review process.

- Document the process. Plan fiduciaries should document the selection and review process, including how they reached decisions about individual investment options.

TARGET-DATE STRUCTURES VARY BY PLAN SIZE

Consultant target-date fund type recommendations vary based on the size of a plan. As shown in Figure 4.1 for plans with assets over $500 million, the majority of consultants believe plan sponsors will select custom and semicustom strategies most frequently. For plans with less than $500 million but more than $200 million, the majority of consultants believe plan sponsors will select custom, semicustom, or a packaged active/passive blend. Notably, for plans under $200 million, less than half of consultants believe clients will select single manager passive strategies.

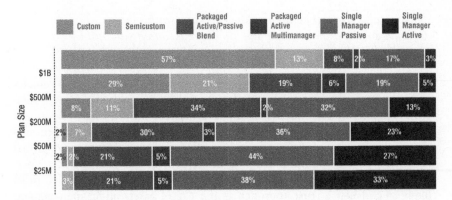

FIGURE 4.1　What Type of Target-Date Offering Will Be Selected Most by Plan Sponsors? *Source:* PIMCO, 2016 DC Consulting and Trends Survey.

CUSTOM TARGET-DATE STRATEGIES

Plan sponsors and consultants often value the control and cost savings gained through custom strategies. Custom target-date strategies offer the plan fiduciary complete control over both the glide path—the asset allocation changes made automatically within the target-date fund as the participant ages—and the underlying investment management lineup. These strategies typically are created using a mix of the plan's core investment offerings, although adding noncore lineup assets is often possible. From an investment perspective, plan sponsors note the benefits of leveraging core manager selection and monitoring, blending investment structures and styles, and the ability to broaden asset diversification beyond the core lineup. Custom strategies also allow flexibility in selecting the types of investment structures; for instance, they can include nondaily traded strategies such as highly concentrated portfolios that require less frequent trading. Packaged funds generally do not have access to these nondaily investments.

In PIMCO's February 2007 DC Dialogue called "To Build, or to Buy: That Is the Question," Stuart Odell, assistant treasurer, Retirement Investments at Intel Corporation, explains the benefits of custom target-date strategies:

> *By building one's own, the plan sponsor both has the flexibility to determine the active-passive mix, and maintains control over the offered asset classes and allocations by age group. You determine your plan's glide path.*
>
> *You also have the flexibility to add asset classes that some managers may not choose to provide because the manager isn't qualified to provide a particular asset class, or it doesn't have expertise in real estate or commodities, for example. Providers may exclude an*

asset class from their off-the-shelf product simply because they don't have professionals to manage it; whereas, when you build it yourself, you have the flexibility.

Custom target-date strategies may be implemented using trust vehicles (e.g., separate accounts) or a model portfolio approach. From a participant perspective, trust-based target-date strategies show a single investment holding (such as "Target-Date 2030"), whereas a model portfolio approach shows the breakout of the target-date allocation (e.g., 50 percent global equity, 20 percent inflation-hedging, 20 percent global bonds, and 10 percent capital preservation). Plans with assets over $500 million are most likely to consider a trust approach as the size of assets under management allows for cost-efficient setup and ongoing operation of target-date trust structures. As custom strategies have grown in prevalence, custodians and recordkeepers have improved and simplified the process of launching these structures, whether trust-based or a model portfolio approach.

While the benefits of custom strategies are clear, the work required to create them often is not. It is important to recognize that creating custom investment blends is not new; large plan sponsors have taken this approach in one asset category or more since the inception of DC plans. Custom funds require the plan sponsor to address several issues, including:

- Structuring, developing, and monitoring asset allocation
- Establishing and maintaining operations
- Rollout and ongoing participant communication
- Cost considerations
- Legal issues

All of the above issues and more are addressed in our 2010 book, *Designing Successful Target-Date Strategies for Defined Contribution Plans.*

SEMICUSTOM TARGET-DATE

Semicustom strategies offer plan fiduciaries partial control, typically allowing selection of the underlying investment managers but no control over the glide path design. This structure may be most attractive to mid-size plans as they lack sufficient assets to reap cost efficiencies within a trust structure, but they retain the significant advantage of tapping into their selection of best-in-class asset managers. This set of strategies may include white label/multimanager structures, stand-alone core funds, and possibly funds beyond the core (i.e., an investment strategy that the plan offers only in custom options, such as alternative investments).

PACKAGED TARGET-DATE

Packaged target-date strategies include both mutual funds and collective investment trusts (CITs). Unlike custom and semicustom options, packaged target-date strategies do not allow the plan sponsor to control the glide path or the underlying investments. Rather, the target-date provider packages both the glide path and the lineup of managers. Packaged funds vary significantly. They are often compared based on the following attributes:

- Glide path structure: to or through retirement
- Open or closed architecture
- Active, passive, or blended packages
- Static or tactical glide path oversight

In Figure 4.2, you can see that consultants expect selection of one type versus another based on plan size. Consultants expect mid-size plans to migrate toward a blend of active and passive, rather than purely active

FIGURE 4.2 Consultants' View on Selection of Target Dates

	Custom	Semicustom	Packaged
Plan Size	Large to mega	Small to large	Small to large
Glide Paths	Controlled by sponsor, customized to plan demographics and investment goals	Sponsor selects characteristics such as risk level to/through and rebalancing frequency	Set by provider
Underlying Investments/ Diversification	Controlled by sponsor, can select best-in-class managers per asset class from core lineup or outside options	Controlled by sponsor; limited to core lineup	Limited to capabilities of one provider for all asset classes
Ease of Use	Participants: Easy Sponsors: More effort	Participants: Easy Sponsors: Modest	Easy for sponsors and participants
Fees	Controlled by sponsor, benefit from DB/DC aggregation, strategic use of active/passive	Sponsor has influence; varies from flat fee to basis point expense	Expense ratios, and value, vary widely

Source: PIMCO, 2016.

or passive. A blend offers the benefits of both active management in asset classes where plan fiduciaries and consultants believe active management is most important (i.e., fixed income and small-cap equity), and the cost efficiencies of passive in asset classes where active management may be less important (e.g., large-cap U.S. equities).

TARGET-DATE SELECTION AND EVALUATION CRITERIA

As plan fiduciaries consider which target-date structure and approach is right for their plan, consultants in PIMCO's 2016 Defined Contribution Consulting Support and Trends Survey help by ranking the most important factors fiduciaries should consider: the glide path structure (92 percent), diversification of underlying investments (79 percent), and fees (79 percent). Notably, the Department of Labor (DOL) target-date tips for fiduciaries also highlight the importance of considering the glide path, diversification, and fees. Unsurprisingly, they also note the importance of considering the risk of loss, which falls within a fiduciary's duties. As addressed in Chapter 1, one of the ERISA fiduciary duties or rules is that "a fiduciary must diversify plan investments in such a manner that the risk of large losses is minimized to the extent possible, with the exception of certain circumstances when it is clearly not prudent to do so." In this section, we will take a look at each of the factors identified here, beginning with the most important: the glide path structure.

We agree with the consultants and the DOL that evaluating the glide path is most important, as both the risk and opportunity for return will be driven primarily by this structure. As discussed in Chapter 2, we believe investment portfolios should be evaluated relative to their objective. With this in mind, as shared earlier, we also asked consultants in PIMCO's 2015 Defined Contribution Consulting Support and Trends Survey what they believe is the number-one glide path objective: They answered to "maximize asset returns while minimizing volatility relative to a retirement liability." We illustrated in Chapter 2 how to evaluate target-date funds relative to this measure. In this chapter, we will introduce additional analyses and considerations for evaluating glide paths and target-date strategies more specifically.

Before we get into the analytics, however, we need to address the active versus passive target-date debate. Since some plan fiduciaries may believe the first decision to make is whether they should select actively or passively managed funds, we would like to emphasize that in our view, there's no such thing as a passively managed target-date fund.

NO SUCH THING AS PASSIVE

In 2011, we published "No Such Thing as Passive Target-Date Funds: Three Active Decisions Plan Sponsors Must Make," in which we argue that there is "no such thing" as a passively managed DC program. Instead, plan fiduciaries must make many critical—and active—decisions to define the structure of and select the suitable investments for their plan, including the investment default. While some in the DC market may argue to keep it simple and just go passive, we suggest that there are at least three active decisions plan fiduciaries must make as they structure their DC plans and select the investment default.

As discussed in the paper, we believe plan sponsors should consider the plan's risk relative to its objective, how to allocate the risk among asset classes to gain the greatest return potential, and whether shortfall relative to a retirement income goal (e.g., replacing less than 30 percent of final pay when 50 percent is needed) or other risks should be managed beyond relying upon only asset allocation and diversification. We share the following:

> *First, the plan sponsor must decide what the plan's risk level will be relative to the plan's objective; that is, decide the "risk budget" or tolerable shortfall relative to meeting a retirement income replacement goal. For instance, if participants need 50 percent of final pay replaced during retirement, what's the tolerance if the plan falls short of this need and only provides 30 percent—or worse, 20 percent—of final pay? This first and most critical active decision begins with deciding the types of employer-provided retirement plans that will be offered and how they will be funded, and concludes with determining the investment design—in particular, the plan's investment default asset allocation, or "glide path."*
>
> *Once the risk budget is set for the plan, the sponsor is ready to make the second active decision: how to allocate the risk among asset classes to gain the greatest return potential. For example, with the default investment, the plan sponsor will determine which asset allocation provides the greatest expected return, given the risk budget. Whether the sponsor creates custom strategies or selects off-the-shelf target date strategies, this evaluation and active decision regarding the asset allocation must be made.*
>
> *Finally, the plan sponsor must make an active decision as to whether shortfall or other risk should be managed beyond asset allocation and diversification. This active decision-making may include considering risk-hedging strategies, such as buying investment instruments or insurance to cushion participant assets against market shocks.*

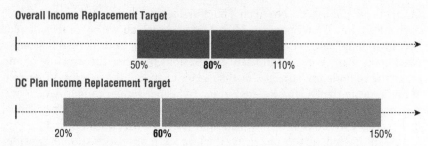

*Q: What is the appropriate **overall income replacement goal**?* (n=51) Assuming no DB plan and no retiree medical, what **income replacement** percent should the **DC plan** alone target? (n=51)*

Overall Income Replacement Target

50%   80%   110%

DC Plan Income Replacement Target

20%   60%   150%

FIGURE 4.3 Consultants Suggest a DC Plan May Need to Replace 60 Percent of Final Pay
Source: PIMCO, 2016 Defined Contribution Consulting Support and Trends Survey.

In working with plan sponsors, we often ask, "What is the investment objective for the DC plan?" Most tell us the DC plan is the primary retirement program for their workers, yet a specific income replacement target has not been identified or stated—let alone identifying how much risk the plan should take relative to that goal. As discussed, we believe plans should begin with the objective and, at minimum, evaluate and compare how the glide paths may deliver or fall short of that objective. As mentioned in Chapter 1, consultants suggest (as shown in Figure 4.3) that a DC plan replace 60 percent of final pay when assuming the participant lacks both a DB plan and retiree medical. Thus the questions that plan sponsors need to ask when evaluating glide paths include:

- Are plan participants likely to succeed?
- Will they have sufficient DC assets to cover the PRICE of a lifetime income stream?
- Are the glide paths designed to build retirement income or to maximize wealth without regard to downside risk?

LOW COST AND LOW TRACKING ERROR DOES NOT EQUAL LOW RISK

As discussed earlier, the Employee Retirement Income Security Act (ERISA) guides plan fiduciaries to act with prudence in selecting the investments for a DC plan. The goal of meeting a plan's objectives should drive investment selection. While managing plan costs is an important component of prudently selecting a plan's investment lineup, we believe cost is only one factor to consider when selecting investments. The ERISA also specifically identifies the need to diversify in an attempt to help minimize the risk of large losses. Note that the rules do not define risk as *tracking error relative to an index*, but rather the *actual risk of incurring large losses in absolute terms*.

As mentioned, the asset allocation structure and underlying investments drive both risk and return. Unfortunately, as discussed earlier, recent fee litigation against DC plan sponsors may have prompted some sponsors to shift their plan's default to passively managed index funds, with the belief that this typically low-cost and low-tracking-error investment approach may reduce litigation risk to the plan sponsor. In our view, this belief and resulting action are misguided, as ERISA attorney Brad Huss of Trucker Huss APC explains in PIMCO's DC Dialogue (April 2010):

> *With the focus on fees, some plan sponsors may believe the government is providing a safe harbor if they select low-cost index investment vehicles rather than actively managed investments. I don't think choosing all passive is inherently a fiduciary safe harbor. What's important is that plan sponsors use a prudent process to select the investment lineup and that they document their approach. Keep in mind, even if the plan sponsor selects passive funds, fiduciary oversight requirements remain. There's not a "set it and forget it" approach with index funds.*

We agree with attorney Huss and suggest a framework for selecting and evaluating target-date strategies, including three active decisions plan sponsors must make.

FRAMEWORK FOR SELECTING AND EVALUATING TARGET-DATE STRATEGIES: THREE ACTIVE DECISIONS PLAN SPONSORS MUST MAKE

Indeed, there are many active decisions plan sponsors must make. We suggested plan sponsors consider three questions as they evaluate target-date strategies (see Figure 4.4):

- How much risk can plan participants take?
- How is risk best allocated across investment choices?
- Should risk be actively managed or hedged?

As plan sponsors consider each question, we suggest the following process for the selection and evaluation of a target-date glide path or packaged fund. Active decisions are required at each step.

Step 1:	Step 2:	Step 3:
Determine appropriate risk level and budget for target-date strategies based on income adequacy target (i.e., set glide path and capacity for loss)	Given risk budget, select the set of assets that maximize return potential and provide inflation protection as well as diversification: ▪ Capital Preservation ▪ Global Bonds ▪ Inflation Protection ▪ Global Stocks ▪ Global Opportunities	Add active management and tail-risk hedging to mitigate volatility and systemic market shock impact: ▪ Reduce Risk Assets ▪ Add Direct or Indirect Hedges

FIGURE 4.4   Suggested Process for Asset Allocation Strategy Selection or Creation
Source: PIMCO.

ACTIVE DECISION #1: HOW MUCH RISK CAN PLAN PARTICIPANTS TAKE?

There are many ways to think about risk. As discussed in Chapter 2, beyond what's suggested by DOL we believe it is most important to think about risk, first and foremost, relative to the plan's objective. For nearly all DC plans, the objective is to meet a retirement income goal. For instance, they may target the DC plan to replace 50 percent of a worker's final pay in sustainable income during retirement or as noted above even 60 percent of pay. Once this income-replacement goal is set, plan sponsors can then determine how much risk may be appropriate relative to the goal.

By using this framework, we can define risk in most DC plans as *the failure to meet the needed real income-replacement target*; that is, a shortfall relative to the inflation-adjusted income goal that we have quantified using PRICE. A central consideration for fiduciaries thus becomes what amount of retirement income shortfall risk they are willing to allow in the plan design, particularly in the plan's investment default. For instance, if the goal is to replace 50 percent of final pay, is reaching a 20 percent replacement level acceptable?

As we consider the income-replacement objective, we also can consider a participant's risk capacity by asking, "If they need 50 percent of their final pay at retirement, how much can they afford to lose in any one year and still meet this goal by their planned retirement date?" To answer this question, our models need to consider three factors: a worker's pay and how it changes over time, the contribution rate and employer match, and investment horizon. In PIMCO's 2016 Defined Contribution Consulting Support and Trends Survey, we asked consultants, "What is the maximum 12-month loss a participant can withstand and still meet their retirement income goal?" (See Figure 4.5.) At the median the 46 respondents said that participants with 40 years until retirement could lose no more than 40 percent of their account balance in a 12-month period and still retire on time; for those at retirement (e.g., 65 years of age), the group said they could not afford to lose more than 10 percent of their account balance (Figure 4.5).

Plan fiduciaries should understand the risk of loss and compare this relative to participants' risk capacity. We suggest considering a value at risk (VaR) analysis with a confidence level of at least 95 percent. Using this approach and our standard salary, contribution, match, and time horizon assumptions, we believe the consultant-suggested loss capacity in some cases may be too high. What's more, we can analyze any glide path and determine the risk of loss. As we wrote in the PIMCO *Viewpoint* article titled "Loss Capacity Drives 401(k) Investment Default Evaluation" (May 2012), we believe that, based on DC participant savings patterns at the time and a 50 percent final income replacement goal, the value at risk a participant can accept in a year without derailing their retirement plans (such as the planned date of retirement or planned lifestyle in retirement) is about 10 percent

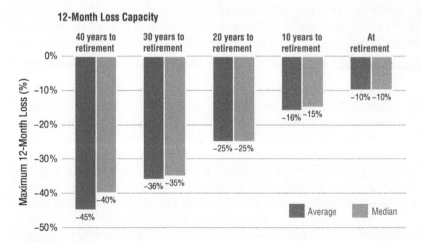

FIGURE 4.5 Participant Risk Capacity: How Much Can Participants Afford to Lose and Still Retire on Time?
Source: PIMCO, 2016 Defined Contribution Consulting Support and Trends Survey.

at 10 years prior to retirement, and less than 7 percent at retirement. We noted that the market-average glide path builds in a risk of loss at a much higher percentage.

In the article, we also calculate the value at risk 10 years from retirement at less than 17 percent, and the at-retirement vintage at a potential loss of more than 11 percent. During the 2008 market downturn, those invested in the market-average at-retirement vintage lost 24 percent of their market value. During this time frame, we also witnessed the greatest outflows from the at-retirement strategies. While we may attribute these transfers to fear or other factors, what's critical to recognize is that many participants in those strategies were subjected to a (realized) *risk of loss that exceeded their capacity for loss.*

Human Capital May Not Be Sufficient: Understanding Risk *Capacity* versus Risk *Tolerance*

In our annual DC consulting trends survey, often at least one consulting firm responds each year that in their view, participants who are 40 years from retirement can afford to lose 100 percent of their account value and still retire on time. The consultants who take this view may differentiate between *human capital* and *financial capital*. Young workers are rich in human capital, but typically poor in financial capital. In PIMCO's February 2009 DC Dialogue "Diversify, Diversify, Diversify," Thomas Idzorek, Chief Investment Officer at Ibbotson Associates, explained the concept of human capital and how to incorporate human-capital thinking in target-date glide paths:

> *There's a rationale behind investing aggressively when a participant is young. Our approach starts by evaluating an individual's total economic worth. Most people are familiar with the idea of financial capital or financial worth. But for a number of people, the largest element of their total economic worth includes the "total value of their human capital." If you discount a person's life-long expected wages into a single number, you'd see that in most cases this value, or the amount of human capital, far exceeds the amount of financial capital.*
>
> *The tradeoff for any given individual between how much human capital and how much financial capital he or she has evolves in a fairly consistent pattern as an investor ages from, say, age 20 into his retirement years.*
>
> *Consider the total economic worth of a 20-year-old. Most 20-year-olds have little financial capital but large amounts of human capital. Next, when you think about cash flows or investment characteristics of*

that human capital, you see that most people's human capital provides a fairly steady stream of inflation-adjusted income.

Conceptually we can think of that human capital as a kind of large inflation-linked bond. Again, that 20-year-old's human capital represents a large proportion of his total economic worth. And so 20-year-olds have an overweight in a bond-like asset.

But in order to diversify his total economic worth, he'd need to invest almost all of his financial capital in equities. Then over time, hopefully, what happens is that this person continues saving a portion of his incoming salary each month and converts some of that human capital into financial capital. Eventually the financial capital grows to the point where, hopefully, it's larger than the amount of human capital.

While young plan participants (e.g., those with 40 years left to work) may have high human capital and thus high risk capacity, that does not mean they have high risk tolerance. Young professionals may have a significant percentage of their assets in a DC plan and may be even more risk averse than older workers who may have other assets such as a home. Taking a loss of 40 percent of their account, or losing 100 percent of their account, may discourage young participants from contributing to or possibly even participating in the plan altogether. As discussed in Chapter 3, the UK NEST target-date design reflects the sensitivity to potential loss for younger workers as the glide path starts out with lower risk capacity and then ramps up the risk as assets build and the participant ages. Some financial experts have supported this lower-risk approach, believing that in the earlier years, risk tolerance may actually matter more than risk capacity.

Rob Arnott, founder and chairman of Research Affiliates, established in 2002 as a research-intensive asset management firm that acts as a subadvisor to PIMCO, has written about the *glide path illusion*, which touches on risk tolerance and risk capacity in early and later years in life. His research examines the range of outcomes for an investor adopting more risk early in life, moving gradually toward more bonds (the classic glide path strategy), an *inverse glide path*, in which the investor ramps up risk over their investing lifetime, and finally a simple balanced strategy that remains unchanged over the investing life cycle:

The basic premise of a "glide path" approach is that a systematic increase in the allocation to bonds over time leads to less risk in our planned spending power in retirement. But does it?

Markets certainly don't care about our glide path, so we're as likely to have our best stock market returns late in our career as early. If the best stock market returns come early, it's self-evident that we'll finish richer with a glide path strategy. And, if the best stock market returns come late in our career, we'll do well to ramp our risk up as our career evolves. But, in our 20s, how can we know whether stock returns will be better early or late in our careers?

Rather than hoping for a repeat of the past, with substantial returns earned on a foundation of far higher yields than today's yields, we should probably shape expectations based on the current outlook.

Today's world of negative real yields is ... neither risk nor uncertainty. It simply is our current reality. We can choose to accept this new reality ... or we can choose to pretend that the invest-ing world hasn't changed in this profound way. For investors who prefer to pretend that the old norms have not changed, this "new normal" will feel like a black swan, and they will suffer accordingly.

Our message remains largely unchanged. Investors who are prepared to save aggressively, spend cautiously, and work a few years longer (because we're living longer), will be fine. Those who do not follow this course are likely to suffer perhaps grievous dis-appointment. Glide path—with less risk taken late in our working lives—is inferior to its counterintuitive inverse. But it is entirely sec-ondary whether we choose a glide path strategy, an Inverse-Glide path, or a simple 50/50 Rebalanced blend. No strategy can make up for inadequate savings or premature retirement.[3]

Other experts may say that plan fiduciaries should not be as concerned with risk tolerance, as participants who are defaulted into a target-date strategy tend to remain invested regardless of the investment environment or any loss incurred. At PIMCO, we studied this belief and found while most do "stay the course," many participants do move, particularly when capital markets correct. Unfortunately, this is the worst time as they then lock in losses. They may also make the mistake of not only selling low, but also—years later—buying back into the markets when prices are high.

In PIMCO's October 2012 Viewpoint article called "Thrown in Over Their Heads: Understanding 401(k) Participant Risk Tolerance vs. Risk Capacity," we evaluate participants' risk capacity and risk tolerance by study-ing whether target-date net flow activity correlates with market movement. Our analyses showed that the market-average glide path may "throw par-ticipants in over their heads, in terms of their tolerance and their capacity for accepting risk." Our analysis on risk tolerance is summarized in the paper:

When we study the correlations between net flows by vintage and by movement in the stock market, using the S&P 500, we observe that the closer the vintage is to the retirement date, the more the net flows are correlated to the market; net flows into the at-retirement target-date funds show the highest correlation to the S&P 500 ... net cash flows into the at-retirement target-date vintage do appear to respond to market movement.

During the 2008 market downturn, investors appear to have responded by shifting money out of the at-retirement target-date funds. It may not be at all surprising that money flows into stable value during such downturns, according to the Aon Hewitt 401(k) Index data over time ... the correlation of flows to the S&P increases the closer participants get to a retirement date.

Over the time frame analyzed, from January 2006 to June 2012, flow activity in the 2050 vintage has a correlation of only 0.18 to the S&P 500, whereas the at-retirement example shows a much stronger 0.47. Even more notable, the correlations appear to tighten in periods of market downturns. During the October 2007 to February 2009 timeframe, the 2050 vintage showed a negative correlation of –0.20, while the at-retirement vintage tightly moved with the market at a 0.80 correlation.

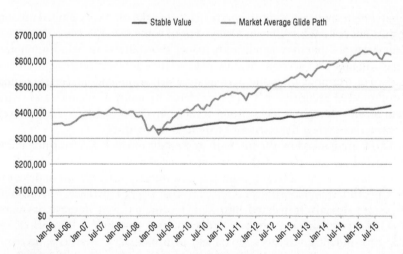

FIGURE 4.6 Accumulated Real Account Balance: Staying the Course versus Moving to Stable Value

Stable value represented by the Hueler Stable Value Index. For Market Average Glide Path index proxies refer to Figure 4.7.
Hypothetical example for illustrative purposes only.

Source: PIMCO and NextCapital, as of December 31, 2015.

> *Our correlation analysis may imply that those closest to retirement have the lowest risk tolerance, and that fear may motivate them to transfer their assets out of the target-date funds. Yet this net cash flow activity may also be explained by the reality that those closest to retirement may be moving out of a DC plan altogether, perhaps simply because of retirement or because they are leaving their current employment for other reasons, e.g., downsizing or job change.*

Regardless of the reason, participants appear to move their DC assets at unfortunate times: when markets are down. Many of these participants may have moved assets out of fear; they lacked risk tolerance to ride out the storm. Those participants with a less aggressive or volatile asset allocation would likely have been more tolerant to the market moves and better off in the long run (Figure 4.6). Unfortunately, those who moved out of fear may have locked in losses and perhaps decided to delay retirement or downscale their retirement lifestyle.

ACTIVE DECISION #2: HOW IS THE RISK BEST ALLOCATED ACROSS INVESTMENT CHOICES?

What if plan sponsors want the participants to take on a very limited amount of shortfall risk? While there is always risk of some sort, there are also investment strategies that may significantly reduce shortfall risk or help "immunize" a participant's DC account against risk, relative to their retirement income needs. For example, investing participant assets in individual Treasury Inflation-Protected Securities (TIPS) is considered by many academics and retirement income thought leaders as one of the relatively less risky available assets for retirement when these securities are held to maturity.

TIPS are backed by the full faith and credit of the U.S. government and contracted to keep pace with inflation as measured by the Consumer Price Index. More specifically, the principal and interest on TIPS are indexed to the CPI-All Urban Consumers (CPI-U) so that overall increases in consumer prices are directly translated into higher principal and interest payments on TIPS. In the unusual event of deflation, or a sustained fall in prices, the U.S. government guarantees repayment of principal; at maturity, investors receive the greater of the inflation-adjusted principal or the initial par (face) amount.

In PIMCO's DC Dialogue (February 2011), Professor Zvi Bodie explains that "we may consider TIPS as the closest we can get to a 'risk-free' portfolio, especially for retirees who need to retain the purchasing power of their assets. Their savings *must* keep pace with inflation."

Bodie goes on to discuss investing for retirement using TIPS:

The natural benchmark to that is starting at the point of least risk and asking the question, "Well, what if I only want to take minimal risk?" One approach would be to invest 100 percent of your retirement assets in inflation-hedged bonds—that is, TIPS. And let's even assume that all you're going to do is keep up with inflation—not earn any real interest above inflation. So whatever you put in, that's what you're going to get out, no matter how many years in the future you withdraw your money.

That is still a very useful place to start because, by definition, if you're going to invest in something that's riskier and that offers a higher rate of return, then you have to recognize that there's a downside to taking on that risk. So, yes, you may earn a higher return, but you also may lose principal or not even keep pace with inflation. That's the downside. And for people who want to anchor their thinking about risk versus reward, the most sensible anchor is a safe rate of return or a minimal-risk portfolio. Again, that's TIPS.

Now, unfortunately, in this country, "safe investing" is often defined as allocating to cash, which may include such short-term instruments as Treasury bills and certificates of deposit. The minimal-risk portfolio may be defined as a 100 percent cash portfolio. Yet that is not necessarily the case, and it certainly is not true in the context of a retirement savings plan.

I believe the safest portfolio is one that locks in an inflation-adjusted rate of return right through to your mortality date. And in my opinion the closest you can get to that is long-term, inflation-protected Treasury bonds, not cash.

While it is conceivable that DC participants could invest in TIPS—and TIPS alone—in an attempt to reach their retirement goals, this strategy is generally not followed. In practice, the majority of DC plans offer access to TIPS via either a pooled fund in the core lineup, or in a blended core or target-date strategy. You can see in Figure 4.7 an allocation of 3.2 percent to TIPS in the Market Average Glide Path. You can also see stocks, bonds, and other diversifying assets. As discussed in PIMCO's DC Research article (December 2013) titled "No Such Thing as Passive: Three Active Decisions Plan Fiduciaries Must Make in Offering a Defined Contribution Plan … and Investment Default," we believe plan participants are best served by asset allocations that are broadly diversified and best use the risk capacity allowable by vintage. The objective in this step is to identify the asset mix that can potentially deliver the highest possible return, given the risk budget. In other words, we want the greatest bang for the buck—we seek to be paid for the risk we are willing to accept.

At PIMCO, we start with the risk budget as a constraint and seek strategies designed to help maximize investment return potential as we identify the asset classes for the glide path. This *risk-budget* or liability-driven approach differs from that taken by many other managers, as they may tend to look first at the asset classes and then at the risk.

In contrast to much of the DC plan landscape, we believe that participants need a glide path that is designed to maximize risk diversification and return opportunity, regardless of the economic environment. That is, participants need a glide path that can offer acceptable risk-adjusted return during periods with heightened inflation and volatility. As plan sponsors determine the appropriate glide path and asset allocation structure for their plan participants, they should consider how the various glide paths might fare during various economic environments.

Further, we believe that to achieve risk-mitigating diversification, it is critical to begin with the risk exposures—drivers of volatility—rather than the asset classes. For instance, if we look at high-yield bonds, others may see a fixed-income asset. But by identifying the drivers of volatility within high-yield bonds, we note the equity market sensitivity as a primary risk factor. By identifying risk factors (or drivers of volatility), our process seeks to produce portfolios that are more appropriately diversified—and thus potentially able to better manage the exposure to any one part of the market. Part of this process is to seek assets that may help reduce risk and maximize expected return potential in various economic environments.

By starting with risk exposures to help determine asset selection, we believe plan fiduciaries may be better able to meet the duty of diversification; that is, they may be able to diversify plan investments in such a manner that the risk of large losses can be minimized.

Let's look at the Market Average Glide Path compared to what PIMCO defines as the Objective-Aligned Glide Path (Figure 4.7). If we consider the asset allocation first, we see that the Market Average Glide Path is heavily concentrated in equities and nominal fixed income. Integration of a meaningful allocation to inflation-hedging assets is generally not done. By comparison, the Objective-Aligned Glide Path approach presents much lower equity exposure in exchange for a higher allocation to inflation-hedging securities. Thus, in the Objective-Aligned Glide Path, we see greater diversification from an asset class standpoint.

Now let's shift our evaluation from an asset-allocation to a risk-allocation view, taking a closer look at the overall tracking error to retirement liability as well as diversification of the sources of this tracking error. You can see in the bar chart in Figure 4.8 that the Objective-Aligned glide path approach appears more diversified, plus the overall level of tracking error is slightly lower, particularly as the retirement date nears.

By determining the asset allocation based on risk diversification, we believe the plan sponsor improves the odds of participants meeting their retirement income goals. A risk-diversified approach may deliver a similar

A. Market Average Glide Path

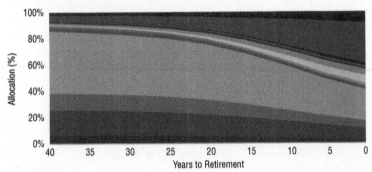

FIGURE 4.7   Market Average Glide Path versus Objective-Aligned Glide Path

Market Average data is as of 30 September 2015. Objective-Aligned data is as of 31 December 2015.

Hypothetical example for illustrative purposes only.

U.S. Large Cap: S&P 500 Index; U.S. Small Cap: Russell 2000 Index; Non-U.S. Equities: MSCI EAFE Total Return, Net Div Index; EM Equity: MSCI EM Index; Real Estate: Dow Jones U.S. Select REIT TR Index; Commodities: Dow Jones UBS Commodity TR Index; High Yield: BofA Merrill Lynch U.S. High Yield, BB-B Rated, Constrained Index; Emerging Market Bonds: JPMorgan Government Bond Index—Emerging Markets Global Diversified (Unhedged); Global Bonds: JPMorgan GBI Global Index (USD Hedged); U.S. Fixed Income: Barclays U.S. Aggregate Index; TIPS: Barclays U.S. TIPS Index; Long Treasuries: Barclays Long-Term Treasury Index; Long TIPS: Barclays U.S. TIPS: 10 Year+ Index; Stable value: Barclays 1–3y G/C Index; Cash: BofA Merrill Lynch 3-Month Treasury Bill Index.

Sources: PIMCO and NextCapital.

B. Objective-Aligned Glide Path

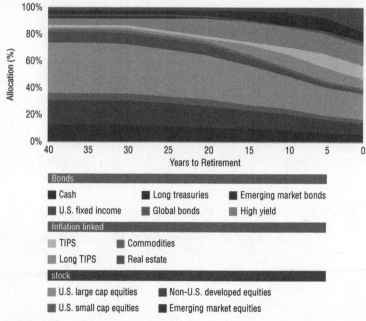

FIGURE 4.7 (*continued*)

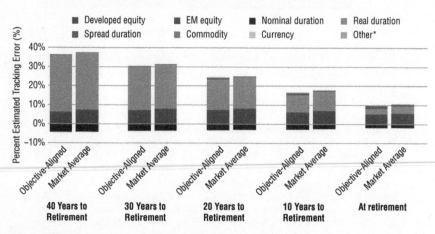

FIGURE 4.8 Risk Factor Decomposition of Tracking Error

Hypothetical example for illustrative purposes only.
Market Average Glide Path was provided by NextCapital as of September 30, 2015, which represents the latest available. For Market Average Glide Path index proxies refer to Figure 4.7.
* Other factors include (among others): Duration, Currency, Idiosyncratic (specific), Country, and Muni factors.

Sources: PIMCO and NextCapital, as of December 31, 2015.

level of expected return as a higher-risk portfolio, yet potentially offer reduced overall tracking error to retirement liability.

Once the glide path and asset classes are set, we finally can turn to how to manage or implement each of the asset classes, including deciding whether to use active or passive management. As plan sponsors consider investment managers and approaches, they may be prone to select both actively managed and passively managed solutions, often based on the asset class. Even Gus Sauter, chief investment officer of Vanguard, one of the largest passive management firms, writes: "We believe both active and index funds can play a role in a balanced and diversified portfolio. They're not oil and water, but more like peanut butter and jelly."[4]

ACTIVE DECISION #3: SHOULD RISK BE ACTIVELY HEDGED?

Asset or risk diversification may be insufficient to guard against losses during systemic market shocks. Plan sponsors can also decide whether to actively seek strategies designed to mitigate market shock risk within a plan. This can be done by introducing a number of hedging strategies or by offering participants insurance strategies that may involve a deferred annuity or other type of similar product.

TAIL-RISK HEDGING STRATEGIES

As explored in our December 2010 DC Research paper, "Designing Outcome-Oriented Defined Contribution Plans (DC 2.0)," tail-risk hedging is an investment management approach that aims to cushion participant assets from systemic market shocks.

At PIMCO, we believe there are three basic approaches to tail-risk hedging that may be effective in helping mitigate market risk. These are:

1. Reduce exposure to risk assets by purchasing Treasury securities. As equity markets correct, this strategy is designed to reduce exposure to the negative impact of equity returns and introduce the potentially heightened return of Treasuries, given the expectation of a likely inflow of assets to this perceived safe haven.
2. Buy direct hedges such as long-dated equity puts, put spreads, or collars. As markets correct, these strategies can increase in value to help offset losses. For instance, S&P 500 Index put options may be added

to a portfolio in an attempt to cushion the impact of an equity market decline.

3. Invest in indirect hedges. These include strategies such as options, swaps, and interest rate swaptions in deep liquid markets sensitive to macroeconomic events. Such strategies are likely to move in the opposite direction from the long exposure they are intended to cushion. For instance, with credit protection, as equity markets correct, corporate bond spreads relative to Treasury securities tend to widen, thus producing a potential offset to the equity market losses.

Active management of tail-risk hedging allows the portfolio manager to actively seek the most attractive combination and pricing for the above strategies. In general, the cost of indirect hedging may be lower than buying a direct hedge; however, along with the potentially lower cost, the portfolio manager takes on the risk of a possible mismatch to the hedged asset. Since the pricing of the hedging approaches can be dynamic, we believe it's important to look at the actual pricing of the hedges to determine the potential impact on a portfolio's return.

INSURANCE

Insurance vehicles are also being introduced into some DC plans. These solutions may offer a degree of market protection (subject to certain conditions), longevity insurance, or both. In our experience, interest in these solutions has been high, but there are obstacles that may still stand in the way of most plan sponsors moving forward with them. According to PIMCO's 2011 DC Consulting Survey, plan sponsors may be reluctant to add these options, given concerns with cost, transparency, fiduciary oversight, and insurance company default risk. More recently, with increased support, especially from government, plan sponsors may be more willing to move forward in offering these potentially risk-reducing solutions.

TARGET-DATE ANALYTICS: GLIDE PATH ANALYZER (GPA) AND OTHER TOOLS

To help plan fiduciaries consider these factors and compare target-date or other asset allocation strategies, PIMCO built DC-tailored financial models including the Glide Path Analyzer (a self-contained software application designed to allow investment professionals to access, analyze, and

FIGURE 4.9 Reports from Glide Path Analyzer

Reports	Description
Asset allocation	Compare the asset allocation of different glide paths
Volatility	Compare the volatility level of different glide paths
Risk diversification	Compare the underlying risk diversification of different glide paths
Drawdown	Compare the potential maximum drawdown of different glide paths
Income replacement	Compare the estimated income replacement ratio distribution of different glide paths

Source: PIMCO.

compare the glide paths of major target-date providers over varied market environments).

As suggested by the DOL, our models allow for plan-specific considerations such as salary, wage growth, employee contribution rates, employer match rates, and employee tenure. Then users of these models may input any glide path or static asset allocation to show how a participant's assets may grow, the risks they may face in various economic environments, and the probability of reaching various income replacement levels. The user can compare a custom glide path to a mutual fund company's glide path as well as to the Market Average Glide Path, which is constructed by NextCapital and is an average of the 40 largest target-date strategies in the market. We suggest considering the reports shown in Figure 4.9.

When evaluating income replacement distributions, in PIMCO's 2015 Defined Contribution Consulting Support and Trends Survey the vast majority (85 percent) of consultants indicated that a tighter distribution (fewer extremes—both unfortunate and fortunate) is more attractive (Figure 4.10). For example, given a choice of hypothetical distributions, over four times (4.3×) as many consultants selected the one with the highest worst case and lowest best case income replacement level than the one with the greatest upside.

GLOBAL DC PLANS: SIMILAR DESTINATIONS, DISTINCTLY DIFFERENT PATHS

In July 2014, I coauthored, along with Will Allport and Justin Blesy, CFA, PIMCO Product Manager Asset Allocation, a DC Design article titled "Global DC Plans: Similar Destinations, Distinctly Different Paths," in

Distribution	99% (Worst Case)	95%	Median	5%	1% (Best Case)
A	25%	30%	50%	100%	140%
B	23%	28%	50%	115%	160%
C	20%	25%	50%	120%	180%
D	15%	20%	50%	135%	200%

FIGURE 4.10   Which Is the Most Attractive Income Replacement Distribution?
Source: PIMCO, 2015 Defined Contribution Consulting and Trends Survey.

which we compared asset allocation glide paths across the three largest DC markets: the United States, the UK, and Australia. Unlike the United States, Australian superannuation programs often offer a dynamic balanced allocation as shown in Figure 4.11, rather than a target date that reduces risk as retirement dates near. By contrast, the UK offers a glide path shown in Figure 4.12 that often shifts fully to fixed income in the 5 to 10 years prior to retirement. Comparing the Australian and UK glide paths to both the Market Average and Objective-Aligned target-date glide paths, we note the need to better align each to the retiree need for purchasing power in retirement. We also note for the Australian glide path that the level of risk at retirement may exceed both the participant's risk capacity and tolerance.

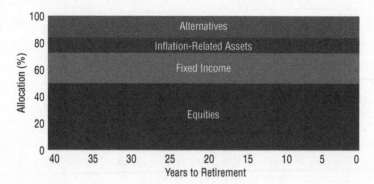

FIGURE 4.11 Australian Balanced Allocation
Source: PIMCO. Sample for illustrative purpose only.

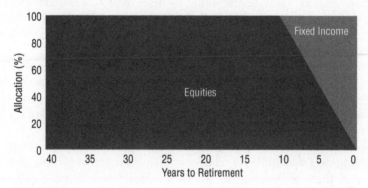

FIGURE 4.12 UK Traditional Lifestyle Glide Path Allocation
Source: PIMCO. Sample for illustrative purposes only.

At PIMCO, our glide path analytics allow comparison of DC asset allocation structures globally. This work is valued and important as multinational plan sponsors consider their offerings country by country. They ask whether the asset allocation is aligned to the objective for each market.

IN CLOSING

In this chapter, we have discussed considerations for selecting and evaluating target-date strategies, whether custom, semicustom, or packaged. Regardless of the structure, we explain why there is no such thing as a passively managed DC plan—and more specifically, no such thing as a passive target-date or other asset allocation solution. The plan sponsor must make many active decisions, including:

1. How much risk employees should take
2. How risk is most appropriately allocated
3. Whether risk should be actively mitigated

The active decisions a sponsor makes about a plan's defaults, including savings and investment options, may influence the success or failure of the participants in meeting their retirement income needs. When it comes to plan design, we believe that plan sponsors, as ERISA fiduciaries, cannot simply "set it and forget it." Moreover, in managing a DC plan, risk should not be defined as the tracking error relative to a benchmark. Rather, we define risk as participants failing to meet their real retirement income needs—an inflation-sensitive liability. As presented in Chapter 2, we suggest plan fiduciaries consider glide paths that maximize investment returns while minimizing volatility relative to the retirement liability, PRICE.

For plan sponsors to act in the best interest of their participants, including helping them meet their income goals, we suggest that sponsors employ and document their procedural prudence using a three-step process to build or select the appropriate target-date strategies or other plan default.

1. Sponsors should set a risk budget for their plan default investment. This risk budget should be set relative to a real retirement income goal.
2. Given the risk budget, plan sponsors should seek to maximize return potential by first identifying the allocation of risk and then fitting the assets to this risk allocation. Only then do we believe they can be ready to select which managers will be responsible for the plan and to decide which asset classes should be actively or passively managed. While passive management may make sense in developed markets such as large-cap U.S. equities, we believe money may be left on the table and risk may be elevated in less efficient markets as well as in fixed income.
3. Plan sponsors should actively evaluate whether to add risk mitigation approaches such as tail-risk hedging or insurance strategies. Active tail-risk hedging may help cushion participant accounts during market turbulence, as well as enhance return potential over time.

QUESTIONS FOR PLAN FIDUCIARIES

1. Have you read and do you understand the Department of Labor's guide "Target Date Retirement Funds: Tips for ERISA Plan Fiduciaries"?

2. What target-date investment structures can you consider?
3. What are your participants' risk capacity and tolerance given your target-date fund's objective (e.g., income replacement of 50 percent)?
4. What glide path structure is appropriate for your participants' risk capacity and tolerance?
5. What assets and risk factors are included in the glide path? Is it well diversified, especially across various economic environments?
6. Should market risk be actively hedged?

NOTES

1. United States Government Accountability Office (GAO) Report to Congressional Requesters, "Defined Contribution Plans: Key Information on Target Date Funds as Default Investments Should Be Provided to Plan Sponsors and Participants," document GAO-11-118, published January 31, 2011, publicly released February 23, 2011. Available at www.gao.gov/products/GAO-11-118.
2. Available at www.dol.gov/ebsa/newsroom/fstdf.html.
3. Rob Arnott, "The Glidepath Illusion," *Research Affiliates* (September 2012).
4. Gus Sauter, "Active and Index Funds: No Contradiction," *Vanguard Markets and Economy* (May 4, 2011).

Building Robust Plans: Core Investment Offerings

Capital Preservation Strategies

I'm more concerned with the return of my money than the return on my money.

—Mark Twain

Part One of this book provided a DC design framework along with suggestions for governance, investment structure, and target-date strategies. In Part Two, we will consider how to fill the core investment lineup with a chapter dedicated to each of the four core risk pillars: capital preservation, fixed income, equity, and inflation hedging (as shown in Figure 5.1). Plus, we provide a chapter on additional strategies such as global balanced and alternatives. In each chapter, we'll consider a range of strategies, share

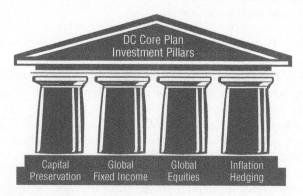

FIGURE 5.1 The Four Pillars of Well-Balanced Core Lineups
Source: PIMCO.

insights from plan sponsors, consultants, and other experts, then offer an analytical framework to evaluate potential investment choices. We start off with a look at capital preservation choices, including money market funds (MMFs), stable value, and short-term bond alternatives.

CAPITAL PRESERVATION: IMPORTANCE

The aphorism by Mark Twain that opens this chapter presents a common sentiment, one that explains why capital preservation strategies, long a cornerstone in DC plans, are also among its most popular offerings. As the name implies, these strategies are meant to allow participants to prioritize the preservation of invested principal; return may be of secondary importance. Participants may also use them to help generate income, offset riskier investments, or as a low-risk investment during volatile markets. In the 1980s, capital preservation strategies yielded upwards of 13 percent or more—but that changed dramatically as interest rates fell over the following decades, with the Federal Funds rate at the end of 2015 near zero.

Prior to the Pension Protection Act of 2006 and the introduction of the Department of Labor's Qualified Default Investment Alternative (QDIA) regulations, DC plans commonly used the capital preservation alternative as the plan's investment default. As discussed in prior chapters, the QDIA regulations made it clear that plans should offer an asset allocation choice with greater long-term real return potential. Even so, capital preservation investment options continue to play an important role in plans today, particularly for retiree assets.

In considering any capital preservation strategy, we believe sponsors should emphasize the following three characteristics to help ensure long-term success and positive outcomes:

1. **Liquidity:** Defined as the degree to which a significant portion of invested capital can be easily sold or converted into cash.
2. **Low risk:** The value of invested principal should be reasonably assured over an appropriate time horizon as determined by the sponsor—daily, monthly, or quarterly.
3. **Real return:** Investments should maintain participants' purchasing power by generating returns that at a minimum are close to or above inflation.

Focusing on selecting capital preservation strategies with these characteristics will help participants maintain and potentially grow the purchasing power of their retirement assets.

Within the capital preservation pillar, there are different options that can help meet the overall goal of preserving capital. Most prevalent are money market funds (MMFs) and stable value, but plans may also consider other short-term investments or even blend a variety of strategies to create white-labeled versions.

CAPITAL PRESERVATION: WHAT IS PREVALENT AND WHAT IS PREFERRED?

Money market funds are perhaps the most widely known capital preservation option, whether in a DC plan or not. These are mutual funds, heavily regulated by the U.S. Securities and Exchange Commission (SEC) that seek to maintain a constant net asset value (NAV) of $1 per share while earning a market interest rate for shareholders. Such funds are comprised of high-quality, highly liquid debt and monetary instruments with a very short average maturity. As discussed later in this chapter, the SEC has made changes to their governing rules and generally low interest rates at the time of writing have resulted in extremely low nominal MMF yields and negative real yields, making their use less attractive in DC plans.

Stable value, the other more common alternative, is generally available only to defined contribution plans and some tuition assistance plans. Historically, stable value has generated returns higher than MMFs but with similar volatility. While stable value may be managed or structured in a variety of ways, the important commonality is stable value investment contracts, sometimes called GICs or wrappers, which convey the ability to carry certain assets at the contract's value, sometimes known as book value. In short, these contracts provide book value accounting characteristics to the portfolio, which is what enables a stable value investment option to maintain principal value and minimize return volatility.

Shorter duration bond portfolios are, of course, fixed income strategies with relatively short average maturities, albeit longer than MMFs. In a DC context, few sponsors have historically used shorter duration bond portfolios as the sole capital preservation option and have instead favored combining an MMF with a short-term or a low-duration bond fund. However, with the compressed returns in MMFs, short bond offerings are evolving in ways that may make these options attractive as stand-alone capital preservation options, including "60-day" funds and ultra-short bond offerings.

A last alternative, particularly for larger plans, is to create a white-labeled capital preservation option that seeks to optimize a blend of solutions and create a customized level of expected risk and return. These types of solutions could include MMFs, shorter duration bonds, and even stable value.

In PIMCO's 2016 Defined Contribution Consulting Support and Trends Survey virtually all consultants (98 percent) concurred that plan sponsors should offer capital preservation strategies (note: the one that did not suggest capital preservation may have suggested a short-term bond fund as sufficient). As a single, stand-alone core option, consultants favor stable value (97 percent) and MMFs (68 percent) over low duration and ultra-short bond options. Yet, notably, a third indicated that low duration and over a quarter indicated ultra-short bonds (26 percent) were appropriate capital preservation options.

In practice, 63 percent of U.S. DC plans offered stable value funds (up from 58 percent in 2012), while 47 percent offered cash equivalents, primarily MMFs, according to the Plan Sponsor Council of America's 58th Annual Survey (reflecting 2014 plan experience). Notably, the larger the plan, the more likely it is to offer stable value with 74 percent of the largest plans (5,000-plus participants) offering this choice. Together, stable value and MMFs capture 13.9 percent of overall DC plan assets. Retiree assets likely represent the bulk of these assets as they often leave assets in their DC plan to invest in stable value, as this option is not available in Individual Retirement Accounts (IRAs).

THE $1 NAV: SHARED BY STABLE VALUE AND MMFs

One reason MMFs and stable value historically have been attractive is that they seek to earn competitive interest for participants while maintaining a constant-dollar net asset value (NAV).[1] What this means is that participants typically expect to see a steady value for assets held in these strategies, plus receive a positive daily return or yield on the assets. However, the financial crisis in 2008 to 2009 presented significant challenges to both strategies, as it became clear these investments both could lose money and that the constant-dollar NAV may not always be possible.

For MMFs, if the underlying money market assets lost enough value the fund may be forced to "break the buck" or fall below the constant-dollar NAV. With this reality in mind, the SEC introduced a series of reforms, the most recent of which were introduced in 2014 and became effective October 2016. These reforms forced a flurry of activity among plans that had offered a *prime* MMF, that is, a fund comprised of securities representing high-quality, liquid debt and monetary instruments from government issuers, as well as banks and corporations, with a weighted average maturity of less than 60 days.

While technically plans could retain a prime money market fund, given the new SEC requirements and potential for the imposition of liquidity gates or fees, they often did not. Rather, most plans were likely to move away from a prime money market fund to a *government* money market fund (see definition below). In other instances, fund complexes transitioned prime funds to government funds, preempting active decisions by the invested plans.

We believe that many plans that had a prime MMF either moved their assets, or passively allowed their assets to be moved, to a government money market fund. However, according to PIMCO's 2016 Defined Contribution Consulting Support and Trends Survey, if a plan sought advice from consultants, almost two thirds (63 percent) were likely or very likely to recommend a capital preservation alternative for plans invested in a prime (nongovernmental) MMF; over three-quarters of consultants (81 percent) were likely or very likely to recommend a switch to stable value.

SEC MMF REFORMS: A CLOSER LOOK

Approved on July 23, 2014, the set of reforms require institutional prime and municipal MMFs to have variable NAVs, in contrast to a constant fixed $1 NAV. Retail prime and municipal MMFs and all government MMFs, however, are exempt. The SEC defines retail MMFs as those with policies and procedures reasonably designed to limit investors to "natural persons." Importantly, for plan sponsors, the SEC identifies participant-directed DC plans as generally beneficially owned by natural persons and, therefore, likely eligible for investment in retail MMFs. Other provisions include:

- All MMFs may temporarily suspend redemptions (i.e., "gate" the fund) if an MMF's "weekly liquid assets" were to fall below 30 percent of total assets, with such gates permitted for up to 10 business days but limited to 10 business days in any 90-day period.
- All MMFs may impose a liquidity fee of up to 2 percent if the MMF's weekly liquid assets were to fall below 30 percent of total assets.
- All MMFs (including retail MMFs, but excluding government MMFs) must impose a 1 percent liquidity fee if the MMF's weekly liquid assets were to fall below 10 percent of total assets.

Furthermore, the reforms redefine government MMFs as those that invest 99.5 percent (formerly 80 percent) or more of their total assets in

(*continued*)

(continued)

cash, government securities and repurchase agreements collateralized with government securities or cash. The SEC also approved additional MMF reforms that include (1) enhanced disclosure of various events, such as gates or MMF sponsor support, (2) tightened diversification requirements, and (3) strengthened stress testing.

The following figure provides more detail on how the world of MMFs has changed as a result of the 2014 reforms.

	Investor Type:	Prime/Municipal		Government Only	
	Fund Type:	Institutional	Retail	Institutional	Retail
Current Structure	NAV	Fixed	Fixed	Fixed	Fixed
	Fees on redemption	No	No	No	No
	Liquidity	Daily	Daily	Daily	Daily
Future Structure	NAV	Floating	Fixed	Fixed	Fixed
	Fees on redemption	Up to 2%[1]	Up to 2%[1]	Up to 2%[2]	Up to 2%[2]
	Liquidity	Daily – with exceptions[3]	Daily – with exceptions[3]	Daily – with exceptions[2]	Daily – with exceptions[2]

Prime/Municipal funds will be required to impose a liquidity fee and permitted to impose redemption gates depending on liquidity conditions

Government funds will be permitted, but not required, to impose fees or redemption gates

Figure A: Impact of Money Market Reform on DC Plans
Source: SEC.

---

[1] Subject to liquidity conditions, prime and municipal funds would be required to impose a 1 percent liquidity fee, and in certain circumstances up to 2 percent.

[2] Subject to liquidity conditions, government funds are permitted but not required to impose fees or redemption gates.

[3] Subject to liquidity conditions, all money market funds can impose redemption gates at the discretion of the fund's board of directors.

Historically, MMFs have delivered on the capital preservation objectives of liquidity, low risk to investment principal, and providing real, after inflation returns. However, in the recent economic environment, changing risks in the financial markets, compressed short-term bond yields, structural changes to issuance in the money markets and several amendments to the 1940 Investment Company Act Rule 2a-7 (which regulates MMFs) have potentially limited future returns and eroded the ability of MMFs to deliver on those critical aims.

Most MMF complexes reacted to the MMF reforms by broadly switching their DC offerings to government MMFs (G-MMFs), which can maintain a $1 NAV and not be subject to fees or redemption gates. Unfortunately, this development will likely increase demand for government paper (bonds

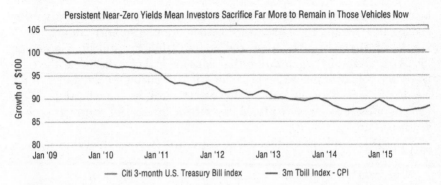

FIGURE 5.2 True Capital Preservation Needs to Include the Protection of Purchasing Power
Source: Bloomberg Finance L.P., as of December 31, 2015.

or other promissory certificates issued by the government) amid limited supply, and may keep the nominal yields from G-MMFs low and real (inflation-adjusted) yields negative.

STABLE VALUE OFFERS MORE OPPORTUNITY IN A LOW-INTEREST-RATE ENVIRONMENT

Unfortunately, while MMFs may preserve *nominal* capital, in the recent low-yield environment, they may fail to preserve purchasing power as they have yielded less than inflation (Figure 5.2). By comparison, stable value funds offer more return opportunity and historically have kept ahead of inflation. From January 1983 to December 2015, the Hueler Stable Value Index delivered an annualized 3.2 percent *real* return. For more than three decades now, stable value funds have been designed to provide MMF-like liquidity and investment risk, while aiming to deliver returns over time similar to intermediate-maturity bonds, keeping returns ahead of inflation. Yet stable value funds, which like MMFs faced challenges during the financial crisis, have some unique risks and contractual obligations associated with stable value investment contracts that may render them less attractive for some plans.

In the early days of stable value, participants may have been offered one or many guaranteed investment contracts (GICs) with a set yield and return of principal guaranteed typically by an insurance company. Over time, stable value evolved with traditional asset managers as well as insurance companies offering a variety of product structures. Today, many stable value managers use "synthetic GICs" that invest in high-quality, diversified fixed income portfolios that seek protection against interest rate volatility using stable value "wrap" contracts issued by banks and insurance companies.

As of December 31, 2014, the Stable Value Investment Association (SVIA), a nonprofit organization that educates policymakers and the public on the role of stable value in saving for retirement, reported that of the nearly $779.4 billion in stable value assets across its membership, 37.51 percent of these assets were placed in synthetic investment contracts such as synthetic GICs.

The SVIA explains synthetic wrap contracts (www.stablevalue.org):

The synthetic investment contract has two components: first, a portfolio of bonds that are owned by the plan or trust (i.e., the underlying investments) and second, a contract issued by a financial institution (such as an insurance company or bank) that wraps the underlying investments to provide the principal preservation and steady yield expected of stable value.

Unlike GICs, this type of contract typically does not provide for a fixed rate of interest over the term of the contract. Instead, these contracts provide a credited rate of return, known as the crediting rate that changes periodically to reflect the ongoing performance of the underlying investments and smooths the returns of the bonds over time.

These wraps also are designed, subject to limitations outlined in the contract, so that qualified participant transactions occur at contract value (which is the participant-invested principal plus any accumulated earnings) and the interest credited to participants does not drop below zero percent. Performance of the synthetic investment contracts, or the rate of growth of the contract at its credited rate of interest, typically depends upon the underlying investments, largely a fixed-income portfolio. Since the fixed-income portfolio's value fluctuates daily, DC participants often ask how the synthetic investment contract's yield remains stable on a day-to-day basis. The SVIA explains:

The terms of the synthetic investment contract specify how the market fluctuations of the underlying investments will be "smoothed" by the crediting rate over time. The contract yield is recalculated on a periodic basis, generally monthly or quarterly. [As shown in Figure 5.3,] the market value of the underlying investments and contract value will naturally diverge and converge over time. The magnitude may differ during certain periods when interest rates are

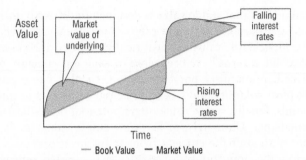

FIGURE 5.3 Market Value of Underlying Investments Fluctuates, but a Stable Value Investment Option's Assets Grow at a More Constant Rate

Book Value: Also known as *contract value*, book value is the value of initial deposited principal, plus accumulated interest, plus additional deposits, minus withdrawals and expenses. The book value of a stable value investment contract is the amount owed by the issuer to the contract holder on behalf of the plan participants, subject to certain terms and conditions.

Asset Value/Market Value: With respect to an investment (e.g., a bond, stock, or fund share), market value is the cash value that selling such investment at a given price in the open market generates. As prices for investments tend to fluctuate daily, the actual or implied market value of an investment will likewise tend to fluctuate daily.

Source: SVIA.

rising or falling quickly or based on the level of withdrawals and deposits from the contract. It is important to note that even though the market value of the underlying investments fluctuates, synthetic investment contracts are designed to protect participants' principal (deposits and earnings) and provide a steady credited yield under normal circumstances.

In June 2010, we spoke with Gina Mitchell, President of the Stable Value Investment Association, about the contribution that stable value funds can make in achieving retirement income goals. She provided detail on the origin of stable value funds:

Stable value started with the advent of employee benefit plans following World War II, and it really hit its stride with the passage of the Employee Retirement Income Security Act (ERISA) of 1974. The structural foundation of stable value is the guaranteed investment contract (GIC). Stable value evolved from the GIC, an insurance company contract that promises to pay a set level of interest based on an investment over a defined period of time.

Mitchell told us that stable value is designed to deliver a positive return regardless of the market cycle, and offers three primary benefits for plan participants: First, stable value has historically outperformed money market securities. Second, returns have been close to what a participant would earn in an intermediate-maturity bond strategy, yet stable value generally has lower short-term volatility and risk to principal compared to intermediate-maturity bonds. Finally, stable value offers potential diversification benefits to DC participants. Ultimately, in her view stable value funds may offer an opportunity to shift the efficient frontier for investors' asset allocation mix, providing the opportunity for greater risk-adjusted returns. She also explained how stable value funds operate: "Stable value has evolved into a synthetic structure, which is typically a diversified bond portfolio owned by the plan, combined with wraps or investment contracts that guard against interest-rate swings."

LOOKING FORWARD: THE CHANGING ROLE OF STABLE VALUE

Stable value, Mitchell told us, has always been considered a valued investment option. In contrast to short bond funds and MMFs, the use of stable value within DC plans can entice retirees to stay in those plans, as stable value doesn't generally exist outside of the employer DC plan framework. Retirees may rely on the diversifying effects of stable value funds, or use the stable value option to help meet income needs without the complexity of an annuity.

Looking forward, Mitchell cautions that "we need to think about how well stable value continues to meet the needs of an aging and mobile workforce." Increasingly, employees may seek liquidity as well as stable, positive returns:

> So the ongoing challenge is to try and mesh the great things that stable value works to provide—principal preservation, consistent positive return, diversification effects—while maximizing the flexibility for plan sponsors and minimizing the drag of some of the bells and whistles of stable value funds, like competing strategies and plan events. Somehow we have to make stable value more universal, more plug-and-play for the 401(k) sponsor. We need to think about the big picture, where stable value should be, and how we can improve this asset class.

During the financial crisis, many stable value funds struggled due to the volatility of the fixed income markets, which prompted some wrap providers to cease wrap issuance, change wrap contract terms and guidelines, or even exit the wrap market completely. Both this decline in wrap availability and the change in the quality of terms challenged and frustrated some plan fiduciaries. Worried about the complexities of investment contracts, limited plan flexibility and lower returns, some plan sponsors decided to exit stable value. A few consulting firms even predicted the end to stable value funds altogether, but Mitchell said such predictions were premature, commenting:

> *Amid the 2008 market meltdown, financial markets seemed to throw out the baby with the bath water. Stable value was one of the few asset classes that continued to perform, despite the market stress—and that's really important. Even though stable value was not immune to market stresses such as plan events, duration, tightening of guidelines and some of the capacity issues with wraps, it continues to serve an important role in defined contribution plans, and I believe we will see more resilient stable value funds come from these challenges.*

In 2016, stable value is thriving, with wrap providers re-entering the market along with new entrants. More plans are considering or offering stable value especially in light of the money market reforms and the continued low rate environment. As plan fiduciaries consider stable value, consultants, according to PIMCO's 2016 Defined Contribution Consulting Support and Trends Survey, viewed the following issues as "very important": fees and diversified wrap providers (both at 63 percent), depth of investment resources (62 percent), clearly understands book value risk (61 percent), and fixed income management expertise and wrap provider credit quality (both at 60 percent). Current crediting rate, diversified fixed income subadvisors and past performance are all noted as less important by the majority of consultants.

Of course, there are risks associated with stable value options, which are important to understand. Some of these risks are inherent in any fixed income portfolio, others result from the book value accounting characteristics of the stable value investment contracts, and still others arise from the terms and conditions of the contracts themselves, which, like all types of insurance, may have limited coverage for certain events.

In October 2010, PIMCO interviewed Donald Stone, President of Plan Sponsor Advisors (now Pavilion), for DC Dialogue and asked about the selection of capital preservation options. He commented:

> *I don't think of a money market fund as a good substitute for a stable value product, because in today's environment, money market*

funds are paying virtually zero. But having said that, stable value requires a much closer evaluation than it did in the past. You have to pull back the covers and look at the quality of the underlying fixed-income manager and the quality of the portfolio. You also have to look at the restrictions being placed on the movement of monies. Stable value certainly is not just a simple decision based on, oh, my vendor offers this product and it's paying X, so we'll take it.

In order to maintain the investment contract issuers' promise to pay participant withdrawals and transfers at book value, the contract may subject the plan sponsors and participants to certain restrictions. For example, withdrawals prompted by certain events (e.g., layoffs, early retirement windows, spin-offs, facility closings, plan terminations, partial plan terminations, changes in laws or regulations) may be paid at the market value of the contract's securities, which may be less than a participant's invested book value balance.

Some plan sponsors may find these preconditions associated with stable value contracts overly challenging. For instance, if sponsors are at risk of bankruptcy or have a participant population with unattractive underwriting demographics and cash flows, then they may be unable to secure sufficient or attractive wrap capacity. Sponsors also may be concerned with the potential risk that mergers, acquisitions, spinoffs, or other corporate actions could contravene provisions in the wrap contract. Some plan sponsors may object to possible prohibitions against managed accounts, income solutions, or other competing strategies that many sponsors view as desirable. Other sponsors may simply be concerned with the ability of the issuers of investment contracts to meet their obligations to their plan.

The bottom line is that some plan sponsors may prefer alternatives to stable value. This may be due to the perceived complexities of using investment contracts, a preference for more flexibility and freedom to administer the plan without periodic negotiation with the contract providers, or concerns with the limitations of contract coverage. Regardless, given the complexity of these contracts and how these potential risks can affect participant returns, if a sponsor is considering a stable value option it is critical to seek help from experts such as consultants and stable value managers.

MAKING LOW-RISK DECISIONS: VIEWS FROM THE FIELD

Other options plan fiduciaries may consider besides MMFs and stable value include short-term, low-duration, and low-risk bond strategies. In evaluating options, we believe plan sponsors should consider potential nominal and real return, volatility, risk of loss, and other factors. Importantly, active management has the potential to further increase both the nominal and real return opportunity in such structures. Weighing trade-offs among these elements will guide prudent decision-making. Nonetheless, depending on the needs of a particular plan, these strategies may present a viable and possibly more attractive capital preservation solution, potentially providing more return and potential to keep ahead of inflation, albeit with a slight step away from stability of the NAV.

A common question we hear from plan fiduciaries is, "Must a DC plan offer a constant dollar NAV investment option such as an MMF or stable value?" In the June 2013 DC Dialogue, we spoke with Marla Kreindler, ERISA attorney and partner at Morgan, Lewis & Bockius, LLP, about capital preservation investment choices, including stable value, money market, and short-term fixed income strategies.

Kreindler points out that while nearly all DC plan sponsors offer a perceived low-risk constant-dollar NAV strategy—either a stable value or a money market strategy—plans are not legally required by law to do so. Further, she notes that the Department of Labor does not provide guidance mandating the selection of low-risk strategies. Says Kreindler:

> *DC plans are not required to offer a capital preservation-focused option. Yet, traditionally, we know that nearly all plans offer a low-risk investment choice, such as a money market or stable value strategy. Often, plan fiduciaries are guided by the duties of prudence with the belief that offering a low-risk choice is in fact prudent. Or they may reference ERISA section 404(c), which can offer plan fiduciaries, who comply with the required provisions, protection from losses resulting from a participant's investment choices. Despite what some may think, 404(c) does not expressly require the plan to offer an investment option that maintains a stable or constant dollar net asset value.*
>
> *Instead, when you actually look at 404(c), some of the points to consider include whether the plan offers a broad range of investment alternatives sufficient to provide a participant or beneficiary with a reasonable opportunity to materially affect the potential return and degree of risk to meet their investment objectives. While 404(c) requires that the plan offer at least three investment alternatives, 404(c) does not mandate that any specific type of asset class be offered. Each of the three investment options meeting these minimum requirements must be diversified and have materially different risk and return characteristics. As well, the three investment options meeting this broad-range requirement are expected to enable the*

participant to construct a portfolio with aggregate risk and return characteristics within a range that's normally appropriate for the participant. And of course, there is no legal requirement to comply with 404(c)—it's an optional provision.

Kreindler also outlined certain steps that fiduciaries may take when considering and evaluating capital preservation options, reminding us that the "basic concepts that the Department of Labor has set out for fiduciaries when reviewing any type of DC investment choice generally apply to capital preservation options too":

First and foremost, a plan fiduciary needs to act prudently when reviewing the plan's investment options, including the capital preservation option—that is, act in the way other similarly situated fiduciaries would act under the circumstances then prevailing. Sponsors who lack the ability to evaluate these investment options are supported in seeking out and obtaining advice from experts in the area, be that a consultant or another type of provider to whom that responsibility might be outsourced.

Once you've gone through that prudent process and analysis, step number two is to make sure that you've documented the various different decisions you've made. This is an important step in making fiduciary decisions more defensible. Thoroughly documenting decisions when they are made makes it easier to prove you employed a prudent process if your decisions are challenged later, and not take the risk of failing memory or leaving room for misinterpretation. So, maintaining supporting records is key in defending any fiduciary decision-making process.

In addition to the "procedural prudence" steps that we have already discussed, there are other considerations plan fiduciaries can take into account. For example, plan fiduciaries should consider whether participant disclosures for any capital preservation investment option are appropriate, whether it is a constant or variable NAV solution. Even if a fund is prudently selected, participants who lose money may later claim that the fiduciaries failed to adequately disclose the fund's risks. While a fiduciary isn't a guarantor of return, other considerations may include whether an appropriate disclosure of risk has been made to participants.

What's important, she maintains, is that plan sponsors build DC plans that can provide improved participant outcomes: "When that is the overriding goal of the plan sponsor, participant outcomes can be improved and also provide for effective fiduciary risk management. That's not to say that losses are not possible, but meeting the objective of better participant outcomes and also disclosing the risks along the way are two of the best protection practices for a plan sponsor in the industry today."

Finally, Kreindler told us that in the current atmosphere of change for capital preservation options, there is a good opportunity for sponsors and others who are interested to use today's market as an opportunity to understand the many different options that are out there and the ways in which plan fiduciaries can improve upon what they currently have: "From my perspective, opportunity brings good things."

WHITE LABELING: A CAPITAL PRESERVATION SOLUTION

In Chapter 3 we discussed the benefits and challenges of white label investment options. Plans can certainly consider such an approach in capital preservation, too, as it can result in a custom solution that reflects a plan's unique needs or characteristics. White labeling historically has been the province of larger plans, which tend to have scale, pricing power, and more administrative resources; but technology is changing this dynamic and allowing customization to occur with smaller plans as well.

In either case, the benefits to consider are customization to a plan's particular risk and return preferences, possibly increased manager diversification, lower costs, increased flexibility from an administrative perspective, and clarity for participants if, for instance, such an option is named the Capital Preservation Fund. These custom solutions could include MMFs, shorter-duration bonds, and even stable value. So what types of white-labeled solutions make sense? One possibility to consider is when a plan offers both an MMF and a low-duration option to participants, but wishes to simplify the investment menu. In this case, combining both options into a blended, single capital preservation option may be a reasonable step—reducing the number of investment options but without fully moving only to an MMF, an option which has generally lagged at providing real returns and maintaining participant purchasing power. Another case to consider is a plan for which stable value is preferred, but the plan characteristics and underwriting make a full implementation challenging or even risky. Here, the plan can consider having only a portion of the fund invested in stable value investment contracts and allocating the balance to cash, short bonds, or a combination of both. Again, the result is a structure that seeks to optimize inputs (MMFs, short bonds, stable value) to create the best risk and return characteristics for that particular plan.

AN ANALYTIC EVALUATION OF CAPITAL PRESERVATION SOLUTIONS

Typically, plan sponsors evaluating capital preservation strategies begin by contrasting money market and stable value funds. After all, both seek to deliver a constant dollar NAV to participants. But they achieve it in different ways: MMFs follow extremely conservative credit guidelines and invest in bonds with very short average maturities; stable value strategies use insurance contracts, or wraps, that help to assure the return of invested principal, albeit with conditions, and smooth the returns of intermediate-duration fixed income investments, through book value accounting.

When it comes to performance, stable value funds have been the clear winner. Over the 10 years ended December 31, 2015, stable value outpaced MMFs by 192 basis points, or bps (see Figure 5.4). Critically, especially since one of the key objectives of any capital preservation option is maintaining and growing the purchasing power of retirement assets, stable value stayed 120 bps ahead of inflation as measured by the Consumer Price Index (CPI). By contrast, MMFs failed to keep pace with inflation, losing ground in purchasing power by around 72 bps each year.

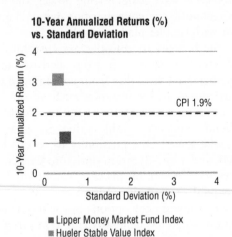

FIGURE 5.4 Stable Value Has Delivered More Return and Less Volatility Than Money Market Funds

The Consumer Price Index represents the rate of inflation of U.S. consumer prices.
Based on current yields, stable value also looks better on a prospective basis. On December 31, 2015, money market yields (based on the yield to maturity of the Bank of America Merrill Lynch U.S. 3-Month T-Bill Index) were near zero, while the Hueler Stable Value Index crediting rate was 1.8 percent, according to Hueler Analytics.

Sources: PIMCO, Hueler Analytics, Lipper, Bloomberg Barclays, U.S. Bureau of Labor Statistics, and Bloomberg Finance L.P. as of December 31, 2015.

For an individual participant, this difference could have been consequential. A $100,000 investment in a stable value fund over the 10-year period could have grown to $135,702, compared with $112,447 in an MMF—a difference of $23,255. On an inflation-adjusted basis, the variance is even starker: The stable value investment could have grown a participant's purchasing power to $112,669, while the money market investor might have lost ground, left with only $93,029 in real terms.

When we compare the risks of money market and stable value funds, they may appear low and roughly equal given the constant NAV objective. As shown in Figure 5.5, the Lipper Money Market and Hueler Stable Value indexes report low volatility as measured by standard deviation (0.5 percent and 0.3 percent, respectively) and zero negative return days. However, these low volatility numbers reflect the constant NAV objective that helps mitigate risk.

Looking under the hood at the underlying money market and stable value portfolios reveals a different story. An MMF, for instance, may hold a portfolio including Treasuries. As shown in Figure 5.5, the 0.6 percent volatility of Treasury bills (as represented by the Bank of America Merrill Lynch Three-Month U.S. T-Bill Index) was higher than that of the Lipper Money Market Index—but not by much. The T-Bill Index also had 461 negative return days, with the most extreme at –0.3 percent. Plan sponsors also should be aware of important, if highly unlikely, risks.

Of course, investment contracts are a key component of a stable value option's ability to provide protection of invested principal. However, if one

January 06 - December 15	Money Market Lipper Money Market Index	Stable Value Hueler Stable Value Index	Money Market Proxy BofA ML 3 Month U.S. T-Bill Index	Short-term BofA Merrill Lynch 1 Year T- bill Index	Low duration Barclays 1-3 Year U.S. Government/ Credit Index	Low risk blend 50% BofAML 3 Month US T-Bill Index 50% Barclays 1-3 Year U.S. Government/ Credit Index
Annualized Return	1.2%	3.1%	1.2%	1.8%	2.7%	2.0%
Annualized Volatility	0.5%	0.3%	0.6%	0.8%	1.2%	0.8%
Annualized Real Return	–0.7%	1.2%	–0.6%	–0.1%	0.9%	0.2%
Duration (years)	N/A	N/A	0.22	0.92	1.94	1.08
# Of negative days (out of 2616 trading days)	0	0	461	901	1077	1024
% Of positive days	100.0%	100.0%	82.4%	65.6%	58.8%	60.9%
Worst calendar day performance	N/A	N/A	–0.3%	–0.5%	–0.7%	–0.5%
Average performance for negative days	N/A	N/A	–0.01%	–0.02%	–0.05%	–0.03%
Worst calendar date	N/A	N/A	9/19/2008	9/19/2008	9/19/2008	9/19/2008
Maximum drawdown	N/A	N/A	–0.3%	–0.8%	–1.7%	–0.7%

FIGURE 5.5 Historical Performance of Money Markets, Stable Value, Short-Term, Low-Duration, and Low-Risk Blend Strategies (January 2006–December 2015)

As of December 31, 2015. Hypothetical example for illustrative purposes only.

Sources: PIMCO, Hueler Analytics, Lipper.

excludes the wraps, the low- to intermediate-duration bonds comprising the fixed-income component of these funds generated volatility as high as 2.8 percent (based on historical 10-year annualized volatility for Barclays Intermediate Government/Credit Index from January 2006 to December 2015), which is more than four times that of Treasury bills. Moreover, both the number of negative days and the magnitude of daily volatility were higher than those for MMFs.

The stable value option's returns can be affected by poor market value returns of the fixed income investments, potentially pushing a contract's market value below its book value. Although the investment contracts seek to assure an investor's principal and smooth the fixed income portfolio's returns, if the contract value of the fixed income portfolio falls and stays below the book value of the wrap contract, crediting rates for participants will be reduced over time. There are other risks (which we detail above) including the risk, however remote, that the wrap provider could become insolvent.

So while the risks of MMFs and stable value funds may appear similar and equal in magnitude due to the constant NAV, the underlying portfolios differ and have different, although still relatively low, levels of risk. For plan sponsors with attractive plan characteristics and who are comfortable with the terms and conditions of wrap investment contracts, stable value will likely continue to be the more attractive capital preservation strategy compared to MMFs.

SHORT-TERM, LOW-DURATION, AND LOW-RISK BOND STRATEGIES

Short-term, low-duration, and other low-risk bond strategies may also warrant consideration for the capital preservation DC seat. Unlike current money market and stable value funds, these bond strategies do not have constant NAVs as an objective. Rather, their holdings are marked to market (i.e., the underlying bonds are priced at the end of each trading day).

Without a doubt, it is the price volatility and risk of loss—particularly the risk of negative short-term returns—that may give plan sponsors pause. Yet DC plan sponsors are under no statutory obligation to provide a constant NAV option to participants (see our conversation with ERISA attorney Marla Kreindler in this chapter).

We suggest plan sponsors carefully consider nominal and real return, volatility and risk of loss for bond strategies. As shown in Figure 5.6, over the past 10 years index returns for a short-term, low-duration bond portfolio and a low-risk bond blend outpaced MMFs in nominal returns, yet only low duration kept ahead of inflation. (Details on the composition of

Cumulative Return (January 06 - December 15)

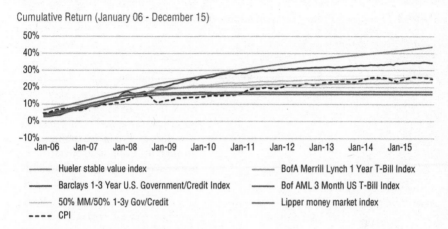

- Hueler stable value index
- Barclays 1-3 Year U.S. Government/Credit Index
- 50% MM/50% 1-3y Gov/Credit
- - - - CPI

- BofA Merrill Lynch 1 Year T-Bill Index
- Bof AML 3 Month US T-Bill Index
- Lipper money market index

FIGURE 5.6 Strategy's Performance and Risk Comparison

As of December 31, 2015. Hypothetical example for illustrative purposes only.

Sources: PIMCO, Hueler Analytics, Lipper.

portfolios and blends are provided in Figure 5.7) Moreover, the volatility, negative daily returns and maximum drawdown for the low-duration strategy exceeded those of the other range of fixed income sectors including investment grade credit, mortgages, and Treasuries.

Of course, moving beyond MMFs and stable value by embracing investment opportunities in the short-term space engenders additional risk, particularly interest rate risk and management risk, but it also provides participants with the potential to realize improved risk-adjusted returns, particularly in a low-yield environment. And, when compared to stable value, the plan thus avoids the cost of wraps and the complexities of investment contract covenants.

In the end, a DC-tailored short-term bond strategy is likely to fall short of stable value returns, even in a low interest-rate environment, but it would likely generate returns closer to inflation than those of MMFs. As shown in Figure 5.6, stable value has handily won on a nominal and real return basis for the past decade. What's more, stable value has excelled on a risk-adjusted return basis given its constant NAV-enabled low volatility. All in all, over long-term investment horizons we expect stable value's relative risk-adjusted return performance advantages to continue.

Plan sponsors may conclude stable value is optimal when compared to both MMFs and short bonds, so long as they can secure a wrap provider and accept the covenants of wrap contracts. For those who do not, a DC-oriented low-risk bond strategy may provide a better alternative for participants than MMFs.

FIGURE 5.7 Capital Preservation Strategies and Index Proxies

Capital Preservation Strategies	Index Proxies	Description
Money market	Lipper Money Market Index	Seeks to limit exposure to losses and maintain a net asset value (NAV) of $1 per share for government-focused money market strategies and retail investors through investing in financial instruments with high quality, high liquidity, and very short maturities
Money market proxy	BofA ML 3-Month U.S.T-Bill Index	Seeks to provide exposure to short-term government Treasury bills of about 90-day maturity
Stable value	Hueler Stable Value Index	Seeks to provide principal preservation and a stable rate of return through investing in short-to-intermediate-term fixed income instruments associated with stable value investment contracts that provide book-value accounting and stability of invested principal
Short-term	BofA Merill Lynch 1-Year T-Bill Index	Seeks to protect capital while achieving a return that compares favourably with a relevant benchmark such as a Treasury bill index through exposure to short-term instruments with high quality and low risk
Low duration	Barclays 1–3 Year U.S. Government/Credit Index	Seeks to produce low volatility of returns and minimal credit risk without sacrificing liquidity through exposure to a diversified range of fixed income securities with average duration of one to three years
Low-risk blend	50% BofAML 3 Month US T-Bill Index 50% Barclays 1–3 Year U.S. Government/ Credit Index	Seeks to produce enhanced returns over money markets while providing greater liquidity and principal stability than longer duration bond strategies

Note: Description refers to the strategy and not the index proxy. It is not possible to directly invest in an unmanaged index.
Source: PIMCO.

INCLUSION OF STABLE VALUE IN CUSTOM TARGET-DATE OR OTHER BLENDED STRATEGIES

As assets in target-date funds surpassed stable value in 2014 (according to the Aon Hewitt 401(k) Index), many wondered whether stable value has lost its footing in DC plans. Yet, many consultants and plan sponsors believe stable value may plan an important role in target-date and other blended strategies.

In PIMCO's 2016 Defined Contribution Consulting Support and Trends Survey, we asked what types of capital preservation strategies are recommended for inclusion within blended strategies such as multimanager/white-label core options or in a sleeve of a custom target-date/risk portfolio. Half of the respondents suggested stable value or ultra-short bond strategies should be included in these blended strategies, while only 42 percent suggested the inclusion of MMFs. Nearly two thirds suggested low-duration bond strategies as bond funds.

In a June 2008 DC Dialogue with Dan Holupchinski, formerly the Retirement Plans Manager at Deluxe Corporation, he explained the structure of their custom target-date funds and the inclusion of stable value: "Our target-date strategies are made up of a mixture of the core investment options. So each of the target-date-fund glide paths is made up of the majority of the core options. However, at one end of the spectrum, for instance, with the 2055 and the 2050 funds, we don't have the stable value as a component. But as time progresses, the stable-value fund is incorporated into them."

He is not alone: many other plan sponsors and consultants include stable value primarily as an alternative to cash. Stable value is designed to provide principal preservation plus higher yield than MMFs. By adding stable value to custom target-date or other blended strategies, participants may benefit by experiencing lower volatility yet without a full "give-up" in return. Let's consider a market average glide path with the addition of stable value in place of cash, half of the U.S. fixed income and 10 percent of the overall equity allocation as shown in Figure 5.8.

By adding stable value to the glide path, participants indeed may benefit from a reduction in the value at risk. As shown in Figure 5.9, stable value reduces the risk of loss for those at retirement from 18.9 to 14.8 percent.

What's perhaps more important, by adding stable value to the glide path, the longevity potential of the assets increases by a year regardless of market environment (Figure 5.10).

We encourage plan fiduciaries to consider stable value assets as one component of custom target-date or other blended strategies.

A. Market Average Glide Path

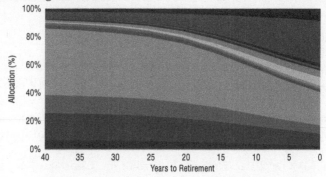

B. Market Average Glide Path with Stable Value

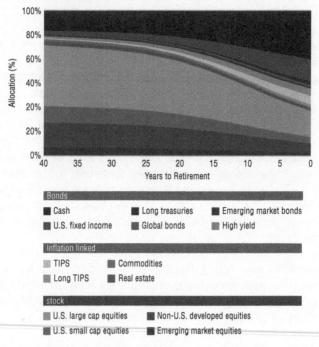

FIGURE 5.8   Market Average Glide Path versus Market Average Glide Path with Stable Value

Market average data as of September 30, 2015, which represents the most current data available from NextCapital.

Hypothetical example for illustrative purposes only.

U.S. Large Cap: S&P 500 Index; U.S. Small Cap: Russell 2000 Index; Non-U.S. Equities: MSCI EAFE Total Return, Net Div Index; EM Equity: MSCI EM Index; Real Estate: Dow Jones U.S. Select REIT TR Index; Commodities: Dow Jones UBS Commodity TR Index; High Yield: BofA Merrill Lynch U.S. High Yield, BB-B Rated, Constrained Index; Emerging Market Bonds: JPMorgan Government Bond Index—Emerging Markets Global Diversified (Unhedged); Global Bonds: JPMorgan GBI Global Index (USD Hedged); U.S. Fixed Income: Barclays U.S. Aggregate Index; TIPS: Barclays U.S. TIPS Index; Long Treasuries: Barclays Long-Term Treasury Index; Long TIPS: Barclays U.S. TIPS: 10 Year+ Index; Stable value: Barclays 1–3y G/C Index; Cash: BofA Merrill Lynch 3-Month Treasury Bill Index.

Sources: PIMCO and NextCapital.

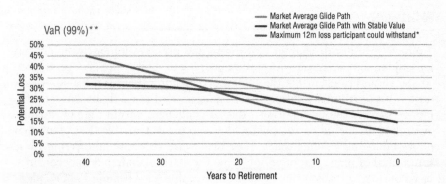

FIGURE 5.9 Potential Loss

As of December 31, 2015.
MarketGlide data as of September 30, 2015 is provided by NextCapital.
Hypothetical example for illustrative purposes only.
*From 2016 PIMCO DC Consultant Survey.
**Value-at-Risk (VaR) is an estimate of the minimum expected loss at a desired level of significance over a 12-month time horizon. Shown as positive percentage.

Sources: PIMCO, NextCapital, 2016 PIMCO DC Consultant Survey.

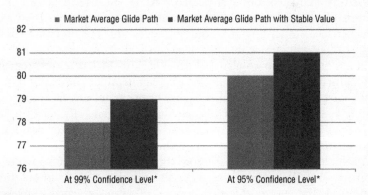

FIGURE 5.10 Estimated Longevity

As of December 31, 2015.
Market average data as of September 30, 2015, which represents the most current data available from NextCapital.
Hypothetical example for illustrative purposes only.
* Based on percent confidence interval of a distribution scenario analysis in the post-retirement decumulation phase.

Sources: PIMCO and NextCapital.

IN CLOSING

We have seen in this chapter that the capital preservation environment has undergone significant transformation over the past few years. For plan sponsors, it should be clear that the capital preservation space is not as simple as it once was. Optimal solutions have changed, and not only because of SEC money market reforms, but also due to challenges within the interest-rate environment, including the potential real returns available. For plans that offer stable value funds today, they may want to continue offering these solutions. For plans that offer only a money market fund, they may consider, or reconsider, a stable value option. Stable value has been used in DC plans for more than three decades and has provided participants with money market-like liquidity and investment risk, while delivering returns over time similar to intermediate maturity bonds. Historically, stable value has protected purchasing power far better than MMFs. However, stable value may not be the optimal solution for every plan; sponsors need to understand the unique risks and contractual obligations associated with stable value wrap contracts.

What are viable alternatives? A plan may consider a shorter-duration bond option, but with a key caveat: sponsors should carefully select a fund specifically designed to address the low volatility needs of plan participants. Typical off-the-shelf enhanced cash or low-duration funds, whether actively or passively managed, often have unattractive short-term NAV volatility. Additionally, the most popular short-duration passive strategies may expose participants to static, buy-and-hold strategies and the potential for NAV losses as rates rise. Active management can seek to manage this risk while providing the flexibility to also seek to exploit inefficiencies inherent in the short-maturity fixed income universe to generate alpha, or excess return. In recent years, a variety of new approaches have capital preservation and low volatility as stated objectives. These new strategies generally invest in similar securities as MMFs, but with more flexible investment guidelines designed to provide the opportunity to deliver returns closer to inflation.

A last alternative, particularly for larger plans, is to create a white-label capital preservation option that seeks to optimize a blend of solutions—including MMFs, shorter-duration bonds, and even stable value investment contracts—and create a customized level of expected risk and return.

QUESTIONS FOR PLAN FIDUCIARIES

1. What capital preservation option does your plan offer today?
2. Does your capital preservation option offer a positive real return?

3. Should the capital preservation option be changed, for example, money market to stable value or short-term bonds?
4. Are there obstacles for stable value, for example, wrap availability, corporate actions, and so forth?
5. Would a floating net asset value solution (i.e., short-term bonds) be appropriate for your plan?
6. Should you consider a short-term bond fund that is tailored to a DC plan need for stability?
7. Should you consider a white-label or blended solution that combines money market funds, shorter-duration bonds and possibly stable value?

NOTE

1. Stable value options may also be offered with a variable NAV, but the characteristics of the stable value investment contracts results in the NAV growing each day at the yield of the portfolio.

CHAPTER 6

Fixed-Income Strategies

It's what you learn after you know it all that counts.

—John Wooden

One of my earliest career responsibilities was managing municipal bond settlements. This included checking signatures and counting bearer bonds in the basement of the California State Treasurer's office in Sacramento, bringing the multimillion-dollar settlement check to the closing, and then distributing the bonds to syndicate members who, in turn, would deliver them to investors, often retirees.

Unlike today, at the time municipal bonds had a series of coupons attached that allowed the investor to literally clip a bond coupon and then redeem it for the promised payment of interest on the bond. In the 1980s, these municipal securities often paid over 8 percent interest pretax—with an assumed tax rate of 25 percent, this equates to a tax equivalent yield of nearly 11 percent. Not bad! For a retiree, buying a ladder of municipal bonds with maturity dates spread out perhaps over a decade offered a fixed and steady income. This approach to buying bonds built a fixed income for the retiree.

Today, fixed-income investing continues to be at the center of retirement investing, although many aspects have changed:

- Investors are more likely to buy into a bond mutual fund or other pooled vehicle rather than buying individual bonds . . . and coupons are no longer clipped from bearer bonds but rather are electronically paid out to the registered owners.

- Retiree assets are likely invested via a tax-deferred account such as a DC plan or IRA . . . in which the tax advantages of municipal bonds are negated, and taxable fixed-income securities are more attractive (note that municipal bonds continue to be a popular retiree investment choice for after-tax accounts).
- Bond markets now exceed $100 trillion globally and have evolved to offer more choice and opportunity for investors who seek to improve risk-adjusted returns.
- Yields have dramatically fallen from when 401(k) plans were first established, requiring investors to develop new approaches to fixed income—and plan sponsors to take a fresh look at DC plan offerings. (Figure 6.1 provides an overview of the history of interest rates and DC plans in the United States.)

As discussed in Chapter 3, fixed income is a primary risk pillar in DC plans—one that has been present in plans since inception. In PIMCO's 2016 Defined Contribution Consulting Support and Trends consultant survey, respondents unanimously supported the inclusion of fixed-income offerings within the investment lineup. Yet many raise questions such as "How many fixed-income offerings and what types are appropriate for DC investors? Should the offerings be available as stand-alone core investment choices or included as part of blended strategies such as white label/multimanager core or custom target-date/risk strategies?"

While the term *fixed income* is often used synonymously with the term *bonds*, technically, fixed income includes bonds with maturities of 12 years

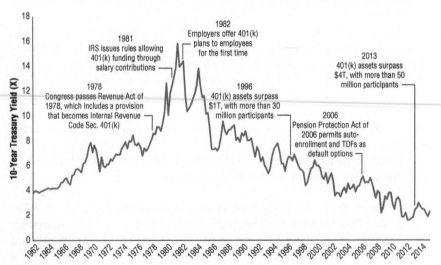

FIGURE 6.1 History of Interest Rates and DC Plans
Source: PIMCO, as of December 31, 2015.

or longer, notes that have maturities of between 1 and 12 years, and money market instruments maturing in at least 1 year. In Chapter 5, we considered capital preservation alternatives including stable value, money market, and short-maturity fixed-income strategies. In this chapter, we'll investigate the important role other types of fixed-income securities can play in DC plans. We'll also consider the bond strategies DC plans offer today, what additional types of bonds may add value in plans, and how plan fiduciaries may evaluate these strategies. Finally, we review why active bond management is so important—recall that in Chapter 3, we noted that among the consulting firms surveyed in 2016, not a single one recommended a passive-only approach to bond management.

As one of the largest fixed-income investment managers in the world, PIMCO offers a wealth of education on bond investing at www.pimco.com. We'll draw upon this material to provide an overview of the bond market, as well as guidance on the importance and types of bonds.

WHAT ARE BONDS, AND WHY ARE THEY IMPORTANT FOR RETIREMENT INVESTORS?

A bond is a loan that the bond purchaser, or bondholder, makes to the bond issuer. Governments, corporations, and municipalities issue bonds when they need capital. An investor who buys a government bond is lending the government money. Likewise, an investor who buys a corporate bond is lending the corporation money. Like a loan, a bond pays interest periodically and repays the principal at a stated time, known as the bond's maturity date.

The modern bond market was born in the early twentieth century, when governments began to issue bonds more frequently, and as the market developed and evolved, investors have purchased bonds for three principal reasons: capital preservation, income, and diversification.

> **Capital preservation:** Unlike equities, bonds repay principal at a specified date absent default, which is their maturity. This feature makes bonds appealing to investors who do not want to risk losing capital, as well as to those who must meet a liability at a particular time in the future. In addition, bonds also offer interest at a set rate that is often higher than short-term savings and money market rates.

> **Income:** Most bonds provide the investor with "fixed" income. On a set schedule—whether monthly, quarterly, twice a year, or annually—the bond issuer sends the bondholder an interest payment, which can be spent or reinvested. Stocks can also provide income through dividend payments, but stock dividends tend to be smaller and less frequent than bond coupon payments. Companies also make stock dividend payments

at their discretion while bond issuers are contractually obligated to make coupon payments.

Diversification: Including bonds in an investment portfolio can help diversify the portfolio. Many investors diversify among a wide variety of assets, from equities and bonds to commodities and alternative investments, in an effort to enhance the long-term risk-adjusted returns of their portfolio.

Diversification across stocks and bonds is effective because stocks and bonds have typically been low or negatively correlated—so when one is not doing well, the other tends to. Bonds typically do well during economic slowdowns, while equities do not, and vice versa. This is typically most evident during a "flight to safety" event when the stock prices fall dramatically, leading investors to pull their money out of stocks and put them in bonds, which are considered safer assets. During these times, bond prices rise because of increased investor demand.

One additional and important potential benefit to investors—*price appreciation*, also known as *capital appreciation*—emerged as the bond market became larger and more diverse in the 1970s and 1980s, when bonds began to undergo greater and more frequent price changes.

Capital appreciation: Bond prices can rise for several reasons, including a drop in interest rates and an improvement in the credit standing of the issuer. If a bond is held to maturity, any price gains over the life of the bond are not realized; instead, the bond's price typically "reverts to par" (its original value) as it nears maturity and the scheduled repayment of the principal. However, by selling bonds after they have risen in price, and before maturity, investors can realize capital appreciation on bonds. Capturing the capital appreciation on bonds increases their *total return*, which is the combination of income and capital appreciation. Investing for total return has become one of the most widely used bond strategies over the past 40 years. (For more, see the section on "Bond Investment Strategies" later in this chapter.)

WHAT ARE THE DIFFERENT TYPES OF BONDS IN THE MARKET?

As noted above, the modern bond market began to evolve in the 1970s, when the supply of bonds increased, and investors learned there was money to be made buying and selling bonds in the secondary market and realizing price gains. Until then, however, the bond market had primarily been a place for governments and large companies to borrow money. The main investors in bonds were insurance companies, pension funds, and individual investors seeking a high-quality "landing spot" for money needed for some specific future purpose.

As investor interest in bonds grew in the 1970s and 1980s (and faster computers made bond math easier), finance professionals created innovative ways for borrowers to tap the bond market for funding, and new ways for investors to tailor their exposure to risk and return potential. The United States has historically offered the deepest bond market, but Europe's market has expanded greatly since the introduction of the euro in 1999, and more recently, developing countries that are undergoing strong economic growth have become integrated into the global bond marketplace.

Broadly speaking, government bonds and corporate bonds remain the largest sectors of the bond market, but other types of bonds, including mortgage-backed securities, play crucial roles in funding certain sectors, such as housing, and meeting specific investment needs. It's important to understand that any time there is a risk that a borrower may not repay as promised, for example, by failing to make a payment or fully repaying a loan, there is credit risk. The degree of credit risk varies depending on the issuer, for example, corporations, mortgage borrowers, municipalities, or foreign governments. Independent credit rating services assess the default risk, or credit

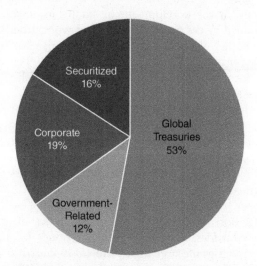

FIGURE 6.2 The Composition of the Global Bond Market, 2016
Source: Bloomberg Barclays Global Aggregate, as of 31 December 2015.

risk, of bond issuers and publish credit ratings that not only help investors evaluate risk, but also help determine the interest rates on individual bonds. An issuer with a high credit rating will pay a lower interest rate than one with a low credit rating. Again, investors who purchase bonds with low credit ratings can potentially earn higher returns, but they must bear the additional risk of default by the bond issuer.

Government bonds: The government bond sector is a broad category that includes sovereign debt, which is debt issued and generally backed by a central government. Examples of sovereign government debt include Government of Canada Bonds (GoCs), U.K. gilts, U.S. Treasuries, German bunds, Japanese government bonds (JGBs), and Brazilian government bonds. The United States, Japan, and Europe have historically been the biggest issuers in the government bond market.

A number of governments also issue sovereign bonds that are linked to inflation, known as inflation-linked bonds or, in the United States, Treasury Inflation-Protected Securities (TIPS). In Chapter 8, we take a closer look at inflation-linked securities.

In addition to sovereign bonds, the government bond sector includes subcomponents, such as agency and quasi-government bonds, which allow central governments to pursue various specific goals such as supporting affordable housing or the development of small businesses. Some agency bonds are guaranteed by the central government while others are not. Local governments—whether provinces, states, or cities—also borrow to finance a variety of projects, from bridges to schools, as well as for general operations. The market for local government bonds is well established in the United States, where these bonds are known as municipal bonds. European local government bond issuance has grown significantly in recent years.

Corporate bonds: After the government sector, corporate bonds have historically been the largest segment of the bond market and this market is evolving rapidly, particularly in Europe as well as in many developing countries.

Corporations borrow money in the bond market to expand operations or fund new business ventures. Corporate bonds fall into two broad categories: investment-grade and high-yield (also known as *junk*) bonds. High-yield bonds are issued by companies perceived to have lower credit quality and higher default risk than more highly rated, investment-grade companies. Within these two broad categories (investment grade and high yield), corporate bonds have a wide range of ratings, reflecting the fact that the financial health of companies can vary significantly. While a high-yield credit rating indicates a higher default probability, higher coupon payments on these bonds aim to compensate investors for the higher risk.

Emerging market bonds: Sovereign and corporate bonds issued by developing countries are also known as emerging market (EM) bonds. Since the 1990s, the emerging market asset class has developed and matured to include a wide variety of government and corporate bonds issued in major external currencies (including the U.S. dollar and the euro), as well as in local currencies (often referred to as emerging local market bonds). Because they come from a variety of countries, all of which may have different growth prospects, emerging market bonds can help diversify an investment portfolio—and can potentially provide attractive risk-adjusted returns.

Mortgage-backed and asset-backed securities: Another major area of the global bond market comes from a process known as *securitization*, in which the cash flows from various types of loans (mortgage payments, car payments, or credit-card payments, for example) are bundled together and resold to investors as bonds. Mortgage-backed securities (created from the mortgage payments of residential homeowners) and asset-backed securities (created from car payments, credit card payments, or other loans) are the largest sectors involving securitization.

After an issuer sells a bond, it can be bought and sold in the secondary market, where prices can fluctuate depending on changes in economic outlook, the credit quality of the bond or issuer, and supply and demand, among other factors. Broker-dealers are the main buyers and sellers in the secondary market for bonds, and DC participants typically purchase bonds through mutual funds or other pooled strategies such as collective investment trusts or separately managed accounts.

WHAT TYPES OF BONDS SHOULD BE OFFERED TO DC PARTICIPANTS?

Now that we know what type of bonds make up the majority of the market, which type of bond strategies should be offered to DC participants? After all, participants are not investing in individual bonds, but rather mutual funds or other pooled vehicles.

As discussed in Chapter 3, what's important in structuring a DC menu—whether lengthy or brief—is to offer a risk-balanced investment set. In the event that participants evenly divide their assets across the investment menu

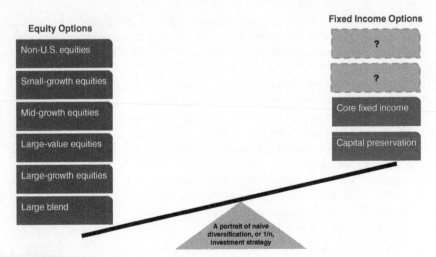

FIGURE 6.3 Balancing Investment Menu Risk by Adding Diversifying Fixed Income Assets

Sample for illustrative purposes only.

Source: PIMCO.

(i.e., the *naive rule* or 1/*n* portfolio strategy), the result should provide a reasonably balanced portfolio (Figure 6.3). Many DC plans offer just one U.S.-centric bond choice, which can lead to equity-heavy allocations by participants. Plan sponsors may find many participants benefit when offered a balanced ratio between stock and fixed-income options, including the capital preservation option, to ensure that investors implementing a naive diversification strategy have a balanced portfolio. While there is no rule of thumb, a 3:2 ratio of stock to bond options would match the commonly referenced *60/40 portfolio.*

So what options should plan sponsors offer? In PIMCO's 2016 Defined Contribution Consulting Support and Trends consultant survey, nearly all consultants (98 percent) recommend a core or core-plus strategy as a stand-alone investment option (Figure 6.4).

In addition, consultants at the median would offer one more bond strategy on the core lineup; they suggest plan sponsors consider income-oriented strategies such as investment-grade corporate bonds, high-yield, multisector, and foreign/global bonds (hedged or unhedged). Blended white-label or custom target-date/risk strategies, core or core-plus, high-yield, and multisector strategies are recommended by over 70 percent of consultants. In addition, foreign or global (unhedged), unconstrained, investment-grade credit, and emerging-markets bonds (unhedged) are suggested by over 60 percent of consultants. Notably, over half of consultants (55 percent) also recommend that

Fixed Income

Stand-alone*		Blended**	
Core or core plus	98%	Core or core plus	81%
Investment grade credit	40%	High yield	76%
High yield	38%	Multi sector	71%
Multi sector	37%	Foreign or global—unhedged	69%
Foreign or global—hedged	35%	Unconstrained	64%
Foreign or global—unhedged	33%	Investment grade credit	62%
Unconstrained	24%	Emerging markets—unhedged	60%
Emerging markets—hedged	14%	Emerging markets—hedged	57%
Emerging markets—unhedged	13%	Foreign or global—hedged	57%
Long duration	11%	Long duration	55%

FIGURE 6.4   Consultants' Recommended Fixed Income Offerings

*Used as a stand-alone option on the core investment menu.
**Used in a multimanager/white label core option or in a sleeve in a custom target-date/risk portfolio.

Source: PIMCO, 2016 DC Consulting and Trends Survey.

long-duration bonds be included in blended strategies. This addition may be most appropriate for the long-dated vintages of target-date strategies.

We'll look at each of these most-recommended strategies in turn to review the goals and benefits to DC investors.

Capital Preservation

As discussed in Chapter 5, capital preservation-focused strategies typically include money market funds, stable value strategies, and possibly short-duration bond funds. For plans that offer stable value, potentially competing investment choices such as money market, short-term, and low-duration bond strategies may be precluded. Stable value strategies (as discussed in the previous chapter) not only offer capital preservation potential, but also historically higher risk-adjusted returns than money market and low-duration strategies.

For plan menus that include a money market fund, we suggest fiduciaries consider adding a short-term or low-duration bond strategy, either as a replacement or complement. We believe it important for these replacements to have real return potential, low volatility, and small risk of negative single-day performance.

Core and Core-Plus Bonds

The most-recommended bonds strategy for DC plans, core fixed-income strategies are offered by the vast majority of DC plans and, given their limited volatility and downside risk, are often viewed as the "anchor" of a portfolio. Some plans offer a core bond strategy that is passively managed or tightly tethered to the Barclays U.S. Aggregate Index (BAGG), or a "core-plus" bond strategy that adds some discretion to add other instruments—such as high yield or global debt—for greater risk-adjusted returns. (The Barclays U.S. Aggregate Index is composed of U.S. government, corporate, and securitized debt.)

Core strategies provide investors the potential for benefits of capital preservation, income, and diversification, plus these strategies have potential capital appreciation. However, because these strategies are often tethered to the Barclays U.S. Aggregate Index, the low-rate environment (Figure 6.5) that PIMCO expects to persist for some time at time of writing will drag on expected returns (because, as we will discuss later in this chapter, a portfolio's yield typically accounts for 80 to 90 percent of future return). As such, we agree with consultants that more, higher-returning bond strategies should be considered for core menus.

FIGURE 6.5   Decline in Yield on BAGG Index (1996–2015) Shows That Forward-Looking Expected Returns Are Lower

*Yield-to-Worst of Barclays U.S. Aggregate Index.

Source: Bloomberg Barclays.

INVESTMENT-GRADE AND HIGH-YIELD CREDIT

The second and third most-recommended bond strategies from consultants for stand-alone plan options are investment-grade and high-yield credit (see Figure 6.4). As discussed previously, corporate credit falls into two broad categories: investment-grade and high-yield bonds. Investment-grade bonds are issued by companies perceived to have higher credit quality and lower risk of default than high-yield rated bonds. However, given the additional risk they represent, high-yield bonds have (unsurprisingly) a higher yield than investment-grade bonds.

The potential benefits of this asset class for participants include higher expected returns than core bond strategies, as well as the overall diversification benefits presented by bonds. While these strategies are typically more volatile (and have higher drawdowns—or the peak-to-trough declines during a specific recorded period—than core bond strategies), at the same time they have historically displayed lower volatility than U.S. equities, and thus offer a nice balance between the two. In today's environment, the income from corporate credit is also meaningfully higher than dividends from U.S. stocks, as shown in Figure 6.6, which illustrates and compares the yields on various asset classes.

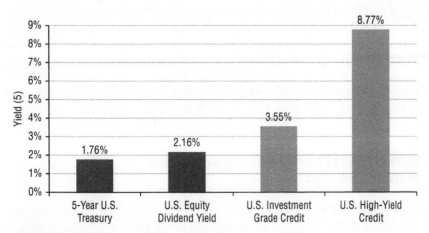

FIGURE 6.6 Comparing Yields across Asset Classes

As of 31 December 2015; U.S. Equity: S&P500 Index (dividend yield), U.S. Investment Grade Credit: Barclays U.S. Credit Index, U.S. High-Yield Credit: Bank of America Merrill Lynch High-Yield Constrained Index

Sources: PIMCO, Bloomberg Finance L.P., Bloomberg Barclays.

Multisector

Because the global bond market is so vast, but plan sponsors want to maintain a simplified core menu and participant communication, a single strategy that commingles high-yield, investment-grade corporate bonds and emerging-market debt—or a combination of these and other asset classes—could increase participant diversification, minimize the volatility of individual strategies, and provide professional asset allocation across market segments.

For participants seeking higher returns or income, a multisector bond strategy may serve as a risk-managed, income-oriented, and global complement (or possible replacement) to traditional core bond holdings. This type of strategy may pursue a global opportunity set, focusing on sectors that provide: higher yield than government securities, income, and low correlation with equities and other asset classes.

Foreign/Global

Investing globally in fixed income can help plan members reach common retirement goals through the potential for higher returns, greater diversification of risks, and inflation hedging. Global bond strategies invest in all bond markets, including the United States, while foreign bond strategies invest in all global bond markets except the United States.

As capital markets have deepened around the world, the U.S. share of the global fixed-income market shrank to only 37 percent at the end of September 2015, according to data from the Bank for International Settlements. Just as U.S. companies have focused overseas to capture broader, global sources of growth, so too should DC plan participants turn their focus globally—as the vast global bond market presents opportunities to enhance returns and reduce overall portfolio volatility. Figure 6.7 illustrates the scope of the opportunity that may be available from "going global."

BOND INVESTMENT STRATEGIES: PASSIVE VERSUS ACTIVE APPROACHES

Plan fiduciaries can choose from many different investment strategies, depending on the role or roles they desire bonds to play in the DC plan.

The next decision is whether to utilize passive or active management. In passive bond strategies, or *index funds*, portfolio managers typically only buy and hold bonds, changing the composition of their portfolios if and when the corresponding indexes change. They do not generally make independent decisions on buying and selling bonds. Passive approaches may suit

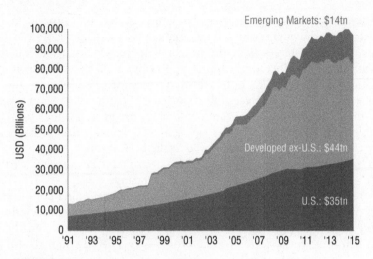

FIGURE 6.7 Global Bond Diversification

Estimated $94 trillion global debt market.

Sources: PIMCO, BIS, Bloomberg Finance L.P.

investors seeking some of the traditional benefits of bonds, such as capital preservation, income, and diversification, but they do not attempt to capitalize on changes in the interest rate, credit, or market environment. The most common bond index in U.S. DC plans is the Barclays U.S. Aggregate Index, or BAGG, which invests in government, securitized, and corporate bonds (see Figure 6.8 for a more detailed breakdown).

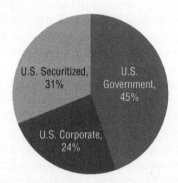

FIGURE 6.8 Composition of Barclays U.S. Aggregate Index

As of October 2015.

Source: Bloomberg Barclays US Aggregate Index Factsheet (available at www.index.barcap.com).

Active investment strategies, by contrast, try to outperform bond indexes, often by buying and selling bonds to take advantage of price movements. These strategies have the potential to provide many or all of the benefits of bonds, including capital appreciation in excess of their index benchmark. However, to outperform indexes successfully over the long term, active investing requires the ability to: (1) form opinions on the economy, the direction of interest rates, and/or the credit environment; (2) trade bonds efficiently to express those views; and (3) manage risk. Bringing all of these elements together is challenging in the best of times.

One of the most widely used active approaches, mentioned earlier in this chapter, is known as "total return" investing, which uses a variety of strategies to maximize capital appreciation, while retaining bond-like risk profiles. Active bond portfolio managers seeking price appreciation try to buy undervalued bonds, hold them as they rise in price, and then sell them before maturity to realize the profits—thus ideally implementing the advice to buy low and sell high. Active managers can employ a number of different techniques in an effort to find bonds that could rise in price. These include:

- **Macroeconomic analysis:** Portfolio managers use top-down analysis to find bonds that may rise in price due to favorable economic conditions, interest-rate environment, or global growth patterns. They will look at economic factors such as national output (GDP), inflation, unemployment, and monetary and fiscal policies to determine which countries offer the most favorable investment potential.
- **Credit analysis:** Using fundamental bottom-up credit analysis, active managers attempt to identify bonds that may rise in price due to an improvement in the credit standing of the issuer. They will look at factors such as a company's balance sheet, cash flows, use of capital, business model, competition, and quality of the management team. Bond prices may increase, for example, when a company chooses to reduce the debt on their balance sheet or develop a product or competitive advantage that allows them to gain market share.
- **Duration, or interest rate, management:** To express a view on and help manage the risk in interest-rate changes, portfolio managers can adjust the duration, or interest-rate exposure, of their bond portfolios. Managers anticipating a rise in interest rates can attempt to protect bond portfolios from a negative price impact by shortening the duration of their portfolios, possibly by selling some longer-term bonds and buying short-term bonds. Conversely, to maximize the positive impact of an expected drop in interest rates, active managers can lengthen duration on bond portfolios.

- **Yield-curve positioning:** Active bond managers can adjust the maturity structure of a bond portfolio based on expected changes in the relationship between bonds with different maturities, a relationship that is illustrated by the yield curve. While yields normally rise with maturity, this relationship can change, creating opportunities for active bond managers to position a portfolio in the area of the yield curve that is likely to perform the best in a given economic environment.
- **Roll down:** When short-term interest rates are lower than longer-term rates (known as a normal interest-rate environment), a bond is valued at successively lower yields and higher prices as it approaches maturity or "rolls down the yield curve." Thus a bond manager can hold a bond for a period of time as it appreciates in price and sell it before maturity to realize the gain. This strategy has the potential to continually add to total return in a normal interest-rate environment.
- **Sector rotation:** Based on their economic outlook, bond managers invest in certain sectors that have historically increased in price during a particular phase in the economic cycle, and avoid those that have underperformed at that point. As the economic cycle turns, they may sell bonds in one sector and buy in another.
- **Technical market analysis:** Portfolio managers can analyze the changes in supply and demand for specific asset classes or individual bonds, as these changes may cause advantageous price movements.
- **Derivatives:** While derivatives developed somewhat of a negative association during the financial crisis, when they were used to create leverage, many managers have been able to effectively use futures, options, swaps, and other derivatives in portfolio management. Furthermore, with the implementation of the Dodd-Frank Wall Street Reform and Consumer Protection Act ("Dodd-Frank") and the evolution of central counterparty clearinghouses, the regulatory framework has reduced risk for select derivatives. In mutual funds and ETFs, derivatives are most typically used for substitution of physical securities and risk control. Derivatives can be more liquid and have lower transaction costs than certain physical securities, in which case it can be better to use them as a substitute for cash bonds. They can also be used to "hedge out" undesired risk characteristics in a portfolio—which means that derivatives (a "risky" asset) can be used to actually lower the overall risk profile of the portfolio.

As you can see, there are many potential ways for active bond managers to enhance returns and reduce risk for DC participants. Given these many techniques, it's not surprising that active bond management dominates in DC plans and, as noted earlier, that consultants believe active bond

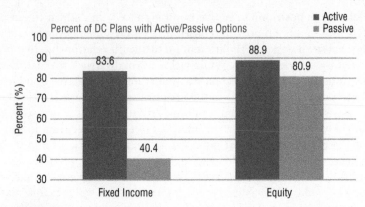

FIGURE 6.9 Plan Sponsors Prefer Active Management for Fixed Income by a Wider Margin Than for Equities
Source: PSCA's 57th Survey.

management is important. As shown in Figure 6.9, DC plans tend to offer active, rather than passive fixed-income strategies.

As shown in Figure 6.10, passive intermediate-term bond strategies underperformed active core and core-plus strategies over the past five and 10 years. Without doubt, passive bond management typically offers lower expense ratios than active strategies. Nonetheless, reduced returns and exposure to rising rates may hit participants with significantly higher hidden costs. In contrast, active core bond managers can manage risk

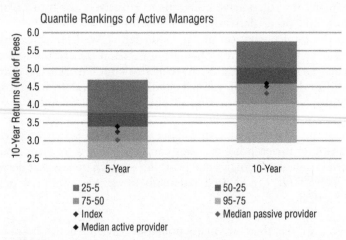

FIGURE 6.10 Active Core Bond Management May Improve Risk and Return
Source: Morningstar.

while seeking to increase returns relative to their benchmark over time and during most market downturns.

For investors in actively managed strategies, this can mean one important thing: the potential for more assets at retirement. Consider that during the past 28 years, the active bond strategies with the most assets in 401(k) plans collectively on average outpaced the BAGG Index, including during periods of rising rates (see Figure 6.11). Indeed, $100,000 invested in these active managers in May 1987 would have grown, on average, to $645,757 by 2015. If it had been invested in the BAGG Index only, however, it would have grown to just $622,689—or a difference of just under $24,000. The best-performing active strategies returned more.

Of course, while active management has the potential to result in higher returns than a passive investment over the longer term, investors should expect active managers to periodically underperform passive ones. It is for this reason that a manager's risk management program is of critical importance. A robust risk management program will help guide and monitor the risk profile of a portfolio so that it aligns with the manager's and investor's expectations. It involves the evaluation of investment risks present in a portfolio and forecasting how the portfolio might behave in different market environments (i.e., "stress testing" a portfolio). An active manager also must

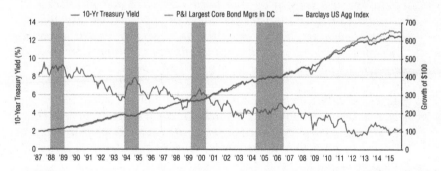

FIGURE 6.11 The Largest Actively Managed Strategies Have Beaten the Barclay's Aggregate over the Past 28 Years

Hypothetical example for illustrative purposes only.

The "Pensions & Investments Domestic fixed-income mutual funds most used by DC plans"("P&I" on figure) composite performance was calculated as follows: PIMCO took the list of the 50 largest domestic fixed-income strategies held within U.S. DC plans, as identified by P&I as of June 30, 2014, and identified the 17 strategies that represent active core managers as defined by Morningstar. Then, using publicly available data for the commingled vehicle run by each manager, we averaged monthly returns for each of the 17 strategies over a 28-year period. Commingled vehicles with a track record shorter than 28 years were added to the composite based on their inception date.

Source: PIMCO, as of December 31, 2015.

evaluate trades on the basis of the risk/reward trade-off. In other words, a trade may have a high return potential but at a risk to the portfolio that is too great for the targeted risk profile of the strategy.

Of course, managers do not have to choose either active *or* passive. Instead, some plan sponsors offer both active and passive bond options, that is, a "mirror" approach. As noted in Chapter 3 (Figure 3.12), however, the majority of consultants in PIMCO's 2016 Defined Contribution Consulting Support and Trends Survey (83 percent) advised against mirroring fixed-income offerings, as the sentiment is that doing so can create unnecessary communication and selection complexity for participants.

What about lessons from the field? In a November 2009 DC Dialogue we spoke with Kevin Vandolder, CFA, principal and leader of the DC research practice area at Aon Hewitt Investment Consulting (formerly principal at Ennis, Knupp & Associates), about fixed-income investing. He shared the following observations on active fixed-income management:

> [T]here are several arguments that support active management of bonds. First, not all segments of the bond market are included in the major bond indexes (e.g., nondollar and bonds rated below BBB), and these segments can provide opportunities for active managers to diversify and tactically outperform the indexes. Secondly, fixed-income markets tend to be somewhat segmented and no market index adequately captures the full range of opportunities available to active managers. Therefore, active managers, and particularly "core-plus" managers with significant skill, can add value. Core-plus managers are managers who opportunistically invest in segments of the fixed-income market that are not included in the major bond indexes, including high-yield and nondollar bonds. Overall we believe that the optimal mix for a particular client depends on factors such as risk control preferences, the desired number of platforms provided to participants, the client's level of confidence in active management and the client's sensitivity to investment manager fees.

Vandolder went on to discuss the types of bond offerings plan sponsors were adding to their plans, saying: "Over the last 18 to 24 months, more of our clients have added a complementary fixed-income alternative into their DC plans. The two highest-frequency additions we see to the DC investment option structure are TIPS alternatives and core-plus bond alternatives (e.g., adding in high-yield, non-U.S. fixed income, etc.)."

Today consultant interest in adding diversifying fixed-income options continues as plan fiduciaries seek opportunities for enhancing returns, improving diversification and reducing risk.

Bonds Unleashed

Benchmarks play a very important role in fixed income. Passive managers seek to match the holdings and returns of a benchmark while active managers can take active positions around the benchmark, with varying degrees of discretion, or take out-of-benchmark positions.

However, benchmarks are not static and often change to reflect changes in the bond market. For example, the most common fixed-income benchmark used today (as noted earlier) is the Barclays U.S. Aggregate Bond (BAGG) Index. The BAGG is a market capitalization-weighted index comprising U.S. investment-grade bonds. This means that as the U.S. bond market changes, so does the index. In fact, U.S. Treasuries in the index hit a 10-year high of 36 percent at the end of 2012 as the U.S. government continued to finance its deficits through debt issuance. Notwithstanding increasing levels of U.S. debt and the downgrade of the U.S. government's credit rating in 2011, yields have fallen to historic lows, while duration, or interest rate risk, has increased over time, demonstrating the changing risk and return characteristics of the benchmark.

Like the BAGG, the JPMorgan Government Bond Index Global—the most widely used global government bond benchmark—provides another example of why reviewing benchmarks is critically important. As a result of the accommodative central bank policies taken by the global central banks after the financial crisis, many rates are negative today. In a negative rates environment, the JP Morgan Government Bond Index Global may no

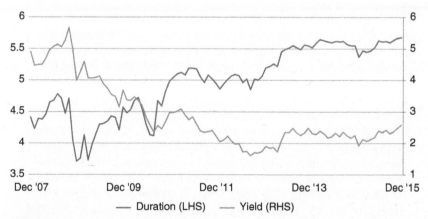

FIGURE 6.12 Decline in Yield and Rise in Duration of BAGG Index (2007–2015) Demonstrates Changing Risk Profile of Indices over Time
Sources: Bloomberg Barclays and PIMCO, as of 31 December 2015.

longer represent the index that a plan sponsor may wish to use for a global bond allocation.

In order to address issues such as these, active managers have also evolved their investment offerings by enhancing benchmarks to better reflect a particular asset class, composition of asset classes (in the case of multiasset or multisector strategies), or top-down view. On the latter, alternative indexes not tied to traditional weightings such as outstanding debt can align investors with global growth trends and potentially reduce exposure to highly indebted countries. This strategy seeks to help bond investors gain greater exposure to areas of global growth and higher yields, as its GDP-weighted index is more inclusive of emerging market countries with stronger underlying fundamentals and is less exposed to highly indebted developed countries. It's a more forward-looking approach harnessed to evolving growth opportunities.

As commonly used benchmarks evolve with the markets, and managers develop potentially improved benchmarks, we recommend that plan sponsors regularly review the risk profile of the benchmarks used in plan investment options and alternatives. Monitoring how benchmarks change over time can help sponsors ensure plan options continue to meet the desired risk-return profile for participants. A framework for doing so is presented in the next section in this chapter.

In the January 2013 DC Dialogue, we spoke with Chris Lyon, CFA, Partner and Head of Defined Contribution Research, and Lisa Florentine, Partner and Head of Fixed Income Research at Rocaton Investment Advisors, about evaluating benchmarks. They shared the following observations:

> In the fixed income part of the menu, we suggest that plans offer some kind of core fixed income strategy plus several other funds— for example, a global fund, a non-U.S. developed or emerging market debt fund, and a high-yield fund. While the Barclays U.S. Aggregate remains the broadest and most popular measure of the taxable U.S. investment grade fixed-income opportunity set and is commonly used as the benchmark for the core DC plan bond fund, we suggest that plan sponsors take a careful look at both the return expectations and the risk that participants may face in the Aggregate, especially in a rising interest-rate environment. We attribute this worsening risk/return profile largely to the overall level of interest rates and the growing concentration within the Barclays U.S. Aggregate of U.S. Treasury and other government-related bonds (approximately 75 percent as of December 31, 2013).
>
> By reconfiguring how plan sponsors define "core" fixed income, we believe there are ways to adjust fixed income allocations

or benchmarks to potentially improve the risk/return trade-off for DC participants. This could include redefining the benchmark and/or complementing the core with diversifying strategies that might provide higher yield and, in some cases, less interest rate sensitivity.

Behavioral finance studies have shown us that too many options can lead to reduced participation rates, so we strive to offer the right mix of options. Fixed income in general is somewhat underrepresented relative to other asset classes in DC plans. When it comes to investment selection, participants tend to choose a limited number of options (typically, three or four), and a lineup with a disproportionate number of options in one asset class may influence how the participant allocates among asset classes.

In implementing these approaches, plans may retain their actively managed core fund and add a GDP-weighted strategy and/ or a diversifying bond fund. Some plans may want to have a multimanaged fixed income option that has a core-plus type of manager as the anchor and then the GDP-weighted and diversifying strategies blended in. Or, you could add additional categories into that multimanaged option, depending on the plan design you're going to implement.

In the September 2012 DC Dialogue, PIMCO spoke with Bradley Leak, CFA, Managing Director, Public Markets at The Boeing Company, about alternative benchmarks. He shared the following observations:

Our bond allocation in the glide path is primarily active, as we have a fairly high target for alpha in the fixed income space. As for global versus U.S. bonds, our optimization suggested a higher allocation to global bonds within the longer-dated funds, and a shift to lower-volatility U.S. bonds as our participants approach retirement.

As you know, our global bond option is managed against the PIMCO Global Advantage Bond Index that allocates assets on a more forward-looking basis, investing more in emerging markets based on their contribution to global GDP. We studied this approach and found that it added the greatest diversification relative to our existing fixed income options in the plan. Traditional global bond offerings did not offer the diversification benefits we needed. Also, we questioned the logic of the traditional bond indexes, in that the more debt an issuer issues, the higher the weight within the index.

ANALYTIC EVALUATION: COMPARING BOND STRATEGIES

What are the evaluation criteria that plan sponsors might use to evaluate different bond strategies and managers? Here we suggest four:

1. **Return Expectations:** What return expectations should plan sponsors have for different bond strategies and managers? To answer this critical question, we suggest evaluating the return potential of current and potential plan offerings by looking at the yield-to-maturity (YTM). Although YTM is an incomplete measure of the total return potential of bond strategies, it may be used as a good first step to comparing indexes and different bond strategies as, over long horizons, it explains 85–90 percent of returns.

2. **Diversification:** Does the bond strategy and/or manager offer diversification benefits relative to other asset classes, such as stocks, diversifiers, or other fixed-income strategies? To determine this, we recommend looking at correlations. The lower the correlation with stocks and other asset classes already on the menu, the greater value the strategy and/or manager will likely add.

3. **Downside Risk or Loss Potential:** Managing volatility to offer a "smooth ride" and limit the magnitude of potential losses for DC participants may reduce fear and flight (i.e., shifting assets out of a strategy) in rougher markets. To determine what the downside risk might be in various market environments (that is, what type of loss participants might expect), we suggest assessing the volatility and the value-at-risk (VaR) at a 95 percent confidence level (VaR estimates the minimum expected loss at a desired level of significance over 12 months), or using similar appropriate downside risk measures.

4. **U.S. rate exposure:** Is your bond strategy sufficiently diversified to reduce exposure to U.S. interest rate risks? As previously discussed, there is a very large global bond market that offers participants a vast opportunity set. We propose plan sponsors consider nominal duration, both overall and U.S.-specific. Based on our index analysis, low duration, and the blended index of global credit, high-yield and Emerging Markets bond strategies all offer lower duration-risk potential than the BAGG.

As you can see in Figure 6.13, there are typically trade-offs when comparing different bond strategies. For example, a low-duration strategy will have lower duration (exposure to interest rates) than a core strategy, which leads to lower estimated volatility and potential drawdown. However, it also has a lower yield to maturity. Likewise, a multisector strategy may provide a higher yield to maturity than a core strategy, but it also

FIGURE 6.13 Diversifying Approaches May Improve Risk and Return Opportunities

	U.S. Core Bond BAGG	Low Duration Bond BofA Merrill Lynch 1-3 Yr Treasury Index	Diversifying Bond 1/3 Barclays Global Credit Hedged USD Index 1/3 BofA Merrill Lynch Global High Yield BB-B Rated Constrained Index 1/3 JPMorgan EMBI Global Index	Foreign Bond JPMorgan GBI Global ex-U.S. USD Hedged
Yield to maturity	2.6%	1.1%	5.3%	1.6%
Nominal Duration (years)	5.3	1.9	5.3	8.5
U.S. Nominal Duration (years)	5.3	1.9	4.4	0.1
Estimated correlation to S&P 500	−0.2	−0.5	0.5	−0.3
Estimated Volatility[1]	3.9%	1.7%	8.2%	3.8%
VaR (95%)[2]	−4.2%	−1.1%	−10.4%	−4.4%

As of December 31, 2015. Hypothetical example for illustrative purposes only.

[1]We employed a block bootstrap methodology to calculate volatilities. We start by computing historical factor returns that underlie each asset class proxy from January 1997 through the present date. We then draw a set of 12 monthly returns within the dataset to come up with an annual return number. This process is repeated 25,000 times to have a return series with 25,000 annualized returns. The standard deviation of these annual returns is used to model the volatility for each factor. We then use the same return series for each factor to compute covariance between factors. Finally, volatility of each asset class proxy is calculated as the sum of variances and covariance of factors that underlie that particular proxy. For each asset class, index, or strategy proxy, we will look at either a point in time estimate or historical average of factor exposures in order to determine the total volatility. Please contact your PIMCO representative for more details on how specific proxy factor exposures are estimated.
[2]Value-at-Risk (VaR) is an estimate of the minimum expected loss at a desired level of significance over a 12-month horizon.

Source: PIMCO.

FIGURE 6.14   A Summary of Diversifying Fixed-Income Strategies and Benefits

Diversifying Strategies	Higher Yield Potential	Reducing Exposure to U.S. Rates	Potential for Low Correlation to Equities	Potential for Low Volatility	Potential Downside Risk Reduction
Credit or MultiSector Complement core bonds with allocations to higher-yielding strategies and sectors to enhance source of income	X	X	X	X	
Global Diversification Broadens diversification and reduces concentration to U.S. interest rates by increasing exposure to global markets	X	X	X	X	
Low Duration Exposure to shorter maturity bonds can structurally reduce interest rate sensitivity		X	X	X	X

Source: PIMCO. For illustrative purposes only.

has a higher estimated volatility and potential drawdown. Figure 6.14 provides another view of the potential risk-reward trade-off of various approaches.

FIXED INCOME WITHIN TARGET-DATE GLIDE PATHS

Fixed income also plays a very important role within asset allocation strategies such as target-date glide paths. As participants approach and enter retirement, the overall allocation to fixed income should increase. As presented in Chapter 2, Figure 6.15 shows that the allocation to fixed income increases as participants approach retirement for both the Market Average and Objective-Aligned Glide Paths. For the Market Average Glide Path, the majority of fixed-income assets is allocated in domestic core bonds while for the Objective-Aligned Glide Path, it is more diversified across global, high-yield, and emerging market bonds. In a manner similar to the approach used by defined benefit plans, we can develop a typical retiree's liability, based on a deferred real annuity of 20 years, which then serves as the basis for determining the optimal asset portfolio in the Objective-Aligned Glide Path. Tracking the retirement liability over time allows for a glide path that is designed to significantly reduce the income risk of retirement savings. The lower the real interest rate at the time of retirement, the more wealth is needed to support a given real income expectation. To increase outcome certainty for retirees, the asset allocation should be sensitive to changes in interest rates and provide more income when more is needed. Then, an income focus leads to long-duration securities (both real and nominal) in the portfolio for their liability-matching characteristics. These long-duration bonds tend to increase in value precisely when rates are low or retirement income is most expensive.

OBSERVATIONS FOR FIXED INCOME ALLOCATION WITHIN TARGET-DATE STRATEGIES

In Figure 6.15, we present a comparison of the total and breakout of the nominal fixed income allocation between the Market Average and Objective-Aligned Glide Paths. The total allocation identifies the top-level allocation to fixed income as an asset class, while the breakout allocation identifies the specific type of fixed income that makes up the overall allocation. On average, the total allocation to nominal fixed income across the vintages is about equal at 23.6 percent and 23.1 percent respectively. However, compared to the Market Average Glide Path, the weighting to nominal fixed income for the Objective-Aligned Glide Path is slightly higher in the early vintages (e.g., 40 years from retirement comparing at 13.0 percent versus 9.2 percent) and lower in the closer to retirement vintages (e.g., 0 years to retirement at 43.0 percent versus 48.7 percent).

When we consider the breakout of allocations within nominal fixed income, we see more differences. The Market Average Glide Path has a higher allocation to cash and U.S. fixed income, while the Objective-Aligned has a greater weight in long treasuries, global bonds, and high-yield bonds. Neither has a significant allocation to emerging market bonds. As we consider a real (i.e., inflation-adjusted) liability framework, adding more diversifying bonds such as long treasuries, global, and high-yield offers the opportunity for improved risk-adjusted returns and better alignment to PRICE. In the upcoming chapters, we'll take a closer look at the allocation to the allocation to equities, and inflation-hedging strategies.

FIGURE 6.15 Market Average Glide Path and Objective-Aligned Glide Path

Years to Retirement	40	35	30	25	20	15	10	5	0	Average
Allocation Percentage to Nominal Fixed Income										
Market Average Glide Path	9.20%	10.30%	11.80%	14.30%	18.60%	25.00%	33.10%	41.60%	48.70%	23.60%
Objective-Aligned Glide Path	13.00%	13.00%	13.00%	17.00%	21.00%	25.00%	29.00%	34.00%	43.00%	23.10%
Breakout Allocations within Nominal Fixed Income										
Cash										
Market Average Glide Path	1.90%	2.10%	2.40%	2.80%	3.50%	4.30%	5.50%	6.80%	8.40%	4.19%
Objective-Aligned Glide Path	0.00%	0.00%	0.00%	0.00%	0.00%	0.00%	0.00%	0.00%	0.00%	0.00%
U.S. fixed income										
Market Average Glide Path	4.10%	4.70%	5.40%	6.90%	9.50%	13.70%	19.30%	25.50%	30.40%	13.28%
Objective-Aligned Glide Path	2.00%	2.00%	2.00%	2.00%	2.00%	2.00%	3.00%	7.00%	18.00%	4.44%
Long treasuries										
Market Average Glide Path	0.20%	0.30%	0.40%	0.50%	0.80%	1.20%	1.70%	2.20%	2.60%	1.10%
Objective-Aligned Glide Path	3.00%	3.00%	3.00%	3.00%	4.00%	7.00%	10.00%	10.00%	7.00%	5.56%
Global bonds										
Market Average Glide Path	0.50%	0.50%	0.50%	0.60%	0.70%	0.90%	1.10%	1.30%	1.30%	0.82%
Objective-Aligned Glide Path	1.00%	1.00%	1.00%	1.00%	1.00%	1.00%	1.00%	2.00%	3.00%	1.33%
Emerging market bonds										
Market Average Glide Path	1.10%	1.20%	1.30%	1.40%	1.40%	1.50%	1.40%	1.20%	1.10%	1.29%
Objective-Aligned Glide Path	2.00%	2.00%	2.00%	2.00%	1.00%	0.00%	0.00%	0.00%	0.00%	1.00%
High yield										
Market Average Glide Path	1.40%	1.50%	1.80%	2.10%	2.70%	3.40%	4.10%	4.60%	4.90%	2.94%
Objective-Aligned Glide Path	5.00%	5.00%	5.00%	9.00%	13.00%	15.00%	15.00%	15.00%	15.00%	10.78%

Market Average data is as of September 30, 2015. Objective-Aligned data is as of December 31, 2015.

Sources: PIMCO and NextCapital.

The Objective-Aligned Glide Path favors long-duration bonds across the vintages. Understanding risk not as volatility or loss of capital, but instead as lack of income in retirement, the emphasis is steadily shifted toward liability-aware asset classes. This aims to reduce tracking error relative to PRICE (refer to Chapter 2 for an in-depth discussion on PRICE), which ultimately serves to preserve purchasing power. At the individual asset class level, we see lower U.S. fixed income in the Objective-Aligned Glide Path across the board compared to the Market Average. Again looking through the lens of PRICE, domestic credit has a relatively high correlation to equities, and a low correlation to PRICE. The focus of the objective-aligned construction is to increase the correlation to PRICE, especially nearing retirement, not to increase equity beta to seek solely higher returns.

IN CLOSING

The challenges of strengthening bond lineups in DC plans can be complex, but needn't be overwhelming. We suggest looking first at the current mix of investment options and ways to improve it. This may lead sponsors to replace suboptimal solutions, possibly money market funds and passively managed core bond strategies. It also may prompt sponsors to offer more choices, either as stand-alone core menu offerings or blended within a custom core strategy. As you consider your core, we suggest that fiduciaries model the potential effects of adding or combining solutions.

In the end, there may be no correct answer to the question of how many offerings should be on a DC plan's investment menu. The "correct" number depends on many factors. But if sponsors can offer a range of options consistent with the needs of plan participants, and present them in a way that reduces the risk of naive diversification, these actions may go a long way toward helping employees achieve their retirement savings goals.

QUESTIONS FOR PLAN FIDUCIARIES

1. What role do you want bonds to play in your investment lineup?
2. Does your current investment lineup have sufficient bond options relative to the number of stock options offered? What would the allocation of a "1/n" investor look like?
3. Which fixed-income strategies complement or complete your lineup?
4. If you offer stable value, would certain fixed-income strategies raise wrap provider concerns?

5. What management style—active or passive—makes the most sense for the fixed-income options on your plan?
6. For income-oriented investors such as near-retirees or retirees, do you offer a bond option that is income-oriented?
7. Given the size of the global bond market, do you offer sufficient access to foreign bonds?
8. Have you evaluated the benchmarks used by your bond investment options—and do they continue to provide the risk-return profile that you are expecting?

CHAPTER 7

Designing Balanced DC Menus: Considering Equity Options

Being average means you are as close to the bottom as you are to the top.

—John Wooden, *Wooden: A Lifetime of Observations and Reflections On and Off the Court*

The third of four pillars of a well-balanced core lineup is equity investments, the focus of this chapter. Offering access to the equity markets within a defined contribution (DC) plan is fundamental—but what's challenging is determining the number and types of equity choices. Whatever the number, the choices should provide participants with the opportunity to reap both capital appreciation and income from equity markets worldwide. Broadening the opportunity set beyond developed markets opens the door to the world's most rapidly expanding economies and return opportunities. Unfortunately, today's DC equity lineups often lack broad access to global markets. What's more, lineups are often shackled to market-capitalization-weighted indexes, which may further hamper returns and heighten volatility.

By restructuring the equity lineup to include global, dividend, and enhanced index strategies, plan sponsors may improve DC participants' risk-adjusted return opportunity and the likelihood of retirement success. In this chapter, we'll examine how equity options fit in DC plan design and what strategies are available and in use today, and how they may evolve in the future. We'll also consider the role of active and passive management in equity options, how behavioral economics influences the ways in which we evaluate market efficiency, and questions plan sponsors may have about currency hedging.

WHAT ARE EQUITIES AND HOW ARE THEY PRESENTED IN DC INVESTMENT MENUS?

Equity investments are also referred to as *stock* investments. Stocks represent an ownership stake in and a claim on profits of companies. Stocks may be issued in *common* or *preferred* shares. The latter combines the features of equities and bonds, as preferreds generally must pay dividends (which must be paid out before dividends paid to common shareholders), and have the potential of price appreciation (although usually do not carry voting rights). By contrast, common shares may or may not pay dividends and the dividends are never guaranteed. When people talk about stocks, they're usually referring to common stock. Equity investors seek capital appreciation and possibly dividend income.

Stocks are issued by small, medium-, and large-size companies all around the world. Equity investors may prefer *value* stocks that have relatively lower price-to-book (P/B) and price-to-earnings (P/E) ratios, and identify those as the best bargain stocks the market has to offer. Or they may prefer *growth* stocks from industries with strong price momentum and higher P/E ratios and P/B ratios as indicative of the market's confidence in a company's ability to continue increasing earnings at an above-average pace. Depending on the market cycle, growth stocks may outperform value stocks or vice versa. DC plan fiduciaries often prefer offering a blend of value and growth stocks as this approach may reduce price volatility for participants.

Given the current expectations of slow global growth at the time of writing, equity markets have the potential to be meaningfully lower than their long-term, pre-2008 averages. In this light, achieving target returns will rely on thoughtful asset allocation with total return coming from some combination of beta (a measure of the volatility, or systematic risk, of a security or a portfolio in comparison to the market as a whole), alpha (the excess returns of a stock relative to the return of the market as a whole), and/or income.

As discussed in Chapter 3, DC plan design historically has been driven by "filling the equity style box" (see Figure 7.1) and offering a range of equity

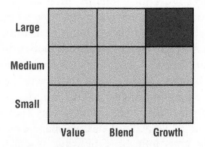

FIGURE 7.1 Equity Style Box
Source: Morningstar.

choices, including U.S. large-, mid-, and small-capitalization stocks, and possibly value and growth strategies. Typically, there is at least one index strategy—commonly the S&P 500 Index, which falls into the large-cap blend style box—plus a non-U.S. developed market equity choice. While the style box approach provides many choices—filling the box would provide nine equity choices plus international equity—the long list of equity choices may unintentionally expose participants to excessive equity risk, including price volatility.

In our 2016 DC Consulting Trends Survey, at the median, consultants recommended that plans include six equity investment choices. Blended equity strategies are suggested more often than a style-based strategy (value or growth) for all market capitalization segments. As shown in Figure 7.2, consultants also recommended non-U.S. developed equity, either unhedged (70 percent) or hedged (35 percent). Given six seats in the stand-alone core lineup, consultants may suggest the following choices: a large-cap blend passive (typically the S&P 500 Index), large-cap dividend or blend active, mid-cap blend active, small-cap blend active, non-U.S. developed active, and emerging markets active. Others would suggest a shorter list of four strategies by combining mid- and small-cap into a "smid" strategy and blending non-U.S. developed and emerging into a non-U.S. fund. As you can see in Figure 7.2, just over half of respondents

Equity

Stand-Alone*		Blended**	
U.S. large-cap blend	92%	U.S. large-cap blend	83%
U.S. small/mid-cap blend	92%	U.S. small/mid-cap value or growth	81%
U.S. large-cap value or growth	81%	Emerging markets—unhedged	81%
U.S. small/mid-cap value or growth	71%	U.S. small/mid-cap blend	79%
Non-U.S. developed—unhedged	70%	U.S. large-cap value or growth	76%
Global	51%	Non-U.S. developed—unhedged	74%
U.S. All Cap	43%	U.S. all-cap	52%
Emerging markets—unhedged	40%	Global	50%
Non-U.S. developed—hedged	35%	Emerging markets—hedged	43%
Emerging markets—hedged	27%	Non-U.S. developed—hedged	36%

FIGURE 7.2 2016 DC Consulting Trends Survey—Investment Recommendations: Equity
Source: PIMCO, 2016 Defined Contribution Consulting Support and Trends Survey.

recommend inclusion of a global (51 percent) and 43 percent recommended a U.S. all-cap fund; consultants recommending the broader blends are also likely to recommend a shorter list of core equity offerings. Within blended strategies, consultants' recommendations are similar to those suggested for the stand-alone lineup.

In practice, plans offer a range of equity options, according to data from the Plan Sponsor Council of America, including actively managed domestic equities and international/global equities (with 80 percent and 75 percent of plans offering these), and indexed domestic and international/global equities (at 78 percent and 51 percent of plans, respectively). In comparison, plans are less likely to offer a stand-alone emerging markets fund (at 37 percent of plans). With the exception of emerging markets, the larger the plan size, the more likely it is to offer each of these options. PSCA also reports the number of choices in each category, showing plans on average offer 9.2 equity funds, including 4.8 actively managed domestic equity funds and 1.8 passively managed domestic equity funds. Similarly, actively managed international equity offerings are more prevalent than passively managed (at 1.6 and 0.6 of funds, respectively). Only 19 percent of plans offer company stock, yet the larger the plan, the more likely this offering at 44 percent of the largest plans (those with 5,000 or more participants).

Asset allocation to equity offerings was reported at 58 percent with the majority of the allocation made to actively managed domestic equity (19.4 percent), company stock (16 percent), and passively managed domestic equity (14.1 percent). International equity captures the remainder of the allocation with actively managed international equity at 4.3 percent, passively managed at 3.2 percent, and emerging markets at 0.6 percent. These low levels may raise concern that DC participants may be underallocated to international equity, with only 14 percent of the equity allocation to international equities (as shown in Figure 7.3), given that the MSCI ACWI is composed of approximately 50 percent U.S. equities. (The Morgan Stanley Capital International All-Country World Index, or MSCI ACWI, is a market capitalization weighted index designed to provide a broad measure of equity-market performance throughout the world.) If we consider smaller plans (with less than 5,000 participants) that are not as likely to offer company stock, we still see an underweight to international stocks, at 17 percent of the equity allocation according to PSCA. The typical reason for this is simple: Individual DC investors express the home-market bias possessed by all investors across geographies, investing in assets they are most familiar and comfortable with and that they understand best.

In designing equity offerings, sponsors may first consider the balance of investment choices within their plan. By offering more domestic equity

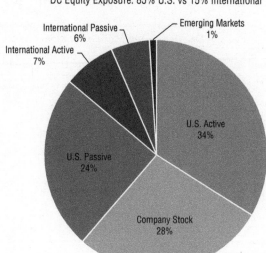

DC Equity Exposure: 85% U.S. vs 15% International

FIGURE 7.3   Equity Investment Trends
Source: PSCA's 58th Annual Survey of Profit Sharing and 401(k) Plans.

choices, it's not surprising that the allocation to these funds overall is higher than international offerings. What also influences participant allocation is the tenure of the option on the investment menu; international funds are likely to be more recent additions and thus may lack the active allocation or investment growth relative to domestic equity offerings—these may have been offered for decades and have experienced not only early allocations but also asset growth.

As discussed in earlier chapters, menu design will influence a participant's investment decisions. As discussed previously, given 10 investment options, many participants will allocate an equal percentage to each; thus, a DC plan with 10 investment choices, including seven equity options, may encourage participants to weight 70 percent of their assets to equities. Figure 7.4 provides the result of an experiment in which one group of employees was offered four fixed-income funds and one equity fund, while another group was offered four equity funds and one fixed-income fund. Consistent with the theory of naive diversification, the second group selected significantly more equity options than the first group—by a 25 percentage-point spread.

FIGURE 7.4   Lineup Design May Have Meaningful Influence on Asset Allocation Decisions

Version	Fund Description and Mean Allocation					Mean Allocation to Equities
	Fund A	Fund B	Fund C	Fund D	Fund E	
Company 1:	Money markets	Savings	Insurance contracts	Bonds	Diversified equity	43%
Multiple fixed-income funds	14%	14%	11%	18%	43%	
Company 2:	Diversified fixed income	Conservative equity	Equity index	Growth stock	International equity	68%
Multiple equity funds	32%	15%	16%	26%	11%	

Sources: PSCA's 57th PSCA Survey; Benartzi and Thaler, 2001; Iyengar, Sheena, and Wei Jiang, "How More Choices Are Demotivating: Impact of More Options on 401(k) Investments," working paper, Columbia University, 2003.

Given menu design concerns, plan sponsors are increasingly moving away from the style-box approach to either a risk-pillar menu or, more commonly, an asset-class-focused core lineup. One reason for the move away from the style box approach is that plan sponsors witness how the style-box construct inadvertently promotes performance chasing (entering or exiting a trend after the trend has already been well established). As noted above, growth and value moves in cycles, but so does large-cap versus small-cap, U.S. versus non-U.S., and developed market versus emerging market equities. The potential for participants with varied levels of sophistication to exclusively select funds with the best three-year past returns is significant. This decision is, however, often followed by a period of underperformance, after which time the fund is sold and the proceeds placed into another fund that now has the best three-year return, and the cycle continues. It's also important to point out that style-box diversification has decreased over time as the correlation among equity styles has increased. Figure 7.5 shows that the average rolling three-year correlation to the S&P 500 Index among equity styles has increased since 2000. This reality is prompting more plan fiduciaries toward equity lineup consolidation, and to seek more diversifying assets.

Plans with a risk-pillar approach may offer a single equity choice, plus the three other diversifying risk pillars: capital preservation, fixed income, and inflation-hedging assets. This selection may be refined further by folding inflation-hedging strategies such as Treasury Inflation-Protected Securities

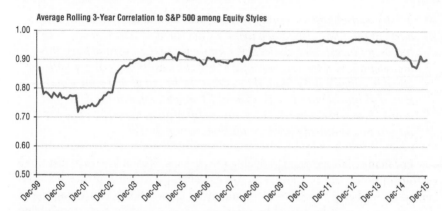

FIGURE 7.5   Correlation among Equity Styles Has Increased
Sources: Bloomberg Finance L.P. and PIMCO, as of December 31, 2015.

(TIPS) into a broad income category, and risky assets such as real estate and commodities into a growth bucket. Plan sponsors with risk-pillar lineups often have sufficient scale to create multimanager (that is, white-label) investment strategies that blend investment approaches and best-in-class managers within each strategy. This approach may clean up the menu by combining many of the managers into a single offering, after which plans may seek additional investment managers or approaches to complete the risk pillar. In a DC Dialogue from September/October 2015, Gary Park, Director of Trust Investments at Schlumberger, described his plan's streamlined core investment lineup:

> *We have four white-label investment options that serve as our core lineup. These include a short-term bond fund, a core bond fund, a U.S. equity fund and a global equity fund. Each fund is made up of select asset classes from our group trust. The trust has a broad range of asset classes, including large cap, small cap, low-volatility equity, international equity, emerging markets equity, Treasury Inflation-Protected Securities (TIPS), and intermediate bonds.*

He goes on to explain the makeup of the two equity funds:

> *Yes, we have a U.S. equity fund that is broadly diversified to include all cap sizes and investment styles. There is not a bias toward a cap size or style, such as value or growth. We also offer a global equity fund that is made up of non-U.S. developed and emerging market equity plus U.S. equity, so participants gain broad exposure to the entire global equity market.*

> *By including U.S. equity in the fund, we dampen volatility for participants. We also don't want to overwhelm participants with too many investment choices. We know that when people have too many choices, they may not make any choices. By offering a globally diversified equity fund, they access the broad global equity markets without having to ask "Should I move between the U.S. and non-U.S. markets now?" The fund we offer gives them the opportunity to invest outside the U.S. without as much risk.*

For many plan sponsors, reducing the core investment lineup to just three or four options may be viewed as too extreme, particularly if they are concerned about being perceived as taking away choice. Some plans may lessen the concern of a "take away" by offering access—possibly even transferring allocations—to favorite brand-name mutual funds via a brokerage window. For plans lacking the necessary scale for white-label strategies or preferring to offer more choice, an asset-class-focused menu may be more desirable. This approach often still requires at least some paring down of equity choices, possibly combining equity styles and eliminating redundancies, and then adding more diversifying assets such as global equity, inflation hedging, and fixed income. As discussed in Chapter 3, Figure 7.6 shows the movement from a style-box to an asset-class or risk-pillar focused core lineup.

Simplifying a menu can help participants make better selections and improve their ability to stay the course—rather than chasing performance or, more likely, fleeing an investment during a sudden market decline, and thus locking in losses. Combining investment strategies and styles may help dampen abrupt swings in performance.

GETTING THE MOST OUT OF EQUITIES

Once sponsors have determined the structure, they may focus on selecting the best strategies for each asset or risk category. When considering equity returns—which are driven largely by capital appreciation and possibly by income—the opportunity set (all risk-and-reward combinations that can be constructed with the available assets and within the environmental constraints) is a good place to start. As Figure 7.7 shows, total global stock market capitalization was $66.9 trillion at the end of Q4 2015, according to the World Federation of Exchanges. Non-U.S. equities, including Asia-Pacific and EMEA (Europe, the Middle East, and Africa), accounted for over half of global stock market capitalization.

To maximize capital appreciation opportunities, DC participants may benefit by accessing high-growth markets, including many emerging markets (EM). Figure 7.8 shows that many developing countries are projected to have

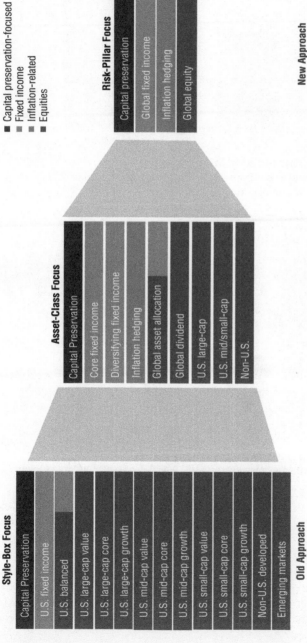

FIGURE 7.6 Evolution of DC Plan Core Investment Structure

For illustrative purposes only.

Source: PIMCO.

FIGURE 7.7   Size of Global Stock Markets
Source: World Federation of Exchanges as of December 2015. See
www.world-exchanges.org.

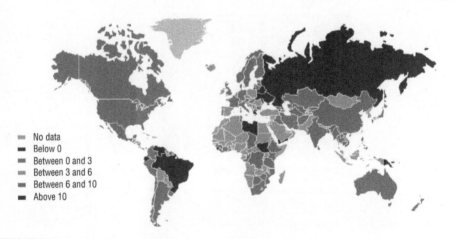

FIGURE 7.8   Emerging Markets Are Growing Fastest
Source: International Monetary Fund (IMF), World Economic Outlook, October 2015.

faster GDP growth than developed countries in North America and Western
Europe. Given that EM represent over half of the world's GDP, investing in
these markets—directly or via developed market companies that source earnings from EM—may offer a significant opportunity for capital appreciation.

These markets, however, also may expose participants to greater risk.
Thus it may be preferable (and advisable, given naive diversification) to offer
a blend of higher-growth markets and more stable—if slower-growing—
developed markets. Figure 7.9 shows that over the more than 15 years ending

FIGURE 7.9 Performance and Risk Comparison for U.S. Large-Cap, Non-U.S. Developed, and Emerging Market Equities

Equity Strategies	Traditional Market-Cap-Weighted Index	Annualized Return	Annualized Volatility*	Return/Volatility	Correlation to S&P 500	Maximum Drawdown	VaR 95%**	Average Dividend
				January 1999–December 2015				
U.S. Large-Cap Core Equity	S&P 500	4.5%	15.1%	0.29	1.00	-50.9%	-22.8%	1.9%
Non-U.S. Developed Equity	MSCI EAFE	3.3%	17.2%	0.19	0.86	-56.4%	-30.1%	2.8%
Emerging Market Equity	MSCI Emerging Markets	7.9%	23.0%	0.34	0.77	-61.4%	-34.9%	2.4%
1/2 U.S. Large-Cap Core Equity	1/2 S&P 500	4.0%	15.6%	0.26	0.96	-53.7%	-25.4%	2.3%
1/2 Non-U.S. Developed Equity	1/2 MSCI EAFE							
1/2 Non-U.S. Developed Equity	1/2 MSCI EAFE	5.6%	21.5%	0.26	0.84	-58.9%	-30.7%	2.6%
1/2 Emerging Market Equity	1/2 MSCI Emerging Markets							
1/3 U.S. Large-Cap Core Equity	1/3 S&P 500	5.5%	17.4%	0.31	0.91	-56.2%	-26.7%	2.4%
1/3 Non-U.S. Developed Equity	1/3 MSCI EAFE							
1/3 Emerging Market Equity	1/3 MSCI Emerging Markets							

Hypothetical example for illustrative purposes only.
*Volatility is measured by calculating the monthly historical volatility of the index.
**Value-at-Risk (VaR) is an estimate of the minimum expected loss at a desired level of significance over a 12-month horizon.

Sources: PIMCO and Bloomberg Finance L.P., as of December 31, 2015.

December 31, 2015, a strategy that blended U.S. large-cap, non-U.S. developed, and EM equities had lower volatility and maximum drawdown than an EM-only strategy. Notably, participants gained 150 basis points (bps) in return relative to a blend without EM, with a slight increase in volatility.

Going forward, consultants expect these general relationships to continue; in 2016, consultants forecast over a three- to five-year horizon both higher expected returns and volatility for EM and non-U.S. developed equities compared to U.S. large-cap equities, with median forecast returns of 9.9, 7.3, and 6.6 percent, and volatility of 26.5, 20.2, and 17.7 percent, respectively, based on PIMCO's 2016 Defined Contribution Consulting Support and Trends Survey. Given the level of historic as well as expected volatility for EM, it's not surprising that few plans offer this investment option as a stand-alone core option. Blending EM along with developed-market equity or also with a U.S. large-cap core allows plans to potentially capture the enhanced return opportunity, yet with dampened volatility.

CONSIDER DIVIDEND-PAYING STOCKS

DC participants, retirees in particular, also may benefit by seeking income, including via dividend-paying stocks. Against a backdrop of low interest rates and slow growth, these may offer more attractive and more stable total returns than non-dividend-paying companies. In a low-growth environment, dividend payments may provide a larger percentage of equity returns. Even as rates rise, dividend-paying stocks may offer higher return potential than non-dividend-paying peers—and even fixed income (see Figure 7.10). Further, dividend-paying equities usually have lower volatility and lower correlation with broad equity markets.

EVALUATING EQUITY STRATEGIES

As discussed, DC plans may get the most out of equities by restructuring core menus to provide access to equities in markets globally, including dividend-paying stocks. But before doing so, we suggest plans evaluate a range of statistical measures, both historically and prospectively. The key measures include:

- **Risk-adjusted return** measures the return delivered relative to the risk taken.
- **Correlation to the S&P 500** shows the potential diversification benefits of different equity strategies relative to a common core equity investment offering.

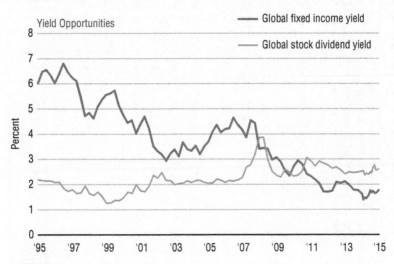

FIGURE 7.10 Divided-Paying Equities May Be an Attractive Long-Term Income Solution

As of December 31, 2015. Global fixed income yield is represented by the Barclays Global Aggregate USD yield to worst. Global stock dividend yield is represented by the MSCI All Country World Index.

Sources: Bloomberg Finance L.P., MSCI, Bloomberg Barclays.

■ **Downside risk** measures potential loss. We suggest using a forward-looking measure of potential risk exposure, for example, value-at-risk (VaR) at a 95 percent confidence level. (VaR estimates the minimum expected loss at a desired level of significance over 12 months.)
■ **Dividend yield** can be an important component of total return from equities. Over the 15-year period, the MSCI ACWI High Dividend Index had an average dividend yield of 3.9 percent, the highest among the 14 equity indexes listed in Figure 7.11.

In addition, plan sponsors should consider metrics for actively managed strategies. These include *active share*, which helps determine potential for outperformance relative to benchmarks, and the *upside-versus-downside capture ratio*, which shows whether, and by how much, a strategy has gained or lost relative to a broad market benchmark during rising and falling markets.

Figure 7.11 offers a comparison of these measures across various slices of the global equity markets.

FIGURE 7.11 How Different Equities Compare across Key Measures

Equity Strategies	Traditional Market-Cap-Weighted Index	January 1999–December 2015						
		Annualized Return	Annualized Volatility *	Return/ Volatility	Correlation to S&P 500	Maximum Drawdown	VaR 95% **	Average Dividend
U.S. Large-Cap Value Equity	Russell 1000 Value	5.4%	15.2%	0.36	0.93	−55.6%	−23.4%	2.4%
U.S. Large-Cap Core Equity	S&P 500	4.5%	15.1%	0.30	1.00	−50.9%	−22.8%	1.9%
U.S. Large-Cap Growth Equity	Russell 1000 Growth	3.5%	17.4%	0.20	0.95	−61.9%	−23.7%	1.2%
U.S. Mid-Cap Value Equity	Russell Mid-Cap Value	8.6%	16.5%	0.52	0.88	−57.4%	−25.3%	2.3%
U.S. Mid-Cap Core Equity	Russell Mid-Cap	8.1%	17.1%	0.48	0.93	−54.2%	−25.7%	1.6%
U.S. Mid-Cap Growth Equity	Russell Mid-Cap Growth	6.3%	21.7%	0.29	0.85	−61.3%	−25.9%	0.8%
U.S. Small-Cap Value Equity	Russell 2000 Value	7.8%	18.3%	0.43	0.80	−64.0%	−27.8%	2.3%
U.S. Small-Cap Core Equity	Russell 2000	6.7%	20.1%	0.33	0.82	−52.9%	−29.6%	1.5%
U.S. Small-Cap Growth Equity	Russell 2000 Growth	5.1%	23.3%	0.22	0.79	−62.6%	−32.4%	0.7%
U.S. Mid/Small Cap Equity	Russell 2500	8.1%	18.7%	0.43	0.87	−55.2%	−29.4%	1.6%
Non-U.S. Developed Equity	MSCI EAFE	3.3%	17.2%	0.19	0.87	−56.4%	−30.1%	2.8%
Emerging Market Equity	MSCI Emerging Markets	7.9%	23.0%	0.34	0.77	−61.4%	−34.9%	2.4%
Global ex-U.S. Equity	MSCI ACWI ex-U.S.	3.8%	17.7%	0.22	0.87	−57.4%	−29.7%	2.7%
Dividend Equity	MSCI ACWI High Dividend	5.8%	15.9%	0.36	0.88	−57.4%	−21.1%	3.9%

*Volatility is measured by calculating the monthly historical volatility of the index.

**Value-at-Risk (VaR) is an estimate of the minimum expected loss at a desired level of significance over a 12-month horizon.

Sources: PIMCO and Bloomberg Finance L.P., as of 31 December 2015.

LESS IS MORE: STREAMLINING EQUITY CHOICES

Reducing the number of equity choices may help improve returns and reduce risk. In Figure 7.12, assuming a naive diversification approach, we can see that streamlining from six options (current equity portfolio, which is equally weighted across six asset classes) to four options (consolidated equity portfolio, which is equally weighted across four asset classes) provided a better risk-adjusted return, lower correlation to the S&P, and a higher dividend yield over the more than 15 years ended December 2015.

SHIFT TO ASSET-CLASS MENU MAY IMPROVE RETIREMENT OUTCOMES

We suggest plan sponsors evaluate the current plan lineup relative to one that includes global equity and dividend strategies. For example, a lineup may include six equity options, two fixed-income options, one capital preservation choice, one inflation-hedging strategy, and one global balanced option. Figure 7.13 shows this current or typical DC lineup, which, if naively diversified, would have 60 percent allocated in equities, three-quarters of which are in domestic stocks.

Consolidating domestic equity strategies and adding global equity options can give participants a more balanced DC menu (Figure 7.14) with the potential for better risk-adjusted return, lower correlation with the S&P, lower maximum drawdown, and lower VaR (95 percent) than the current portfolio under the "typical menu" (see Figure 7.15 for asset allocation details).

ACTIVE VERSUS PASSIVE—THE ONGOING DEBATE

In addition to the plan design considerations such as style-box, asset-class, or risk-pillar approaches, other important considerations are whether plans and participants should use actively managed equity strategies, passive strategies, or strategic betas instead—or a blend of some of each, depending on the asset class. (*Strategic beta* is an approach that mixes elements of both passive and active investing, usually incorporating one or more factor tilts relative to standard market indexes.) As shown in Figure 7.16, while 37 percent of consultants believe active management is not important for U.S. large cap equities, 63 percent believe it is at least somewhat important. By comparison, the participating consultants believe active management of EM, non-U.S. developed, and U.S. small-cap equity is important or very important at 96, 88, and 80 percent, respectively.

FIGURE 7.12 Performance and Risk Comparison of Current Equity Portfolio and Consolidated Equity Portfolio

Equity Portfolios	January 1999–December 2015						
	Annualized Return	Annualized Volatility *	Return/ Volatility	Correlation to S&P 500	Maximum Drawdown	VaR 95% **	Average Dividend
Current equity portfolio[1]	5.4%	15.9%	0.34	0.97	-52.5%	-24.8%	1.9%
Consolidated equity portfolio[2]	5.7%	15.9%	0.36	0.95	-54.4%	-23.9%	2.5%

Hypothetical example for illustrative purposes only.

[1] The current equity portfolio is equally weighted across six asset classes: the S&P 500, Russell 1000 Value, Russell 1000 Growth, Russell Mid-Cap, Russell 2000, and the MSCI EAFE Index.

[2] The consolidated equity portfolio is equally weighted across four asset classes: the S&P 500, Russell 2500, MSCI ACWI ex-U.S., and the MSCI ACWI High Dividend Index.

*Volatility is measured by calculating the monthly historical volatility of the index.

**Value-at-risk (VaR) is an estimate of the minimum expected loss at a desired level of significance over a 12-month horizon.

Sources: PIMCO and Bloomberg Finance L.P., as of December 31, 2015.

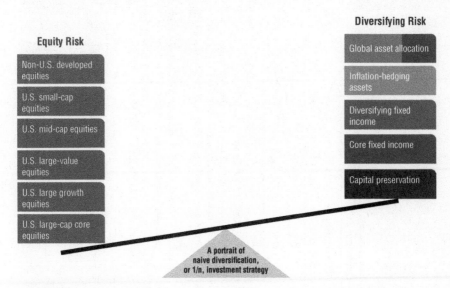

FIGURE 7.13   A Typical DC Core Menu Is Dominated by Domestic Equity Risk
For illustrative purposes only.
Source: PIMCO.

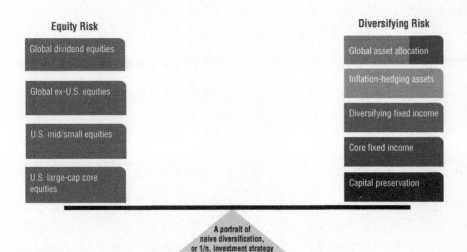

FIGURE 7.14   Consolidate Domestic Equity Options and Add Global
For illustrative purposes only.
Source: PIMCO.

FIGURE 7.15 Strategy Performance and Risk Comparison

Equity Portfolios	January 1999–December 2015					
	Annualized Return	Annualized Volatility*	Return/ Volatility	Correlation to S&P 500	Maximum Drawdown	VaR 95%**
Current portfolio[1]	5.4%	10.6%	0.52	0.96	−38.4%	−15.9%
Consolidated portfolio[2]	5.5%	9.5%	0.58	0.92	−36.0%	−13.7%

Hypothetical example for illustrative purposes only.

[1]The current portfolio is equally weighted across 11 asset classes: the S&P 500, Russell 1000 Value, Russell 1000 Growth, Russell Mid-Cap, Russell 2000, MSCI EAFE, global asset allocation (60 percent MSCI World Index, and 40 percent Barclays U.S. Aggregate Index), inflation hedging (1/3 Barclays U.S. TIPS Index, 1/3 Dow Jones UBS Commodity TR Index, 1/3 Dow Jones US Select REIT Index), diversifying fixed income (1/3 Barclays Global Aggregate Credit USD Hedged Index, 1/3 BofA Merrill Lynch Global High Yield BB-B Rated Constrained USD Hedged, 1/3 JPMorgan EMBI Global Index), Barclays U.S. Aggregate, and the BofA ML 3-Month U.S. T-Bill Index.

[2]The consolidated portfolio is equally weighted across nine asset classes: the S&P 500, Russell 2500, MSCI ACWI ex-U.S., the MSCI ACWI High Dividend, global asset allocation (60 percent MSCI World Index and 40 percent Barclays U.S. Aggregate Index), inflation hedging (1/3 Barclays U.S. TIPS Index, 1/3 Dow Jones UBS Commodity TR Index, 1/3 Dow Jones US Select REIT Index), diversifying fixed income (1/3 Barclays Global Aggregate Credit USD Hedged Index, 1/3 BofA Merrill Lynch Global High Yield BB-B Rated Constrained USD Hedged, 1/3 JPMorgan EMBI Global Index), Barclays U.S. Aggregate Index, and the BofA ML 3-Month U.S. T-Bill Index.

*Volatility is measured by calculating the monthly historical volatility of the index.

**Value-at-risk (VaR) is an estimate of the minimum expected loss at a desired level of significance over a 12-month horizon.

Sources: PIMCO and Bloomberg Finance L.P., as of December 31, 2015.

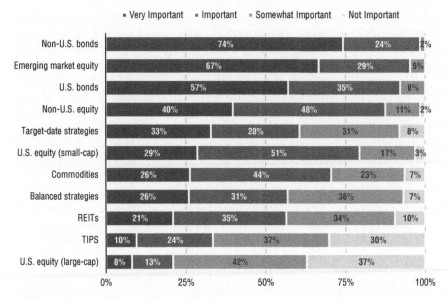

FIGURE 7.16   Consultants Underscore Importance of Active Management for Equity
Source: PIMCO, 2016 Defined Contribution Consulting Support and Trends Survey.

Consultants may explain that they assign lower importance to actively managing large-cap U.S. equity as they may view these markets as more efficient. Few consultants believe all equity markets are efficient; those that do may follow the efficient market hypothesis (EMH) formulated by academic Eugene Fama in 1970. The EMH holds that it is impossible consistently to "beat the market" over time, as stock market efficiency causes existing

FIGURE 7.17   Top Performing Equity Managers Outperform Their Passive Peer Average

	Average 10-Year Equity Return for Top Quartile of Active Managers	Average 10-Year Passive Equity Manager Return
Large-Cap	8.30%	6.62%
Small-Cap	8.50%	6.05%
International	4.70%	2.95%
Emerging Market	6.92%	5.64%

Performance is limited by a specified date range; different time periods may produce different results.

Source: Morningstar, as of December 31, 2015.

share prices to always incorporate and reflect all relevant information. Yet over time, top performing portfolio managers have been able to beat the market—that is, they have been able to outperform the benchmark for their strategy. (see Figure 7.17)

In April 2015, as part of our DC Dialogues series we spoke with Professor Richard H. Thaler, Charles R. Walgreen Distinguished Service Professor of Economics and Behavioral Science at the University of Chicago Booth School of Business, about his most recent book, *Misbehaving: The Making of Behavioral Economics* in which he writes about market efficiency and why he doesn't believe markets are efficient. We asked him to explain his thinking:

> *It's important to stress that there are two aspects of the efficient market hypothesis. I like to refer to these as the "no free lunch" component and the "price is right" component. The "no free lunch" component is that you cannot beat the market, a belief held by noted colleagues at the University of Chicago. Much of academic debate has been about this component. I think the real question is whether beating the market is impossible or hard. My colleagues argue impossible, and I would say hard.*
>
> *On average, studies have shown that large-cap equity managers tend to underperform the market after fees. This means that investors should be cautious. And people who invested in Ponzi schemes should have known better. No one can beat the market by 10 percent a year every year for whatever number of years in a row. The markets are too efficient for that.*
>
> *Now, we know that certain parts of the market are more efficient than others. Large caps are more efficient than small caps. Liquid traded equities are more efficient than less liquid private equity. Emerging markets are less efficient than developed markets. Overall, I would give the "no free lunch" component of the efficient market theory something like a B+ or A–, so mostly true.*

When we asked him about the "price is right" component of the efficient market hypothesis, he said:

> *The "price is right" component refers to the fact that prices are supposed to be equal to their intrinsic value. This one is much harder to test because who knows what the intrinsic value is. If I ask you what the intrinsic value of Apple is and whether it's really worth its $700 billion market cap or whatever that number is, nobody can answer that question.*

That means this component of the efficient market hypothesis can be harder to evaluate. . . . There's lots of research on mispricing, including the market bubbles we have experienced over the last 30 years. . . . Market bubbles are of enormous importance as a public policy matter. Central bankers and policy makers have to be worried about frothy markets. We've seen what can happen when a frothy market—especially one that's accompanied by substantial leverage—crashes. We're still digging our way out of one seven years later. So I think we need to worry a lot more about that. And when it comes to that part of the efficient market hypothesis, I think it's quite dubious.

Fischer Black, the co-inventor of the Black-Scholes option pricing model, once said that stock markets were efficient, by which he meant prices were correct within a factor of two. But, as I write in my book Misbehaving, *I think that had he lived to see 2000, he would have revised that to within a factor of three. And that's not a very efficient market.*

Rather than moving to fully active equity management, many may be interested in an approach that falls in between active and passive, often referred to as *smart beta* or what Morningstar thought leader John Rekenthaler refers to as *strategic beta*. Rekenthaler explains that strategic beta means "investing in indexed portfolios—but not the usual variety of index that copies an entire market. Strategic-beta funds own part of a marketplace, those securities that are exposed to a particular factor (or factors). . . . The concept is actually quite simple. A value-style index fund is a strategic-beta fund that uses the single factor of value."[1] Other options include multifactor strategic-beta funds that use more than one factor, such as the two factors of small and value.

In Rekenthaler's view, the strategic beta approach is the simplest of paths for those who wish to invest actively, as this approach is less complex and more transparent than many other investment innovations. Instead, with a strategic beta approach, a model that sorts for the factors that drive active performance, including low liquidity, cheap stock-price multiples, and high stock-price momentum.

"Today's investors," comments Rekenthaler,

recognize the importance of cost as never before, and they are equally aware of the struggles of active management. . . . Some will opt for fully passive portfolios. Most, however, will retain some thrill of the chase by blending passive with active. And that active portion might well take the form of strategic beta, particularly as investing actively through strategic-beta funds reduces surprises and eases information-gathering.

Using a strategic beta approach such as a fundamentally weighted index may enhance participant returns and reduce risk.

STRATEGIC BETA: CONSIDER ADDING FUNDAMENTALLY WEIGHTED EQUITY EXPOSURE

By investing in broadly diversified portfolios that de-link stock price from portfolio exposure, participant outcomes may improve. Traditional indexes weight stocks in proportion to their market capitalization. Because weights in a market-cap index are proportional to a company's market value, distortions in stock prices flow into investors' portfolios. Portfolios that select stocks based on fundamental measures, in contrast, gauge a company's economic footprint using publicly available financial data, including, for instance, sales, cash flow, book value, and dividends.

The primary source of outperformance over long periods for non-price-weighted portfolios is trading against the market's most extravagant bets—which are also those most likely to be wrong. As Figure 7.18 shows, adding fundamentally weighted U.S. equity indexes may provide notably better risk-adjusted returns.

Incremental alpha (excess return), compounded over the years, can be substantial. As Figure 7.19 demonstrates, a January 1999 investment of $100,000 in the consolidated portfolio with fundamental indexing could have grown to $280,018 by December 2015, compared with $246,353 and $248,427 in the current and consolidated portfolios, respectively.

PIMCO: HOW TO TELL IF SMART BETA IS SMART

Selecting active managers requires significant due diligence and a deep understanding of how they may add value. In July 2016, PIMCO published a "Feature Solution" paper, written by Markus Aakko and Andy Pyne, titled "Detecting a 'Smart' Investment Strategy," designed to help understand how and why a "smart beta" approach might make sense—and how to select smart beta managers and strategies.

The prevailing view in the industry is that one should select managers with quality research, consistent investment criteria, and high active share, emphasizing potential returns arising from stock selection. The analysis should also acknowledge the manager's factor tilts, with the manager fully aware of these factor biases and able to articulate why they should exist in their portfolios, and why they ultimately should benefit portfolio performance.

Selecting the right systematic equity or smart beta provider demands similarly careful analysis and quantitative evaluation. Good questions to serve as a guide to manager selection include:

- Is the strategy over-reliant on back-tested results or is there a live track record to evaluate?

- Does the manager offer an intuitive and rational explanation as to why the strategy should work in the future, or is the model more of a black box?

- Is the strategy overly simplistic, which could lead to unintended consequences such as high industry concentration or exposure to "value traps"?

- Does the strategy take into account liquidity and transaction costs, which affect capacity and implementation?

- Are the models static or do they evolve and incorporate new insights driven by ongoing research?

Factor-based strategies are not a silver bullet that leads to consistent outperformance . . . but over time these factor exposures have the potential to be accretive to portfolio performance.

CURRENCY HEDGING: AN ACTIVE DECISION

In addition to management style (active versus passive), plan sponsors and participants need to make decisions about whether it makes sense to implement currency hedging for non-U.S. strategies. In PIMCO's 2016 Defined Contribution Consulting Support and Trends Survey, we also asked consultants why plan sponsors should consider hedging non-U.S. currency exposure (Figure 7.20). Notably, we were not specific as to fixed income or equity. The majority of consultants (53 percent) said plan sponsors should consider currency hedging given the potential for reduced volatility. They also noted concern that "plan participants do not understand" (and thus should not be exposed to) currency risk (39 percent), and the reality that "plan participants live in the United States" and can be expected to spend their retirement dollars there.

When asked whether they would recommend hedged or unhedged fixed-income options, an approximately equal percentage of consultants suggested

FIGURE 7.18 Add Fundamentally Weighted Equity Indexes

Equity Strategies	Fundamental-Weighted Index	January 1999–December 2015						
		Annualized Return	Annualized Volatility*	Return/ Volatility	Correlation to S&P 500	Maximum Drawdown	VaR 95%**	Average Dividend
U.S. large-cap equity	FTSE RAFI US 1000	7.4%	16.2%	0.46	0.94	−55.5%	−23.9%	1.9%
U.S. mid/small-cap equity	FTSE RAFI US 1500	11.4%	20.4%	0.56	0.83	−69.5%	−28.2%	1.7%

Equity Portfolios	January 1999–December 2015					
	Annualized Return	Annualized Volatility*	Return/ Volatility	Correlation to S&P 500	Maximum Drawdown	VaR 95%**
Current portfolio[1]	5.4%	10.6%	0.52	0.96	−38.4%	−15.9%
Consolidated portfolio[2]	5.5%	9.5%	0.58	0.92	−36.0%	−13.7%

Consolidated portfolio with fundamental-weighted indexes[3]	6.2%	9.8%	0.64	0.90	–37.1%	–13.9%

Hypothetical example for illustrative purposes only.

[1]The current portfolio is equally weighted across 11 asset classes: the S&P 500, Russell 1000 Value, Russell 1000 Growth, Russell Mid Cap, Russell 2000, MSCI EAFE, global asset allocation (60 percent MSCI World Index and 40 percent Barclays U.S. Aggregate Index), inflation hedging (1/3 Barclays U.S. TIPS Index, 1/3 Dow Jones UBS Commodity TR Index, 1/3 Dow Jones US Select REIT Index), diversifying fixed income (1/3 Barclays Global Aggregate Credit USD Hedged Index, 1/3 BofA Merrill Lynch Global High Yield BB-B Rated Constrained USD Hedged, 1/3 JPMorgan EMBI Global Index), Barclays U.S. Aggregate, and the BofA ML 3-Month U.S. T-Bill Index.

[2]The consolidated portfolio is equally weighted across nine asset classes: the S&P 500, Russell 2500, MSCI ACWI ex-U.S., the MSCI ACWI High Dividend, global asset allocation (60 percent MSCI World Index and 40 percent Barclays U.S. Aggregate Index), inflation hedging (1/3 Barclays U.S. TIPS Index, 1/3 Dow Jones UBS Commodity TR Index, 1/3 Dow Jones US Select REIT Index), diversifying fixed income (1/3 Barclays Global Aggregate Credit USD Hedged Index, 1/3 BofA Merrill Lynch Global High Yield BB-B Rated Constrained USD Hedged, 1/3 JPMorgan EMBI Global Index), Barclays U.S. Aggregate Index, and the BofA ML 3-Month U.S. T-Bill Index.

[3]The consolidated portfolio with fundamentally-weighted indexes is equally weighted across the FTSE RAFI US 1000, FTSE RAFI US 1500, MSCI ACWI ex-U.S., MSCI ACWI High Dividend, global asset allocation (60 percent MSCI World Index/40 percent Barclays U.S. Aggregate Index), inflation hedging (1/3 Barclays U.S. TIPS Index, 1/3 Dow Jones UBS Commodity TR Index, 1/3 Dow Jones US Select REIT Index), diversifying fixed income (1/3 Barclays Global Aggregate Credit Component USD Hedged, 1/3 JPMorgan EMBI Global Index, 1/3 BofA ML BB-B US Dollar Global High Yield Constrained Index), Barclays U.S. Aggregate Index, and BofA ML 3-Month T-Bill Index.

*Volatility is measured by calculating the monthly historical volatility of the index.

**Value-at-risk (VaR) is an estimate of the minimum expected loss at a desired level of significance over a 12-month horizon.

Sources: PIMCO and Bloomberg Finance L.P., as of December 31, 2015.

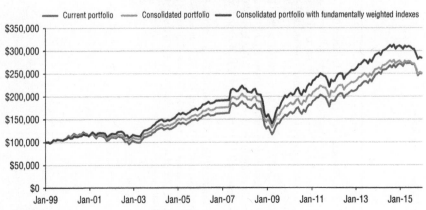

Growth of $100,000 (January 99–December 15)

FIGURE 7.19   Portfolio's Performance and Risk Comparison

Hypothetical example for illustrative purposes only

[1]The current portfolio is equally weighted across eleven asset classes: the S&P 500, Russell 1000 Value, Russell 1000 Growth, Russell Mid Cap, Russell 2000, MSCI EAFE, global asset allocation (60 percent MSCI World Index and 40 percent Barclays U.S. Aggregate Index), inflation hedging (1/3 Barclays U.S. TIPS Index, 1/3 Dow Jones UBS Commodity TR Index, 1/3 Dow Jones US Select REIT Index), diversifying fixed income (1/3 Barclays Global Aggregate Credit USD Hedged Index, 1/3 BofA Merrill Lynch Global High Yield BB-B Rated Constrained USD Hedged, 1/3 JPMorgan EMBI Global Index), Barclays U.S. Aggregate, and the BofA ML 3-Month U.S. T-Bill Index.

[2]The consolidated portfolio is equally weighted across nine asset classes: the S&P 500, Russell 2500, MSCI ACWI ex-U.S., the MSCI ACWI High Dividend Index, global asset allocation (60 percent MSCI World Index and 40 percent Barclays U.S. Aggregate Index), inflation hedging (1/3 Barclays U.S. TIPS Index, 1/3 Dow Jones UBS Commodity TR Index, 1/3 Dow Jones US Select REIT Index), diversifying fixed income (1/3 Barclays Global Aggregate Credit USD Hedged Index, 1/3 BofA Merrill Lynch Global High Yield BB-B Rated Constrained USD Hedged, 1/3 JPMorgan EMBI Global Index), Barclays U.S. Aggregate Index, and the BofA ML 3-Month U.S. T-Bill Index.

[3]The consolidated portfolio with fundamentally weighted indexes is equally weighted across the FTSE RAFI US 1000, FTSE RAFI US 1500, MSCI ACWI ex-U.S., MSCI ACWI High Dividend, global asset allocation (60 percent MSCI World Index/40 percent Barclays U.S. Aggregate Index), inflation hedging (1/3 Barclays U.S. TIPS Index, 1/3 Dow Jones UBS Commodity TR Index, 1/3 Dow Jones US Select REIT Index), diversifying fixed income (1/3 Barclays Global Aggregate Credit Component USD Hedged, 1/3 JPMorgan EMBI Global Index, 1/3 BofA ML BB-B US Dollar Global High Yield Constrained Index), Barclays U.S. Aggregate Index, and BofA ML 3-Month T-Bill Index.

Sources: PIMCO and Bloomberg Finance L.P., as of December 31, 2015.

FIGURE 7.20   Consultants' Views on Currency Hedging

Why Hedge Currency Exposure?	
Potential for reduced volatility	53%
Participants do not understand currency risk	39%
Participants live in the United States	24%
Over the long run, currency risk adds little value	17%
Potential for enhanced returns	14%
We do not recommend hedging currency exposure	29%

Source: PIMCO, 2016 Defined Contribution Consulting Support and Trends Survey.

the inclusion of foreign or global hedged (35 percent) as those who suggested unhedged (33 percent). Similarly, with emerging markets, fixed income hedged (14 percent) was suggested by about the same percentage as unhedged (13 percent). For equity, nearly three-quarters of consultants (70 percent) recommended unhedged non-U.S. developed as a stand-alone core fund, and 40 percent suggested unhedged emerging-markets equity; about a third suggested hedged non-U.S. developed (35 percent) and hedged emerging markets (27 percent). Notably, for blended portfolios such as white-label core or custom target-date strategies, consultants preferred unhedged strategies for both non-U.S. fixed income and equity strategies whether developed or emerging markets.

Why the difference between hedging fixed income and equity strategies? Some may argue that equity strategies are already volatile, so the currency hedging wouldn't make much of a difference, or that the risk will wash out over time, so why do it? As you can see in Figure 7.21, the currency hedging of MSCI EAFE and the Barclays Global Aggregate significantly reduces volatility. In percentage terms, the fixed income volatility is cut in half, declining from 6 percent to less than 3 percent; although not as dramatic, the equity volatility dropped from 16 percent to 13 percent by hedging currencies. Hedging may add or subtract from returns depending on the relative movement of the U.S. dollar. As noted in Figure 7.20, only 14 percent suggest hedging for the "potential to enhance returns" and 17 percent said that "over the long run, currency risk adds little value."

You may also hear that currency hedging is expensive. Currency hedging costs are currently minimal as we write; your consultant or investment managers can tell you current costs. Given a low hedging cost, we believe plan sponsors should consider hedging currencies for both fixed income and equity. The volatility reduction benefit is clear and is an important consideration for plan participants.

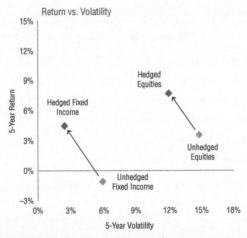

Index	1-year return	1-year volatility	3-year return	3-year volatility	5-year return	5-year volatility	10-year return	10-year volatility
MSCI EAFE Unhedged Net Div Index in USD (%)	−0.81	14.53	5.01	12.46	3.60	14.86	3.03	18.40
MSCI EAFE Hedged USD (%)	5.02	15.31	12.02	11.23	7.75	12.05	3.81	14.71
Barclays Global Aggregate ex-USD (%)	−5.03	5.36	−4.22	5.70	−1.11	5.99	3.25	8.00
Barclays Global Aggregate ex-USD Hdg USD (%)	1.68	2.93	4.25	2.63	4.49	2.46	4.42	2.52

FIGURE 7.21   Why Should Plan Sponsors Consider Hedging Their Non-U.S. Currency Exposure?

As of December 31, 2015.
Hedged Equites: MSCI EAFE USD Hedged Index. Unhedged Equities: MSCI EAFE Index. Hedged Fixed Income: BC Global Aggregate ex-USD Hdg USD Index. Unhedged Fixed Income: BC Global Aggregate ex-USD Index.

Sources: Bloomberg Finance L.P. and PIMCO

OBSERVATIONS FOR EQUITY ALLOCATIONS WITHIN TARGET-DATE STRATEGIES

In Figure 7.22, you see the total and breakout allocations of equities within the Market Average and Objective-Aligned Glide Paths. The average allocation to equities across the Market Average glide path is 69.6 percent, while the Objective-Aligned has an average of 60.0 percent. Looking at individual vintages, the difference is greatest at the beginning, with a 12 percent difference 40 years from retirement, diminishing noticeably by 10 years from retirement, to a final difference of below 5 percent at retirement.

Segmenting the equity allocation further, the comparison is even starker. The Market Average glide path has a higher allocation to U.S.

FIGURE 7.22 Glide Path Allocation to Equities

Years to Retirement	40	35	30	25	20	15	10	5	0	Average
Allocation Percentage to Equities										
Market Average Glide Path	86.00%	84.70%	82.90%	80.10%	75.40%	68.20%	58.90%	49.00%	40.90%	69.57%
Objective-Aligned Glide Path	74.00%	74.00%	73.00%	69.00%	65.00%	58.00%	50.00%	41.00%	36.00%	60.00%
Breakout Allocations within Equities										
U.S. large-cap equities										
Market Average Glide Path	47.40%	46.70%	45.70%	44.30%	42.20%	38.30%	33.50%	28.10%	23.80%	38.89%
Objective-Aligned Glide Path	38.00%	38.00%	37.00%	35.00%	33.00%	30.00%	25.00%	21.00%	19.00%	30.70%
U.S. small-cap equities										
Market Average Glide Path	12.80%	12.60%	12.40%	12.00%	11.10%	10.00%	8.40%	6.90%	5.70%	10.21%
Objective-Aligned Glide Path	5.00%	5.00%	5.00%	5.00%	5.00%	4.00%	4.00%	3.00%	3.00%	4.30%
Non-U.S. equities										
Market Average Glide Path	19.20%	18.90%	18.50%	17.80%	16.60%	15.00%	12.90%	10.70%	8.80%	15.38%
Objective-Aligned Glide Path	18.00%	18.00%	18.00%	17.00%	16.00%	14.00%	12.00%	10.00%	8.00%	14.60%
Emerging market equities										
Market Average Glide Path	6.60%	6.50%	6.30%	6.00%	5.50%	4.90%	4.10%	3.30%	2.60%	5.09%
Objective-Aligned Glide Path	13.00%	13.00%	13.00%	12.00%	11.00%	10.00%	9.00%	7.00%	6.00%	10.40%

Market Average data is as of September 30, 2015. Objective-Aligned data is as of December 31, 2015.
Sources: PIMCO and NextCapital.

large cap throughout the glide path, as well as more U.S. small cap. The differences are relatively small within non-U.S. equities, but again with higher exposures in Market Average. In emerging market equities we see a higher allocation in the Objective-Aligned throughout, but especially in earlier vintages. Viewing this through the lens of real liability, less exposure to U.S. equities and more relative exposure to emerging markets as a diversifier improves correlation to PRICE without compromising the risk/return profile.

IN CLOSING

Plan sponsors should consider designing core investment menus that offer equity choices that are balanced relative to other DC investment offerings, and maximize DC participants' opportunity to gain from both capital appreciation and income. Often DC plans offer too many equity choices, yet fall short of providing sufficient opportunity to maximize returns and minimize risk. By studying historical and forecasted future risk/return relationships among equity markets—as well as between passive and active management—plan sponsors may craft a set of equity strategies that offers both total return and risk-mitigation potential and helps DC participants meet their retirement income objectives. To reduce volatility in international equities, plan fiduciaries should consider currency hedging back to the U.S. dollar—a hedging policy may be just as relevant in equity as it is in fixed income.

QUESTIONS FOR FIDUCIARIES

1. What is the overall investment structure of your plan? Do you want a style-box, asset-class, or risk-pillar core lineup?
2. Is the number of equity options overwhelming relative to other investment choices?
3. Are the equity choices overlapping in market size or approach? Has "style drift" occurred, and the choice diverged from their stated investment style or objective?
4. Would white-label or multimanager strategies make sense?
5. Does your plan offer access to non-U.S. developed and emerging market equity?
6. Do participants have the opportunity to invest in dividend-focused strategies?

7. Should you hedge non-U.S. equity strategies back to the U.S. dollar?
8. Is your small cap strategy capacity constrained?
9. Do you offer passive investment strategies?
10. Are there better approaches to maximize value for participants?

NOTE

1. John Rekenthaler, "Why Strategic Beta Makes Sense and How It Departs from Other Investment 'Innovations,' " May 5, 2016.

CHAPTER 8

Inflation Protection

Inflation is as violent as a mugger, as frightening as an armed robber and as deadly as a hit man.

—Ronald Reagan

In 1978, when then–presidential candidate Ronald Reagan likened inflation to a mugger, it struck a nerve. Inflation was running at a 9 percent annual clip, on its way to nearly 15 percent two years later. Inflation was a harsh reality.

In 2016 as I write this book, inflation is tame, and the voices of monetary hawks have been drowned out. The modernization of banking over time now means there is a much lower likelihood that we could ever experience high single- or double-digit inflation as in the 1970s. Instead, the "mugger" is more likely to be a "stealthy pickpocket" that can significantly erode an individual's purchasing power over time. But for retirees, who often depend on income that does not adjust with inflation, even relatively tame inflation—the stealthy pickpocket, not the armed robber—can be devastating. Consider: After 20 years of 3 percent annual inflation, $50,000 in retirement income would buy only about $27,000 worth of goods and services; with 5 percent inflation, the value shrivels to only about $18,000 (Figure 8.1 shows the impact of inflation on your purchasing power over time).

Thus when it comes to investing for retirement, consultants concur: Inflation is one of the greatest risks, and inflation-fighting assets should be part of retirement portfolios. Given the long-term nature of retirement investing, it becomes clear why consultants worry so much about this risk and

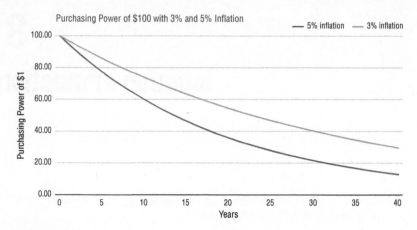

FIGURE 8.1 Inflation Can Cripple Purchasing Power in Retirement
Source: PIMCO.

work hard to address it by recommending the use of inflation-related assets in participant portfolios. In fact, 84 percent of respondents to PIMCO's 2016 Defined Contribution Consulting Support and Trends Survey support offering an inflation-hedging choice in a DC plan's standalone core investment menu. Inflation-fighting asset classes can help portfolios in other ways, too—they may diversify risk from traditional stocks and bonds, and potentially reduce overall portfolio volatility and mitigate downside risk.

As discussed in Chapter 3, we consider inflation-hedging assets to be one of four primary risk pillars. In this chapter, we'll take a closer look at the breadth of inflation-fighting assets available today, and we'll present some evaluation methods for these important securities.

WHAT IS INFLATION AND HOW IS IT MEASURED?

Inflation is an increase in the price of goods and services. In the United States, a widely accepted measurement of inflation is the Consumer Price Index (CPI), a measure of the average change over time in the prices paid by urban consumers for a market basket of consumer goods and services. Calculated and reported by the U.S. Bureau of Labor Statistics (BLS), the broadest and most comprehensive CPI is called the "All Items Consumer Price Index for All Urban Consumers," or CPI-U, and it reflects spending patterns for all urban consumers. (Most references to "CPI" are to the CPI-U index.) This index is made up of goods and services such as housing (37 percent), food and beverages (15 percent), transportation (12 percent), and medical

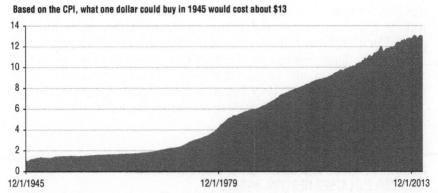

FIGURE 8.2   The Rising Cost of a Dollar over Time
Source: Bloomberg Finance L.P., as of December 31, 2015.

care (9 percent) (all percentages are as of December 31, 2015, according to the BLS), while the "all urban consumer group" represents about 87 percent of the total U.S. population, including professionals, the self-employed, the poor, the unemployed, and retired people, as well as urban wage earners and clerical workers. As Figure 8.2 shows, the changing CPI over time means that "price of a dollar" has risen steadily in the United States since the end of World War II.

In addition to the All Items CPI (CPI-U), BLS publishes thousands of other consumer price indexes. CPI-U is often referred to as "headline" or "top line" inflation as it tends to get the most attention in the media, yet often considered more valuable is "core inflation," which is measured by an index called "All Items Less Food and Energy." Some users of CPI data use this index because food and energy prices are relatively volatile, and these users want to focus on what they perceive to be the "core" or "underlying" rate of inflation. Core inflation is thought to be an indicator of underlying long-term inflation.

In effect, no matter which index you select, inflation shrinks the value of your money. The dollar you invest today will be worth less tomorrow, posing a serious threat to investors. For bondholders, inflation is a particular concern, as it can erode the purchasing power of future interest and principal payments.

WHY INFLATION PROTECTION IN DC?

The intuition behind retirement investors' need to consider inflation protection in their portfolios is quite apparent when considering the ultimate purpose of the assets. Specifically, retirement investors are saving to support a portion of their consumption needs in retirement; essentially, these needs include a basket of goods and services that permits them to maintain an equivalent lifestyle to their working years. This basket of goods and services may contain things like rent (or the equivalent), food, gasoline, movie tickets, medical services, and so on. While consumption patterns may vary by individual, the Consumer Price Index, or CPI, measures the U.S. national average and provides a useful guide to contemplating inflation-related asset portfolios.

HISTORY OF INFLATION: INFLATION SPIKES UNDERSCORE NEED FOR INFLATION-HEDGING ASSETS

Many readers may recall the high inflation period of the 1970s. Throughout history, there have been many more periods of high inflation. Over the past century, hyperinflation also hit post-World War II Europe. The history of inflation in the United States is shown in Figure 8.3. As you can see, inflation, when it occurs, may strike quickly and unexpectedly . . . but also creeps along in the background even when no spikes are occurring. This dual reality underscores why DC plan participants' assets should be "inflation aware" at all times.

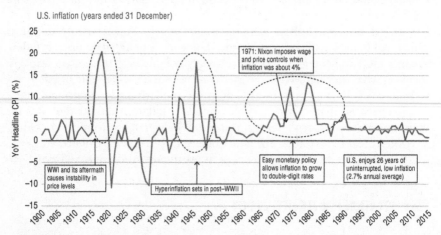

FIGURE 8.3   U.S. Inflation 1900–2015
Sources: Bloomberg Finance L.P. and U.S. Bureau of Labor Statistics, as of December 31, 2015.

INFLATION PROTECTION WHEN ACCUMULATING AND DECUMULATING, AND IN DIFFERENT ECONOMIC ENVIRONMENTS

In PIMCO's July 2008 Defined Contribution Dialogue, Matthew Rice, Principal and Chief Research Officer at DiMeo Schneider & Associates, LLC, speaks about the need for inflation protection in DC. He shares that "in a DC plan, participants' liabilities are real, or after inflation. Retiree assets need to keep up with inflation as much as possible. That's why you need to have asset classes that do better during stretches of unanticipated inflation, in addition to traditional asset classes."

For retirement savers, those who are accumulating assets to fund their retirement spending, the benefits of using inflation-related investments may not be obvious—as over very long time horizons (i.e., 20-plus years), traditional assets such as equities tend to outperform inflation. Nevertheless, Rice suggests that relying on equities may not be a suitable catch-all inflation hedge:

> *Equities aren't a great inflation protector because when you get periods of rising inflation, you frequently get periods of rising interest rates [and] higher discount rates. . . . If you go through a decade of unanticipated rising inflation like we had in the 1970s, it's typically not a great period for equities. Participants approaching or in retirement absolutely need more inflation protection. Regardless of time horizon, some inflation protection is wise in any portfolio.*

As noted above, however, inflation-related assets do more than just provide a hedge against inflation. These assets can also provide an important source of portfolio diversification, particularly relative to the asset classes that typically dominate DC participant portfolios: equities and bonds.

In Chapter 3, we set out a framework (in Figure 3.6) for constructing well-diversified portfolios that are able to generate returns in a variety of economic environments. The underlying message of that framework is that there's no one "silver bullet" portfolio that will perform well in all economic conditions, whether inflation and growth are high or low. This framework is important to consider when contemplating long-term asset allocation decisions that will ultimately define the retirement investor's quality of lifestyle. We believe it is prudent to allow participants the ability to cover all four growth/inflation scenarios when constructing long-term strategic portfolios. Inflation-related assets tend to perform well during times when "traditional" portfolios, consisting primarily of nominal stocks and bonds, underperform.

This message is underscored by the deeper work undertaken by PIMCO to investigate inflation "regime shifts," or large, abrupt, persistent changes in how inflation rises and falls over time. In October 2012, we published a white paper investigating the implications for asset allocation of inflation regime shifts. The underlying thesis of this work is that investors who are concerned about inflation should focus on increasing their exposure to asset classes that provide a positive beta to changes in inflation—and asks whether stocks, the traditional inflation hedge over the long term, are still an effective tactic for inflation protection.

In his paper "Inflation Regime Shifts: Implications for Asset Allocation," author and PIMCO portfolio manager Nicholas Johnson finds that "domestic U.S. financial assets—stocks and bonds—tend to perform poorly when inflation is higher than previous expectations, compared to real assets, foreign currencies, and TIPS, which tend to perform quite well." Instead of "high inflation," the paper concludes that inflation surprises (the difference between expected and actual inflation) are a "more significant driver of asset returns than just the level of inflation, because it is changes in inflation expectations that tend to matter to the security returns. For example, high inflation isn't the enemy of bonds. If inflation is high, it is likely that interest rates are high and already factored into the price of bonds. Instead, it is the unanticipated move from low inflation to high inflation that is particularly negative for the returns of bonds or stocks."

Turning from inflation surprises to the relationship between equities and inflation, the paper notes that numerous academic studies have documented a negative beta between stocks and inflation—that is, stock values go down when inflation goes up. Johnson shares:

> Yet despite a plethora of academic studies and historical evidence, this negative relationship remains somewhat of a puzzle to financial economists. A common question is whether inflation shocks tend to occur when other equity factors are at play. If so, then in order to assert the existence of a negative correlation today investors must be confident the recurrent—but perhaps not universal—negative factors that give rise to the negative beta between inflation and stocks are prevalent in the current market environment.

The paper ultimately finds that "historically, investors worried about inflation perhaps shouldn't have bought stocks as a hedge. While most studies were performed on U.S. data, international evidence also supports this conclusion. The negative beta of stock returns to inflation was documented in Japan, the UK, and in large-scale studies involving major stock markets globally." However, it also concludes that:

. . . none of this analysis suggests that an investor should not own stocks or that they are not an attractive asset class that can provide long-term returns due to the presence of an equity risk premium. The main takeaway should be that equities historically have not been a good inflation hedge and that the process of moving from low inflation to high inflation will likely be detrimental to the returns of financial assets like equities and bonds, particularly relative to physical assets.

In the remainder of this chapter, we investigate how DC plans can effectively provide inflation protection for members in light of the regime shifts for inflation we are pointing to here.

ECONOMIC ENVIRONMENTS CHANGE UNEXPECTEDLY— AND REWARD OR PUNISH VARIOUS ASSET CLASSES

Inflation-hedging assets offer important benefits to DC participants, including the opportunity for improved diversification, risk reduction, and the potential for higher returns in certain economic environments. Most economic environments are defined by two key factors: growth and inflation. Depending on the combination of these factors, different investments tend to perform well or poorly. In high growth and low inflation environments, stocks tend to do well (as experienced in the 1980s and 1990s); but in other economic environments stocks have not fared as well. For instance, the 1930s and 2000s are "lost decades" in terms of stock returns.

In periods of high inflation, inflation-linked bonds, commodities, and real estate tend to do far better than stocks and bonds. Figure 8.4 shows asset class performance in various economic environments: inflationary, an equity bull market, and a turbulent market environment. What's critical is that participants are prepared for all economic environments, not just one.

As you can see in Figure 8.5, looking not too far back in history, nominal bonds did not fare well in the inflationary environment from 1962 to 1980, as this asset class didn't maintain its purchasing power over time. In fact, while it's difficult to see on this chart, bonds fell short of inflation by almost 50 percent. What did well? Commodities—even though oil was not included in the CPI-U index until 1983.

Looking ahead, we need to prepare for the possibility of an inflationary environment. What's more, we need to look for opportunities to find attractive investment returns, not only in the United States but around the globe. Looking for opportunities and discovering how to steer clear of danger is critical as the economic horizon and markets around the world change.

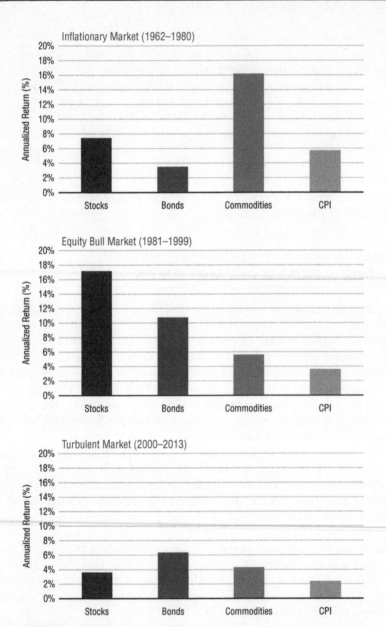

FIGURE 8.4 Asset Class Performance in Various Market Environments
Sources: Haver Analytics and PIMCO, as of 31 December 2015.

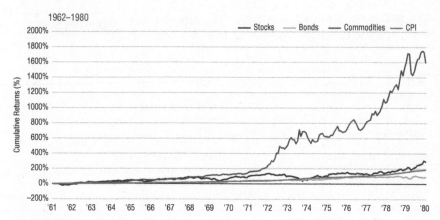

FIGURE 8.5 During an Inflationary Environment, Commodities Outperform Other Asset Classes

Hypothetical example for illustrative purposes only.

Source: Haver Analytics and PIMCO, as of 31 December 1980.

CONSULTANTS FAVOR TIPS, MULTI-REAL-ASSET STRATEGIES, REITS, AND COMMODITIES

We asked participants in our 2016 PIMCO Defined Contribution Consulting Support and Trends Survey which inflation-protection strategies they recommend (Figure 8.6). For stand-alone strategies as part of core menus, a majority of consultants suggest Treasury Inflation-Protected Securities, or TIPS (67 percent), a multi-real-asset strategy (60 percent), and Real Estate Investment Trusts, or REITs (51 percent). Only 14 percent suggest commodities as a stand-alone offering. In addition, a small percentage of consultants recommend natural resource equity (11 percent), private real estate (11 percent), bank loans (7 percent), and infrastructure (4 percent).

In blended strategies, commodities top the list, with 84 percent of consultants recommending this asset class. In addition, over three-quarters suggest that REITs (82 percent), a multi-real-asset strategy (78 percent), and TIPS (78 percent) be included, while the majority suggest including natural resource equity (60 percent), bank loans (58 percent), private real estate (56 percent), and infrastructure (53 percent). Just over a quarter of consultants (27 percent) recommend currency or gold for blended strategies.

Stand-Alone*		Blended**	
TIPS	67%	Commodities	84%
Multi-real-asset strategy	60%	REITs	82%
REITs	51%	Multi-real-asset strategy	78%
Commodities	14%	TIPS	78%
Natural resource equity	11%	Natural resource equity	60%
Private real estate	11%	Bank loans	58%
Bank loans	7%	Private real estate	56%
Infrastructure	4%	Infrastructure	53%
Currency or gold	0%	Currency or gold	27%
None of the above	5%		

FIGURE 8.6   Consultant Support for Inflation-Fighting Assets
Source: PIMCO, 2016 Defined Contribution Consulting Support and Trends Survey.

REAL RETURN ASSETS: MORE ON TIPS, COMMODITIES, AND REITS

Real Return Assets are physical or financial assets that have either an *explicit* or *implicit* link between their cash flows and/or valuations and inflation. Examples of real return assets include TIPS and global Inflation-Linked Bonds, commodities, and real estate. The primary inflation-hedging assets—TIPS, Commodities, and REITS—have many benefits and differences. Here we provide a brief definition of each and a comparison of their characteristics (also see Figure A).

WHAT ARE INFLATION-LINKED BONDS?

Inflation-Linked Bonds (ILBs) are fixed-income instruments whose returns are contractually linked to the rate of inflation in order to protect investors from the negative effects of inflation. Most ILBs are indexed to a nationally recognized inflation measure, such as the CPI, and any increases in price levels directly translate into higher principal values. Additionally, while the coupon rate remains fixed, the dollar value of each interest payment changes as each coupon is paid on the inflation-adjusted principal value.

WHAT ARE TREASURY INFLATION-PROTECTED SECURITIES, OR TIPS?

Treasury Inflation-Protected Securities (TIPS) are a form of inflation-linked bond issued by the U.S. government. More specifically, TIPS are a treasury security that is indexed to inflation in order to protect investors from the negative effects of inflation. TIPS are considered an extremely low-risk investment as first, they are backed by the U.S. government, and second, because their par value rises with inflation, as measured by the Consumer Price Index, while their interest rate remains fixed. Interest on TIPS is paid semi-annually. TIPS can be purchased directly from the government in $100 increments with a minimum investment of $100 and they are available with 5-, 10-, and 30-year maturities.

WHAT IS A COMMODITY?

A commodity is a basic good used in commerce and interchangeable with other commodities of the same type. Commodities are most often used as inputs in the production of other goods or services. The quality of a given commodity may differ slightly, but it is essentially uniform across producers. When they are traded on an exchange, commodities must also meet specified minimum standards, also known as a basis grade.

WHAT IS A REAL ESTATE INVESTMENT TRUST, OR REIT?

A REIT is a type of security that invests in real estate through property or mortgages and often trades on major exchanges like a stock. Publically traded REITs provide investors with a liquid stake in real estate. More specifically, a REIT is a tax designation for a corporate entity investing in real estate that reduces or eliminates corporate tax; in turn, REITs are required to distribute at least 90 percent of their taxable income to their shareholders. These dividends are taxed at the investor level using a combination of ordinary income and capital gains tax rates rather than at the individual's corporate dividend tax rate. For an investor, this is an investment vehicle that essentially securitizes the owning, operating, and/or financing of real estate, and a REIT mutual fund specializes in owning publicly traded REITs.

(continued)

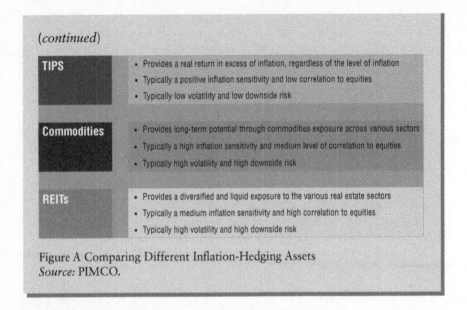

Figure A Comparing Different Inflation-Hedging Assets
Source: PIMCO.

HOW SHOULD PLAN SPONSORS ADDRESS INFLATION RISK IN DC PORTFOLIOS?

As plan sponsors consider adding inflation-hedging strategies, they may consider one of three strategies: an *asset class orientation*, a *multiasset or hybrid blend*, or an *outcome orientation*. Figure 8.7 illustrates this spectrum of choice.

In our July 2008 DC Dialogue, Matthew Rice provided some "on-the-ground" examples of how a DC plan addresses inflation protection. He shared:

> *When they create custom target retirement-date strategies, our clients typically use their underlying core funds or managers within their target retirement-date funds. In addition, most also*

Spectrum of Inflation Hedging

Asset Class Orientation	Multiasset Blend	Outcome Orientation
Distinct asset classes that provide an explicit or implicit return linkage to inflation	Strategies that employ some asset class diversification and tactical flexibility, but typically are limited to a real asset opportunity set	Strategies that employ broad asset class diversification and tactical flexibility to deliver a real return objective
Example: • TIPS • Commodities • REITs	Example: • Real Asset Blend (TIPS, Commodities, and REITS) • Expanded Real Asset Blend (real assets plus currency, gold, ...)	Example: • Global Asset Allocation aimed to beat CPI

FIGURE 8.7   A Range of Inflation-Hedging Strategies for Consideration
Source: PIMCO.

include other asset classes they don't want to include in the core menu, such as emerging markets, real estate, high-yield bonds, foreign bonds, Treasury Inflation-Protected Securities (TIPS) or commodity futures.

He explained the use of inflation-hedging assets within a glide path:

We allocate portfolio assets to inflation-protection securities along the entire glide path—not necessarily for the same reason. Early on with more aggressive portfolios, we view TIPS as a tremendous diversifier to equities. When we look at periods of time when equity markets struggle, typically TIPS frequently perform better than nominal bonds. TIPS also should do particularly well in periods of unanticipated rising inflation.

He also comments on the inclusion of commodities and importance of managing to a real liability:

Commodity futures can be a good diversifier, long term. When stocks fall 10 percent, commodity futures are frequently positive and can dampen some of the volatility. As you approach retirement it's essential to have a portfolio that hedges your liabilities. In a DC plan, participants' liabilities are real, or after inflation. Retiree assets need to keep up with inflation as much as possible. That's why you need to have asset classes that do better during stretches of unanticipated inflation, in addition to traditional asset classes.

Rice also notes the value of real estate as a potential inflation hedge, but places it behind inflation-linked bonds and commodities. He explains:

Real estate doesn't provide the same inflation protection you get from TIPS or commodity futures, but you get a little more inflation protection than from pure equity. Assuming that rising rents accompany higher overall inflation, real estate can be a solid inflation hedge. However, higher inflation usually accompanies higher interest rates and discount rates, which causes the present value of future rents to fall. Real estate is a mixed bag at least, whereas many other financial assets are just plain bad inflation hedges.

In PIMCO's December 2010 DC Dialogue, we spoke to Dave Zellner, then CIO of the General Board of Pension and Health Benefits of the United Methodist Church, now Westpath Benefits and Investments.

Dave told us about how his plan addresses inflation risk through a separate fund for inflation hedging. He also shared his views on using real estate for inflation hedging and the appropriateness of non-U.S. inflation hedging for a mainly U.S.-based population:

> Within the Inflation Protection Fund, 50 percent is in U.S. Treasury inflation-protected securities (TIPS), but then 50 percent of the portfolio is set aside for other inflation-sensitive strategies, including 30 percent in a global inflation-protected strategy and 10 percent in a dedicated commodity strategy. For the remaining 10 percent, we invest in emerging market inflation-linked bonds. For instance, we may invest in bonds from Brazil, Mexico, Turkey, Poland, South Africa, Korea, Uruguay and Argentina, among others.
>
> We thought about including REITs in the Inflation Protection Fund, but our benchmark for the Inflation Protection Fund is the Barclay's U.S. Government Inflation Bond Index. Since we have a pretty tight risk budget, we didn't want to use most of it on REITs. We preferred adding real estate to the equity funds.
>
> Our primary motivation with the non-U.S. inflation assets is to increase portfolio diversification via exposure to foreign currencies. I know there have been a lot of folks who are concerned about the currency risk, but our view is that currency is a way to provide further diversification to the portfolio.

At the time of writing, we caught up with Zeller, who shared with us that since 2010 "we have brought additional sources of diversification into the fund. Specifically, we have added allocations to floating rate senior secured loans (bank loans) along with timber and infrastructure. We have funded these strategies by reducing the TIPS allocation from 50 to 35 percent."

IMPLEMENTATION CHALLENGES

No matter your preferred strategy, adding inflation-hedging assets to DC menus requires thoughtful analysis. First, individual inflation-fighting assets respond to inflation in different ways. Then, as we have discussed in previous chapters, there's the "1 over n," or naive diversification, consideration or the tendency of DC participants to allocate their assets evenly among fund choices. Broadly speaking, in order to counter the potential negative impacts of inflation on retirement income, we suggest offering a balanced menu of investment choices designed to boost the odds that participants create reasonably balanced portfolios—even when blindly allocating equal sums across menu options.

FIGURE 8.8 Key Questions and Metrics We Believe Plan Sponsors Should Evaluate

Benefit or Drawback Question	Statistical Measure
How well may this asset or blend of assets respond to an inflation surprise?	Inflation beta, which represents sensitivity of asset class excess returns (above the risk rate) to inflation surprises*
Will this asset or blend add diversification relative to equity?	Equity correlation, which measures how the asset moves relative to the S&P 500 Index
How volatile is this asset or blend?	Volatility, which measures the variation and risk of an asset's value
What is the potential 12-month loss that may be incurred by investing in this asset or blend?	Downside risk, measured by value-at-risk (VaR), is an estimate of the minimum expected loss at a desired level of significance over 12 months

*We define *inflation surprise* as the difference between actual inflation and expected inflation as measured by the Philadelphia Fed Survey. (The Philadelphia Fed Survey is a business outlook survey used to construct an index that tracks manufacturing conditions in the Philadelphia Federal Reserve district, and is used by investors to provide insight on equity markets.) When inflation surprises by +1 percent, an asset with an inflation beta of 1.5 is expected to have an additional excess return of 1.5 percent (all else equal).

Source: PIMCO.

To help plan fiduciaries as they evaluate inflation-fighting assets both for stand-alone core options and blended strategies, we suggest considering a set of measures: *inflation beta, equity correlation, volatility,* and *downside risk.* These measures, along with the questions we suggest plan sponsors use to evaluate how they might apply to portfolios, are set out in Figure 8.8.

EVALUATING REAL ASSET STRATEGIES

Let's take a look at how inflation-hedging asset classes and blends perform against these measures:

- **Inflation beta:** At PIMCO, as mentioned above, we believe asset prices are much more sensitive to inflation surprises (that is, unexpected and sudden increases in inflation, which have not been factored into economic projections) than actual levels of inflation—in other words, investors react strongly when outcomes differ from expectations. Historically, inflation spikes have occurred quickly and unexpectedly. Therefore, we believe the most important factor for DC participants in selecting a real asset is its sensitivity to unexpected inflation. Asset classes with a positive beta to inflation surprises—they rise in value in response to unexpected inflation—have historically tended to perform well, thus preserving purchasing power, during inflationary market environments. (Inflation beta quantifies the magnitude of an asset's response to inflation; for every 1 percent change in the rate of inflation, returns move by a multiple reflected by its inflation beta.)

As Figure 8.9 shows, the inflation beta of a stock/bond portfolio (composed 70 percent of the MSCI World and 30 percent of the Barclays Aggregate Global Corporate Bond Index, or BAGG) was –2.09 as of December 31, 2015. By contrast, all of the asset types and blends except for infrastructure and natural resource equities showed a higher inflation beta. Commodities and gold stood out with the highest inflation betas—they moved the most in response to changes in the rate of inflation.

- **Equity correlation:** To reap the potential diversification benefits of real assets, each asset type and blend should be evaluated for its correlation to equities. Viewed through this lens, the stock/bond portfolio shows a tight correlation of 0.94, to the S&P 500, while other assets or combinations show lower correlations (thus offering improved diversification potential). Assets with the lowest correlations include TIPS, gold, and commodities.
- **Volatility:** Selecting an individual asset class or blend with relatively low volatility is important to lessening the risk of participants selling out with a sudden shift in returns. As Figure 8.9 shows, the stock/bond portfolio had volatility of 11.8 percent, while other asset types or blends offered smoother rides. Of note, TIPS, bank loans, and the expanded multi-real-asset blend showed lower volatility.
- **Downside risk:** Although there are many ways to measure tail risk (defined as the risk of an asset or portfolio of assets moving more than three standard deviations from its current price), we suggest evaluating risk exposure by assessing value-at-risk (VaR) at a 95 percent confidence level. (VaR estimates the minimum expected loss at a desired level of significance over 12 months, while a 95 percent confidence level represents how often the true percentage of the population who would pick an answer lies within the confidence interval. The 95 percent confidence level means you can be 95 percent certain.) Applying this measure, we observe that the stock/bond portfolio has potential downside risk of –17.9 percent. Other asset types and blends may have less downside risk. TIPS, bank loans, and the expanded multi-real-asset blend stand out again.

FIGURE 8.9 How Different Asset Classes Compare across Key Measures

Asset Classes	Inflation Beta[1]	Estimated Correlation to S&P 500	Estimated Volatility[2]	VaR 95%[3]
Commodities	6.17	0.30	17.2%	−30.3%
TIPS	1.00	−0.19	4.7%	−5.1%
REITs	−1.26	0.86	14.8%	−26.5%
Infrastructure	−2.13	0.85	16.4%	−28.9%
Bank loans	−0.26	0.62	6.2%	−7.4%
Private real estate	−0.77	0.55	15.1%	−26.4%
Natural resource equities	−2.10	0.78	25.7%	−39.3%
EM currency	0.82	0.44	7.9%	−10.4%
Gold	6.17	−0.10	15.5%	−24.6%
High yield	−1.44	0.58	10.5%	−19.3%
Multi-real-asset*	1.97	0.61	9.3%	−15.7%
Expanded multi-real-asset**	2.30	0.33	6.9%	−10.1%
70% Equity/30% Bond	−2.09	0.94	11.8%	−17.9%
50% Equity/30% Bond/20% Expanded multi-real-asset	−1.20	0.90	9.1%	−13.7%

As of December 31, 2015.

Hypothetical example for illustrative purposes only.

*The multi-real-asset blend is an equally weighted mix of the Barclays U.S. TIPS Index, the Dow Jones UBS Commodity TR Index, and the Dow Jones US Select REIT index.

**The composition of the expanded multi-real-asset blend is 45 percent Barclays U.S. TIPS Index, 20 percent Dow Jones UBS Commodity TR Index, 15 percent JP Morgan Emerging Local Markets Index, 10 percent Dow Jones US Select REIT Index, and 10 percent Dow Jones UBS Gold Sub Index.

Other asset classes are defined as follows: Equities: MSCI World Index; Bond: Barclays U.S. Aggregate Index; TIPS: Barclays U.S. TIPS Index; Commodities: Dow Jones UBS Commodity TR Index; REITs: Dow Jones US Select REIT Index; EM Currency: JP Morgan Emerging Local Markets Index (Unhedged); Gold: Dow Jones UBS Gold Sub Index; Natural Resources: MSCI ACWI Commodity Producers Sector Capped Index; Bank Loans: Credit Suisse Institutional Leveraged Loan Index; High Yield: BofA Merrill Lynch U.S. High Yield, BB-B Rated, Constrained Index; Private Real Estate: NCREIF/Townsend Core Index; Infrastructure: S&P Global Infrastructure Index.

[1]Inflation beta represents the sensitivity of asset class excess returns (above the "risk-free" rate) to inflation surprises (the difference between actual inflation and expected inflation as measured by the Philadelphia Fed Survey); when inflation surprises by +1 percent, an asset with an inflation beta of 1.5 is expected to have an additional excess return of 1.5 percent (all else equal).

[2]We employed a block bootstrap methodology to calculate volatilities. We start by computing historical factor returns that underlie each asset class proxy from January 1997 through the present date. We then draw a set of 12 monthly returns within the data set to come up with an annual return number. This process is repeated 25,000 times to have a return series with 25,000 annualized returns. The standard deviation of these annual returns is used to model the volatility for each factor. We then use the same return series for each factor to compute covariance between factors. Finally, volatility of each asset class proxy is calculated as the sum of variances and covariance of factors that underlie that particular proxy. For each asset class, index, or strategy proxy, we will look at either a point in time estimate or historical average of factor exposures in order to determine the total volatility. Please contact your PIMCO representative for more details on how specific proxy factor exposures are estimated.

[3]Value-at-risk (VaR) is an estimate of the minimum expected loss at a desired level of significance over a 12-month horizon.

Source: PIMCO.

SUMMARY COMPARISON OF INDIVIDUAL AND MULTI-REAL-ASSET BLENDS

By comparing asset classes across these metrics, Figure 8.9 underscores that when it comes to fighting inflation, a multipronged approach may be best. It lists individual asset types followed by multi-real-asset and expanded multi-real-asset categories.

These data go a long way in explaining why the consultants we polled are strongly supportive of adding multi-real-asset strategies to a DC plan's core lineup. A well-diversified portfolio should hold assets that perform well in different economic environments, but plan sponsors don't always want core options for each. That's where a multi-real-asset solution might come in: It offers a convenient way to provide diversification across inflation-fighting assets, protect purchasing power, and limit volatility that might result from holding a single asset class (such as commodities) in isolation.

Relative to the stock/bond portfolio, both the multi-real-asset and expanded multi-real-asset blends offer inflation hedging (positive inflation betas) and potential diversification benefits (i.e., equity correlations of less than 1). What's more, both blends show the potential for lower volatility and less risk of loss (VaR) than the stock/bond portfolio. Notably, the blends may offer volatility and risk-of-loss levels below those of many individual real assets. To simplify a core lineup and reduce the risk that a participant will either chase or flee an investment at the sight of enticing or unfortunate returns, these multi-real-asset blends may be preferable to individual assets.

In addition to adding the multi-real-asset blend or the expanded multi-real-asset blend to the core lineup, a plan sponsor should evaluate their investment default for its ability to stand up to inflation. Plan sponsors may want to add these multi-real-asset blends to the investment default glide path or may prefer adding individual asset classes in different weights based on target-date vintage. As Figure 8.9 shows, shifting 20 percent of the 70/30 stock-and-bond allocation to the expanded multi-real-asset blend allows the potential inflation-fighting and diversification benefits to shine through. Most notably, volatility decreases from 11.8 percent to 9.1 percent while the potential loss (VaR) drops from –17.9 percent to –13.7 percent and the inflation beta increases from –2.09 to –1.2.

Figure 8.10 shows how a multi-real-asset solution might look in practice, consistent with their place as one of the most consultant-recommended inflation-hedging options for DC core menus.

In Figure 8.11, we list the inflation-fighting assets consultants rated "important" along with suggested index proxies. In addition, we show two multi-real-asset blends, as well as a stock and bond portfolio.

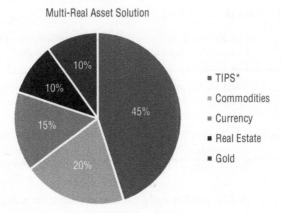

Multi-Real Asset Solution

- TIPS*
- Commodities
- Currency
- Real Estate
- Gold

FIGURE 8.10 Real Asset Diversification for Inflation Protection

*Treasury Inflation-Protected Securities
Hypothetical example for illustrative purposes only.
The chart does not represent a fixed allocation and is only meant to highlight a potential portfolio allocation.

Source: PIMCO.

FIGURE 8.11 Diversifying Real Asset Strategies and Index Proxies

Diversifying Real Asset Strategies	Index Proxies	Description
Commodities	Dow Jones-UBS Commodity Index	Provides long-term return potential and high inflation sensitivity through commodities exposure across various sectors
TIPS	Barclays U.S. TIPS Index	Designed to provide a predictable real return in excess of inflation and portfolio diversification through low correlation to other asset classes
REITs	Dow Jones U.S. Select REIT Index	Provides a diversified inflation hedge and consistent income through exposure to the various real estate sectors
Infrastructure	S&P Global Infrastructure Index	Provides exposure to companies that represent the listed infrastructure universe including utilities, transportation, and energy

(continued)

FIGURE 8.11   *(continued)*

Bank loans	Credit Suisse Institutional Leveraged Loan Index	Provides exposure to institutional leveraged bank loans
Private real estate	NCREIF/Townsed Core Index	Provides exposure to private equity real estate funds pursuing core investment strategies
Natural resource equities	MSCI ACWI Commodity Producers Sector Capped Index	Provides equity exposure across equally weighted commodity-related sectors including energy, metals, and agriculture
Emerging Markets currency	JP Morgan Emerging Local Markets Index (Unhedged)	Provides inflation hedge through exposure to a broad range of Emerging Markets currencies
Gold	Dow Jones UBS Gold Sub Index	Provides inflation hedge through exposure to gold futures
High yield	BofA Merrill Lynch U.S. High Yield, BB-B Rated, Constrained Index	Provides exposure to BB-B Rated U.S. dollar-denominated corporate bonds publicly issued in the U.S. domestic market with total allocation to an individual capped at 2%
Multi-real-asset	1/3 Barclays U.S. TIPS Index, 1/3 Dow Jones UBS Commodity TR Index, 1/3 Dow Jones US Select REIT Index	"2-in-1" TIPS, U.S. commodity, and real estate exposure looks to hedge inflation risk and provide diversification
Expanded multi-real-asset	45% Barclays U.S. TIPS Index, 20% Dow Jones UBS Commodity TR Index, 15% JP Morgan Emerging Local Markets Index, 10% Dow Jones US Select REIT Index, 10% Dow Jones UBS Gold Sub Index	Provides a comprehensive portfolio strategy to seek diversified exposure to inflation-related investments, including assets that respond to different types of inflation
Stock/bond portfolio	70% MSCI World Index, 30% Barclays U.S. Aggregate Index	Provides a balanced strategy to seek exposure to traditional stocks and bonds

Source: PIMCO.

INFLATION-HEDGING ASSETS IN TARGET-DATE GLIDE PATHS

We now look at historical portfolio experience with and without the inclusion of inflation-related assets; please note our data set is somewhat limited as TIPS were first issued in 1997. In the following table, we consider a 60 percent equity and 40 percent bond portfolio versus a 50 percent equity, 30 percent bond, and 20 percent inflation-related asset portfolio.

As you can see from Figure 8.12, the diversification benefit of including inflation-related assets in a traditional stock and bond portfolio is clear based on the 0.7 percent lower volatility while exhibiting similar returns. Additionally, the return-to-risk ratio improves by over 5 percent and the max drawdown (or the peak-to-trough decline during a specific recorded period) is improved by roughly 2 percent, which speaks to the downside that risk mitigation inflation-related assets can cause to portfolios. Importantly, all of these enhancements from the inclusion of inflation-related assets into a traditional stock and bond portfolio were achieved in a benign inflation environment when the full value proposition of holding such assets was not necessarily realized (i.e., inflation not advancing and/or surprising to the upside).

While the benefit of adding real assets may be clear, plan fiduciaries may worry in markets that reward a less-diversified investment approach such as 60 percent equities and 40 percent bonds. In an NEPC June 2016 article, "The Disease of Doubt," Chief Investment Officer Timothy F. McCusker, FSA, CFA, CAIA, discusses how plan fiduciaries may experience doubt "whenever a portfolio position has not played out as expected." He says,

FIGURE 8.12 Adding Inflation-Related Assets to a Traditional Nominal Stock and Bond Mix May Improve Portfolio Diversification (From January 1997 to December 2015)

Hypothetical Portfolios	Annualized Return	Annualized Volatility	Return/ Risk	Max Drawdown
60% equities/40% bonds	6.9%	9.3%	0.74	−33%
50% equities/30% bonds/ 20% inflation-related assets	6.7%	8.6%	0.78	−31%

As of December 31, 2015.
Equities: S&P 500 Index; Bonds: Barclays U.S. Aggregate Index; Inflation-related assets: Inflation Response Index (45 percent Barclays U.S. TIPS, 20 percent Bloomberg Commodity Index [formerly Dow Jones UBS Commodity Total Return], 15 percent JP Morgan Emerging Local Markets Plus, 10 percent Dow Jones Select REIT, 10 percent Bloomberg Gold Subindex Total Return [formerly Dow Jones UBS Gold Subindex Total Return]

Source: Bloomberg Finance L.P.

"After watching U.S. equities repeatedly outshine global markets, and witnessing the losses racked up by emerging markets and real assets, it is intuitive for investors to question their allocation and philosophy." McCusker encourages plan fiduciaries to "embrace approaches that depart from average asset allocations," and he specifically comments on the importance of inflation-hedging assets:

> *With high commodity production, tepid global growth, and spending constrained by debt levels, deflationary pressures have recently outweighed inflationary concerns. That said, inflation can rear its head with a change in monetary policy, amid a strong spurt of global growth, or unforeseen commodity supply shocks. While these scenarios may seem unlikely in the near term, we cannot rule them out. In most cases, a portfolio of growth-centric assets (even if balanced with nominal bonds) would suffer meaningfully if inflation appeared. The critical strategic decision for inflation protection is whether program objectives have an inflationary component. If they do, exposure to real assets should be considered a strategic imperative, even when suffering through losses.*

OBSERVATIONS FOR INFLATION-HEDGING ASSETS IN TARGET-DATE GLIDE PATHS

Looking at Figure 8.13, you will find a comparison of the total and breakout allocations to Inflation-Hedging Assets for the Market Average and Objective-Aligned Glide Paths. In total, the Objective-Aligned series contains a substantially higher allocation, 16.9 percent on average, compared to 6.8 percent for the Market Average. In early vintages, the difference between the Market Average and Objective-Aligned allocations is lower than at later points, as the Objective-Aligned glide path increases its allocation faster, decreasing again just before retirement.

In the breakout allocation, we see a similar story. While the allocations are higher, on average, for the Objective-Aligned glide path for each of the individual allocations, there are some differences. TIPS, Long TIPS, and Commodities all begin with relatively small differences between the two glide paths and increase through time, while the difference is great in Real Estate at the beginning. Then as we near retirement, the difference decreases as both glide paths reduce their allocations to Real Estate. At retirement, the Objective-Aligned glide path also reduces exposure to Long TIPS while the Market Average continues to increase exposure. Understanding that the

FIGURE 8.13 Glide Path Allocation to Inflation-Hedging Assets

Years to Retirement	40	35	30	25	20	15	10	5	0	Average
Allocation Percentage to Inflation-Hedging Assets										
Market Average Glide Path	4.80%	5.00%	5.30%	5.60%	6.00%	6.80%	8.00%	9.40%	10.40%	6.81%
Objective-Aligned Glide Path	13.00%	13.00%	14.00%	14.00%	14.00%	17.00%	21.00%	25.00%	21.00%	16.89%
Breakout Allocations within Inflation-Hedging Assets										
TIPS										
Market Average Glide Path	0.50%	0.60%	0.80%	1.10%	1.60%	2.40%	3.60%	4.90%	6.00%	2.39%
Objective-Aligned Glide Path	2.00%	2.00%	2.00%	2.00%	2.00%	2.00%	5.00%	10.00%	10.00%	4.11%
Long TIPS										
Market Average Glide Path	0.30%	0.30%	0.40%	0.50%	0.60%	0.80%	1.20%	1.60%	1.80%	0.83%
Objective-Aligned Glide Path	1.00%	1.00%	2.00%	2.00%	2.00%	7.00%	10.00%	10.00%	7.00%	4.67%
Commodities										
Market Average Glide Path	1.40%	1.50%	1.50%	1.40%	1.40%	1.30%	1.20%	1.10%	1.00%	1.31%
Objective-Aligned Glide Path	2.00%	2.00%	2.00%	2.00%	2.00%	2.00%	2.00%	2.00%	2.00%	2.00%
Real Estate										
Market Average Glide Path	2.60%	2.60%	2.60%	2.60%	2.40%	2.30%	2.00%	1.80%	1.60%	2.28%
Objective-Aligned Glide Path	8.00%	8.00%	8.00%	8.00%	8.00%	6.00%	4.00%	3.00%	2.00%	6.11%

Market Average data is as of September 30, 2015. Objective-Aligned data is as of December 31, 2015.
Sources: PIMCO and NextCapital.

goal of the Objective-Aligned Glide Path is to more closely match the liabilities of a retiree, it makes sense that we would wish to decrease the duration risk as the duration of the liabilities decreases. This change, along with the higher overall allocation to inflation-hedging assets, serves to increase correlations to PRICE, the PIMCO Retirement Income Cost Estimate discussed in Chapter 2, while also improving risk-adjusted returns throughout.

IN CLOSING

Inflation-fighting strategies are fundamental to DC investment lineups and participants' need to build and preserve purchasing power in retirement. Plan sponsors should evaluate inflation-fighting assets, separately and in combination, to determine how best to offer them.

Whatever choices are made, selected assets or blends should be designed to deliver the primary benefits of inflation responsiveness, diversification relative to stocks, volatility reduction, and downside risk mitigation. To deliver these and ward off the inflation robber baron, plan sponsors may find multi-real-asset blends attractive both as core options and as additions to asset allocation strategies such as target-date funds.

QUESTIONS FOR FIDUCIARIES

1. Does our plan include inflation-hedging assets?
2. What inflation-hedging options are available on the core lineup?
3. Should inflation choices be made available as stand-alone core asset classes, as multi-asset blends, or as an outcome orientation?
4. How are inflation-hedging assets blended into the plan's investment default?

CHAPTER 9

Additional Strategies and Alternatives: Seeking Diversification and Return

Is that all there is?

—Miss Peggy Lee

In 1969, American singer Peggy Lee won the Grammy Award for the Best Female Pop Vocal Performance for her version of the song "Is That All There Is?" Originally written during the 1960s by American songwriting team Jerry Leiber and Mike Stoller, who were inspired by the 1896 story "Disillusionment" (*Enttäuschung*) by Thomas Mann, the lyrics capture a person's disenchantment with life's events. The song begins with a little girl witnessing her family's home burning down, then seeing her first circus—and later, falling in love for the first time. In the song's refrain, with each experience she asks, "I that all there is?" expressing her successive disappointment.

* * *

As we consider DC investment offerings, we may ask the same question, "Is that all there is?" Many DC programs anchor heavily on mainstream stocks and bonds, both in the target-date allocations and the core investment line-ups. Unfortunately, at the time of writing, we are in a low-yield world, with core U.S. bond yields of 1 to 2 percent, which center return expectations on 1 to 2 percent (net of inflation, that's near 0 percent). U.S. stock valuations are similarly high, with dividend yields near 2 percent and cyclically adjusted P/E multiples well above 20x, which, based on history, may mean 10-year future returns of 5 percent or less. Yet, investors don't expect returns of 2 to 5 percent; and many require much more to meet their retirement goals. Where might they turn? In this book thus far, we have discussed the four *pillar* asset classes: capital preservation, fixed income, equities, and inflation-hedging assets. In this chapter, we'll take a look at a fifth pillar—alternative strategies a plan fiduciary may consider to help participants achieve either higher returns or reduced risk—or both—all with a continued focus on our objective of increasing the probability that participants will attain sustainable spending in retirement.

Thus instead of asking, "Is that all there is?" we may ask ourselves, "What are the alternatives to stocks and bonds?" When we say *alternatives*, most may think primarily of less-liquid investment strategies, such as hedge funds and private equity. There are, however, many additional components of the alternatives bucket for DC plans. For our purposes in this discussion of alternatives, we would start by considering *alternative ways to invest* such as, for example, adding a global tactical asset allocation strategy to a core lineup or a blended strategy. Then, we would consider *liquid alternatives* such as multistrategy solutions. Finally, we would take a look at potential *less-liquid alternatives*, such as hedge funds and private equity, while also taking into account the operational and other issues associated with these strategies.

Overall, our mission with alternatives is to find incremental return potential and/or risk diversification away from mainstream stocks and bonds. In the following pages we'll take a look at what alternatives are, why to consider them in DC plans, and consultant views on alternatives. We'll also review alternative investment approaches, consider how liquid and less-liquid alternatives compare, and explore how alternatives may be folded into a DC plan as core assets and/or within blended investment options.

WHAT ARE ALTERNATIVE ASSETS?

A 2013 paper from the Defined Contribution Institutional Investment Association (DCIIA), titled "Is It Time to Diversify DC Risk with Alternative Investments?" focuses on three primary categories of alternatives: *absolute- and total-return, private equity*, and *real estate strategies*. Consultants would add many more alternatives to this set. In our 2014 DC Consulting Support

FIGURE 9.1   Investment Strategies Defined as "Alternatives" by Consultants

Strategies Defined as Alternatives	# of Firms	# of Firms
Hedge funds	41	93%
Private equity	41	93%
Long/short equity	39	89%
Private real estate	39	89%
Absolute return	37	84%
Currencies	31	70%
Infrastructure	27	61%
Commodities	26	59%
Managed volatility	25	57%
Multi-real assets	24	55%
Unconstrained equity	13	30%
Unconstrained bond	12	27%
REITs	11	25%
Tactical asset allocation	9	20%
n = 43		

Source: PIMCO, 2014 Defined Contribution Consulting Support and Trends Survey.

and Trends Survey, we asked consultants to identify which investments they consider to be "alternatives." As shown in Figure 9.1, nearly all respondents (95 percent) identified hedge funds and private equity as alternatives. The vast majority of firms also defined long/short equity (90 percent), private real estate (90 percent), absolute return (86 percent), and currencies (86 percent) within the alternatives set, while a minority added unconstrained equity (29 percent) and bonds (26 percent), REITs (24 percent), and tactical asset allocation (21 percent) to the list.

As you can see, this list is a bit of a hodgepodge, as it includes less-liquid, liquid, and alternative investment approaches. You may also notice that this list includes several of the inflation-hedging asset classes, such as commodities and REITs, that we addressed in Chapter 8. As discussed in that chapter, real assets offer diversification and other benefits relative to stocks and nominal bonds. In this chapter, we'll look at additional ways to add benefit beyond liquid real assets. Given this focus, and as noted in the introduction to this chapter, we will group alternatives into three broad categories: *alternative ways to invest*, *liquid alternatives*, and *less-liquid alternatives*.

A WIDER LENS ON ALTERNATIVES

Let's start with alternative ways to invest. At PIMCO, Asset Allocation Product Manager John Cavalieri and retired Managing Director Sabrina Callin explain in their 2013 paper, "In an Era of Uncertainty and Lower Returns, It's Time for Alternative Approaches," that when "traditional approaches to investing are not going to get investors where they need to go, it's time for alternative approaches." They address alternative ways to invest, telling us that by "investing alternatively," they mean not only selecting nontraditional asset classes and strategies, but also nontraditional approaches to portfolio construction itself, including:

- Alternative asset allocation approaches
- Alternative index-construction processes
- Alternative sources of alpha, or excess return
- Alternative return and risk objectives
- Alternative risk-mitigation tools

The paper addresses the alternative asset allocation approaches and tactical allocation as follows: "The traditional approach to portfolio construction focuses on the percentage of capital allocated to each investment strategy and, collectively, to each asset class or category. The classic example is the 60/40 stock/bond portfolio. However, while such a portfolio may appear balanced, from a risk standpoint the allocation is clearly dominated by equities" (see Figure 9.2).

The authors continue by emphasizing the importance of identifying and allocating portfolio assets based on their risk characteristics:

To truly reap the power of diversification, we believe investors should allocate based on the risk contributions of the assets in their portfolio, not their percent of capital. We find that a focus on risk factors, which are the elemental components of risk within an asset class or strategy, is a more effective approach, enabling better risk targeting and diversification.

In addition, we believe it is important to evaluate the prospective risk/reward trade-off offered by different exposures, and to emphasize those that offer more attractive prospective risk-adjusted returns while still maintaining a diversified portfolio. Approaches that rigidly apply equal weights to portfolio risk exposures, as an

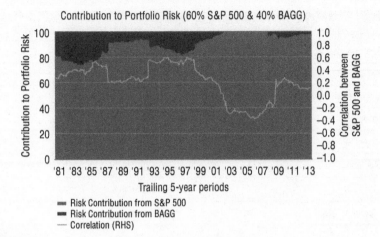

FIGURE 9.2   Equity Risk Dominates Traditional Portfolios

Note: Reflects the contribution of variance from stocks and bonds to the total variance of the 60/40 blend, after adjusting for correlation.

Sources: PIMCO, Bloomberg Finance L.P., and Bloomberg Barclays, as of March 31, 2013.

example, ignore the fluidity of economic conditions and variability of risk-adjusted returns across assets over time.

In DC plans, offering a global tactical asset allocation strategy (GTAA) is a common alternative asset allocation approach and is the additional strategy most recommended by consultants as a stand-alone investment choice (as shown in Figure 9.3). While many plan fiduciaries that offer target-date strategies may believe there is no need to offer another balanced fund in the core, others see many benefits. Not all participants will participate in the target-date strategies, as they may prefer building their own allocations to meet personal risk preferences. Others may desire a manager to actively seek opportunities or manage risk over time based on the global market environment, rather than based on the participant's presumed time horizon. Yet others may find value in a GTAA approach that differs in philosophy and construction from what is offered via the target-date strategies. Plan fiduciaries may thus view a GTAA strategy as appropriate for the "do-it-yourself" participants who desire the diversification relative to other core investment choices—and who may also like how the strategy is diversified to reduce aggregate risk while tapping into additional return drivers.

Stand-Alone		Blended	
Global balanced (e.g., GTAA)	39%	Multistrategy liquid alternative	61%
Multistrategy liquid alternative	27%	Global balanced (e.g., GTAA)	53%
Absolute return	15%	Absolute return	45%
Long/short equity	12%	Hedge funds	39%
Managed futures	10%	Risk parity	34%
Hedge funds	5%	Long/short equity	32%
Private equity	5%	Managed futures	32%
Risk parity	5%	Private equity	26%
None of the above	41%	None of the above	16%

FIGURE 9.3 Consultant Support for Additional Strategies and Alternatives
Source: PIMCO, 2016 Defined Contribution Consulting Support and Trends Survey.

CONSULTANT SUPPORT FOR ADDITIONAL STRATEGIES AND ALTERNATIVES

In our 2016 DC Consulting Support and Trends Survey, nearly half of the respondents (44 percent) recommended that plans include, in their core lineup, a balanced option—and over a quarter (27 percent) suggested an alternatives fund. Notably, when asked what type of additional strategy or alternative they would suggest as a *stand-alone core* option, as mentioned above, global balanced (e.g., global tactical asset allocation strategies or GTAA) topped the list (39 percent), followed by a multistrategy liquid alternative (27 percent). Within a *blended* strategy, respondents showed greater support for these additional strategies, yet flipped the priority—ranking a multistrategy liquid alternative highest (at 61 percent) followed by a global balanced option (e.g., GTAA) (at 53 percent).

In practice, the Plan Sponsor Council of America (PSCA)'s 58th Annual Survey of Profit Sharing and 401(k) Plans reflecting 2014 plan experience shows that 56 percent of all plans offer a "balanced fund/asset allocation" choice, with 13 percent offering an "alternative asset class." (Note: These investment choices are tallied separately from target retirement date/lifecycle fund, target risk/lifestyle funds, TIPS, real estate, and other sector funds.) Across all respondent plans' total assets (reported at $785 billion), PSCA reports an allocation of 5.3 percent to the balanced fund/asset allocation category and rounding to zero in the alternative asset class.

ALTERNATIVE ASSET ALLOCATION APPROACHES: CONSIDERING GLOBAL TACTICAL ASSET ALLOCATION

John Cavalieri, PIMCO Asset Allocation Product Manager, shared the following comments and discussion about GTAA strategies:

The remarkable adoption and growth of target-date funds as the preferred Qualified Default Investment Alternative (QDIA) for DC plans are reflective of a critical investment tenet—recognition that the asset allocation approach is the most important factor in determining the long-term success of an investor. Yet, target-date funds are not for everyone. For participants who opt out of the QDIA and pursue a "do-it-yourself" asset allocation approach, plan sponsors often provide a simplistic range of core investment options—focusing on major asset classes, typically with a domestic emphasis. The aim of the approach is to make it easier for these participants to first, understand the investment options, and second, combine them in a thoughtful asset allocation mix.

Herein lies one of the most significant, though perhaps most subtle, contradictions in DC core lineup design: In seeking to increase simplicity for participants by limiting core investment options to predominantly major, domestic asset classes, plan sponsors may be burdening participants with arguably the most complicated task of all—the asset allocation process! Furthermore, by limiting the diversity of core options, participants may not have sufficient component parts to construct a robust total portfolio. Even when the list of options is sufficiently broad, it remains a very tall task to combine them in a way that properly accounts for their varying return, risk, and correlation characteristics in order to produce a robust portfolio that is aligned with the individual's long-term goals . . . while also reflecting their tolerances for risk.

A way to address this challenge—and to help simplify things for participants who opt out of the QDIA—is to include in the core lineup a (or some) "prebuilt" asset allocation strategy: a global tactical asset allocation strategy (GTAA) option. In addition to increasing simplicity for investors by presenting a prebuilt portfolio solution, a GTAA strategy also can provide the following three benefits, or a "3D advantage":

1. **Diversification:** Most GTAA strategies do not limit themselves to the traditional mainstays of core lineups—cash, core U.S. bonds, and U.S. stocks—but rather incorporate markets far beyond these

(continued)

(*continued*)

mainstream asset classes. This can include allocations to international stock and bond markets, both developed and developing, credit sectors across global fixed income, inflation-related assets, and other alternative sectors. As a result, GTAA strategies can provide "one-stop" access to a diversifying range of markets that typically are not offered in the core investment lineup. Critically, inclusion of these diversifying markets via GTAA strategies can have both a risk-reducing and return-enhancing role.

In terms of risk reduction, the potential for lower average correlations across this wider range of markets can create a more efficient portfolio, helping to lower total volatility. Also, inclusion of a wider range of markets can help hedge risks across a wider range of economic outcomes, for example, variations in global growth rates and inflation regimes.

In terms of return enhancing, the ability to reach beyond the traditional mainstays of core lineups—cash, core U.S. bonds, and U.S. stocks—into markets with lower starting valuations offers the potential for higher prospective returns. This is particularly relevant at the time of writing, given the extraordinary levels of monetary policy accommodation that have pulled forward the returns of these major domestic asset classes, leaving them with forward-looking return prospects that are definitionally diminished. These lower-return prospects can be observed by noting the historically low yields on cash, core bonds, and U.S. stocks alike—and in addition for stocks, historically high levels of earnings and cyclically adjusted price-to-earnings ratios.

2. **Dynamic:** Return prospects across asset classes are "time varying." Put simply, this term refers to the phenomenon that as valuations in a given market increase, long-term return prospects decrease, and vice versa. These time-varying return prospects are even more notable as we write, given a "multispeed" global economy in which individual countries' economic and financial market conditions may exhibit less correlation to each other than in the past. To complement the largely static holdings within most DC plans, a GTAA strategy can also provide one-stop access to tactical flexibility, helping to better navigate risks and emphasize attractive opportunities in seeking better long-term risk-adjusted returns.

3. **Disciplined:** To be sure, the category for asset allocation/GTAA strategies is a heterogeneous one. There are many ways an investment manager can design a multiasset strategy, both in terms of the markets they emphasize and their style of tactical asset allocation inside the strategy. Key to adding value for participants is incorporating only those GTAA strategies that have a clearly defined asset allocation approach and a disciplined execution. This way, plan sponsors know what investment characteristics each GTAA strategy is bringing to their DC plan and can thoughtfully pair them with the balance of core options.

   For example, traditional GTAA strategies are centered on the classic 60/40 stock/bond blend. Others may seek to strategically diversify away from mainstream stocks, emphasizing less-traditional markets. Yet others may offer a real return or inflation-hedging orientation, emphasizing markets with higher correlations to inflation changes. Each of these can have a role in a DC plan—and while they each have multiple moving parts under the hood, when managed in a defined and disciplined manner, they can provide a smoother ride to investors as compared to the "attempt-it-yourself" approach followed by the average participant.

Plan sponsors recognize the need for professionally managed asset allocation approaches within DC plans, as reflected by the tremendous adoption of target-date funds as the QDIA. Participants who opt out of the QDIA risk losing this benefit. As one means of addressing this potential loss, the inclusion of asset allocation/GTAA strategies in the core lineup can help reroute participants back into professionally managed asset allocation solutions, and in so doing, potentially improve long-term outcomes for that segment of the participant base.

BACK TO BASICS: WHY CONSIDER ALTERNATIVES?

The short answer is that broadening the opportunity set, or the set of all possible portfolios that one may construct from a given set of assets, can mean less risk and more performance. In PIMCO's 2015 Defined Contribution Consulting Support and Trends Survey, respondents identified many potential benefits of adding alternative investment choices into a DC plan. Topping this list is "risk mitigation," which was ranked first or second in importance by 69 percent of the consultants. Risk mitigation is followed

DB versus DC Asset Mix—U.S.

Asset class	Asset mix		Returns	
(Ranked by returns)	DB	DC	DB	DC
Stock U.S. Large Cap or Broad	25%	30%	7.7%	7.5%
Small-Cap Stock	6%	8%	8.9%	9.1%
Stock Non-U.S. or Global	24%	8%	6.1%	6.0%
Employer Stock	0%	20%	n/a	9.5%
Fixed Income	32%	10%	6.5%	5.7%
Stable Value/GICs	n/a	17%	n/a	4.5%
Cash	2%	7%	2.8%	2.7%
Real Assets	5%	n/a	9.6%	n/a
Hedge Funds	3%	n/a	6.9%	n/a
Private Equity	4%	n/a	12.1%	n/a
Total	100%	100%	7.6%	6.4%
Number of Observations	3,430	2,143		

FIGURE 9.4 Defined Benefit and Defined Contribution Plan Returns
Source: CEM Benchmarking, representing 19 years from 1997 to 2015.

by the benefits of equity beta diversification, inflation protection, return enhancement, and rising rate protection. As plan fiduciaries consider alternatives, consultants note as "very important to consider" characteristics such as daily valuation (72 percent) and daily liquidity (67 percent). They also underscore the importance of considering whether the alternatives provider is an established organization, has a strategy track record, offers participant communication, and has a reasonable fee level and structure.

While risk mitigation tops the list of benefits, return enhancement is also noted. Comparing defined benefit (DB) plans to DC plan asset allocations, "alternatives" often garner 10 percent or more of the DB allocation yet are largely absent from DC plan allocations. CEM Benchmarking, a global benchmarking company, also reports DB outperformance by more than 100 basis points over the 1997 to 2015 time frame. As shown in Figure 9.4, the asset allocation within DB plans as reported by CEM Benchmarking reflects an allocation to alternatives of 12 percent compared to the DC plan allocation reported by CEM Benchmarking. It is important to note, however, that alternative assets in DB plans are typically "locked up" in private funds—and DC plans, which generally require liquidity, may focus on liquid alternatives that may not present the same return potential.

In their 2013 paper (noted earlier in this chapter), the DCIIA outlines many of the reasons DC plan fiduciaries should consider alternative investments:

Alternative investments provide an important avenue for effectively diversifying the risk in DC plans. By complementing traditional DC offerings, an alternatives strategy can improve a portfolio's efficiency and serve the interests of DC plan participants. The potential benefits of incorporating a well-executed alternatives strategy include:

- *Potential for Improved Total-Return Performance: Including alternative investments within broad portfolios can contribute to improved plan performance for DC participants, similar to that experienced by institutional investors.*
- *Reduced Reliance on Traditional Equities and Bonds: Alternatives enable DC plans to complement the traditional asset classes to which DC participants have historically been exposed.*
- *Incremental Portfolio Diversification: Alternatives can diversify the risk within DC plans' portfolios, allowing for blended investment portfolios with complementary characteristics.*
- *Lower Portfolio Volatility: Alternatives have the potential to lower the portfolio's volatility, through the plan's investment strategies and through lower correlation to traditional asset classes.*
- *Increased Consistency of Returns: The combination of portfolio diversification and lower volatility may allow DC plans to potentially achieve increased consistency of returns over time. These benefits are important considerations for any investor in today's market. Just as institutional investors refine their approaches in order to diversify risk, DC plans can continue to selectively employ similar strategies to improve portfolio efficiency.*

The DCIIA explains how alternatives may improve portfolio efficiency by sharing the Aon Hewitt Efficient Frontier analyses, shown here in Figure 9.5.

Thus the benefits of including alternatives in a portfolio can have material effects for plan participants over time.

* * *

In 2008, we spoke with Ross A. Breman, CFA and Partner, and Rob J. Fishman, CFA and Partner, at investment consulting firm NEPC, about the role of less-traditional, alternative investments within DC plans. We asked them about how plan sponsors are using these types of assets, and they told us:

First, let's define the different product types, and then discuss when and how it's appropriate to use them. We'll also look at how these

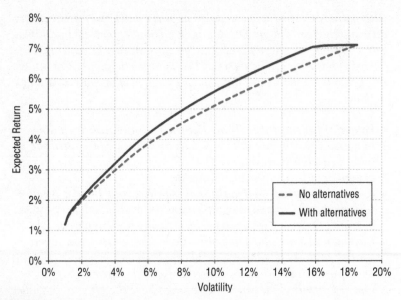

FIGURE 9.5   Alternatives May Improve the Efficient Frontier

Efficient frontier (forward-looking 10 years). For illustrative purposes only. No representation is being made that any account, product, or strategy will or is likely to achieve profits, losses, or results similar to those shown.

Source: Aon Hewitt, as of Q3 2016.

types fit within the framework as potential standalone options. If we consider alternatives in the non-DC sense—say, within a DB plan—we automatically think hedge funds and private equity. The marketplace tends to associate alternatives with high fees, low liquidity, and low transparency.

Today, in DC plans, alternatives refer to less-traditional core offerings. So we could be referring to emerging-market equity, emerging-market debt, commodities, TIPS, [Global Asset Allocation or] GAA, and real estate. These typically are products that are valued daily, offer daily liquidity, and diversify broadly across multiple strategies. In order to identify the roles different types of products play, when we consider alternatives in the DC sense, we often break the category down into two camps: equity alternatives and bond alternatives. Equity alternatives include GAA strategies and unconstrained equity strategies. Bond alternatives include real-return assets such as TIPS and real estate. We should note, however, that while products may fall generally into these broad categories, *products can vary greatly and there are many exceptions to the general themes. While GAA typically might fit in the equity-alternative category, for example, a GAA strategy might look to outperform inflation or a cash benchmark rather than a global equity/fixed benchmark.*

Alternative strategies can help improve the risk-versus-return profile. Equity alternatives include many strategies designed to provide equity-like returns with more bond-like risk levels, which is attractive for a DC plan. Investing in these alternatives gives us a tool to help reduce the traditional equity exposure and improve diversification for participants without sacrificing return potential. We can achieve this particularly well in target-date strategies. But we can't simply instruct DC participants to do it themselves.

Today, the number of alternative products available in the DC world isn't limitless and many DC alternative offerings are expensive. But we also see more competitively priced strategies. While we're willing to pay for liquidity, there's a limit to how high the fees can go before the cost outweighs the benefit.

NEPC returned to this theme with a 2014 paper entitled "The Alternative Route: A Smoother Ride for Defined Contribution Plans." In that paper, the authors note that "now more than ever, alternative asset classes and strategies are deserving of a place in DC plans," commenting:

If plan sponsors and participants are to move beyond traditional stocks and bonds, the question remains, why? In 2008 we said it was to improve return potential and smooth the ride for participants. That core belief hasn't changed. Alternatives are essential to institutional portfolios, and within a participant's portfolio they can improve expected outcomes to and through retirement.

. . . Take for instance the average target-date fund in Morningstar's U.S. Open-Ended 2046–2050 universe, which according to NEPC's 2014 assumptions has an expected return of 6.6 percent, expected risk of 15.5 percent, and a Sharpe ratio of 0.3. When you add an alternatives allocation to this portfolio, the overall expected portfolio rises to 6.8 percent and the risk actually drops to 14.9 percent, with an expected Sharpe ratio of 0.4, indicating more efficient returns.

While 20 basis points of added return may not seem like much, consider a 25-year-old employee with $10,000 in assets today. In 40 years, a 20 basis point different in return results in an 8 percent larger asset balance when they retire at age 65. This figure does not

*give consideration to the expected return in portfolio risk from add-
ing the alternatives allocation, which has the potential to increase
the ending wealth differential by even more.*

LIQUID ALTERNATIVES: TYPES AND SELECTION CONSIDERATIONS

PIMCO Product Managers Justin Blesy and Ashish Tiwari address liquid alternatives in their 2015 paper "Liquid Alternatives: Considerations for Portfolio
Implementation." In the paper, they note that liquid alternatives is "one of the
fastest-growing categories in the investment world." Since 2008, the number
of funds in the United States has tripled to more than 865, and as shown in
Figure 9.6 assets under management have swollen to about $493 billion.

Blesy and Tiwari differentiate and provide the underlying rationale for
liquid alternative *assets* and *strategies* as follows:

> *Alternative asset classes, such as commodities and emerging mar-
> ket currencies, provide exposure to alternative risk premia whose
> returns are driven by different economic drivers than traditional
> portfolios. Alternative investment strategies, on the other hand,
> are typically actively managed and not constrained by traditional
> benchmarks. These strategies may provide diversification through
> the manager's individual security selection (or active management
> alpha), with much less reliance on broad stock and bond expo-
> sures to deliver returns. Examples of alternative strategies include
> absolute return fixed income, equity long/short and managed fu-
> tures [see Figure 9.7].*

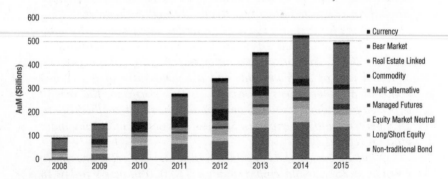

FIGURE 9.6   Liquid Alternatives Come to Main Street
Sources: PIMCO and Morningstar, as of December 2015.

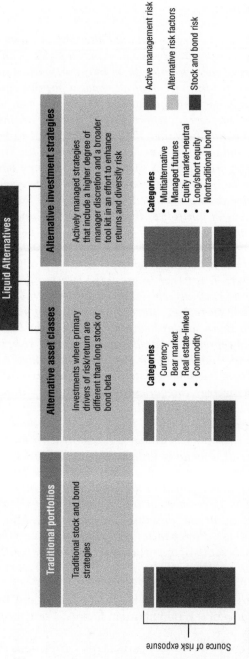

FIGURE 9.7 The Liquid Alternatives Landscape
Source: PIMCO.

Blesy and Tiwari go on to help readers understand the risk characteristics of liquid alternatives:

> *The varied risk characteristics of liquid alternatives—which reflect an array of asset classes, strategies and manager styles—can complicate the process of incorporating them into portfolios. Long/short equity managers, for instance, typically have a positive equity beta (they are normally net long equities [i.e., they will benefit when the price of equities increases]), whereas equity market-neutral strategies target zero equity beta [i.e., they are constructed to have zero systematic risk and thus the same expected return as the "risk-free" rate]. Other categories, such as managed futures, may have more dynamic equity beta; equity beta may be positive in strong bull markets and negative during sustained market sell-offs. Implementing liquid alternatives in portfolios, therefore, requires understanding not only the different categories of strategies but, perhaps more importantly, comprehending how their key risk characteristics vary across different market environments.*
>
> *In many ways, it is easier to grasp the risk profile of alternative asset classes, such as real estate investment trusts (REITs), commodities and currencies, since investment products in these categories often share similar benchmarks. While the benchmarks themselves often represent nontraditional sources of risk, investors have a better understanding of the risks they are taking.*
>
> *However, there is a much greater challenge across most alternative investment strategy categories, as risks can vary dramatically even within the same category. Many of these strategies are often benchmarked to cash or LIBOR [the London Interbank Offered Rate, which is a primary benchmark for short-term interest rates around the world], providing little anchor for the risks in the underlying strategies. For example, a review of the top 10 managers by Assets under Management in the nontraditional bond category reveals significant differences in total volatility and the risk contributions from credit and duration [see Figure 9.8]. Multiple factors can drive these discrepancies, including differences in investment processes, breadth of opportunity set, investment outlook and product structure.*

As plan fiduciaries consider liquid alternatives, Blesy and Tiwari suggest they have a solid grasp of several important factors. These include:

■ Total volatility and mix of risk, particularly correlations to traditional portfolio risks—equity risk and interest rate risk

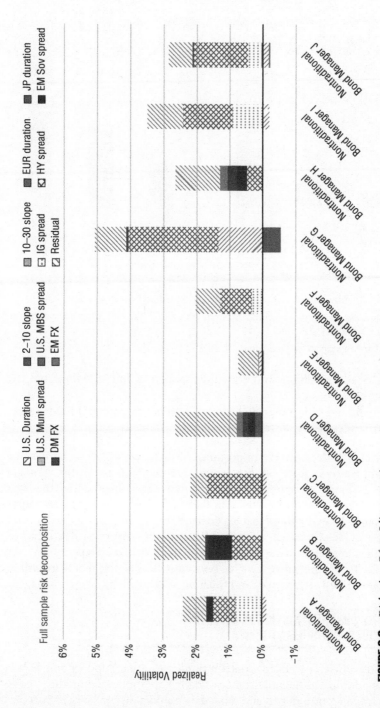

FIGURE 9.8 Risks Are Often Idiosyncratic

Sources: PIMCO and Bloomberg Finance L.P., as of December 31, 2015.

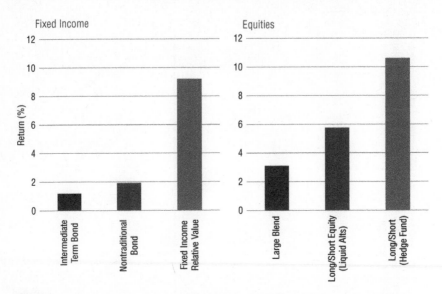

FIGURE 9.9 In Alternative Strategies, Manager Skill Plays an Important Role

Return dispersion: Difference in returns between 20th and 80th percentile managers by category from June 2010 to December 2015.

Source: Morningstar, as of December 31, 2015.

- Historical drawdowns and drawdown potential and how they compare with expectations
- Level and use of leverage and options to identify potential hidden risks
- Performance across different market environments

They also underscore the importance of manager selection, noting that "many alternative strategies are more dependent on portfolio manager expertise—a larger component of returns may derive from active manager decisions, not market returns." They note the return dispersion across alternatives managers may be many times that experienced among traditional fixed-income and large-cap blend managers. Figure 9.9 shows this dispersion. For example, over this time frame return dispersion between the 20th and 80th percentile long/short (hedge fund) equity managers has been more than double that of long/short managers in liquid alternatives and fourfold in large blend equity managers.

IMPORTANT CHARACTERISTICS IN SELECTING ALTERNATIVES: CONSULTANT VIEWS

In our 2015 PIMCO Defined Contribution Consulting Support and Trends Survey, in addition to the importance of daily valuation and liquidity, nearly all of the respondents (96 percent) ranked as "important" or "very important"

FIGURE 9.10 Important Characteristics in Selecting Alternatives

Characteristics of Alternatives	Importance			
	Very Important	Importance	Somewhat Important	Not Important
Daily valuation	72%	20%	7%	0%
Daily liquidity	67%	24%	9%	0%
Established organization	57%	39%	4%	0%
Three-year minimum track record	38%	47%	15%	0%
Participant communication support	36%	38%	19%	8%
Fee level similar to other plan options	32%	40%	23%	6%
Fixed fee structure	21%	53%	23%	4%
"One-stop-shop" multistrategy solution	9%	39%	28%	24%
n = 54				

Source: PIMCO, 2015 Defined Contribution Consulting Support and Trends Survey.

when adding alternatives to a DC plan that fiduciaries hire a manager from an established organization; plus, the vast majority (85 percent) deemed it "important" or "very important" that the alternatives manager provide at least a three-year track record (Figure 9.10).

For their part, Blesy and Tiwari suggest looking for liquid managers with the following key attributes:

- Exceptional and proven *manager experience* (defined as returns generated in a consistent and diversified manner, and strong performance during periods of market shocks)
- A well-defined and repeatable *investment process*
- Depth of research and a demonstrated ability and process to *convert research themes into profitable trades*
- *Understanding of the underlying risk factors* and the ability to dynamically adjust such exposures within the portfolio as warranted
- *Trading efficiency*, often achievable through economies of scale
- A robust *risk management framework*
- Proper *alignment with investor incentives*
- *Ability to clearly communicate* strategies, objectives, and risks to investors
- Regulatory/compliance *processes and experience* in managing mutual funds and ETFs

You'll note that among the important selection characteristics in Figure 9.10 is "participant communication support" which is also noted by Blesy and Tiwari suggesting plans consider the "ability to clearly communicate strategies." While we expect that alternatives are most likely to be blended into custom strategies such as white-label core and target-date funds, it remains important to make available communication materials for participants who seek this information. In addition, consultants believe it is important or very important that alternatives offer a "fee level similar to other plan options" (72 percent), and they also believe that alternatives should have a "fixed fee structure" (74 percent).

Fee levels are a critical consideration for plan fiduciaries. As noted in earlier chapters, the fiduciaries should seek reasonable fees for the investment offerings and other plan services. It's important to consider the fee relative to the expected value—both returns and risk management—that an investment may deliver. Blesy and Tiwari note the significant variance in fees across liquid alternatives. They note that "some managers aggregate third-party strategies, passing through underlying fees to end investors. In contrast, other structures that focus on individual securities may offer lower fees." Figure 9.11 shows a fee comparison for liquid alternatives.

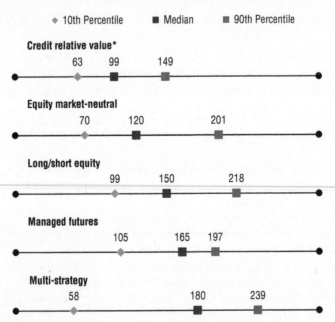

FIGURE 9.11   Liquid Alternatives Fees and Expenses Range Widely

Credit relative value is a subset of nontraditional bond. Fee structures for other investment products and jurisdictions may vary.

Source: Lipper, as of December 31, 2015.

Plan fiduciaries may consider adding liquid alternatives to a DC plan either as a stand-alone investment option or to a blend such as white-label core or custom target-date strategies. As noted in Figure 9.3 at the outset of this chapter, for the stand-alone lineup, consultants recommend a global balanced (e.g., GTAA) strategy (39 percent) or a multistrategy liquid alternative (27 percent).

As mentioned, consultants are far more likely to recommend additional strategies as components of blended strategies. They place multistrategy liquid alternatives at the top of the list with support from nearly two thirds of consultants (61 percent) and this is followed by a global balanced (e.g., GTAA) strategy (53 percent).

ILLIQUID ALTERNATIVES: TYPES AND CONSIDERATIONS

Often referred to as *illiquid investments*, in our view these are best thought of as "less-liquid" alternatives as they typically have less liquidity than daily—ranging from as little as a week to 10-year waiting periods. This category is composed of private market investments such as hedge funds, private debt, private real estate, and private equity. These investments generally are not traded on public exchanges, nor are they valued daily or traded daily. Despite the lack of daily valuation and trading, DC plans can—yet rarely do—include less-liquid alternatives; DC plans that include less-liquid alternatives typically include them in blended strategies such as custom target-date and target-risk/balanced funds.

Reasons to include less-liquid alternatives mirror those discussed above, including added return opportunity, diversification improvement, and volatility reduction. For less-liquid investments, there's another added benefit: an *illiquidity premium*, that is, higher returns in exchange for a longer commitment of capital. In Figure 9.12, in the DCIIA presentation "Capturing the Benefits of Illiquidity," they provide the following overview of hedge funds, private real estate, and private equity along with the key merits of each. Although not included in the DCIIA presentation, private debt is another increasingly important segment of the alternatives opportunity set largely created by bank retrenchment (such as when banks exit certain markets or cease operations in a specific business sector). The key merits for investors include high income, illiquidity premia, and, for some types of debt, low correlations to equity and bonds.

DC plans present a challenge as nearly all are valued each day and also offer participants daily access to transfer out of the investment offered. Notably, while participants have the ability to trade daily, record keepers report that the vast majority do not trade even once a year. Given this reality, many have questioned whether daily valuation and trading are appropriate for DC plans; fiduciaries may ask, "Why are all participants

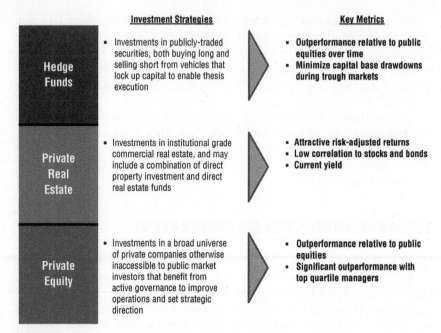

FIGURE 9.12 Overview and Merits of Hedge Funds, Private Equity, and Real Estate Alternatives
Source: DCIIA, "Capturing the Benefits of Illiquidity," September 2015.

paying for daily liquidity when few use or need it?" In the 1980s and early 1990s, DC plans were not valued daily. Instead, most were valued monthly or even quarterly. In PIMCO's 2014 Defined Contribution Consulting Support and Trends Survey, over half of the consultants (53 percent) expected the ability to offer alternatives with greater ease may influence DC plans to move from daily valuation to "some extent" or "a significant extent." Regardless of whether plans shift back to less-frequent valuation, consultants are unlikely to suggest that less-liquid alternatives be added to the stand-alone core lineup. Rather, they are more likely to combine them within the blended strategies.

DCIIA notes that the valuation and trading issues are manageable: There are "numerous precedents for nonmarket pricing methods" and "liquidity needs can be managed as part of a broader allocation." Yet we also learn that the risks in offering less-liquid alternatives are "related primarily to inflexibility during a severe downturn" in the markets. Plan fiduciaries are told that participant-level liquidity is needed through all market cycles, and the importance of communicating and documenting decision-making to "minimize litigation risk" is also emphasized. With the added complexity of selecting and monitoring less-liquid alternatives, plus litigation that has focused largely on fees, in general we anticipate slow adoption of less-liquid alternatives within DC plans. Rather, plans may look to global balanced and liquid alternatives for the sought-after benefits.

CONTRASTING LIQUID ALTERNATIVE STRATEGIES WITH HEDGE FUND AND PRIVATE EQUITY INVESTMENTS

Finally, Blesy and Tiwari contrast liquid alternative strategies with less-liquid alternatives: hedge funds and private equity investments. They comment:

> *Initially, hedge funds and private equity funds were the primary way investors accessed alternative investments. Neither was widely available beyond institutional or accredited individual investors, in part because both typically required large minimum initial investments and lengthy lock-ups and offered little transparency. Relative to these semiliquid and illiquid alternatives, liquid alternatives may provide a number of benefits, including:*

> - *Lower investment minimums*
> - *Daily liquidity in most vehicles*
> - *Improved transparency*
> - *For U.S. investors, simplified tax reporting (typically a 1099, not a K-1)*

> *However, there are trade-offs. Not all traditional hedge fund and private equity strategies can be responsibly offered in a liquid alternatives vehicle. Many require capital lock-ups to align the liquidity provided to clients with the horizon of the fund's investments. Often, this embedded illiquidity premium can offer the potential for more attractive returns than can be achieved in liquid strategies, and in a world of lower-return prospects, this higher return potential may be an attractive benefit of hedge fund and private equity strategies.*

> *It is important to note, though, that several strategy types, including managed futures and equity long/short strategies, increasingly can be implemented in liquid vehicles without a significant reduction in return potential, whereas private real estate, infrastructure and private equity strategies may necessitate reduced liquidity to achieve investment objectives (see Figure 9.13).*

Typical Attributes	Traditional 60/40 Portfolio*	Liquid Public Fund Alternatives*	Private Fund Alternatives
Potential diversification benefits vs. traditional 60/40 portfolio	None	Moderate/high	Moderate/high
Daily liquidity (most vehicles)	Yes	Yes	No
Transparency	High	High	Moderate
Accessibility	Broad	Broad	Accredited investors only
Tax reporting (U.S. investors)	Typically 1099	Typically 1099	Typically K-1
Long/short flexibility	None/limited	Yes	Yes
Potential capture of illiquidity premium	Low	Low	High
Potential capture of nontraditional betas	Low	High	High

FIGURE 9.13 Comparing the Benefits of Various Liquid Alternative Strategies

*Benefits limited to when implementing in an investment product offering the underlying characteristics. An investor should thoroughly review offer documents prior to making an investment decision.

Source: PIMCO.

IN CLOSING

We started this chapter by asking, "Is that all there is?" But as we have seen, for plan sponsors, there is in fact a lot to consider when asking the question "What else?" Alternatives in their various forms have the potential to improve outcomes for participants—especially in a low-return environment for mainstream U.S. stocks and bonds. While we tend to call the various portfolio components examined in this chapter "alternatives" by convention, plan fiduciaries recognize that this is not a category of similar strategies—it is instead a very heterogeneous array of investments. What perhaps unifies them under a single moniker, aside from convenience, is generally *what they don't offer*—dedicated exposures to traditional stock and bond asset classes—and not what they do.

In considering alternatives in DC plans, in our view it is key for plan sponsors to consider, relative to other DC investment offerings, the following attributes that alternatives may bring to a portfolio:

- Ability to add diversification and reduce volatility relative to other DC investment offerings.
- Opportunity to add return, especially through different market environments.
- Liquidity available relative to the plan or blended strategy liquidity needs.
- Valuation frequency and methodology.
- Merits and risks of each strategy type and stand-alone asset.
- Manager skill compared to traditional active strategies and certainly versus passive approaches. To warrant the higher fees associated with these strategies, plan sponsors must have (relatively) greater confidence in the underlying manager's ability to achieve the strategy objectives.

In addition to evaluating the potential alternatives, a plan fiduciary should also consider the plan's ability to stay the course. While diversifying into alternatives may add value across market cycles and, at times, deliver impressive results relative to mainstream stock and bonds, plan fiduciaries are likely to experience concern or even frustration when these strategies lag behind. Fiduciaries will need to manage behavioral tendencies to chase returns for the recent winners, and more importantly avoid "fleeing" from strategies when they lag behind. This chasing and fleeing behavior would assuredly hurt long-term returns as plans would buy high and sell low. You also may hear of adding diversification as a "regret maximization exercise," in that you may regret having any diversification when you don't need it . . .

and then you regret not having more when you do. We hope plan sponsors will look beyond the stocks and bonds to reap the diversification and return opportunities within alternatives.

QUESTIONS FOR PLAN FIDUCIARIES

1. Are there additional investment strategies that may offer risk mitigation or return benefits to plan participants?
2. Should a global balanced (e.g., GTAA) strategy be added to the stand-alone lineup?
3. Should a multistrategy liquid alternatives fund be added to the stand-alone lineup?
4. Is the investment default asset allocation optimal? Would the addition of a global balanced strategy, multistrategy liquid alternatives, or individual liquid alternatives improve potential outcomes?
5. Should less-liquid alternatives such as hedge funds, private real estate, or private equity be considered as additions to blended strategies?

Bringing It All Together: Creating Retirement Income

Retirement Income: Considering Options for Plan Sponsors and Retirees

I advise you to go on living solely to enrage those who are paying your annuities. It is the only pleasure I have left.

—Voltaire

In April 2007, I had the pleasure of interviewing, for PIMCO's DC Dialogue, a friend and former fellow board member at the Financial Planning Association: Susan Bradley, CFP. Susan is a nationally recognized financial planner, esteemed author, and founder of the Sudden Money Institute, which is dedicated to working with individuals to address the emotional and financial impacts of receiving "sudden money." Now, when we think about the idea of sudden money, what normally comes to mind are events such as winning a lottery or receiving a large inheritance—but for most Americans, receiving their retirement savings, such as funds in a defined contribution pension plan, is about as close to lottery winnings or an inheritance as they'll ever get. Yet sudden money in all its forms—from unexpected windfalls to carefully saved retirement accounts—changes lives and adapting to this change requires transition.

In this book thus far, we have focused on how plan sponsors and participants can work to ensure the best outcomes from their DC plans, from the point of view of ensuring those plans are sufficiently funded and designed to provide the retirement income plan that participants will need. But what happens to participants, plan sponsors, and plans at the point of retirement? Should retirees leave their assets in DC plans, roll them over to an individual retirement account (IRA) to invest in capital markets, or buy an annuity to create retirement income? What are plan sponsors' preferences? What are the options to create income in retirement that participants need, and plans should provide? Is the range of existing investment choices appropriate and sufficient?

In this chapter, we will address these questions as we shift our focus from DC plan design for the accumulation years to the *decumulation* or distribution phase—when DC plans may transform to delivering a retirement paycheck. We will focus on what both advisors and consultants have told us is important for retirees. Then we provide suggestions for plan sponsors as they work to retain retiree assets. We suggest an approach and analytics for evaluating the appropriateness of at-retirement target-date or other retiree-intended asset allocation strategies, and close with a discussion of the potential beneficial role of deferred income annuities (i.e., longevity insurance).

ADVISOR AND CONSULTANT RETIREMENT INCOME SUGGESTIONS

As participants get closer to retirement, their financial lives become more complex and thus the importance of individual planning comes sharply into focus. Some plan sponsors make available either internal or external financial planners, via phone or in-person meetings, to help meet individual planning needs. Preretirees can benefit from working with financial planners who are trained not only in investment management, but also broader financial planning issues such as insurance and risk management, tax and estate planning. Susan Bradley notes the importance of providing financial planning as a boost to employee loyalty—as a way to attract talented people and keep them. Ideally, she says, a preretiree has a company professional or financial planner work with them to model retirement scenarios and evaluate the possible paths. The planner may ask, "If we take this option, retire at this point, live in this house, and spend at this level, how long does our money last?" Participants may use scenarios to test whether they are both emotionally and financially ready to retire, as well as the likely longevity of their money. Providing this professional help to support the retirement decision may also benefit the employer to manage their workforce engagement and attrition.

As plan fiduciaries consider offering participants access to advisors, it is important to understand the compensation structure for those advisors who are engaged to provide advice; plans should seek advisors who will act in the best interest of their participants. In April 2017, the Department of Labor (DOL)'s conflict of interest rule is scheduled to become effective. The DOL's intention in putting this rule into place is to help protect investors by requiring all those who provide retirement investment advice to plans and IRAs to abide by a fiduciary standard—putting their clients' best interest before their own profits. To fulfill this fiduciary duty, advisors should make participants aware of the benefit of retaining assets throughout retirement in a former employer's DC plan. While not all DC plans offer cost or invest-ment advantages relative to rolling over to an individual retirement account, at a minimum DC plans provide fiduciary oversight of the investment menu and, in many states, may protect assets from creditors where IRAs may not.

In the DC Dialogue noted above, Bradley discusses the issues retirees face and how they can transition to and remain in retirement successfully. She also considers how plan sponsors can help. Among her suggestions is a call for automated asset allocation or rebalancing choices, as she observes that "people will spend less time managing their money" in retirement. She also advocates offering a diverse set of investment choices, including those that provide inflation protection. Finally, she advises plan sponsors to con-sider offering conservative income-paying investment or annuity choices. Bradley underscores the value plan sponsors can deliver by offering institu-tionally priced investments and group annuity rates, and she is not alone in her suggestions.

In PIMCO's 2016 Defined Contribution Consulting Support and Trends Survey, consultants reported that 51 percent of their clients either actively seek to retain client assets (21 percent) or prefer retaining these assets, but do not actively encourage (30 percent) clients to keep their assets in their plans; only 16 percent of clients prefer retirees move their assets out of the plan. Notably, compared with 2015 survey results, consultants reported a 50 percent higher percentage of clients actively seeking to retain assets in the plans at retirement, up from just 14 percent in 2015 (see Figure 10.1).

The consultants, as with Bradley, also emphasize the importance of offer-ing asset allocation and income-focused strategies in retirement; as shown in Figure 10.2, among investment and insurance retirement income strategies, they actively promote at-retirement target dates (30 percent), cash manage-ment (29 percent), and multisector fixed income (19 percent) strategies.

At-retirement target-date strategies are all the more important given the growing percentage of retiree (i.e., participants aged 60 and up) assets allocated to these strategies. As shown in Figure 10.3, target-date funds as of year-end 2014 captured over 16 percent of assets for participants 60 years of age or older. Combined with balanced funds, these asset allo-cation strategies surpassed stable value assets with 24 percent versus

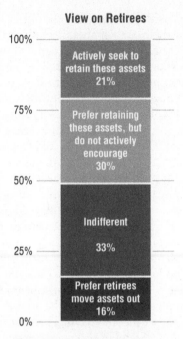

View on Retirees

FIGURE 10.1 Plan Sponsor Attitudes toward Retaining Client Assets at Retirement *Source:* PIMCO, 2016 Defined Contribution Consulting Support and Trends Survey.

21 percent, respectively. If we combine money market assets (2 percent) with stable value (21 percent), the asset allocation strategies still slightly exceed these capital preservation vehicles. We anticipate this trend to continue over the coming decade.

Consultants also generally support managed accounts and a range of insurance solutions for retirement income such as out-of-plan annuities, asset allocation with lifetime income guarantee, in-plan deferred income annuities, and in-plan immediate annuities. (Note that in-plan deferred income annuities may be a component of a target-date fund or a distribution option; in-plan immediate annuities refers to purchasing an annuity at the point of retirement.) Immediate and deferred income annuities can be offered as either a plan distribution option—a qualified plan distributed annuity, or QPDA—or as a rollover to an IRA.

However, the consultants also noted in Figure 10.4 many concerns with in-plan accumulation insurance products, including portability (67 percent), cost (63 percent), and insufficient government support (62 percent).

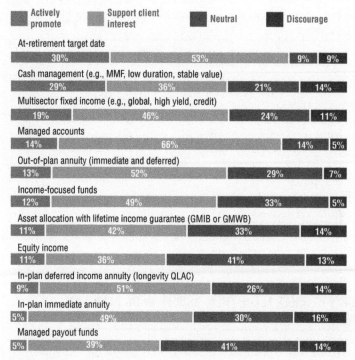

FIGURE 10.2 Consultants Report on Support for Retirement Income Strategies
Source: PIMCO, 2016 Defined Contribution Consulting Support and Trends Survey.

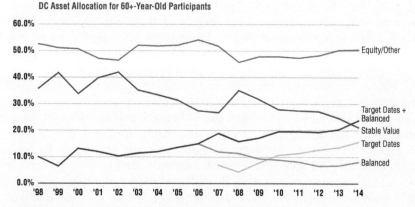

FIGURE 10.3 Retiree Assets May Be Building in Target-Date Strategies
Source: EBRI/ICI Participant-Directed Retirement Plan Data Collection Project, 1998–2014. Available at www.ici.org/research/investors/ebri.

FIGURE 10.4   Consultants Report on Primary Concerns with In-Plan Insurance Products

Primary Concerns with In-Plan Insurance Products

Portability	67%	Operational complexity	35%
Cost	63%	Communication complexity	27%
Insufficient government support (e.g., safe harbor)	62%	Monitoring/benchmarking	25%
		Low interest rate environment	16%
Perception of added liability	40%	Transparency	14%
Insurance company default risk	37%	Selection criteria unclear	10%
Lack of liquidity and control	37%	Lack of insurance company commitment	3%
Lack of participant demand	35%		

Source: PIMCO, 2016 Defined Contribution Consulting Support and Trends Survey.

WHY DON'T RETIREES LEAVE THEIR ASSETS IN DC PLANS AT RETIREMENT?

While advisors and consultants generally agree with the benefits of retaining retiree assets in a DC plan, retirees are often quick to roll their money out of the DC plan—often to higher-priced investment products within a retail IRA. In November 2013, PIMCO dug into why retirees may fail to retain their assets in DC plans once they hit the retirement stage of their investing lifecycle, and we published our results in an article titled "Sponsors Ask Retirees, 'Why Don't You Stay?' Seven Questions for Plan Sponsors." In our paper, we noted that while the term used to describe plan assets leaving as members enter retirement is *leakage*, it may be better termed a *deluge* as every year hundreds of millions of dollars spill out of defined contribution plans. Yet retaining 401(k) participants' assets may yield big cost savings and other benefits, both for sponsors and investors. In an era of increased focus on fees and fiduciary obligations, we suggest that plan sponsors actively consider whether to encourage retirees to stay in their plans. Regardless of the decision, sponsors need to make sure their plans are appropriately structured for retirees.

Plans with more participants and assets generally can benefit by commanding better pricing on investment management and services. According to financial information company BrightScope (www.brightscope.com), in an analysis based chiefly on 2014 government filings, the average total cost for the largest 401(k) plans (those with more than 5,000 participants) was 52 basis points (bps). In contrast, the average cost for the smallest plans, with fewer than 200 individuals, was 107 bps, or more than double the cost in the largest plans. Because they do not share the benefits of scale in purchasing services, it stands to reason that IRA costs may be similar to those of the smallest 401(k) plans. But the cost difference can certainly add up: Compounded over many years, a reduction in fees from 100 basis points to 50 basis points could extend the potential of participants' 401(k)s to provide retirement income by several years.

In addition, retirees who stay in 401(k) plans may access stable value, custom target-date, and other strategies that are not available in IRAs. As noted above, they may also enjoy the investment due diligence and oversight of the plan sponsor fiduciary and as plans that are qualified under the Employee Retirement Income Security Act (ERISA), 401(k)s may offer superior asset protection from creditors for retirees and beneficiaries, at least in some states. (While assets in qualified retirement accounts cannot be pursued in bankruptcy proceedings, outside of bankruptcy the extent to which creditors can pursue assets held in IRAs varies by state.)

Despite plan sponsors' ability to force terminated vested participants out of the plan at age 65, the majority of plans allow retirees to stay. Notably, the larger the DC plan, the more likely retirees will be allowed to retain assets in the plan; two thirds of all DC plans allow retirees to retain their assets in-plan, which rises to 74 percent for plans with more than 5,000 participants. In the July 2014 DC Dialogue interview with Pete Apor, Director of Retirement Services at Fujitsu, he told us about the retirement income projections, planning workshops, and other efforts his company has pulled together to help retirees prepare for and successfully remain in retirement. Among these efforts, Fujitsu works together with the plan's recordkeeper to help retirees understand the benefits of retaining assets in the plan:

> *We have worked with our recordkeeper to help communicate the benefits of remaining in the plan relative to rolling over to an IRA. We tend to retain DC assets for the majority of our retirees. Retirees understand the many benefits of remaining in the plan, including our institutionally priced investment management, custom target-date funds, stable value and the oversight we provide. In an IRA, they would pay a lot more and not have access to funds like stable value. They realize that we evaluate our funds and that, as a fiduciary, we have a responsibility to oversee the plan in a way that they may not get in an IRA or from an advisor.*
>
> *There are other important benefits to keeping assets in an ERISA plan, including creditor protection—although you hope this isn't an issue for retirees. Many who roll to an IRA may not realize they are giving this up. We have had retirees roll assets out of the plan to an*

IRA and then regret doing so, saying "If I could do it over again, I would not have left [the Fujitsu DC plan]." In response, one of our recent plan enhancements now allows terminated participants to roll their money back into our plan. And retirees are rolling money back into the plan from IRAs.

In addition to written communications, our recordkeeper trains its phone reps on how to educate participants on the benefits of remaining in the plan. The reps actively encourage participants to stay in the plan, and also help them to roll in an IRA or other retirement assets. It's critical to find a recordkeeper that's on your side and wants to help retain the assets in the plan. We had to change recordkeepers to get the asset retention support we needed. Our prior recordkeeper seemed to work hard to move assets out of our plan to its proprietary IRAs. At one point, this created negative cash flows in our DC plan. This negative flow stopped once we changed to our current provider, and now we experience positive cash flows. It's been truly refreshing to have a partner that shares our objective to retain assets. They've been extremely helpful.

Of course, retaining assets as well as rolling in IRAs and other retirement assets also provides a lot of benefit to our active participants. They too enjoy the benefits of scale—our lower institutional investment management and service costs.

Unlike Fujitsu, however, most plans do little to actively encourage asset retention. One reason noted anecdotally by some plan sponsors for this is plan sponsors' apprehension about extending their fiduciary responsibilities to additional participants, which is a reasonable concern. However, given that most plans already keep many participants beyond retirement, it is prudent to make sure that plans meet the needs of retirees.

SEVEN QUESTIONS FOR PLAN SPONSORS AS THEY CONSIDER RETAINING RETIREE ASSETS

As plan sponsors consider whether and how to retain retiree assets, we suggest they address seven questions:

1. Will retaining retiree assets improve economies of scale, thus potentially reducing both per-participant administration and investment management costs?

As we have noted, all-in DC fees (i.e., recordkeeping and invest-ment management) tend to fall steadily as the number of partici-pants increases. Whereas the smallest plans (those with fewer than 200 participants) paid 107 bps in fees, those with 200 to 999 mem-bers paid 95 bps, while those with 1,000 to 4,999 paid 77 bps, and the largest plans paid just 52 bps, according to BrightScope. Sponsors should consider the total cost to their plan of retaining retirees. They may also consider whether an annual administra-tive fee and other relevant costs should be paid by retirees.

2. Do participants have access to their money?

For retirees to remain in the plan, they should have the abil-ity to take periodic partial withdrawals and set up installment payments. The Plan Sponsor Council of America (PSCA) reports in their 58th Annual Survey of Profit Sharing and 401(k) Plans (reflecting 2014 plan experience) that only 59 percent of all plans allow partial withdrawals, and about the same percentage (58 percent of all plans) allows installment payments; however, among those with more than 5,000 participants, the figures jump to 69 percent and 67 percent, respectively. Plans that seek to retain retiree assets should ask their recordkeeper about these distribution features.

3. Do you offer sufficient investment choice?

Plan fiduciaries should seek to offer participants sufficient choice as part of their efforts to help meet investment objectives and minimize the risk of large losses. As discussed throughout this book, we believe the core lineup should provide access to the four primary risk pillars: that is, capital-preservation-focused, global fixed income, global equity, and inflation-hedging strategies. In addition, as supported in the results of the 2016 DC Consulting Support and Trends Survey, we believe retirees need appropriate at-retirement target-date strategies and a multiasset fixed-income strategy. In addition to these options, about half of consultants (47 percent) in PIMCO's 2016 Defined Contribution Consulting Support and Trends Survey suggest a brokerage window to pro-vide significant investment flexibility whether restrained to mutu-al funds or open to individual securities as well. (Note: Investment expenses may be higher in the window than the plan; participants should be made aware of this difference and understand that they will bear this additional cost based on the investments they select on the brokerage platform.)

(*continued*)

(*continued*)

4. Does the plan adequately balance risk and return? Among risks to consider, we believe market volatility, sudden shocks, inflation, and longevity should be priorities. These considerations are especially important for the default option, which many participants may blindly trust. It's also essential to consider the core lineup offerings for participants who desire to build their own asset allocation. Given the propensity of participants to allocate assets on an equal-weighted basis (i.e., as discussed in Chapter 3, the "naive diversification" or the $1/n$ assumption in practice), the following questions are key:

■ What is the potential return for the investment?

■ What is the volatility embedded in the investment?

■ What is the risk of loss?

■ How inflation-responsive is the investment?

■ How long may the money last?

(We will address each of these questions in the analytic section later in this chapter.)

5. Is guidance or advice available?

Retirees may need handholding to understand how to structure their investment income at retirement. As discussed, offering access to unbiased financial planners may be desirable as these planners can help address a range of issues—from retirement income and taxation to home ownership, health care insurance, and investments.

Managed account solutions should be evaluated similarly, by asking providers how they would allocate assets for retirees if they had no information other than their age. This allocation and the underlying investment selections should then be evaluated over time. As with any asset allocation or investment choice, the value of the service and reasonableness of the fees must also be evaluated by the plan fiduciary.

6. Can retirees consolidate DC, IRA, and spousal assets into the plan?

Take a look at whether plan rules allow participants to roll-in DC and IRA assets. PSCA reports that while 98 percent of plans allow participants to roll-in profit sharing/401(k) plan balances, only 62 percent accept IRA assets. Does the plan offer Roth accounts that can consolidate external Roth assets and accommodate additional after-tax contributions? A retiree may also want to consider adding a "deemed IRA," which allows contributory IRA assets, as well as spousal IRA assets, to be commingled under the institutional plan umbrella. Deemed IRAs were considered as part of the Economic Growth and Tax Relief Reconciliation Act of 2001 (EGTRRA), and several public plans have rolled out deemed IRAs, as discussed below.

7. Are retirees aware of the ability and value of remaining in the plan?

Naturally, for plan sponsors, communicating the value of your program relative to retail offerings is critical. As noted above, an increasing percentage of plan sponsors actively encourage participants to remain in the plan. In reviewing options to increase retiree assets remaining in the plan, look at how the rollover process is managed, including via a benefit website, a call center, or paper form. Is the retiree being made aware of the value the plan offers? Does the call center help retirees understand its value or encourage the retiree to roll over to an IRA? Consider using webcasts, seminars, and other ways to educate retirees on plan benefits and how to manage assets during retirement.

In PIMCO's 2016 Defined Contribution Consulting Support and Trends Survey, we asked consultants what strategies they thought plan sponsors should take to encourage retirees to retain their assets in DC plans after retirement. The most popular response was "add retirement education/tool," followed by "allow distribution flexibility" and "offer drawdown retirement advice." The results are shown in Figure 10.5—and cover a range of suggestions, from providing direct advice to the preretiree, training plan member staff to encourage retention, and offering a brokerage window. Notably, just 4 percent responded that they do not recommend that plan sponsors encourage retention.

RETAINING A RELATIONSHIP WITH YOUR EMPLOYER IN RETIREMENT: AN INNOVATIVE AND CARING PLAN SPONSOR

In February 2010, we spoke with Georgette Gestely, director of the New York City Deferred Compensation Program about the deemed traditional and Roth IRAs offered within its plan to employees, as well as to retirees

FIGURE 10.5 Consultants Report on What Actions Plan Sponsors Should Take to Encourage Retirees to Retain Their Assets in the Plan

Actions to Encourage Retiree Asset Retention	
Add retirement education/tool	80%
Allow distribution flexibility (e.g., partial and installments)	73%
Offer retirement drawdown advice	66%
Add retiree-focused investment options (e.g., income fund)	61%
Offer one-on-one advice	52%
Allow consolidation of non-plan assets (e.g., IRA roll-in)	48%
Offer insurance/annuity choice	39%
Offer managed accounts	34%
Train call center to encourage retention	25%
Offer brokerage window	14%
Require signature to roll over	9%
None—we do not recommend that plan sponsors encourage retention	4%

Source: PIMCO, 2016 Defined Contribution Consulting Support and Trends Survey.

and spouses. Gestely stands out in the public plan community as a leader in retirement plan design. She explains how her organization set up its deemed IRA programs, and why employees and retirees alike find the programs attractive. We asked her whether her organization encourages participants to remain in the plan after retirement:

> *Yes, we do. Our IRA programs help us do it by enabling partici-pants to consolidate and continue building retirement assets in our institutionally priced programs. From an altruistic point of view, participants may be much better off remaining in our plan than they are moving outside of it because the plan aggregates those par-ticipants' assets with everyone else's. You're not in an individual account but, rather, a deemed IRA within a group plan. Keeping your assets in our plans may be good for all other participants, too, as the plan receives better breakpoints on investment fees when we have more money in the plans.*

In her comments, Gestely emphasized the support that her organiza-tion provides to employees considering retirement, and the importance of educational efforts that accompany the discussions employees have about their plans:

> *Our financial planning department provides seminars on retirement and distribution planning. The seminars walk people through each program offered by the plan, discussing the roles and characteristics—the "different pots of money," as we call them— from pension to Social Security to DC and IRA programs. We help people understand the tax issues as well as how to access their money in retirement. This includes how to make money last throughout retirement.*
>
> *Employees also can obtain program educational materials from the financial planning department that explain the accounts' advantages and differences. People need to take some time to figure out what's best for them.*

Gestely mentioned that the New York City Deferred Compensation Program also provides an online financial planning software tool that helps estimate the amount of money employees may have in retirement: "It's helpful software, especially when employees also attend a retirement planning seminar. We use a program that's customized for our plans and participants." Overall, she emphasized the importance of support and education as participants work their way through the retirement choices they need to make:

> *Education is very important. I can't stress that enough. To make any of this work, you must have in place a robust educational program because it's impossible for people to understand all the benefits, pros and cons of each of the programs. Make sure people don't make any decision until they understand each plan's benefits. It's easy to give this message: People must take time to go through the choices. But you also need education with it.*

MUTUAL BENEFITS: RETAINING RETIREE ASSETS MAY HELP BOTH RETIREES AND PLAN SPONSORS

In summary, our findings (published in our November 2013 "Why Don't You Stay?" paper) are that retaining retirement assets in a DC plan may offer significant benefits to both retirees and other plan participants. Doing so may allow retirees to maintain access to institutional investment strategies and, if the sponsor allows, a drawdown plan that can provide consistent monthly income. For plan sponsors, retaining retiree accounts can increase assets and bolster leverage to negotiate lower fees. This benefits all participants—and may help employers attract and retain workers. By raising retiree awareness of the many benefits of remaining in the plan, more retirees are likely to retain their money in the plan and potentially increase the life of their retirement assets. More retirees will likely respond, "Thank you, I think I will stay."

TURNING DC ASSETS INTO A LIFETIME PAYCHECK: EVALUATING THE DC INVESTMENT LINEUP FOR RETIREE READINESS

For retirees who "stay"—that is, keep their assets in the DC plan—they likely will need help in creating a lifetime income stream. In our 2015 DC Research paper, "Turning Defined Contribution Assets into a Lifetime Paycheck: How to Evaluate Investment Choices for Retirees," we suggest an approach for evaluating the DC investment lineup for retiree readiness.

We note that to generate steady and sustainable retirement income—that is, a lifetime paycheck—retirees seek opportunity for return as well as the ability to manage specific risks, chief among them: market, longevity, and inflation risk. Each imposes unique demands on a retiree's portfolio.

- Managing *market risk* requires structuring an investment portfolio to seek retirement income with stable payouts and minimal disruption from market shocks.
- Managing *longevity risk* requires assessing how long assets might last.
- Managing *inflation risk* requires populating a portfolio with assets that seek to keep pace with inflation.

We propose a set of measures to evaluate portfolios on their appropriateness to retirees' needs:

1. Correlation to retirement liability: How well does the strategy correlate to the PIMCO Retirement Income Cost Estimate (PRICE)?
2. Information ratio relative to retirement liability: What is the information ratio relative to PRICE?
3. Downside risk: What level of value-at-risk (VaR) is appropriate given a retiree's risk capacity?
4. Asset longevity: How long are assets likely to remain during the distribution phase?

5. Inflation beta: To what extent is a retiree's account likely to keep pace with inflation and retain purchasing power?

In the analysis that follows, we examine four strategies. First, we take two approaches: target-date (at-retirement vintage) and fixed-income strategies. For each of these two approaches, we look at two strategies: For target-date funds, these are the Market Average and the Objective-Aligned glide paths (at-retirement vintage); for diversified fixed-income strategies, we model the Barclays Aggregate Bond Index and a multisector bespoke blend of major U.S. and non-U.S. bond indexes. This gives us a total of four strategies to evaluate, as outlined in Figure 10.6.

The concept of the PIMCO Retirement Income Cost Estimate (PRICE) is discussed in Chapter 2. In short, the PRICE methodology proposes that the cost of retirement can be defined as the amount an individual must pay to buy an annuity that provides lifetime income sufficient to maintain his or her lifestyle during retirement. Interest rates, in turn, will largely determine the cost.

Figure 10.7 shows the correlation of the four retirement income strategies noted in Figure 10.6 to the objective of securing retirement income as defined by PRICE. Between the target-date strategies, the Objective-Aligned approach correlates better than the Market Average glide path. Between the diversified fixed-income strategies, the Barclays U.S. Aggregate Index has a slightly higher correlation than the multisector bond portfolio.

Next, we modeled how well each of these four strategies perform relative to PRICE, including excess return, tracking error, and information ratio. Information ratio is basically defined as excess return divided by tracking error. (See Figure 10.8.) It is a measure of the risk-adjusted return. Given the amount of risk taken (measured by tracking error), as the information ratio climbs, so does the excess return of the portfolio. Given the amount of excess return, the higher the information ratio, the lower the tracking error of the portfolio. Between the target-date strategies, the Objective-Aligned glide path (at-retirement vintage) had a higher information ratio than the Market Average glide path (at-retirement vintage). For the diversified fixed-income strategies, the multisector bond portfolio had a higher information ratio.

To measure potential loss, we modeled risk exposure by assessing VaR at the 95 percent confidence level (VaR estimates the minimum expected loss at a desired level of significance over 12 months). As Figure 10.9 shows, among the target-date strategies, the Objective-Aligned glide path has a similar downside risk compared to the Market Average glide path. For the diversified fixed-income strategies, the multisector bond strategy has slightly more downside risk than the Barclay's U.S. Aggregate Index.

FIGURE 10.6 Asset Allocations: Target-Dates (At-Retirement Vintage) and Diversified Fixed Income

Asset Class	Target-Date at Retirement Vintage		Diversified Fixed Income	
	Market Average Glide Path (At-Retirement Vintage)	Objective-Aligned Glide Path (At-Retirement Vintage)	Barclays U.S. Aggregate Index	Multisector Bond
Cash	8.4%	0.0%	0.0%	0.0%
Short-term fixed income	0.0%	0.0%	0.0%	0.0%
U.S. fixed income	30.4%	18.0%	100.0%	20.0%
Long treasuries	2.6%	7.0%	0.0%	0.0%
Global bond	1.3%	3.0%	0.0%	0.0%
Global bond ex USD	0.0%	0.0%	0.0%	20.0%
Global credit	0.0%	0.0%	0.0%	20.0%
Emerging market bonds	1.1%	0.0%	0.0%	20.0%
High yield	4.9%	15.0%	0.0%	20.0%
TIPS	6.0%	10.0%	0.0%	0.0%
Long TIPS	1.8%	7.0%	0.0%	0.0%
Commodities	1.0%	2.0%	0.0%	0.0%
Real estate	1.6%	2.0%	0.0%	0.0%

U.S. large-cap equities	23.8%	19.0%	0.0%	0.0%
U.S. small-cap equities	5.7%	3.0%	0.0%	0.0%
Non-U.S. equities	8.8%	8.0%	0.0%	0.0%
Emerging market equities	2.6%	6.0%	0.0%	0.0%
Sum	100.0%	100.0%	100.0%	100.0%

Objective-Aligned Glide Path is represented by PIMCO Glide Path. U.S. large cap: S&P 500 Index; U.S. small cap: Russell 2000 Index; Non-U.S. equities: MSCI EAFE Total Return, Net Div Index; Emerging market equities: MSCI EM Index; Real estate: Dow Jones U.S. Select REIT TR Index; Commodities: Bloomberg Commodity Index; Global credit: Barclays Capital Global Credit Hedged USD Index; High yield: BofA Merrill Lynch U.S. High Yield, BB-B Rated Constrained Index; Emerging market bonds: JPMorgan Government Bond Index—Emerging Markets Global Diversified (Unhedged); Global bond: JPMorgan GBI Global Index (USD Hedged); Global bond ex-USD: Barclays Global Aggregate ex-USD (USD Hedged) Index; U.S. fixed income: Barclays U.S. Aggregate Index; TIPS: Barclays U.S. TIPS Index; Long treasuries: Barclays Long-Term Treasury Index; Long TIPS: Barclays U.S. TIPS: 10 Year+ Index; Short-term fixed income: Barclays 1–3 Year Government Index; Cash: BofA Merrill Lynch 3-Month Treasury Bill Index.

Multisector bond consists of: 20 percent Barclays U.S. Aggregate Index; 20 percent Barclays Global Aggregate ex-USD (USD Hedged) Index; 20 percent Barclays Capital Global Credit Hedged USD Index; 20 percent BofA Merrill Lynch Global High Yield BB-B Rated Constrained Index; 20 percent JPMorgan EMBI Global Index

Market Average Glide Path is as of September 30, 2015 and Objective-Aligned Glide Path is as of December 31, 2015.

Sources: PIMCO and NextCapital.

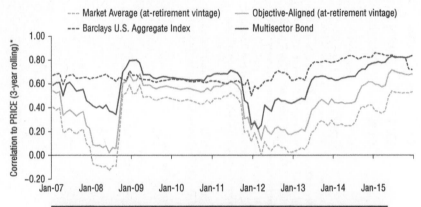

Retirement Income Strategies	Average Correlation
Market Average Glide Path (at-retirement vintage)	0.38
Objective-Aligned Glide Path (at-retirement vintage)	0.51
Barclays U.S. Aggregate Index	0.66
Multisector Bond	0.65

FIGURE 10.7   Four Retirement Income Strategies and Their Correlation to PRICE

*Inflation-adjusted historical returns of the strategies were used to calculate the correlation to PRICE. PRICE is calculated as the discounted present value of a 20-year annual income stream using the historical zero-coupon U.S. TIPS yield curve.
Hypothetical example for illustrative purposes only.

Sources: PIMCO, Bloomberg Finance L.P., Haver Analytics, NextCapital, as of December 31, 2015.

February 2004 - December 2015*	Target-date (at-retirement vintage)		Diversified fixed income	
	Market Average Glide Path (at-retirement vintage)	Objective-Aligned Glide Path (at-retirement vintage)	Barclays U.S. Aggregate Index	Multi-sector bond
Excess return (vs. PRICE)	2.7%	3.2%	1.6%	2.6%
Tracking error (vs. PRICE)	8.2%	7.5%	5.6%	5.6%
Information ratio	0.33	0.43	0.29	0.46

FIGURE 10.8   Four Retirement Income Strategies: Excess Return versus Tracking Error Relative to PRICE

*Period reflects availability of zero-coupon TIPS curve data from Haver Analytics. PRICE is calculated as the discounted present value of a 20-year annual income stream using the historical zero-coupon U.S. TIPS yield curve.
Hypothetical example for illustrative purposes only.

Sources: PIMCO, Bloomberg Finance L.P., Haver Analytics, NextCapital, as of December 31, 2015.

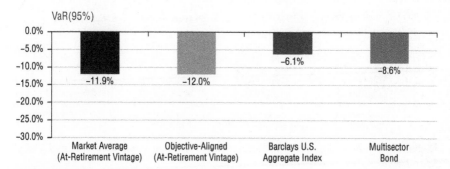

FIGURE 10.9 Four Retirement Income Strategies: Downside Risk (VaR 95 Percent)

Hypothetical example for illustrative purposes only.

Sources: PIMCO and NextCapital, as of December 2015.

EVALUATING PORTFOLIO LONGEVITY

How long might one's money last? To answer this critical question, we modeled the distribution phase to evaluate the likely life of the assets. We assume participants begin retirement at age 65 with an account balance of $680,000 and withdraw 50 percent or 30 percent of a final salary of $74,500. Figures 10.10 and 10.11 illustrate the projected longevity of assets at 95 percent and median confidence for final salary withdrawal levels of 50 percent and 30 percent respectively.[1]

We find that the Objective-Aligned (at-retirement vintage) Glide Path has the same asset longevity under the 95 percent confidence level and

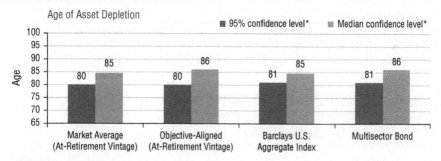

FIGURE 10.10 Asset Longevity in Retirement: 50 Percent Final Salary Annual Withdrawal Rate

As of December 31, 2015.

Hypothetical example for illustrative purposes only

*Based on percent confidence interval of a distribution scenario analysis in the post-retirement decumulation phase.

Sources: PIMCO and NextCapital.

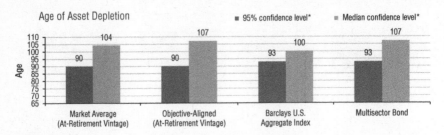

FIGURE 10.11   Asset Longevity in Retirement: 30 Percent Final Salary Annual Withdrawal Rate

As of December 31, 2015.

Hypothetical example for illustrative purposes only.

*Based on percent confidence interval of a distribution scenario analysis in the post-retirement decumulation phase.

Sources: PIMCO and NextCapital.

higher asset longevity under the median confidence level than the Market-Average glide path (at-retirement vintage) for both 50 percent and 30 percent of final salary annual withdrawal rates. The multisector bond portfolio has the same asset longevity as the Barclays Aggregate U.S. Index under the 95 percent confidence level and higher asset longevity at the median confidence level, for both 50 percent and 30 percent of final salary annual withdrawal rates.

As to inflation responsiveness (i.e., "inflation beta"),[2] we believe asset prices are much more sensitive to inflation surprises than actual levels of inflation. Asset classes with a positive beta to inflation surprises[3] have historically tended to perform well, thus preserving purchasing power.

As Figure 10.12 shows, for the target-date (at-retirement vintage) strategies, the Objective-Aligned glide path had a slightly higher inflation beta than the Market Average glide path. Among the diversified fixed income strategies, the multisector bond portfolio had a higher inflation beta.

TURNING DEFINED CONTRIBUTION ASSETS INTO A LIFETIME INCOME STREAM: HOW TO EVALUATE INVESTMENT CHOICES FOR RETIREES

Retirees may benefit from building a retirement income stream from their DC plan, including access to institutional investments, fiduciary oversight, and attractive pricing. For retirees to retain assets in-plan, though, they need appropriate investment choices: that means strategies designed to keep pace with the real cost of retirement, reduce the risk of significant loss, and stay ahead of inflation. Plan fiduciaries should evaluate these strategies relative to retiree needs.

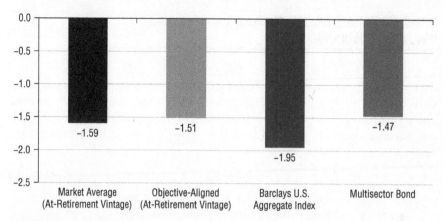

FIGURE 10.12   Four Retirement Income Strategies: Inflation Beta*

Hypothetical example for illustrative purposes only

*Inflation beta represents sensitivity of asset class excess returns (over the "risk-free" rate) to inflation surprises (realized inflation minus Philadelphia Fed Survey inflation forecast), i.e., when inflation surprises by +1 percent, an asset with an inflation beta of 1.5 is expected to have an excess return of 1.5 percent (all else equal); based on quarterly rolling annual data from 1973 to 2015. These numbers are estimated over a one-year horizon; longer term, we expect the numbers to be less negative or even positive.

Sources: PIMCO and NextCapital.

Our analysis shows that an Objective-Aligned glide path (at-retirement vintage) is superior or similar to the Market Average glide path (at-retirement vintage) across all measures analyzed, including in correlation to the cost of retirement (PRICE), risk-adjusted performance, downside risk, asset longevity in retirement, and inflation beta. In addition, our analysis demonstrates that compared to the Barclays U.S. Aggregate Index, a multisector bond strategy may provide higher return, greater asset longevity, and higher inflation protection, albeit with slightly higher downside risk.

In addition to the evaluation factors presented, and as discussed in Chapter 3, we encourage plan fiduciaries to carefully consider the use of active versus passive investment management. As noted, consultants in PIMCO's 2016 Defined Contribution Consulting Support and Trends Survey underscored the importance of active management for all asset classes except U.S. large-cap equity. Retirees may benefit from the potential for increased return opportunity and reduced risk by selecting actively managed target-date and fixed-income strategies. Sponsors also may consider target-date strategies that embed downside hedging intended to guard retiree assets against a sudden market downturn.

GUARDING RETIREE ASSETS AGAINST A SUDDEN MARKET DOWNTURN: SEQUENCING RISK

In December 2013, DC Dialogue interviewed (and updated at time of writing) Michael E. Drew, PhD, Professor of Finance at Griffith University and Director of Drew, Walk & Co. in Australia, about managing asset allocation and risk for preretirees and those in retirement. Professor Drew commented on sequence of return risk and how this must be a concern for retirees as follows:

> When folks from age 50 to 75 have the same asset allocation, this raises concerns about the sequence of returns, as the path may have a dramatic impact on retirement outcomes. As our DC system matures, we need to think about portfolio construction with an eye on retirement income. Recent history has shown us the impact of experiencing returns that have a poor sequence, particularly towards the end of the accumulation phase and early in the distribution phase.

When asked whether he would suggest insurance solutions, and the purchase of annuities in particular, Professor Drew responded:

> Yes. I think it's a building block—one of the prudent ways to manage the risks we have in front of us and the time horizons we have. Building blocks like deferred annuities and mortality pooling are also an important part of the conversation, particularly when we're talking about longevity risk.
>
> For many people, it has to be a combination of these solutions. Some form of insurance (depending on the price), some sensible asset allocation and, critically, how we can frame for people the different liabilities they will face over different time horizons. And that's the really difficult piece. In the accumulation phase, at least you have (hopefully) some idea of when someone's going to retire. The challenging part within the income phase is the largely unknown nature and timing of health and aged-care needs and, obviously, death.
>
> So this is a very complex problem. We need to use different building blocks to provide folks with a happy, healthy, sustainable retirement experience. The building blocks needed to meet one individual's needs are likely to differ from those needed for the next person.

The professor goes on to encourage plan fiduciaries to help retirees and to remind us all that there is no single "right solution":

> *The more work we've done with DC plan providers, with invest-ment managers and policy makers, the more we've seen the need for fiduciaries to assist plan participants with safe passage through the retirement risk zone, I think for me that is the key takeaway.*
>
> *We need to keep in mind that there is no single right solu-tion, no silver bullet. We cannot take a deterministic, static frame to the DC challenge. Our participants face a dynamic path, one where what's considered safe and risky changes over their lifetime. We need our DC plan design, communications, contributions and investment management working in concert to achieve a sustain-able level of retirement income for our participants. And if we can have our risk management clearly informed by the outcomes we're trying to achieve, that is a very positive step forward.*

WAYS TO MANAGE MARKET AND LONGEVITY RISK . . . WITHOUT ADDING IN-PLAN INSURANCE PRODUCTS

There are many approaches and products that may help plan fiduciaries manage market and longevity risk. Some insurance products such as a vari-able annuity with a living benefit feature bring both market shock protection and longevity insurance into a single solution. As noted earlier, consultants raise many concerns with offering these accumulation insurance solutions in-plan; however, they are generally supportive of out-of-plan income annu-ities, particularly deferred annuities. We suggest that plan sponsors first con-sider capital market methods to manage market risk, and second consider making available out-of-plan immediate and deferred income annuities to manage longevity risk.

We have discussed the importance of asset and risk-factor diversifica-tion to minimize risk. Unfortunately, in a financial crisis, often these risk-minimization approaches aren't sufficient to protect retiree assets. To guard against the risk of loss during a sudden market downturn, plan fiduciaries may consider target-date and other investment strategies that include "tail-risk hedging" to their basket of risk management approaches. These strate-gies consist primarily of selectively acquiring options on the various indices that broadly track the assets in a portfolio; these hedges, in turn, may be best purchased during noncrisis times when they are relatively inexpensive. For example, purchasing long-dated out-of-the-money put options on equity

Major Financial Crises since 1980

1982	Mexico defaults on bonds, leading to international debt crisis
1987	Black Monday, Dow drops 22.6% in one day
1989–91	United States S&L and Latin American debt crises
1992–3	European Monetary System crisis
1994–5	Mexican peso crisis, requiring $50 Bn U.S. guarantee
1997–8	Asian financial crisis, requiring $40 Bn IMF bailout
1998	Russian default and LTCM
2001–2	Argentine default, dot-com bust, Sept 11 terrorist attacks
2007–9	Financial market meltdown

10-YEAR ANNUALIZED RETURN FACTORING A 10TH "BAD YEAR"

Portfolio return for nine "good years"	–20%	–25%	–30%
8%	4.8%	4.1%	3.4%
10%	6.5%	5.9%	5.1%
12%	8.2%	7.6%	6.9%

One "bad year" can erase the gains from many "good years"

FIGURE 10.13 Extreme Events Occur More Often Than "Normal" Risk Models Predict

Hypothetical example for illustrative purpose only.

Sources: Bloomberg Finance L.P. and PIMCO.

indices, such as the S&P 500, on an ongoing basis can provide investment-based hedges against equity factor risk (the risk associated with movements in the broad equity market). The intent of tail-risk hedging is not to provide protection against frequent small to medium downswings in the market, but rather to shield against the rare but catastrophic events (Figure 10.13) that can derail retirement security. In general, tail-risk hedging is a cost to the overall portfolio; the pricing of the hedges can be dynamic. It is important for plan fiduciaries to understand the potential impact of the actual pricing of the hedges on a portfolio's return.

LIVING BEYOND 100: PLANNING FOR LONGEVITY

PIMCO's November/December 2015 DC Dialogue focused specifically on the issue of longevity, as we interviewed Professor Joshua Grill, PhD; Associate Professor, Department of Psychiatry and Human Behavior; Director of Education, Institute for Memory Impairments and Neurological Disorders; and Associate Director, Alzheimer's Disease Research Center, University of California–Irvine, on the issue of living beyond 100 years of age. Professor Grill comments that:

> *Unlike any other time in history, people are living longer, healthier lives. Medical science has made incredible strides toward reducing*

*major causes of death, such as stroke and heart disease as well as some
cancers. As a result, the human lifespan continues to increase. If the
pace continues, we expect that over half of the children born this century will celebrate their 100th birthday. We anticipate that by 2050,
the number of Americans age 85 or older will quadruple to 21 million.*

The biggest challenge for retirement income planning posed by an
aging population, according to Dr. Grill, is that of dementia, which he
defined for us as "a clinical phenomenology whereby a person has cognitive
impairment—problems with the way they think—that prevents them from
living life the way they once did." The issues posed by dementia are wide-
ranging and carry significant risk for the success of retirement income
planning through the life span, particularly in the later years for the population who reaches an advanced age:

*People over 65 years of age control a growing percentage of defined
contribution assets and significant additional wealth. As you can imag-
ine, cognitive decline can inhibit sound financial decision-making.
Unfortunately, the elderly are often unaware of diminishing cog-
nition, which may place them at greater risk of making financial
errors or, worse, may open them to fraud risk. Retirement professionals can help reduce these risks.*

*Health care costs are also a significant factor for retirees' re-
tirement planning as well as for employers. [Alzheimer's Disease
International] reports that the worldwide cost of dementia exceeds
$600 billion annually. Covering this escalating expense may fur-
ther increase health and long-term care insurance premiums. Plus,
in most countries, an increasing burden is falling on the younger
working-age populations, as fewer workers support the growing retired population. Providing care for elder loved ones certainly will
add to the retirement savings challenge for the younger populations. There are many issues.*

Dr. Grill also provided some closing words of advice for how retirees
and their loved ones can plan for the potential of diminished mental capacity, including the possibility of dementia, in and through retirement:

*Early in retirement or even prior to retirement, when cognitive abili-
ties are intact, is the best time to plan for managing both medical
and financial decisions. Financial and legal professionals can help
with writing a power of attorney and an advance health care directive, along with other important documents that capture the retiree's*

wishes. Again, the earlier these concerns are addressed, the more the individual can be involved in making sound decisions for their future.

For retirement income professionals, including DC plan sponsors and employers, Dr. Grill advises that "An ounce of prevention is worth a pound of cure":

Professionals can urge or incentivize employees and clients to put plans in place for old age while they are still cognitively healthy. It's best to plan for the worst and hope for the best. If the unthinkable happens, you want everything in place. As people near retirement, we should ask, "Do you have a durable power of attorney? Do you have an advance health care directive? Do you have a living will and trust? Do you have long-term care insurance?"

Employers and insurers can also offer incentives to stay active and healthy. For instance, people can be offered reduced insurance costs if they walk 10,000 steps a day and keep up routine wellness visits. These incentives are expected to cost less than the cost of caring for those who become diseased. Preventive medicine is the way of the future.

MANAGING LONGEVITY RISK: CONSIDERATIONS FOR BUYING AN ANNUITY

Employers also may consider making an institutionally priced annuity purchase program available to retirees. This could enable retirees to access immediate and deferred income annuities. Retirees may gain greater comfort in managing longevity risk by purchasing a deferred annuity that begins paying income, for example, when the retiree reaches age 85. A deferred annuity may allow the retiree to shorten their investment horizon and possibly increase installment payouts. Combining an objective-aligned target-date strategy or a multisector fixed-income strategy with a deferred annuity may create a more secure lifelong retirement income stream.

IMMEDIATE AND DEFERRED ANNUITIES: WHY OUT-OF-PLAN MAKES SENSE

In PIMCO's 2016 DC Consulting Support and Trends Survey, respondents placed "out-of-plan annuities" as most desirable among the insurance-related retirement income choices. Such programs allow employees and retirees to receive competitive bids from multiple insurance companies for immediate or deferred income annuities (DIAs) or longevity insurance (more information on these types of annuities below). Employers may be able to make such programs available through their DC plan record keeper, but without adding the annuity income products as a plan distribution option. Rather, the employer makes available the program benefits, including competitive institutional pricing, and does so without taking on the fiduciary oversight required for insurer selection.

These platforms may offer access to two or more types of annuities, as defined by Hueler Income Solutions®:

> **Immediate Income Annuity.** *A long-term contract between an annuitant and an insurance company for which the annuitant pays a lump sum premium to the insurance company. The insurance company converts the assets into a stream of guaranteed monthly income payments for life or a specified fixed period of time. An Immediate Income Annuity provides income immediately after the premium is received, typically, within 30 days from the date of deposit; however, the annuitant can choose to defer payments for up to 12 months after the date of purchase.*
>
> **Deferred Income Annuity with Death Benefit.** *A long-term contract between an annuitant and an insurance company for which the annuitant pays a lump sum premium payment to the insurance company and the insurance company converts the assets into a stream of guaranteed monthly income payments for life or a specified fixed period of time. A Deferred Income Annuity enables the annuitant to defer income payments for as little as 13 months or up to 40 years. Prior to the income start date, the Death Benefit would be a return of premium. After the income start date, the Death Benefit is determined by the annuity type selected at the time of purchase.*
>
> **Deferred Income Annuity with no Death Benefit ("Pure Longevity Insurance").** *A long-term contract between an annuitant and an insurance company for which the annuitant pays a lump sum premium payment to the insurance company and the insurance company converts the assets into a stream of guaranteed monthly income payments for life. Currently, the only start date available for a Deferred Income Annuity without a Death Benefit through the Income Solutions® platform is on the annuitant's 85th birthday (Pure Longevity Insurance). There is no return of premium to beneficiaries should the annuitant(s) pass away before the income start date.*

Insurance providers may offer participants a range of features, such as a cash refund, joint and survivor benefits at specific percentages, fixed period, and CPI-linked adjustments. The participating companies are often willing to competitively bid based on the desired contract type and features. Prior to 2014, buying longevity insurance or a Deferred Income Annuity within a tax-deferred IRA or DC plan posed a problem given the required minimum distribution rules that compel payments to begin at age 70 years and 6 months. (Required Minimum Distributions, or RMDs, are amounts that the U.S. federal government requires one to withdraw annually from traditional IRAs and employer-sponsored retirement plans.) To address this problem, the Treasury issued regulations under the Code of Federal Regulations (CFR) 1.401(a)(9)-6, declaring that as long as a longevity annuity meets certain requirements, it will be deemed a "Qualified Longevity Annuity Contract" (QLAC) and the contract value will be automatically exempt from the RMD calculations (beginning at age 70 years and 6 months). Hueler Income Solutions defines a QLAC and requirements as follows:

> **Qualified Longevity Annuity Contract (QLAC).** *A Deferred Income Annuity (DIA) with or without a Death Benefit can be designated as a Qualified Longevity Annuity Contract (QLAC). The income start date for a DIA QLAC with a Death Benefit must be after the age of 70 years and 6 months, no later than the first day of the month following the annuitant's 85th birthday. The only available income start date for a DIA without a Death Benefit is on the annuitant's 85th birthday.*
>
> *The premiums per individual are limited to the lesser of $125,000 (lifetime) or 25 percent of your total IRA balances (excluding Roth IRAs and inherited IRAs) as of December 31st of the year prior to purchase. Dollars from either IRAs (excluding Roth IRAs and inherited IRAs) or qualified accounts can be used to fund a QLAC. It is the annuitant's responsibility to ensure QLAC premium limitations are met.*

Today, longevity insurance can be purchased as a qualified plan distribution option (QPDA) or through an IRA rollover. In order to qualify for an IRA rollover, the regulations currently require participants to have opened the IRA in the preceding year and have the appropriate balance to meet the purchase requirements. These requirements have the unfortunate unintended consequence of subjecting the remaining balance (e.g., $375,000 if purchasing a $125,000 QLAC) to retail investment fees—thus we encourage Treasury to amend its ruling so that an IRA QLAC may be purchased directly from the plan.

In our view, offering plan participants the opportunity to purchase income annuities (whether deferred or immediate) allows them to benefit from transparency and competitive bidding while minimizing the fiduciary oversight of such offerings. Keep in mind that although the purchase is made out-of-plan and thus out of the fiduciary oversight[4] of the plan, the participant still benefits from the institutional pricing and the ability to tap DC assets. Given that the annuities pay directly to the participant from the insurance company, holding the contract as an individual outside the plan may make sense, as this direct payment is the simplest option. As shown in Figure 10.14, employees or retirees may gain many of the same benefits of access to an in-plan accumulation annuity program as they would by being offered access to an out-of-plan annuity purchase platform; notably, the latter requires the employer, not the ERISA plan fiduciary, to select and offer the program.

Another consideration for employers is to make annuity purchase programs available within their voluntary health and welfare benefits offerings. As employees make decisions about health, life, disability, and long-term care insurance, that may also be the time to consider whether to purchase longevity insurance.

Decision Factor	In-Plan Accumulation	Out-of-plan
Institutional pricing	Yes	Yes
Individual competitive bidding	No	Yes
Portability	Complex	Yes
Communicated via benefit platform	Yes	Yes
Fiduciary oversight	Yes	No
Employee/retiree product support	Yes	Yes

FIGURE 10.14   Out-of-Plan Annuity Buying Program May Offer More Advantages
Source: PIMCO 2016.

In the March 2007 DC Dialogue "Where's the Beef?" we interviewed Professor Zvi Bodie of Boston University and Kelli Hueler, CEO of Hueler Companies, about building sustainable retirement income using a combination of TIPS, target-date strategies, and annuities. Professor Bodie shares his "big beef" with target-date retirement funds: the marketing of the funds as having a "target date," yet no guarantee of a specific payout. Hueler suggests that participants can add a guaranteed insurance product to their retirement income plans by coupling an annuity purchase with their target-date funds. She shares her views on deferred annuities:

> *A new generation of products is coming that allows participants to gain this guarantee. We believe in offering a strategy that allows individuals to begin the process of building retirement income while they're still employed. For instance, while they're still active in their plans, employees can purchase target-deferred annuities. Ideally, this is accomplished by purchasing from multiple providers at different times at current competitive institutional rates. This reduces exposure to provider and interest-rate risks.*

Bodie and Hueler are not alone in suggesting the complement of target-date strategies and deferred annuities. By purchasing a deferred annuity to start paying out at age 85 (or earlier), the retiree shortens the investment horizon for the at-retirement target-date strategies and may more confidently set up installment payouts, or periodically withdraw assets to fund retirement income. This is one strategy that a financial advisor should help a preretiree consider. An advisor should also help clients understand the pricing differences that may be available when annuities are offered within a company plan as a distribution choice from that plan or via an institutionally priced platform; in some employer-offered programs, women may benefit from unisex pricing (i.e., their gender cannot be taken into account despite their expected longer lives relative to men). Annuities may or may not be attractive for the participant, depending on other income sources, annuity rates, bequest intentions, and other personal factors.

As participants work to create a sustainable retirement income stream, they may express the wish that they had a traditional defined benefit payout. In response, academic thought leaders and retirement experts may tell the participants, "You can create your own income stream using a combination of DC assets and insurance solutions." PIMCO's August/September 2014 DC Dialogue is an interview with Jeffrey R. Brown, the Josef and Margot Lakonishok Professor of Business and Dean of the College of Business at the University of Illinois in Urbana-Champaign, Illinois, about creating a lifetime income stream, including how traditional DB plans measure up to the retirement income needs of the workforce.

Dr. Brown explains that in his 15 years of studying the U.S. retirement system, he's observed that "the system works extremely well for part of the population and not very well at all for other parts of the population:"

> *Full-time workers who have access to and participate in an employer-provided retirement plan—most commonly a defined contribution plan—should be on a very good path to a financially sound retirement. Fortunately, over the last decade, a lot of DC improvements have been made, including automatic enrollment and contribution escalation, improved investment defaults, less reliance on employer stock, and so forth. People who participate in a DC plan should, in theory, be very well set for retirement, with one main caveat—that they successfully transition from accumulation to retirement income.*

Without an employer who provides a workplace retirement plan, which he tells us may represent up to half of the U.S. workforce at any given point in time, individuals are potentially left with Social Security plus whatever retirement savings they amass individually. This may mean retirement income is insufficient. Comments Dr. Brown:

> *A complete do-it-yourself system is just not going to work for lots of people. To help address the coverage issue, we need to make it easier for smaller employers to offer DC plans to their workers. The employer plays a huge role in the success of the retirement system.*
>
> *Most importantly, employers are trusted intermediaries. As plan sponsors, they act in a fiduciary capacity to design and deliver retirement plans. Designing plans with automatic enrollment and contribution escalation, as well as thoughtful match formulas, is clearly helping people participate and increase their contribution rates. Plan sponsor selection and oversight of the investment default is also helping participants by improving diversification—reducing market risk—and simplifying communication. And we know that plan design can positively leverage human behavior.*

Interestingly, Dr. Brown also comments that "While DC plans are not perfect, the DB system also was far from perfect." He points out that when DB plans were the norm, total pension coverage rates were no higher than what we now have in a DC-dominated world. Going forward, Dr. Brown says he encourages plan sponsors, policy makers, and participants "to continue to work on improving the existing DC system" by ensuring DC plans better address, in addition to higher participation and contribution rates (with automatic enrollment and contribution escalation), investment, inflation, and longevity risk:

> Our current DC system has never really been focused on the ultimate objective of providing guaranteed income in retirement. An advantage of the DB system was the default to receive a monthly check for as long as you live. There's absolutely no reason why we couldn't create a monthly income stream within the DC system.
>
> Overall, DC plans can better manage investment and longevity risk. I'd start on the investment side with two suggestions: first, improving the investment default's alignment to the DC plan objective, and second, increasing asset diversification. Then, we need to address longevity risk for participants.

Ultimately, Dr. Brown says he believes we're "at the beginning of an explosion in innovation that will help improve defaults. This may include a combination of financial products and insurance solutions, which may be brought together in simple packages that do not exist today."

IN CLOSING

In this chapter, we've explored the idea that retirees may be best off creating a retirement income stream from their DC plan. Plan sponsors can help retirees by confirming they have appropriate access to their money, together with investment choices that offer attractive risk-adjusted returns. We suggest considering the investment options within the PRICE retirement-income liability framework—that is, confirm, as you plan for retirement, that assets keep pace with retirement cost. We also suggest considering risk of loss, asset longevity, and other factors. Finally, we encourage employers to consider whether it makes sense to make available an institutionally priced annuity purchase program; combining a longevity annuity with an at-retirement target-date strategy or multiasset income fund may offer retirees an attractive lifetime income stream.

QUESTIONS FOR PLAN FIDUCIARIES

1. Do we want to retain retiree assets in the DC plan?
2. Does your record keeper support retiree asset retention or work to pull retirees out of your plan?

3. Will the retiree assets help bring down costs for all participants (active and retired)?
4. Do we offer sufficient access to retiree assets: partial and installment payments?
5. Does our plan offer sufficient and appropriate investment choices for retirees: at-retirement target-date strategies, multiasset fixed income, and capital preservation?
6. Can retirees consolidate DC and IRA assets within the DC plan?
7. Do we have a communication program to help retirees understand the benefit of retaining assets in the plans?
8. Do we offer access to objective financial planning?
9. Do we offer access to an out-of-plan annuity purchasing program?

NOTES

1. Refer to appendix of PIMCO's DC Research (January 2016) paper, "Turning Defined Contribution Assets into a Lifetime Paycheck: How to Evaluate Investment Choices for Retirees," for additional performance and fee, return assumptions, hypothetical example, investment strategy, portfolio analysis, risk, and VaR information.
2. Inflation beta represents sensitivity of asset-class excess returns (over the "risk-free" rate) to inflation surprises (realized inflation minus Philadelphia Fed Survey inflation forecast), that is, when inflation surprises by +1 percent, an asset with an inflation beta of 1.5 is expected to have an excess return of 1.5 percent (all else equal); based on quarterly rolling annual data from 1973 to 2015. These numbers are estimated over a one-year horizon; longer term, we expect the numbers to be less negative or even positive.
3. Inflation surprise is defined as the difference between actual inflation and expected inflation as measured by the Philadelphia Fed Survey.
4. As interpreted under current regulations; the Department of Labor has issued the Conflict of Interest Rule, which will be effective April 2017.

CHAPTER 11

A Global View

The Best Ideas from around the Globe for Improving Plan Design

千里之行，始於足下

A journey of a thousand miles starts with a single step.
— Lao Tzu (6th century BC), Tao Te Ching

As I write this final chapter, I am also preparing to speak at a plan sponsor conference on the future of retirement. This is always a challenging topic, as who can predict the future? Fortunately, I'm not alone in this mission: I'm working with retirement experts Bill Ryan, associate partner at Aon Hewitt, Sabrina Bailey, global head of Defined Contribution at Northern Trust, and Sally Nielsen, Employee Retirement Income Security Act (ERISA) attorney at Kilpatrick Townsend & Stockton LLP. After much debate, together we identified three primary trends that will likely drive the future of retirement:

1. The need for increased retirement plan coverage and participation globally.
2. The importance and evolution of the investment default on achieving retirement outcomes.
3. The search for retirement income solutions to sustain one's lifestyle in retirement.

In this chapter, we consider the shift toward DC plans around the world, and focus in on these three trends in plan design—all with the hope of helping countries improve retirement outcomes in a DC world. We then provide a summary analytic framework for considering investment default and core investment strategies. Finally, we end by summarizing the main lessons learned in Chapters 1 through 10.

DC PLANS: BECOMING THE DOMINANT GLOBAL MODEL

In 2014, the U.S.-based Bipartisan Policy Center launched the Commission on Retirement Security and Personal Savings to examine the U.S. retirement system and offer public policy recommendations to facilitate increased savings and thus improve the financial security of Americans in retirement. The Commission, in its work, has acknowledged the swift change in sources of retirement income over time, noting that defined benefit pensions are now being replaced by defined contribution savings arrangements. They also highlight concerns with the current system, including the access to workplace savings plans, current savings rates, and the risk for retirees of outliving savings. In June 2016 the Commission published a report titled "Securing Our Financial Future" in which they outlined six recommendations to improve retirement security for American workers. In the opening letter from the Commission cochairmen, they write:

> *A large segment of Americans struggle to save for any purpose. Millions are anxious about their preparation for retirement as well as their difficulty accumulating a savings cushion for short-term unexpected needs. Policymakers are concerned about the consequences of insufficient retirement savings for individuals, families, and the nation. Recent economic headwinds—stagnating wages and weak economic growth—have heightened these anxieties.*
>
> *The nation's retirement system has many strengths, but it is also experiencing challenges. Retirement and savings policies have evolved over the decades into a true public-private partnership. Assets in workplace retirement savings plans and Individual Retirement Accounts (IRAs) have grown dramatically over the last four decades, but too many Americans are still not preparing adequately. Social Security remains the base of financial support in old age for most Americans, yet the program faces substantial financing problems. A long history of bipartisanship built these systems to promote savings and improve retirement security, but much work lies ahead.*

To improve retirement security, the Commission suggests the U.S. government take multiple actions; top among them are to improve access to workplace retirement savings plans and to facilitate lifetime-income options to reduce the risk of outliving savings. We'll take a closer look at each of these suggestions and consider how other countries are addressing these issues, but let's first consider the reliance on DC globally.

Tectonic shifts in demographics, policy, and the marketplace have not only transformed the U.S. retirement landscape, but also programs around the world. Today, as a result of those changes, adequate income in retirement must be addressed through the targeted creation of a retirement income stream. This income stream may need to last 20 years or longer in retirement, and potentially even longer in coming years. This is the goal of retirement benefit programs: to help workers retire at their desired age and with sufficient income.

At the PIMCO Global DC Roundtable for Multinational Plan Sponsors, Brigitte Miksa, Head of International Pensions (and Executive Editor of PROJECT M at Allianz Asset Management AG), shared the following observations:

> *We know that DC plans are becoming the dominant global pension model—but how that transition is playing out varies significantly in different markets and economies. For example:*
>
> - *Many Asian countries have young populations, but need to build comprehensive pension systems in relatively short order. Taiwan, for instance, is one of the most youthful countries, with an old-age dependency (OAD) ratio of 16. Yet by 2050, its OAD will be 71, the same as Japan's, both the oldest countries in the world then. [OAD is the ratio of older dependents—people older than 64—to the working-age population—those aged 15-64. Data are shown as the proportion of dependents per 100 working-age population.] DC will be the primary source of retirement income in those countries, and often the only one for low- to mid-income earners.*
> - *In contrast, in the mature pension systems of the industrialized world, with the exception of the United States, demography has pressured state pension systems to adjust—mostly by reducing pension assets substantially. This adjustment has increased the need for private retirement preparation.*
> - *Finally, individuals in countries that provide state-run pension systems are not necessarily able to count on those pensions to provide adequate and comprehensive retirement income—only a handful of countries (such as the Netherlands, Denmark, Norway, Switzerland, and the United States) have been successful in balancing sustainability and adequate pension provision.*

In PIMCO's September 2010 DC Dialogue, we speak with Juan Yermo, Head of the Private Pensions Unit at the Organisation for Economic Co-operation and Development (OECD) in Paris, France, about DC elements that are "givens" in Europe, including the inability to cash out savings prior to retirement, the structure of European plans compared to their U.S. counterparts, and what the two markets (United States and Europe) might learn from each other about plan design and implementation.

In his conversation with us, Yermo noted that for over a decade Europeans have focused on the need for change in their retirement programs, including both public (i.e., social security) and private pensions, with a realization that "demographics are changing, with people living longer and fewer workers to support them, given the lower birth rates." As a result, he said, government leaders understand these demographic changes will affect the pension systems quite severely over the coming decades—and both the OECD and the European Commission have been "playing a leading role in alerting countries about the need to reform pension systems to meet the challenges of new demographics." He continued:

> If we take a quick look around Europe, we can see that some countries have been better at pension reform than others. For example, the Nordic, or Scandinavian, countries—Denmark, Finland, Iceland, Sweden, and even Norway to some extent—are in better shape with respect to the sustainability of their public pension plans and their ability to fund those plans. Some of these countries tend to rely more on prefunding of the public system. Norway, with its government pension fund, is probably the best example of that. A country like Denmark, on the other hand, relies much more on fully funded, mandatory defined contribution arrangements.
>
> As we move on and look at continental Europe, we really have a variety of stories. Some Eastern European countries, like Estonia, Latvia and Poland, also have mandatory, fully funded defined contribution plans, and their public pension systems are in good shape from a sustainability perspective.
>
> Countries like France and Germany have enacted major reforms that don't get talked about much in the international press. However, they have been effectively cutting down replacement rates for future retirees. In fact, someone joining the workforce today in the private sector in France or Germany is going to get a pension that is not going to be that much higher than what a person would get from social security in the United States—somewhere around 40 percent replacement of their final salary.
>
> Then you have some southern Mediterranean countries—like Spain and Greece—which still are promising rather generous

pension replacement rates for someone entering the workforce. In those countries, replacement rates are higher than 80 percent of average salaries.

Finally, when we look at the two Anglo-Saxon countries in Europe, Ireland and the UK, their concern is more about how to improve the coverage and the generosity of the public pension system. In those countries, there is only limited coverage of private schemes, and the public pension itself does not always provide sufficient retirement income.

Ultimately, Yermo concluded by noting "all in all, I think there is some degree of convergence [of trends influencing retirement in the European countries] happening, with a greater emphasis on private pensions and later retirement." Population aging is obviously the main long-term driver of reform, he added, "but most recently, fiscal pressures have been of paramount importance. These pressures have been intensified further by market developments over the last two years." Indeed, since our discussion with Yermo in 2010, multiple factors including pension reform and the European sovereign debt crisis have reduced replacement rates in certain countries; for instance, in 2015 the replacement rate in Greece was 46.2 percent, down from around 100 percent in earlier years.

While circumstances and conditions vary, the need for workers to build their own sources of retirement income through defined contribution plans is growing. Despite a common objective, many differences in program design and investment approaches exist across countries. Let's now take a look at differences in coverage and participation, then we'll consider investments and finally retirement income.

RETIREMENT PLAN COVERAGE AND PARTICIPATION

In the June 2016 report from the Commission on Retirement Security and Personal Savings on "Securing Our Financial Future," the commissioners wrote first about the need to improve workplace retirement savings plan coverage. They report that "about one-third of private-sector workers do not have access to a workplace retirement savings plan" and note that many of those who are not covered work in small businesses or on a part-time or seasonal basis. In the United States, whether an employer offers a retirement program and whether an employee decides to participate in the program is, for the most part, voluntary. In contrast, many other countries have taken a different approach: requiring employers to offer a plan, requiring automatic enrollment into the plan, or both. As shown in Figure 11.1 and briefly discussed in Chapter 2, you see (for example) the voluntary DC and DB plans

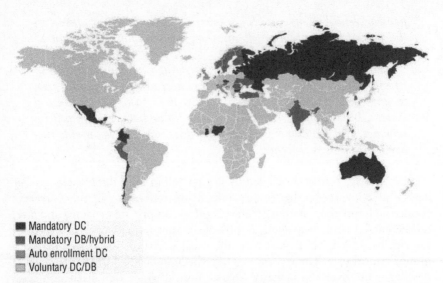

- ■ Mandatory DC
- ■ Mandatory DB/hybrid
- ■ Auto enrollment DC
- ▨ Voluntary DC/DB

FIGURE 11.1   Retirement Plan Structures Vary Globally
Source: OECD, Pensions at a Glance, 2015.

in the United States, Canada, Brazil, France, Germany, and Japan. You also note the mandatory DC programs in Australia, Mexico, Chile, and Denmark. Finally, in the UK and Italy, we see an auto-enrollment DC plan where the government requires employers to offer a plan and automatically enroll ("auto-enroll") participants into the plan, but the participant may opt-out of the program should they desire to do so.

As the U.S. government, both at the state and federal levels, studies ways to improve DC plan coverage, plan designs outside the United States, including consideration of mandatory requirements, have been reviewed. At this point in time the U.S. government is less likely to pursue a fully mandatory program such as Australia's and more likely to pursue an automatic enrollment model such as offered in the UK.

To understand the Australian retirement income system, in PIMCO's September 2010 DC Dialogue we speak with Julie Agnew, Associate Professor of Finance and Economics at the College of William and Mary and who was at that time a Senior Visiting Fellow at the University of New South Wales. Agnew tells us that "many people consider Australia's retirement system as one of the best public retirement systems in the world. It has three pillars, including a means-tested 'Age Pension' that is similar in some ways to Social Security in the United States, a mandatory private superannuation savings vehicle [also known as "super" programs], and a voluntary savings component."

What's important to understand is that unlike the U.S. social security
system, Australian employees and employers do not contribute to the public
"Age Pension" system; rather, this is funded out of general government revenue, that is, taxes paid by the public. Since Australians do not contribute to
the Age Pension, some may think they also do not receive a benefit. Agnew
addresses this misunderstanding, saying:

> *What's not true is that few retirees receive an Age Pension; actually,*
> *over 75 percent of retirees receive this government money today.*
> *Yet, as mentioned, the Age Pension is means-tested, so the govern-*
> *ment looks at both a retiree's assets and income. It's not meant to*
> *replace preretirement standards of living, but to provide a very basic*
> *income, and if you qualify, you may also have access to discounts*
> *on health services and energy costs. Roughly, in inflation-adjusted*
> *dollars, it will replace about 27.7 percent of an average male's earn-*
> *ings for a single person and about 41.3 percent for a couple. That*
> *equates to AUD 19,643 for singles or AUD 29,614 for a couple.*
>
> *Super programs will need to close most of the gap to meet re-*
> *tirement income needs, and given that rate and the means test taper*
> *[which reduces the amount of age pension received if a pensioner*
> *has assets above a predefined upper limit], that gap is much larger*
> *for higher-income individuals. As a result, using some back-of-the-*
> *envelope calculations and assuming a target replacement rate of*
> *80 percent, we estimate that supers will need to replace as much as*
> *30 to 80 percent of final pay, depending on the person's preretire-*
> *ment income.*

Australia's second pillar is similar to the U.S. DC plan and referred
to as a "superannuation" plan or simply "super." This mandatory program began in 1992 and requires a contribution rate that is escalating
up to 12 percent of pay by 2025. Agnew told us that "unless a person is
self-employed, the employer must contribute a percentage of salary for all
workers aged 18 to 70 who earn over AUD 450 a month. This requirement
results in over 92 percent of workers being included in the super programs."
Australia largely has managed the coverage issue with their current retirement system—although this success is more evident with respect to accumulation for retirement, as concerns remain about the adequacy of retirement
income once retirement begins.

Americans appear to be more inclined to pursue a mandatory auto-
enrollment system such as that offered in the UK. As of October 2015, all
UK employers with 30 or more workers were required to automatically
enroll those employees who earn at least 10,000 pounds per year into a

retirement savings plan at a default contribution rate of 1 percent of pay. Employees, for their part, may change contribution rates or opt out entirely. By April 2017, the requirement will apply to all employers; and the minimum default contribution rate will increase to 4 percent of pay by October 2018. Employers are also currently required to contribute 1 percent of pay to these plans for workers who participate. Employer minimum required contributions are set to increase to 3 percent of pay, and the U.K. government will contribute another 1 percent of pay, beginning April 2019. As the UK discussed the rollout of this mandatory DC system, many feared that the opt-out rate would be so high as to undermine the objective of building retirement security broadly. Now that the system has been in place for a number of years, UK reports show that the behavioral power of inertia is alive and well; while workers can opt out of the DC plan, the vast majority do not—rather they remain invested.

It's this "power of inertia" that may also benefit workers in the United States—and, for that matter, other workers around the globe. A system in which the government requires employers to offer a plan, but also allows participants to opt-out may be more palatable for Americans than mandatory plans with no opt-out provisions. In addition to addressing the lack of DC plan access for some American workers, a mandatory plan with opt-out provisions could help address another clear problem in the United States today, which is that fully 17 percent of workers who have access to a DC plan chose not to participate (according to the U.S. Bureau of Labor Statistics).[1]

Bill Ryan, associate partner at Aon, shared observations about the power of automatic enrollment programs. He notes that since the Pension Protection Act (PPA) of 2006, DC participation rates have improved across all demographics. In 2015, U.S. DC plans with automatic enrollment realized an average participation rate of 86 percent, compared to plans without this feature at only 63 percent (Figure 11.2). Unfortunately, the Plan Sponsor Council of America (PSCA) reported in their 58th Annual Survey (reflecting 2014 experience) that just over half of U.S. DC plans (52.4 percent) offer automatic enrollment: So while plans with auto-enrollment typically enroll a majority of eligible participants, only about half of plans offer auto-enrollment! By implementing a UK-like mandatory system, the U.S. workers would benefit from both the availability of and automatic enrollment into a DC retirement plan. (See Figure 11.2.)

Today, a significant initiative is underway within many U.S. states to address the lack of widespread private sector retirement plans (i.e., state-administered retirement programs). Similar to the UK, the majority of approved or proposed state programs incorporate both mandatory employer participation and automatic enrollment for participants.

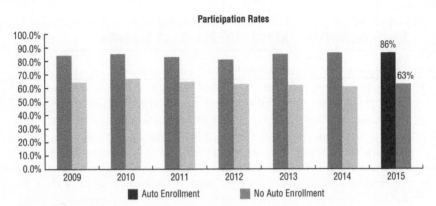

FIGURE 11.2   Auto-Enrollment Improves DC Plan Participation Rates
Source: Aon Hewitt's 2016 Universe Benchmarks—Employee Savings and Investing Behavior in Defined Contribution Plans.

In addition to the state programs, the report "Securing Our Financial Future" from the Commission on Retirement Security and Personal Savings suggests the federal government launch a mandatory federal program as an ERISA-covered multiple employer plan (or MEP); they suggest the program be called "Retirement Security Plans" (RSA) and note that it "would allow small employers to transfer most responsibilities for operating a retirement savings plan to a third-party expert, while still maintaining strong employee protections." (Note: The Commission believes an RSA label for a MEP will help reduce confusion between *multiple employer plans*, or MEPs, and *multi-employer plans*, which are plans organized by more than one employer and a labor union.)

A MEP may be adopted by unrelated employers with some common connection such as being in the same industry or some common ownership, but not to the level of a controlled group ("controlled group rules" identify whether two or more corporations and certain other groups of related trades or businesses are treated as if they were one employer under many provisions of the ERISA and the Internal Revenue Code [IRC] applicable to employee benefit plans). Nondiscrimination and certain limits are tested separately, but service for eligibility and vesting counts with any employer adopting the MEP (see IRC Section 413(c) for more information). This type of program would likely be highly attractive to employers except for one significant drawback: If one employer fails qualification requirements, the entire plan may be disqualified. In the event that the law is changed and this disqualification risk is lifted, a federal MEP (or RSA if you go with the Commission's naming) may become immediately attractive nationwide.

STATE-ADMINISTERED RETIREMENT PLANS: AN OVERVIEW

One option that has been developed to address the shortage of private-sector retirement plans in the United States is the state-administered program. As shared by Sabrina Bailey and Sally Nielsen, these plans are designed to provide more private-sector workers with access to retirement savings through their employer. State programs are specifically meant to serve as a way for private-sector employers that do not currently offer a retirement savings plan to do so.

Private-sector employers typically identify one or more of the following reasons for not offering retirement plan access: administrative burden, fiduciary responsibility, high fees, and/or small company size. However, at the time of writing this book, eight states have enacted retirement plan laws—California, Illinois, Oregon, Massachusetts, Washington, New Jersey, Maryland, and Connecticut—and over 20 additional states have moved forward with legislative proposals or studies to develop programs that help address these employer concerns.

There are generally two predominant plan structures approved or proposed by the various states: Non-ERISA (IRA and Marketplace plans) or ERISA-Covered (DC and multiple employer plans, or MEP). A payroll deduction IRA is exempt from ERISA as only employees are allowed to contribute to the program, but is also limited by the IRA rules in the amount an employee may contribute as set by the Internal Revenue Code (e.g., for 2016 IRA contributions, $5,500 standard limit or $6,500 catch-up limit for those 50 years of age or older). By comparison, an ERISA-covered plan allows for employee contributions (Roth or pretax) of considerably more, that is, in 2016, $18,000 plus an age 50 catch-up of an additional $6,000. If you add in employer contributions, in total all employee and employer contributions have a much higher limit (e.g., for 2016 under Section 415(c)(1) (A) the limit is the lesser of 100 percent of pay or $53,000). Notably, an ERISA-covered approach may allow for nearly 10 times the contribution amount as allowed under a non-ERISA program. Figure A summarizes the differences in these approaches.

Sabrina Bailey notes:

States considered many factors when deciding upon which structure would be most appropriate for these programs. Some of these considerations, such as the need for an institutional fee structure and the ability to set up a non-ERISA covered plan have been well documented. Another critical consideration in the states' decision making models, one that is often over-looked, is the desire for the state-administered program to avoid competing with retirement plans currently offered by private-sector employers. The purpose of these state programs is to provide ease of access to a retirement program for private-sector workers where none exists; it is not to become the retirement program of choice of all employers in the states. The continued benefits of employer sponsored programs to drive improved retirement outcomes, such as higher contribution limits and the ability to provide an employer match or other form of employer contributions, will likely increase the number of employers that sponsor their own DC plan rather than moving into the state-administered program, an outcome that the states view as a positive one for workers in their state.

Sally Nielsen agrees with the need for easy solutions for all employers, commenting:

It goes without saying we are approaching, or in the beginnings of, a retirement savings crisis in the United States, with nearly one-third of those employed in the United States unable to participate in a workplace retirement savings option.

The different state approaches each have their own advantages and disadvantages. But in the end, regardless of the size of the employer, all employers seek the same things: convenient ways to adopt and offer retirement savings plans, administrative ease, but most of all, protection from fiduciary risk.

It is hard to envision that a mix of state approaches will help all but the smaller employers. We need comprehensive federal alternatives to step up the coverage and savings rates, starting with an expanded ability to offer the RSA under one umbrella at the federal level. In effect, we should look at a federal prototype plan that would be available for employers of any size in any state who agreed to make it available to all employees.

Through the use of currently available safe harbor designs under the Internal Revenue Code, such a plan could be designed to be exempt from coverage and contributions testing. Alternatively, Congress should consider a form of safe harbor plan that does not require employer contributions so that employers would at least find it easy and less burdensome to offer some savings vehicle in the workplace.

(*continued*)

(continued)

> *Going further, with guidance and assistance from the Department of Labor, such a plan could offer a safe harbor selection of appropriate investment options that would enable employers to avoid fiduciary risk on investment selection. The DOL has already provided a safe harbor for the automatic roll-over of small benefits to IRAs and defined safe harbor "qualified default investment alternatives." The DOL could continue down that path to offer a safe harbor suite of other investment alternatives in addition to the current list of QDIAs, or at a minimum, provide access to appropriate investment alternatives on a cost effective basis for the smaller market.*
>
> *I am not suggesting that individually designed plans are ineffective or outdated. They are not. But in many cases, a federal prototype plan, coupled with a safe harbor suite of investment alternatives, may be a better solution for an employer that does not have employees with the time, interest, or expertise to make these decisions or a desire to select and monitor investment experts.*

	Non-ERISA (IRA / Marketplace)	ERISA-Covered (MEP / Prototype)

	1. Individual Retirement Account (IRA)
	   Traditional or Roth
	
	2. Marketplace
	   Connects employers with private market
	   retirement plans (ERISA or non-ERISA)
	   Marketplace itself not ERISA-covered
	   State is not fiduciary and not ERISA
	   qualified
		1. Multiple Employer Plan (MEP)
		   Multiple employers join the plan, though plan
		   is run by state or designated third party
		
		2. Prototype
		   Each employer sponsors an ERISA plan
		   (separately)
		   State or designated third party assumes
		   responsibility for administrative and asset
		   management functions

Employer Participation	Mandatory (IRA) Voluntary (Marketplace)	Voluntary
Auto-Enrollment	Permitted (w/ Opt-Out Option)	Permitted (w/ Opt-Out Option)
Default Investment	Permitted	Permitted
Fiduciary Responsibility	State (IRA) Employer (Marketplace using DC)	State (MEP) Employer (Prototype)
Employer Contribution	Not Permitted (IRA)	Permitted
Registered Investments	Required (Typically for most IRA)	Not Required (Collective Investment Trusts permitted)
Investments	Target-date funds, objective-based funds, single funds	Target-date funds, objective-based funds, single funds

FIGURE A   Non-ERISA and ERISA-Covered State Retirement Plan Approaches
Source: Northern Trust, as of 2016.

To date, for the eight U.S. states that passed initiatives, the design features are summarized in Figure B.

	California	Illinois	Oregon	Mass.	Wash.	New Jersey	Maryland	Conn.
Design Approach	IRA	Roth IRA	IRA	Prototype	Marketplace	Marketplace	IRA	Roth IRA
Employers Affected	5 or more employees	25 or more employees	Employers with no plan	20 or fewer employees; Non-profit only	100 or fewer employees	100 or fewer employees	Employers with no plan	5 or more employees
Employer Participation	Mandatory	Mandatory (2+ year old business)	Mandatory	Voluntary	Voluntary	Voluntary	Mandatory (2+ year old business)	Mandatory
Auto-Enrollment	Yes	Yes	Yes	Yes	Not Required	Not Required	Yes	Yes
Fee Limit	1.00%	0.75%	"Low"	0.86%	1.00%	1.00%	0.50%	0.75%

FIGURE B State–Administered Retirement Plans, Summary of Passed Initiatives
Source: Northern Trust DC Solutions, 2016.

(*continued*)

(*continued*)

An IRA design approach for state-sponsored plans will require states to work through a number of issues, some of which may still need to be addressed. These include:

- Administrative fee payments
- Investment options and fees
- Distributions
- Lost employees
- Account balance size
- Seasonal employees
- Rollover
- Implications of the Department of Labor (DOL) fiduciary rule

State-sponsored plans are another area of continuing research, development, and interest for workers, state governments, and all those interested in the development of retirement income solutions.

Going forward, increasing the coverage and participation rates for employer-sponsored retirement plans is a critical first step. Mandatory programs or eased access via MEP structures may change coverage. To improve retirement security success, programs also need to establish a sufficient contribution rate. As discussed, Australia has mandated a contribution rate that is climbing to 12 percent of pay. The UK has also established a default rate that, as noted, will require a total contribution of 8 percent of pay by April 2019; 4 percent of this contribution will be sourced from the employee.

In the United States, we do not have a minimum contribution rate or escalation requirements. Rather, the majority of plans that automatically enroll participants set a default deferral rate of 3 percent of pay (50.7 percent of plans) or higher (40.4 percent), according to the PSCA 2015 survey. About a third of plans that automatically enroll participants also escalate the deferral rate, typically by 1 percent, on an annual basis. A concern with the low default rate—particularly when not coupled with auto-escalation—is that an employee may end up saving less than if they selected their own savings rate.

PSCA reports that the average percentage of salary deferred for all active participants is 6.5 percent of pay; if those participants who are defaulted to 3 percent remain at 3 percent, this rate of pay deferral will decline over time. Fortunately, in addition to the employee deferral, the vast majority of U.S. employers (95.6 percent) also contribute to the DC plan at an average rate of 4.8 percent when a DB plan is not also offered (note: PSCA reports the employer contribution drops to 4.3 percent when a DB is offered in addition to the DC plan). When combining the average employee deferral and employer contribution rates, for those U.S. workers who have a plan and participate, the total average annual contribution rate may exceed 11 percent.

INVESTMENT DEFAULT AND GROWTH OF TARGET-DATE STRATEGIES

As discussed throughout this book, as more assets automatically pour into DC plans, evaluating the investment default is essential. Returning to the January 2014 DC Dialogue with Brigitte Miksa, she notes an expectation that plans will increasingly become "professionalized" in their structure and oversight. Comments Miksa:

> *Another word for professionalization may be institutionalization. This includes moving to institutional investment structures and more sophisticated outcome-oriented DC (income) products. To move in this direction, more advanced trust structures may be used, and the administrative and recordkeeping capabilities may be enhanced. Professionalization also may include outsourcing the asset allocation decision-making to the plan sponsor, investment manager or consulting firm. Acknowledging the global lack of financial literacy and shifting the tough decisions to experts is likely to continue.*

Miksa also notes the importance of investment structures that are outcome-oriented or, as we have said throughout this book, *objective-aligned*. She agrees and goes on to say plan fiduciaries need to consider "what the DC plan is intended to do. For most, that's focusing on meeting the participant's future liability—building plans that deliver adequate and sustainable retirement income. That's why workers are saving for retirement. This understanding is growing and plans are improving, but it's going to take time."

She notes DC design differences among countries, including how participants are enrolled, whether they can access their money both pre- and postretirement, the investment structures offered, and whether guarantees are provided:

> *Despite the differences in enrollment and access rules, the investment choices among the Anglo-Saxon DC plans are similar in shifting the asset allocation decision-making to professionals. In the U.S. and Canada, the focus is on target-date strategies that are designed to reduce risk within the vintage portfolios as the participant ages. The U.K. offers a similar approach by shifting the participant's asset allocation to lower-risk portfolios as participants age. Australia tends not to shift the allocation, but keeps participants in a single diversified portfolio. Notably, the Anglo-Saxon plans generally do not offer guaranteed return of principal, whereas plans in other developed markets often do carry these guarantees.*

Miksa identified two underlying factors that drive the differences among market segments: *culture* and *weight on the public pension pillar.* She noted that from a cultural perspective, continental Europe can be viewed as "more paternalistic and embracing of community risk-sharing. Let's not forget that public pensions started in Germany with von Bismarck in 1889."

She outlined developments in German and Swiss plans, in particular how these plans guarantee that the nominal principal value of a participant's account will be retained—which drives the plan sponsors to reduce risk in these DC plans. The result for plan participants can include two unintended consequences: that "DC participants in these plans may see limited growth in their assets and, most important, may have assets that retain nominal value but fail to keep up with inflation." She also noted innovative hybrid DC/DB structures such as the Netherlands' "Defined Ambition" system, in which (unlike DC) the employer takes responsibility for attempting to deliver a specified retirement outcome, but (unlike DB) the employer is not bound to deliver that outcome at any cost. Other countries including the UK have considered similar systems, yet struggle with who carries the risk when investment returns turn south.

Focusing back on the United States, Bill Ryan at Aon Hewitt shared that DC assets continue building in Qualified Default Investment Alternatives (QDIA) strategies, a category that target-date funds dominate. As shown in Figure 11.3, Ryan notes that from 2005 to 2015, target-date strategies usage by participants (i.e., they invest in at least a dollar in one or more target-date funds) has grown from 40 percent to 70 percent. To further break down usage as a percentage of a participant's account balance (i.e., an average of the percentage allocations to target-dates including zeros), it has grown from 9 percent to 47 percent, likely driven by participants early in their career tenure being defaulted into a target-date fund. Over the same time period, these strategies have grown from 6 percent to 23 percent of total DC plan assets.

Ryan goes on to share Figure 11.4 and the fact that target-date solutions take-up is highest for shorter-tenured workers, at 85% for those with one to two years at an organization, yet still high and growing for longer tenured workers—as shown, in 2015 those with 30 or more years of experience had 51 percent of participants investing in a target-date solution (up from 33 percent in 2005).

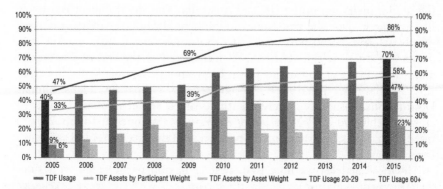

FIGURE 11.3 Target-Date Fund Strategies Capture Growing Share of Participant Account Balance
Source: Aon Hewitt's DC Universe Benchmarks Reports.

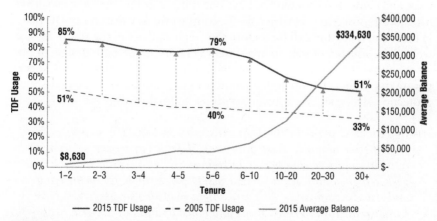

FIGURE 11.4 Tenure's Impact on Target-Date Fund Usage and Average Balance
Source: Aon Hewitt's DC Universe Benchmarks Reports.

Ryan projects these trends to continue, expecting within the next decade to see the vast majority of DC plan assets invested in target-date or other professionally managed solutions. Comments Bill Ryan in an August 17, 2016, post on Aon Hewitt's retirement and investment blog: "Over the next several years we could see closer to 50 percent of DC plan assets held in target-date funds [TDFs]. As the swell of rapid TDF growth continues to consume assets from core funds, we may begin to observe this wave of change introducing a greater divide in fee leverage at the possible expense of the participants invested in core fund options."

As non-U.S. DC plans evolve, we anticipate similar trends. At time of writing, we are witnessing increased usage of target-date strategies around the world, including in the UK and Australia. This development is a likely improvement over the traditional investment defaults in these countries, which either exposed participants to too much or too little market risk, depending on their time horizon. As introduced at the end of Chapter 4, along with PIMCO colleagues Justin Blesy and at the time Will Allport, in July 2014 we published a DC Design article, "Global DC Plans: Similar Destinations, Distinctly Different Paths." An expanded version of this article was published in *The Journal of Retirement* (Summer 2014, pp. 71–88) titled, "DC Plans: International Experience and the Need to Address Retirement Security."

In these articles we note that, despite having participants with similar retirement-outcome goals, the three countries with the greatest reliance on defined contribution (DC) plans—Australia, the United States, and the UK—have adopted dramatically different approaches to plan design and investment management. We evaluate the typical glide paths in these countries, and show that they tend to have one thing in common: They may leave investors exposed to excessive risk. We contrast the key features of DC plans in these countries and call for a more thorough analysis of the risk of loss, as well as the sources of risk, in investment defaults. Glide-path design, in our view, should focus on desired outcomes, respect risk-capacity limits, incorporate risk diversification and inflation hedging, and consider market-shock protection strategies. We conclude with the following observations:

> In sum, DC plans in the U.S., Australia and the UK may benefit from better aligning asset allocation defaults to workers' needed outcomes: purchasing power in retirement. This would likely suggest a higher allocation to real assets for both inflation hedging and risk diversification. The assessment may also suggest a need for earlier reduction in risky assets and consideration of tail-risk hedging in an effort to guard DC assets against potentially devastating market shocks.

As plan sponsors consider the appropriate asset allocation default, they also should consider the possibility that retirees may be likely to move their assets out of the DC default within several years of retirement. In the U.S., money often is cashed out of the DC plan and rolled over to an Individual Retirement Account, while in Australia members may withdraw money for travel or other expenses. Up until recently, U.K. retirees generally did not have the freedom to cash out all of their DC assets; instead, they generally had their assets shifted to government bonds and then used to purchase an annuity. However, we anticipate future U.K. annuity buying to decline materially given the 2014 U.K. legislative changes to tax treatment of pension asset withdrawals. Whether these portfolio shifts are freely chosen or otherwise they underscore the need for a more outcome-focused and risk-managed asset allocation prior to retirement: This need crosses international boundaries and is truly a global phenomenon.

At PIMCO, our Client Analytics group including professionals Steve Sapra and Ying Gao has the ability to model retirement expected outcomes across multiple countries and asset allocation structures. Our capabilities continue to grow and evolve globally. To consider an example of this work, we suggest that you go to the *Journal of Retirement* paper or reach out directly to PIMCO.

RETIREMENT INCOME: THE GLOBAL SEARCH FOR SOLUTIONS

As assets in DC plans build and participants age, we anticipate that all markets will ask the same questions that developed countries are posing now—namely, how do we convert DC savings into a sustainable and adequate retirement income?

The most developed DC markets, which are the United States, Australia, and the UK, have become increasingly similar when it comes to retirement income: All allow participants at retirement age or before to "take their money and run." While the UK formerly had a longstanding annuitization requirement at retirement, this has now been lifted. Australia as we write is considering requiring DC plans to offer dedicated retirement income solutions for participants to choose among at retirement, but these solutions or choices have yet to be fully defined. Depending on the direction a participant intends to take at retirement—cash out, stay in-plan, or buy an annuity—their asset allocation may well vary. This means that plan sponsors need to be prepared, and help participants prepare for the choices they'll make at retirement about where income will source from in the coming years.

These issues were raised in our conversation with Olivia S. Mitchell, International Foundation of Employee Benefit Plans Professor, as well as Professor of Insurance/Risk Management and Business Economics/Policy; Executive Director of the Pension Research Council; and Director of the Boettner Center on Pensions and Retirement Research; all at the Wharton School of the University of Pennsylvania when we spoke to her as part of our DC Dialogues in 2008, and updated at time of writing.

We asked Mitchell whether, given the dramatic shift toward defined contribution plans as the primary employer-provided retirement plan, participants would be able to meet their retirement-income goals by using them. She told us that the answer is a mixed bag:

> *On one hand, DC plans do a much better job for great swaths of the population. In the past, fewer than one in 10 new employees starting work at a firm with a defined benefit plan actually received retiree benefits from the plan due to turnover, job changes, and so forth. DC plans are much better for a mobile workforce. They have great portability and are a powerful tool for diligent savers.*
>
> *Yet if employees don't exercise the option to save, especially in a tax-qualified manner, they won't do workers much good. Consequently, one challenge is getting people to understand the need to save, to comprehend investment opportunities, and to keep money in a plan, so that assets don't leak out of the system early. An additional challenge will be to help Baby Boomers realize they need to manage their assets sensibly during the decumulation or payout phase.*

She also noted that "Baby Boomers are far less certain than their parents' generation about how much they'll need in retirement. The younger generation entering the labor force today probably will be even less certain." In contrast, she added that:

> *My parents' generation was relatively secure when it came to retirement. They expected a strong Social Security system, they could lean on a fairly reliable Medicare program, and many had retiree health benefits from their companies. The Baby Boomers' story has changed dramatically. As a generation, it must be much less complacent about all these institutions, since many face insolvency in our lifetimes. Sadly, the next generations face even more serious risks.*
>
> *This uncertainty suggests that we need substantially higher target saving rates. Each successive generation is likely to live longer and therefore need far more in retirement than one might extrapolate from looking at today's retirees.*

One issue she focused on is the ability of DC plan participants to access their cash before retirement:

> *When I last served on the Social Security Commission, we hotly debated the policy issue of whether a personal-account system should allow people to access their money before retirement age. In the end, we proposed that individuals not be allowed access prior to retirement age except in the case of divorce. In those cases, the money would be treated as a divisible asset, yet people still would have to save it until retirement. There was concern that if you don't give people access to their money in a 401(k) or 403(b) scheme, people may not opt to contribute much in the first place because they feel the need to retain a certain degree of liquidity. Yet if they have easy access through loans and withdrawals, it could erode their accumulations, especially in hard times. So it's a delicate balance.*

She also pointed specifically to the situation in Australia, in which typically "one can't access the funds prior to age 55, rising to 60. Yet the system permits people to take a lump sum from their personal accounts at that age. As a consequence, many people in their 50s embark on the so-called 'overseas experience trip' and draw down their retirement assets. Then at age 65, they present themselves without much money and request the means-tested government old-age benefit. So we need to be extremely careful about structuring the system so that people don't have an incentive to take the money and run, then come back later and ask for aid."

There are two retirement income solutions used outside the United States that are often discussed and we'd like to explore here: the concept of *defined ambition* pension plans, and the old-but-new solution of group self-annuitization, or *tontines*. We'll start with defined ambition plans.

DEFINED AMBITION IN THE NETHERLANDS

In February 2014, we interviewed Tim Burggraaf, DC Leader at Mercer in the Netherlands, an area that is often viewed as providing innovative solutions for retirement income. In the Netherlands about 80 percent of workers participate in a semi-obligatory pension plan: "Basically, workers must participate in a predominantly union-run, industrywide pension fund." That leaves 20 percent of the people who work with employers that are not part of an industrywide fund. That portion of the population may have a voluntary pension system "where employers can decide whether they want to offer a pension plan, and employees can decide whether or not they want to participate in it." In this part of the market, he added, "we're seeing the clear and decisive movement to DC plans."

Burggraaf told us about two types of plans that are replacing traditional DB plans: defined ambition (DA) and defined contribution. While DA plans are presented as defined benefit, he tells us that the financial crisis forced a downward adjustment in the payouts from these plans. He notes that since the benefit is not guaranteed, the plans offer more of a retirement income "ambition" and are closer to defined contribution than traditional defined benefit. He also noted that:

> *Industrywide pension funds are a bit of a black box. Their boards are composed of employer representatives (50 percent) and employee representatives (50 percent). The unions sit in the "employee representative" seats, even though very few workers are actually linked to any union. So, bottom line, the nonunionized workers are represented by the unions. Employers contribute to the plans; for example, 15 percent of pay, regardless of the worker's age or income level. These plans are structured to provide an average-pay defined benefit. However, employers are not on the hook for the payout amount or for maintaining a plan funding level, and therefore DC accounting is allowed—the plans are off the balance sheet of the employer. Unfortunately, no entity stands behind the pension payment—pension payment amounts are not guaranteed.*
>
> *If the pension fund is short relative to its liabilities—say a pension fund needs to be 105 percent of liabilities and is only at 100 percent—then the benefits will be cut by 5 percent for both current and future pensioners. So, in practice, the actual pension payout is based on how well the underlying investments perform and on market interest (through the solvency framework). Payments may go up or down. The plans may offer an adjustment for inflation, but only if there is sufficient money in the plan. If there's no money, there's no inflation indexation.*

Burggraaf told us about how these defined ambition plans work in practice, and the risk that workers may not receive payments they have been expecting.

> *After the financial crisis, several funds had to cut benefits to get back on track. Since the beginning of the financial crisis, many retirees have been unpleasantly surprised to see their pension payouts cut—by as much as 16 percent in extreme cases. As you can imagine, that really hurts. The retiree's cost of living is going up, but their*

pension is going down. It's a pretty bad situation, which is not over. [In 2014] we estimate that another 20 to 30 industry funds may need to cut benefits again this year.

. . . Until the financial crisis, the plans were in great shape. The values and pension payouts were fine—everything went up. There were no significant issues, so everybody felt that our pensions were guaranteed. But that was only because nothing bad had happened. And then suddenly something bad did happen. So the whole economy crashed. And this is where people started to realize, "Oh, wait a minute. It's not guaranteed." It felt like the pension was guaranteed, but that was only because the market was going the right way.

He ended his conversation with us by noting that "a completely unionized system may have been fine in the 1970s and 1980s, but our population and markets have changed. The risk-sharing systems of the past are unlikely to hold, especially when it's the youth that end up ultimately shouldering the risk—or facing the shortfall of retirement savings."

NEW SOLUTIONS IN AUSTRALIA AND BEYOND: TONTINES AND GROUP SELF-ANNUITIZATION

For the past several years, the government of Australia has been reviewing the range of available retirement income products in Australia, with a view to potentially introducing new products that "could help retirees achieve their desired levels of income, provide them with flexibility and help them better manage risk. Currently, barriers are stifling innovation and adding costs to providers developing new products" (as noted by the Australian Financial System Inquiry report released in December 2014). If the goal is to increase the use of products with longevity protection, the Inquiry reports, "Australia needs to have an appropriate and affordable range of products."

In Australia, as the population continues to age, there is increasing pressure on the Age Pension. One option that has gathered interest in Australia is the potential use of tontine or group self-annuitization products. In a group self-annuitization (GSA), participants contribute funds to a pool invested in financial assets—and starting at a qualifying age, retirement income payments are made to surviving members from the pool. This sharing or pooling of mortality risk ensures that participants receive higher income in retirement than many alternative retirement income solutions (such as an accumulation account that is drawn down in retirement at a minimum required rate), while also providing protection against longevity risk (note: This protection is dependent on the pool and is not an insured solution).

This means that at least in theory, superannuation funds could provide lifetime retirement income and protect against longevity risk without using an insurance product.

The income from a GSA might be composed of a mix of investment earnings and return of capital. New products have started to emerge in the Australian market, including a product that provides income via return of capital, investment earnings, and a "living bonus," which is the income paid to surviving members in the pool.

Although the use of group self-annuitization products is new, the underlying idea supporting these products—that of a tontine or an annuity shared by subscribers or participants, the shares increasing as subscribers die until the last survivor enjoys the whole income—is not new and in fact stretches back to the seventeenth and eighteenth centuries, when it was a relatively popular arrangement for raising capital in continental Europe. GSAs differ from other retirement income products such as annuities in that they do not require capital to back guarantees, and because the income is not guaranteed as in an annuity offered by a life insurance company. GSAs can also be offered on a deferred basis like a deferred income annuity.

Recently, retirement income specialists in the United States have started to propose tontines—or "survivor funds"—as an option within 401(k) plans. For example, Jonathan Barry Forman, the Alfred P. Murrah professor of law at the University of Oklahoma–Norman, and Michael J. Sabin, an independent consultant in Sunnyvale, California, have proposed (in a June 27, 2016 article in international money management publication *Pensions and Investments*) a survivor fund that would work as follows:

> At the outset, imagine that 10 65-year-old male participants each invest $8,000 in a pool that buys 10-year Treasuries. At the current Treasury interest rate, that $80,000 investment would return about $100,000 in 10 years, and each participant—or the heirs—will get $10,000, reflecting that pitiful 2.3% yield.
>
> But what if we instead divided that $100,000 only among the participants who survived 10 years to reach age 75? Say eight of our 10 participants will live to 75.
>
> With a survivor fund, those eight survivors will divide the $100,000, and the two participants who died will get nothing. In short, in 10 years, each of the eight survivors will get $12,500 on an $8,000 investment, and that works out to be a 4.6% return, double the 2.3% return.
>
> What happens is this. If you are willing to give up leaving money to your heirs, you can enter into a survivor game with other investors. If you win, you get more; but if you die, your heirs get nothing.

Of course, you could play this kind of survivor game until there is only one survivor who gets all the money. Historically, such last-survivor-takes-all games were often called tontines—after the 17th-century Italian banker Lorenzo de Tonti, who came up with the survivor principle.

But the survivor principle can be used to design financial products that benefit multiple survivors, not just the last survivor. With survivor funds, each time an investor dies, that investor's account balance would be divided among the survivors. These survivor funds would be attractive investments because the survivors would get a greater return on their investments.

And even if no other investors die during the term of the fund, the survivors will never get less than the return on the underlying investment.

They propose that future research should focus on how to create these survivor funds—and how they should be regulated, adding that "survivor funds should find a home with today's 401(k) plan sponsors and with mutual funds that help participants transition to retirement."

Another option identified by Australia's Financial System Inquiry is deferred life annuities, or DLAs: "a form of lifetime annuity where income payments are delayed for a set amount of time. For example, a 65-year-old retiree may purchase a DLA that will provide a steady income stream after the retiree turns 85 and guarantee an income above that of the Age Pension for the remainder of the retiree's life." For the Financial System Inquiry, DLAs are viewed as a complement to age-based pensions, as drawdowns from account-based pensions can be structured so that the balance "is exhausted, or close to exhausted, at the time a DLA begins to make payments." The use of DLAs can cover advanced-age longevity risk without compelling drawdowns in the earlier years of retirement.

The Financial System Inquiry in Australia identified a number of regulatory barriers to the development of new retirement income products in Australia. These include the regulations set out in the Superannuation Industry (Supervision) Regulations established in 1994. Many submissions to the Inquiry called for removing these barriers to product innovation created by the regulations. There are also tax rules that impact how superannuation assets are taxed in both the accumulation and retirement phases. All in all, multiple approvals and regulatory changes would need to be implemented before new retirement income products are likely to enter the Australian market.

The rise of new systems and solutions speaks to the need to continue to find ways to solve the problem of retirement income for workers around the world. At the outset of this chapter, we identified three trends we believe may shape the future of retirement globally: the need for increased plan coverage and participation, the importance of investment defaults and the growth of target-date strategies, and the overarching search for retirement income solutions to sustain lifestyle in retirement. In this chapter, we explored the issues, considerations, and potential answers to multiple facets of the retirement income problem in the United States and around the world. Looking at this chapter together with the chapters that precede it, what have we learned?

"GETTING DC RIGHT": LESSONS LEARNED IN CHAPTERS 1 THROUGH 10

In the preceding chapters, we reviewed the growing need for and importance of DC pensions, how and why to manage a DC plan to meet a retirement income objective, how to structure DC plans effectively, the importance of selecting appropriate qualified default investment alternatives, core investment offerings for capital preservation, fixed income, real assets, equity, and alternatives—and how and why to turn DC plan assets into lifetime income in retirement. In this section, we present our view of the main takeaways from these chapters to guide plan development now and in the future.

Chapter 1: DC Plans Today

The stakes are high . . . and getting higher. Over the past decade, virtually everything about DC plan investing and design has grown: the number of plans, the dollars invested in those plans, the number of people—not only in the United States but also around the globe—who are retired or anticipating retirement in the coming years, and the proportion of lifetime income retirees expect to generate from DC plans. Together these factors mean that the need to understand and appreciate the potential of DC plans has grown, along with the risk of getting DC wrong and the importance of getting DC right.

It is against this backdrop that this guide has been created: to help DC plan sponsors and providers to structure investment menus for participants to meet their retirement goals. In this chapter, we set out a five-step process for DC plan design, supported by seven guiding principles to steer plan design.

"Getting DC right" can be understood as successfully bringing together the various elements of plan philosophy, design, governance, and implementation that ensure plans and retirees both *meet targets* and *avoid failure*. We believe plans should set a target income replacement level and design their plans to minimize the risk of failing to meet this target.

The bottom line: We believe that using an "objective-aligned" framework to build and implement DC plans will lead to improved results for all those with a stake in the outcomes.

Chapter 2: Aligning DC Investment Design to Meet the PRICE of Retirement

How much is enough? In Chapter 2, we delve more deeply into the importance of using an objective-aligned framework for DC plans, starting with the objective to create a real income stream in retirement and seeking appropriate assets to help meet this objective.

If the goal is to meet an income replacement target, how do we know what the target should be? In this chapter, we review all of the elements that should be considered when determining income replacement targets, including the income mix in retirement, the mix of workers in the plan (think about pilots versus professors), the mix of costs workers can expect to encounter in retirement (with healthcare as an example), and the mix of real and nominal income and costs in retirement.

We close the chapter by encouraging readers to consider what plan failure means and how success is defined—what level of shortfall is acceptable?—and to take a prospective, not just retrospective, view. The concepts in this chapter are brought together in PIMCO's methodology to create a proxy for the prospective costs of lifetime income in retirement, the PIMCO Retirement Income Cost Estimate (or PRICE).

The bottom line: Knowing the PRICE of your retirement can help translate plan balances into future retirement income potential. Consider PRICE as a simple but compelling methodology to address the most fundamental retirement income planning question of "how much is enough?"

Chapter 3: Plan Investment Structure

Even the best-designed plan can founder on the shoals of participant behavior. In this chapter, we look at how a plan's design accommodates the ways in which participants interact with plans—including options we call "Do it for me," "Do it with me," and "I'll do it myself." In this way, we bring behavior into the mix of options. We also review participant and plan sponsor preferences, including the choices of active or passive management for various components of the investments in the plan; and the choice of mutual funds, collective investment trusts, or separately managed accounts.

After reviewing the many options, factors, and choices available to plan sponsors and participants and influencing plan outcomes, the conclusion is clear: Plan design, especially when interwoven with participant behavior, is an area where all parties need to make careful and considered decisions. But the most important decision is that of the investment defaults in plans, as those defaults are likely to significantly influence outcomes for plans and participants alike.

The bottom line: Structuring a plan to take real-world factors, such as investor behavior, into account by the thoughtful construction of plan defaults is a critical step for plan sponsors.

Chapter 4: Target Date Design and Approaches

Default investment strategies combine advice and implementation of a plan. A target-date strategy or other asset allocation default investment can be thought of as performing a two-part function: not only offering advice, but also implementing that advice for the participant. Making decisions about how to fulfill this dual function by selecting and evaluating target-date or other asset allocation strategies is anything but passive. Instead, plan sponsors must consider how much risk employees should take, how risk is most appropriately allocated, and whether or not risk should be actively mitigated.

In considering what investment default to select, and in contrast to much of the DC plan landscape, PIMCO counsels taking the long view: We believe that participants need a glide path that is designed to maximize risk diversification and return opportunity, regardless of the economic environment. That is, participants need a path that can offer acceptable risk-adjusted return even during inflationary and turbulent times. As plan sponsors determine the appropriate glide path and asset allocation structure for their plan participants, in our view they should consider how the various glidepaths might fare not only during "normal" times, but also during inflationary and turbulent times. And what's more, we believe that the success of a qualified default investment alternative should be measured by the extent to which participants are able to meet their real retirement income needs as a result of relying on the default, rather than measuring success by noting how closely a savings and investment option matches a specified benchmark.

The bottom line: Selecting the investment default is among the most important roles a plan sponsor will fulfill, as it will influence the outcomes of many plan participants. We urge plan sponsors to think beyond the current situation and "take the long view" in making the active decisions that support the selection and implementation of investment defaults.

Chapter 5: Capital Preservation Strategies

Capital-preservation-focused options have long been a cornerstone in DC plans. As their name implies, these options seek to help participants preserve invested principal, generate income, provide a liquid, low-risk investment during volatile markets, or offset riskier investments in a portfolio.

In our view, plan sponsors should focus on three objectives for capital preservation options: *liquidity* (the degree to which a significant portion of invested capital can be easily sold or converted into cash), *low risk* (the value of invested principal should be reasonably assured over an appropriate time horizon as determined by the sponsor), and *real return* (investments should maintain participants' purchasing power by generating returns that at a minimum are close to or above inflation).

In the past few years, the capital preservation environment has undergone significant transformation and is now a changing cornerstone in DC plans. Optimal solutions for capital preservation have shifted, not only as a result of governmental reforms but also due to a changing interest rate environment. This means that the range of solutions a plan might consider to fill the cornerstone function of capital preservation may include stable value, shorter-duration bonds, money market funds, and even white-label options that seek to optimize a blend of approaches.

The bottom line: The capital preservation environment is no longer one in which "if you do what you've always done, you'll get what you've always gotten." Instead, when evaluating potential capital preservation options, consider a range of solutions and approaches—relying on history and convention may not be sufficient in a shifting environment.

Chapter 6: Fixed Income Strategies

Fixed income is at the center of retirement investing, although many aspects have changed over time. The role of fixed income includes capital preservation, income, the potential for capital appreciation, adding diversification to a portfolio, and providing a hedge against economic slowdown and even deflation.

In contrast to the early days of the modern bond market, now some decades past, the range of fixed-income investments available to investors has grown. Despite these changes, in PIMCO's 2016 consultant survey, respondents unanimously supported the inclusion of fixed-income offerings within the investment lineup. Yet many raise questions such as, "How many fixed-income offerings and what types are appropriate for DC investors? Should the offerings be available as stand-alone core investment choices or within blended strategies such as white-label/multimanager core or custom target date/risk strategies?"

In our view, there is likely no single correct answer to the question of how many fixed-income offerings and options should be on a DC plan's investment menu. Instead, plan sponsors should focus on offering a range of solutions consistent with the needs of plan participants—and present them in a way that reduces the risk of naive diversification resulting in an inappropriate asset allocation.

The bottom line: As the complexity of choices has grown, the need for thoughtful and coherent approaches to fixed-income investing within plans has likewise developed. In selecting the fixed-income lineup, plan sponsors should consider a range of factors including return, volatility and correlations, downside risk, and U.S. rate exposure—to help ensure the potential from fixed income can be realized.

Chapter 7: Designing Balanced DC Menus: Considering Equity Options

Offering access to the equity markets within a DC plan is fundamental, and equity choices have long been the primary focus of discussion and analysis of DC plans. What's challenging, however, is determining the number and types of equity choices—including the choice to expand the opportunity set beyond developed markets, thereby opening the door to the world's most rapidly expanding economies and return opportunities. Today's DC equity lineups often lack broad access to global markets, and lineups are often shackled to market-capitalization-weighted indexes, both of which may hamper returns and heighten volatility.

Here again, too, plan menu design can influence participants' investment decisions. As a result, plan sponsors are increasingly moving away from the *style-box* approach to *a risk-pillar menu* or an *asset-class-focused lineup* for the equity choices in a plan. However the options are arrayed, in our view plan sponsors should consider designing core investment menus that offer equity choices which are balanced relative to other DC investment offerings, and maximize DC participants' opportunity to gain from both capital appreciation and income. Often DC plans offer too many equity choices, yet at the same time fall short of providing sufficient opportunity to maximize returns and minimize risk.

By studying historical and forecasted future risk/return relationships among equity markets—as well as between passive and active management—plan sponsors may craft a set of equity strategies that offers both total return and risk-mitigation potential and helps DC participants meet their retirement income objectives. To reduce volatility in international equities, plan fiduciaries should also consider currency hedging back to the U.S.

dollar—a hedging policy may be just as relevant in equity as it is in fixed income.

The bottom line: Even though equities arguably have received the most focus of any asset class in DC plans, equity choices in plans aren't a "done deal." Rather, plan sponsors and participants need to work to ensure equities deliver on the risk premium they offer for DC plans, by evaluating how all elements of a plan fit and function together.

Chapter 8: Inflation Protection

Retirement income is vulnerable to inflation. The dual nature of inflation—it can both spike quickly and creep along slowly in the background—means DC plan participants' assets should be "inflation aware" at all times, not only when inflation seems high or likely to increase. DC plans can incorporate inflation protection by selecting assets that have either an *explicit* or *implicit* link between their cash flows and/or valuations and inflation.

But inflation-related assets do more than just provide inflation protection: They can also provide an important source of portfolio diversification, particularly relative to the asset classes that typically dominate DC participant portfolios, which are equities and bonds. That diversification is needed because there's no one "silver bullet" portfolio that will perform well in all economic environments, whether inflation and growth are high or low.

This "no-silver-bullet" reality is important to consider when contemplating long-term asset allocation decisions that will ultimately define the retirement investor's quality of lifestyle. We believe it is prudent to allow participants the ability to cover all four growth/inflation scenarios when constructing long-term strategic portfolios. Inflation-related assets tend to perform well during times when "traditional" portfolios, consisting primarily of nominal stocks and bonds, underperform. Plan sponsors should evaluate inflation-fighting assets, separately and in combination, to determine how best to offer them. After consideration, plan sponsors may find multi-real-asset blends attractive both as core options and as additions to asset allocation strategies such as target-date funds.

The bottom line: Whether inflation shows up for DC plans as a stealthy pickpocket depleting assets over time or a robber suddenly devastating the purchasing power of your saved dollars, plans need to be inflation-aware to ensure participant dollars—and spending power—are protected from both kinds of thievery. Inflation-aware assets can also act as important portfolio diversifiers, supporting portfolios through various economic conditions. Today, plan sponsors have a range of solutions to add inflation awareness and protection to plans.

Chapter 9: Additional Strategies and Alternatives: Seeking Diversification and Return

In Chapter 9 we discuss going beyond stocks and bonds. For DC plans, the pillar asset classes are capital preservation, fixed income, equity, and inflation-hedging assets. But increasingly investors need to branch outside of the mainstream in efforts to achieve higher return levels and increase the probability of achieving sustainable spending in retirement. Plan fiduciaries, for their part, are often looking for more choices to further reduce risk and improve return opportunities for plan participants. Thus the move into alternatives, including global tactical asset allocation, nontraditional asset classes, or other alternative investment strategies.

Alternatives in their various forms have the potential to improve outcomes for plan participants—especially in a low-return environment for mainstream U.S. stocks and bonds. In considering alternatives in DC plans, in our view it is key for plan sponsors to consider elements such as the liquidity needs of the plan; the merits and risks of each strategy type and stand-alone asset relative to existing mainstream assets that tend to dominate DC portfolios; and the asset manager, as many of these strategy types have greater reliance on manager skill, compared to traditional active strategies, and certainly versus passive approaches.

The bottom line: Diversification is sometimes referred to colloquially as a regret maximization exercise: *You regret having any diversification when you don't need it . . . and you regret not having more when you do. But the attentive integration of alternative assets within DC plans allows plan sponsors and participants alike to potentially reap the rewards of going beyond mainstream assets.*

Chapter 10: Retirement Income: Considering Options for Plan Sponsors and Retirees

After retirement, a plan still needs to allow retirees to create income to last a lifetime. Most of the chapters to this point have focused on how plan sponsors and participants can work to ensure the best outcomes from their DC plans, from the point of view of ensuring those plans are sufficiently funded and designed to provide the retirement income plan participants will need. But what happens to participants, plan sponsors, and plans at the point of retirement? Should retirees leave their assets in DC plans, roll them over to an individual retirement account (IRA) to invest in capital markets, or buy an annuity to create retirement income? What are plan sponsors' preferences? What are the options to create income in retirement that participants need, and plans should provide? Is the range of existing investment choices appropriate and sufficient?

For retirees who stay—that is, keep their assets in the DC plan—they likely will need help in creating a lifetime income stream. We note that to generate steady and sustainable retirement income—that is, a lifetime paycheck—retirees seek opportunity for return as well as the ability to manage specific risks, chief among them market, longevity, and inflation risk. Each imposes unique demands on a retiree's portfolio.

The bottom line: Retirees may benefit from creating a retirement income stream from their DC plan. Plan sponsors can help retirees by confirming they have appropriate access to their money, together with investment choices that offer attractive risk-adjusted returns. We suggest considering the investment options within the PRICE retirement-income liability framework—that is, confirm, as you plan for retirement, that assets keep pace with retirement cost.

ANALYTIC FACTORS TO CONSIDER: SUMMARY BY ASSET PILLAR

Throughout the book, we introduced a set of analytic factors to help plan fiduciaries evaluate and compare investment strategies. In Figure 11.5 we provide a summary of the factors by asset class.

IN CLOSING

While retirement programs evolve globally, we anticipate the shift to a defined contribution structure will continue. In this chapter we considered three primary trends in retirement plan evolution, including the need for increased coverage and participation, the growing importance of the investment default and target-date strategies in particular, and the ongoing search for retirement income solutions. We can all learn from each other as various programs are tested and evolve in various countries. For instance, the United States can learn about improving plan coverage and participation by observing DC program implementation in Australia and the UK. The former requires participation and retention of assets until retirement age, while the latter now requires enrollment but not ongoing participation. While the United States historically has shunned the idea of any mandatory programs, many states are rolling out programs that include a mandatory participation element.

On the investment side, we expect continued movement toward target-date or similar asset allocation programs that manage the investment risk based on participants' estimated time horizons. As discussed in earlier

FIGURE 11.5 Summary Evaluation Metrics

Evaluation Metrics	Target Date Strategy	Capital Preservation Strategy	Fixed-Income Strategy	Equity Strategy	Inflation Protection Strategy
Excess return (vs. PRICE)	x				
Return		x	x	x	x
Real return		x			
Worst calendar day performance		x			
Average performance for negative days		x			
Dividend				x	
Yield to maturity			x		
Tracking error (vs. PRICE)	x				
Volatility		x	x	x	x
VaR (95%)			x	x	x
Maximum drawdown		x	x	x	x
Nominal duration (years)		x	x		
U.S. nominal duration (years)			x		
Percent of negative days		x			
Correlation to PRICE	x				
Correlation to S&P 500			x	x	x
Inflation beta					x
Information ratio (vs. PRICE)	x				
Return/Volatility		x	x	x	x
Probability of income replacement ratio < 30%	x				
Asset longvetity	x				
Worst calendar date		x			

Source: PIMCO.

chapters, we encourage plan fiduciaries to seek structures that align to the PRICE of retirement and minimize the risk of failing to create a sustainable retirement income stream.

Finally, for retirement income solutions, we have not seen the "silver bullet" solution appear anywhere in the world. Rather, the United States and other countries continue to consider ways to improve the distribution phase. A key question for plan fiduciaries is the choices a participant may be offered: Can they stay in the plan, or must they move their money out of the plan? The answer to this question may drive whichever investment and insurance choices are appropriate.

More countries may consider programs that imbed insurance such as a tontine-like structure now available in Australia or a defined ambition structure that shares payout risk across a participant base. While these programs are intriguing and respond directly to the growing demand for retirement income solutions, they also raise concerns that may slow their adoption. Until new products such as the annuities discussed previously (such as deferred life annuities) become more widely adopted, we anticipate growing use of higher income and capital preservation offerings by those most attuned to the need for current income: more tenured participants and retirees. This will occur in parallel with continued flows into the investment default—once again underscoring the importance of getting the default aligned to the plan objective: helping retirees maintain their lifestyles throughout retirement.

NOTE

1. See "Employee Benefits in the United States—March 2015," www.bls.gov/news .release/pdf/ebs2.pdf.

Closing Comments

What's measured improves.

—Peter F. Drucker

As I write these closing words, it's been over 35 years since I started working in the finance industry and began saving toward retirement. I feel privileged to work in a profession that offers both intellectual challenge and social purpose. Over the past several decades, I have enjoyed working to improve retirement programs alongside plan sponsors, consultants, university professors, government leaders, lawyers, service providers, colleagues and other professionals. In contrast to many other investment areas, DC requires engagement across multiple disciplines and collaboration with other professional experts. It's not just about investing: rather, to design successful DC plans, we must also understand benefits and insurance, behavioral science, communication approaches, regulatory and tax considerations, and administrative complexities. As no one of us can know it all, we look to each other in the DC professional community to work together in an effort to improve these critical retirement programs—to help workers succeed in meeting their retirement goals.

Over these three-plus decades since my financial services career began, DC plans have changed in many ways. They've evolved from being viewed as a supplemental, perhaps even insignificant, component of a retirement income strategy, to being the most-relied-upon private retirement savings program for workers worldwide . . . and thus significantly more serious. Along the way, "cute" education programs designed to "help a participant understand stocks and bonds" so they could pick an asset allocation right for them have been replaced by professionally managed investment defaults and world-class risk management. Gone are the days of individuals going it alone. The importance of DC plans as a source of retirement income, coupled with the dual challenges of capturing investment returns and managing risk, makes DC far more significant. Today, the stakes are much higher as workers have only one chance to save for retirement, only *one chance to get it right*. This reality is unlikely to change.

We anticipate DC plans will continue to be rolled out around the globe and to be relied upon as a primary source of retirement income. Looking forward, many fear that a DC-dependent system will doom workers to fail in reaching their retirement goals. I don't believe this is true. When a DC plan is well structured and managed, workers are likely to succeed. We need to continue working together to make these plans better—and many actions can be taken to continue to improve plans. Here are my three top priorities for where these actions should be focused.

PRIORITY 1: INCREASING PLAN COVERAGE AND INDIVIDUAL SAVINGS RATES

In the preceding chapters, we talked about increasing plan coverage and pumping up savings rates. These goals may be best accomplished through automatic enrollment and contribution escalation programs, while nationally supported and/or state-offered multiple employer programs may also help close the coverage gap. We'll also need to consider leakage from DC plans, including rollovers to (possibly higher-cost) retail retirement programs, and the failure to pay back loans or cash-outs prior to retirement. We applaud efforts by Mark Iwry at the U.S. Treasury in driving regulation to reduce cash-outs and retain assets in the DC system by making it easier to roll money from one DC plan to another. In our view, more work can and should be done in this area—including supporting more plan sponsors that actively work to retain retiree assets within the DC plan.

PRIORITY 2: MOVING TO OBJECTIVE-ALIGNED INVESTMENT APPROACHES

On the investment side, a lot has gone right: in particular, the establishment of qualified default investment alternatives and the movement toward asset allocation strategies that take into account, at minimum, a participant's expected investment time horizon. At time of writing and as discussed throughout the book, target-date strategies are the dominant option in U.S. plans and are growing in prevalence around the globe. We expect that trend to continue. More tailored asset allocation approaches, such as managed accounts and possibly robo advisors, also may attract more assets over time. Regardless of the asset allocation approach, what is critical is for the DC community to help align these strategies and benchmarking to the DC plan's objective. For the vast majority of plans, this means aligning to an income replacement goal. How do we help participants and plan fiduciaries focus and measure to this goal?

In this book, we have outlined an approach for aligning and evaluating an asset allocation strategy—whether target-date, target-risk, balanced, or managed accounts—to a sustainable retirement income objective. We introduced a methodology for quantifying the cost to buy a sustainable retirement income stream, using the acronym PRICE (PIMCO Retirement Income Cost Estimate). This methodology can be used to look at how the cost of retirement has changed historically as well as to show what it may cost for a participant to retire even decades from today.

The concern we hear from plan sponsors in using this *real-liability-aware* or *objective-aligned* framework is the challenge of helping participants understand it. In response, we may argue that participants don't necessarily need to understand this approach, as long as the plan fiduciaries do, and the fiduciaries build or select investment default structures that align the participants' accounts to reach a reasonable income replacement target. Given an objective-aligned investment default coupled with automatic enrollment and a healthy contribution rate, participants may be set on a path to retirement success. An objective-aligned, professionally managed investment default will both increase the probability of success and, importantly, reduce the risk of failure.

What's also critical is for plan fiduciaries to shift their *evaluation* of the investment default to an objective-aligned framework, both historically and prospectively. Whether the investment default outperforms or underperforms relative to a peer group of similar investment alternatives (e.g., target-date vintages) may be irrelevant if the other investments are set to achieve a different objective, such as maximizing wealth with little regard for downside risk. Here again, we need an objective-aligned evaluation approach. We offer the PRICE methodology as an important consideration as you evaluate your target-date or other asset allocation strategies relative to a plan's retirement income objective.

PRICE can be plugged into models to evaluate historic tracking to the real liability, including considering tracking error and return relative to an objective—and then bringing both together in an information ratio (i.e., return relative to risk of failing to meet the income objective). This real-liability-aware approach is most relevant as we consider long timeframes, asking whether participants are on track to meet their retirement income goals—and as we evaluate the closest-to-retirement vintages, which should more closely track PRICE. The PRICE approach can also be used within stochastic modeling to consider the probability of meeting or falling short of a goal. In summary, both implementing and evaluating objective-aligned asset allocation programs will take us a long way toward improving DC plan success.

Unfortunately, for short-term benchmarking, such as quarterly and annual performance, PRICE may be inappropriate given the amount of anticipated and justifiable tracking error. Accordingly, more work is needed to consider and put forth a real-liability-focused approach to short-term benchmarking. As we write, it may be most helpful to identify a peer group of asset allocation strategies that are managed to the same investment objective, that is, meeting a sustainable retirement income goal. Movement to an objective-aligned benchmarking process is critical. As management guru Peter Drucker said, "What's measured improves." For DC plans to improve in delivering retirement income, we need to measure them relative to this objective.

Now, how can we do a better job in communicating with participants? Can they understand PRICE? (Do they need to? Maybe not.) As a DC community, we have talked about the importance of shifting the participant's mindset from *wealth accumulation* to *retirement income building*. We want participants to think not of the total value of their DC account (as a lump sum at a point in time), but rather of the monthly income that account may deliver (as an income stream over time). While clearly important, one's account size is not necessarily the best indicator of the monthly income that it may fund throughout retirement. Many DC recordkeepers show participants a projection of what an account may deliver, yet as an industry we lack clarity and consistency in the methodology used to calculate that amount.

As the Department of Labor considers offering guidelines for this calculation, we again suggest the PRICE methodology as a defensible and capital-market-based approach. As PRICE is derived using current and forward TIPS pricing, it is founded in the market realities participants face. It does not require future return or other assumptions. We believe staying away from backward-looking and static assumptions is in the best interest of participants. Using PRICE shows a better picture of what the participant may actually experience. Importantly, by providing a monthly retirement income estimate using PRICE, participants will be able to see that their income may actually go up *even though their account balance has gone down*. This can be a difficult concept for individuals to grasp. By refocusing their attention to monthly income that is largely driven by the real rate environment they will see a truer, and less volatile, picture of what they may have for retirement, instilling confidence rather than angst.

PRIORITY 3: BROADENING OPTIONS FOR RETIREMENT INCOME

As discussed in the book, retirement income itself is the third area that requires attention and improvement. We believe retirees may be best served by retaining assets within their DC plan and creating an income stream from the plan—particularly for large plans with buying power that can offer lower pricing on investment products and services than a retail account (e.g., an IRA). Plans need to offer the appropriate asset allocation structure (e.g., at-retirement-date strategies), plus capital preservation and income-focused strategies. They need to offer access to account balances through at least partial withdrawals, but also ideally via installment payments, making it easy for a retiree to create a monthly paycheck or automatic deposit to their checking account.

Retirement investment options should account for the retiree's time horizon (to and through retirement) and help manage the risk of loss. In addition, the need for longevity insurance should be considered. For example, an employer may wish to consider offering access to an out-of-plan, institutionally priced annuity platform. This would allow a retiree to gather competitive bids, then buy the insurance that fits their individual needs and lifestyle. Buying a deferred annuity that pays out 20 years post retirement allows the investment horizon for DC assets to constrict and eases the challenge of meeting the monthly income needs. More study is needed of longevity insurance solutions and implementation processes.

NUDGING ONE ANOTHER ALONG A PATH TO SUCCESS

What else is needed to succeed? DC plans will advance by increasing plan coverage and participation, implementing objective-aligned asset allocation strategies, and improving retiree access and solutions. The larger the organization, the more buying power and value can be delivered to help participants succeed. Regardless of the organization's size, the fiduciary oversight by plan fiduciaries brings value to the participants. We can help individual workers by designing plans to increase the likelihood of reaching their objective. Taking these actions, along with practicing good governance and process, should put sponsors in good standing and lessen the risk of present and future litigation.

Employers may also be able to offer more one-on-one retirement and broader financial planning support. One-on-one planning would help address not only retirement issues, but would also consider retirement within a comprehensive financial picture that takes into account budgeting, college financing, home purchase, and more. While some plan sponsors offer access to these programs today, more widespread adoption would improve the financial security and sense of well-being among our workforce. For plan sponsors who do offer such programs, we often hear small usage rates for the programs. Perhaps we need to find an appropriate nudge to get them there? As many readers likely have seen, elephants nudging one another forward along the path is often used as a symbol for automatic enrollment and other programs. It's always a pleasure to share visual images that represent how to move forward. With that in mind, here I share a couple of photos from a recent trip to Africa where the many elephants roam the open plains. They indeed nudge each other forward. They also live in family groups with long and healthy lives. In closing: thank you for the time you have spent reading and studying the material in this book. I know if you comment on the elephants that you have made it to the end, along the path we have laid out. We look forward to working with you and helping your DC plan participants succeed.

FIGURE 1

FIGURE 2

Index